WITHDRAWN

ETHNIC CONFLICT

SOME OTHER VOLUMES IN THE
SAGE FOCUS EDITIONS

8. **Controversy (Second Edition)**
   Dorothy Nelkin

14. **Churches and Politics in Latin America**
   Daniel H. Levine

21. **The Black Woman**
   La Frances Rodgers-Rose

22. **Making Bureaucracies Work**
   Carol H. Weiss and Allen H. Barton

24. **Dual-Career Couples**
   Fran Pepitone-Rockwell

31. **Black Men**
   Lawrence E. Gary

32. **Major Criminal Justice Systems**
   George F. Cole, Stanislaw J. Frankowski,
   and Marc G. Gertz

34. **Assessing Marriage**
   Erik E. Filsinger and Robert A. Lewis

36. **Impacts of Racism on White Americans**
   Benjamin P. Bowser and
   Raymond G. Hunt

41. **Black Families**
   Harriette Pipes McAdoo

43. **Aging and Retirement**
   Neil G. McCluskey and Edgar F. Borgatta

47. **Mexico's Political Economy**
   Jorge I. Dominguez

50. **Cuba**
   Jorge I. Dominguez

51. **Social Control**
   Jack P. Gibbs

52. **Energy and Transport**
   George H. Daniels, Jr., and Mark H. Rose

54. **Job Stress and Burnout**
   Whiton Stewart Paine

56. **Two Paychecks**
   Joan Aldous

57. **Social Structure and Network Analysis**
   Peter V. Marsden and Nan Lin

58. **Socialist States in the World-System**
   Christopher K. Chase-Dunn

59. **Age or Need?**
   Bernice L. Neugarten

60. **The Costs of Evaluation**
   Marvin C. Alkin and Lewis C. Solmon

61. **Aging in Minority Groups**
   R.L. McNeely and John N. Colen

62. **Contending Approaches to
   World System Analysis**
   William R. Thompson

63. **Organizational Theory and Public Policy**
   Richard H. Hall and Robert E. Quinn

64. **Family Relationships in Later Life**
   Timothy H. Brubaker

65. **Communication and Organizations**
   Linda L. Putnam and
   Michael E. Pacanowsky

66. **Competence in Communication**
   Robert N. Bostrom

67. **Avoiding Communication**
   John A. Daly and James C. McCroskey

68. **Ethnography in Educational Evaluation**
   David M. Fetterman

69. **Group Decision Making**
   Walter C. Swap and Associates

70. **Children and Microcomputers**
   Milton Chen and William Paisley

71. **The Language of Risk**
   Dorothy Nelkin

72. **Black Children**
   Harriette Pipes McAdoo and
   John Lewis McAdoo

73. **Industrial Democracy**
   Warner Woodworth, Christopher Meek,
   and William Foote Whyte

74. **Grandparenthood**
   Vern L. Bengtson and Joan F. Robertson

75. **Organizational Theory and Inquiry**
   Yvonna S. Lincoln

76. **Men in Families**
   Robert A. Lewis and Robert E. Salt

77. **Communication and Group
   Decision-Making**
   Randy Y. Hirokawa and
   Marshall Scott Poole

78. **The Organization of Mental
   Health Services**
   W. Richard Scott and Bruce L. Black

79. **Community Power**
   Robert J. Waste

80. **Intimate Relationships**
   Daniel Perlman and Steve Duck

81. **Children's Ethnic Socialization**
   Jean S. Phinney and Mary Jane Rotheram

82. **Power Elites and Organizations**
   G. William Domhoff and Thomas R. Dye

83. **Responsible Journalism**
   Deni Elliott

84. **Ethnic Conflict**
   Jerry Boucher, Dan Landis, and
   Karen Arnold Clark

85. **Aging, Health, and Family**
   Timothy H. Brubaker

86. **Critical Issues in Aging Policy**
   Edgar F. Borgatta and
   Rhonda J.V. Montgomery

87. **The Homeless in Contemporary Society**
   Richard D. Bingham, Roy E. Green, and
   Sammis B. White

88. **Changing Men**
   Michael S. Kimmel

89. **Popular Music and Communication**
   James Lull

90. **Life Events and Psychological
   Functioning**
   Lawrence H. Cohen

91. **The Social Psychology of Time**
   Joseph E. McGrath

ETHNIC CONFLICT

International Perspectives

Edited by

Jerry Boucher
Dan Landis
Karen Arnold Clark

SAGE PUBLICATIONS
The Publishers of Professional Social Science
Newbury Park   Beverly Hills   London   New Delhi

For Amanda Marie, in the hope that she
will not grow up in a world of conflict
—D. L.

For information address:

SAGE Publications, Inc.
2111 West Hillcrest Drive
Newbury Park, California 91320

SAGE Publications Inc.
275 South Beverly Drive
Beverly Hills
California 90212

SAGE Publications Ltd.
28 Banner Street
London EC1Y 8QE
England

SAGE PUBLICATIONS India Pvt. Ltd.
M-32 Market
Greater Kailash I
New Delhi 110 048 India

Printed in the United States of America

Library of Congress Cataloging-in-Publication Data

Main entry under title:

Ethnic conflict.

  (Sage focus editions ; v. 84)
  Bibliography: p.
  Includes index.
  1. Race relations. 2. Ethnic relations.
I. Boucher, Jerry. II. Landis, Dan. III. Clark,
Karen A., 1960-
HT1521.E84 1986   305.8   86-17885
ISBN 0-8039-2817-3
ISBN 0-8039-2818-1 (pbk.)

FIRST PRINTING

Contents

Foreword
ROSS STAGNER   7

Acknowledgments   17

1. Themes and Models of Conflict
DAN LANDIS and JERRY BOUCHER   18

2. Sinhala-Tamil Relations in Modern
Sri Lanka (Ceylon)
SINNAPAH ARASARATNAM   33

3. Intergroup Relations in Hong Kong:
The Tao *of Stability*
MICHAEL HARRIS BOND   55

4. Ethnic Conflict Management in
Yunnan, China
ZHANG SHIFU and DAVID Y. H. WU   80

5. Interethnic Conflict in the
Malay Peninsula
RONALD PROVENCHER   92

6. The Basque Conflict
J. MARTÍN RAMIREZ and BOBBIE SULLIVAN   120

7. Black-White Relations in Mississippi
RONALD BAILEY   140

8. Puerto Rican Ethnicity and Conflict
ANGELA B. GINORIO   182

9. American Indians and Interethnic Conflict
    JOSEPH E. TRIMBLE   208

10. Interethnic Conflict in the
    Philippine Archipelago
    ERIC S. CASIÑO   231

11. Interethnic Conflict in New Zealand
    M. JOCELYN ARMSTRONG   255

12. Twenty-Four Generations of Intergroup
    Conflicts on Bellona Island
    (Solomon Islands)
    ROLF KUSCHEL   280

13. Ethnic Antagonism and Innovation
    in Hawaii
    JOHN KIRKPATRICK   298

14. Some Thoughts on Ethnic Conflict
    WINTHROP D. JORDAN   317

About the Contributors   325

Foreword

ROSS STAGNER

Group conflict is the most pressing problem facing the social sciences today. I refer not only to the overhanging threat of nuclear war, but also to the smaller conflicts that might trigger the final catastrophe. And this refers not merely to nations, although the highest probability attaches to conflicts between small nations that are client states of the U.S. and the U.S.S.R. Thus the war between Iran and Iraq, or the potential war between Syria and Israel, might serve as a trigger for a superpower confrontation. On a still smaller scale the warning applies to conflicts between ethnic groups, as in northern Ireland or Sri Lanka, or the Fleming-Walloon controversy in Belgium.

This volume focuses on the third group—conflicts between ethnic groups that are not for the most part organized as nation-states. It is somewhat easier to identify fundamental issues in these instances; but it seems intuitively obvious that a theoretical and conceptual analysis of these controversies will be relevant to the understanding of superpower or mini-power rivalry and violence.

I do not see any particular value to a simple tabulation of conflicts around the world, or even of the issues salient in a specific conflict, as between Thais and Malays. Rather, we need a more appropriate conceptualization of factors predicting such conflicts and hypotheses regarding the treatments that may minimize the dangers or maximize the constructive outcomes to be anticipated.

This implies that conflict may be either socially disruptive or socially beneficial. Looking at conflict as a psychologist, I see instructive parallels between the development of a child and the development of a nation or other large social entity. As Piaget pointed out long ago, the child does not abandon egocentric thinking until pressure from parents and other adults requires accommodation to "reality" as perceived by societal norms. Similarly, Freud emphasized that infantile narcissism and living by the pleasure principle will persist until conflicts with the adult world require some shift to delayed gratification or the "reality principle." It can be plausibly argued that ethnic conflicts over equal rights for all individuals irrespective of ethnic membership have similarly led to maturation in the functioning of the society.

We need a theoretical framework, then, that will enable us to identify crucial variables in interethnic disputes and also hypotheses for predicting the consequences of manipulating these variables for destructive or beneficent ends. As a psychologist, I am disposed to seek this theoretical framework within psychology. This is not to deny the obvious relevance of economic interests, power seeking, military security, group cohesiveness, and other variables appropriate to a higher-level systems analysis. Rather, I would argue that the human being is the ultimate element in economics and sociology; following the advice of René Descartes, we should therefore examine the problem in terms of this irreducible level of simplicity. The use of analogies across levels is always hazardous; we know that a mechanical engineer putting together a hydraulic press need not worry about the relevance of nuclear physics to his problem. But the minimal elements in social engineering are not so easily disregarded. A leader trying to devise a solution to group violence must be deeply concerned about whether the possible procedures are compatible with what is known regarding individual psychology. On the other hand, some psychologists have overdone their emphasis on solutions at the level of the individual; consider the case of those who advocate psychoanalysis for national leaders to reduce violence. Can we imagine Adolf Hitler or Josef Stalin taking a couple of years off for analytic therapy? And who would compel them to submit to it?

A more promising course seems to be that of identifying the crucial variables in a cross-section of group conflicts; that is the enterprise undertaken by the authors of the chapters included here. Given these variables, we can consider possible political, economic, or social solutions that will minimize the probability of social catastrophe.

From the psychological point of view there are three major components of ethnic conflict: perception, motivation, and action. Perception relates primarily to the process of stereotyping: The outgroup is perceived as possessing various undesirable and unattractive attributes, without regard to any realistic basis. The ethnic distinction may be based on physical categories, such as skin color, facial pattern, and so on. The distinction may also be based on social data: marriage customs, penal system, language, religion, sanitary practices, and dietary habits. Almost any discriminable feature may be used as a basis for ethnic prejudice. The comparison with the ingroup is polarized: "We" have the good attributes; "they" show only bad features.

Ethnocentric perception is a major contributor to group hostility. If the members of the opposing group are seen as ignorant, violent, untrustworthy, greedy, and cruel, peaceful accommodation is unlikely. We cannot believe their offers of cooperation; we quickly exaggerate any threatening action they take. These attributions tend to take a "mirror image" pattern: as various researchers have shown, the Americans "see" the Soviet leadership as belligerent, treacherous, and expansionist; the Soviets "see" American leaders as belligerent, treacherous, and expansionist. Studies of propaganda show that the credibility of a message source modifies the effectiveness of the communication. Given the hostile image we hold of the Soviets, it is not surprising that Americans do not believe offers of peaceful accommodation emanating from Moscow.

We know from the work of Piaget that the earliest form of perception is egocentric; that is, the child sees only his or her own reality, and denies the reality of facts as seen by others. The parents socialize the child in part by teaching him to see events as the adult community sees them. It is difficult to transfer this analogy to group conflict; the opposing leaders are already adult, albeit immature, and they usually refuse to be educated to a different way of perceiving.

As a substitute for ethnocentrism, I have elsewhere proposed teaching children "altrocentrism," that is, the ability to see events as they appear to others. (This is not to be confused with altruism, which implies that one acts to benefit the other; altrocentrism means that one perceives accurately what the world looks like to the other person, but one may still reject the action desired by the other.) Surprisingly good results have been obtained using this conceptual approach; for example, aggressive juvenile delinquents have been taught to behave in a more socialized manner, and disruptive school children have been at least substantially domesticated. Some experiments with this procedure in Black-White relations, for example, in city police forces, have also been quite encouraging. Intensely prejudiced persons will of course resist training toward altrocentrism, and leaders who glean personal benefits from prejudice (power, prestige, etc.) will not readily accept altrocentric thinking.

A second major psychological component of prejudice is motivation. Psychologists have in general abandoned the idea of an aggressive instinct (as espoused by Konrad Lorenz) and even most psychoanalysts have rejected Freud's theory of Thanatos, the "death" instinct. Instead, emphasis is placed on positive motives such as economic gain (the ingroup benefits from denying shares to the outgroup), power (the outgroup is contained in a helpless or ineffectual posture), and security (safety from attack as outgroup members are disarmed or confined). Perception may guide prejudicial action, but motives supply the energy necessary for action.

One general psychological rule is that the degree of violence in conflict situations is a function of intensity of *motivation*. To take an example from the literature of social psychology, an early study of stereotyping showed that American college students perceived Turks as ignorant, cruel, untrustworthy, and so forth—the classic pattern for outgroup perception. But there was no violence directed toward the Turks because there were no important economic, power, or security goals involved. On the other hand, destructively violent conflicts (e.g., northern Ireland, Sri Lanka) involve strong motives as well as hostile stereotypes. In both instances economic advantage held by one group is the dynamic element in the conflict. Political power can also be involved. Cases of nonviolent conflict (e.g., Hong Kong, Singapore) show less economic discrepancy and at least a muted exercise of power by the holders of control.

Another variable that one finds in these case studies of conflict is that *intensity* seems to be a function of the standard of living. There is more violence if the depressed group is kept in physiological deprivation; poor food and housing trigger more aggressive action. Deprivations at the egoistic and status levels are less potent in releasing violence. Thus wealthy minorities denied political power are less prone to physical aggression than impoverished minorities.

The third psychological component of interethnic prejudice is *action*. Action, of course, has been repeatedly mentioned in the foregoing paragraphs. However, another kind of action is important: the institutionalization of violence. Popular news accounts tend to restrict the term "violence" to physical protests by a dissident minority; violence by police and army is labeled "law and order." Political power thus leads to a possibility of action through the legal machinery to establish a monopoly of violence in the hands of the politically ruling group.

Nonviolent action is also important. Mohandas Gandhi found that nonviolence could be used effectively against the British; it is a feasible tactic when the majority accepts some responsibility for harm to nonviolent protesters. One can hardly imagine similar success in Nazi Germany or in Stalinist Russia. Superego controls do not operate in the presence of rigid stereotyping and hostile feelings.

History teaches us that the resort to violence by either contender in a conflict tends to set off *escalation*. That is, when the American Indians fought back against seizure of their lands, even greater violence was mobilized by the European immigrant invaders.

Unfavorable perceptions are transmitted by way of myths and legends about the outgroup. Children's minds are filled with hostile images long before a member of the outgroup is encountered. It is fairly easy to induce escalation of a controversy; it is remarkably difficult to take steps designed to ease the tensions.

Most of the research available has to do merely with the presence and degree of stereotyping. There is a great need for study of these social groups where stereotyping is minimal or nonexistent. It would be interesting to get some insights, for example, into the success of the Amish in maintaining ingroup solidarity without excessive hostile stereotyping of the majority group milieu. It would be worthwhile to compare the German-speaking Tyrol, annexed to Italy after World War I, with Alsace-Lorraine, which has been under both German and French sovereignty alternately. The Tyrol frequently erupts in bombings and other violence, whereas such incidents are virtually nonexistent in Alsace.

One approach to such research is by way of the conceptual scheme of identifying dimensions. If group conflict is an identifiable social phenomenon, it must vary along dimensions that can be identified and labeled, though perhaps not measured. Other sciences show the value of such an approach. Physics, for example, could not progress until basic dimensions—mass, momentum, and reaction, for example—had been defined. In the study of group conflict we must go beyond individual psychology. We need to conceptualize social conflicts at a more complex level. We need to establish some kind of measuring device, and assign dimensional values to differing conflict situations. At that point we shall be able to probe into the hidden variables that account for variance along dimensions.

Just twenty years ago, in 1967, I proposed such a set of dimensions. These ranged from fairly obvious items such as the magnitude of the conflict (number of persons affected), duration over time, and so forth, to more complex variables such as emotional intensity and the proportion of realism or neurotic distortion involved in the controversy. As far as I know, the suggestion fell on deaf ears, if indeed it reached any ears at all.

In that book (*Dimensions of Human Conflict,* 1967) I proposed that a set of dimensions applied to instances of marital, racial, industrial, and international conflict. Three of these were identified as major variables calling for special investigation: emotional intensity, polarization of thinking, and realism versus neuroticism.

Emotional intensity is probably self-explanatory. The only type of conflict in which it has been systematically utilized is in union-management conflict, where it has been referred to as *attitudinal climate*. Briefly, union-management relationships can be assigned places on a dimension from cooperative to conflictful. Some are turbulent, some are "arms-length" dealing, and some are cooperative. In the kinds of interethnic conflicts described in these essays, the best single index might be the occurrence, frequency, and severity of violence. However, intensity can also be evaluated by examination of propaganda attacks and by sampling of individual attitudes toward the groups involved.

Polarization of thinking is an obvious phenomenon, highly correlated with emotional intensity; however, it merits separate consideration. It is manifested by an exaggerated frequency of "Black-White" thinking, in which one side is seen as pure and virtuous while the opponents are perceived as evil and vicious. Osgood (1962) has referred to this mental process as "Neanderthal thinking" because it is primitive. It does not take account of the complexities of most intergroup relations.

Polarization increases as the conflict intensifies. In a study of changing public opinion early in World War II, Stagner and Osgood

(1946) found that public opinion among American adults changed progressively from 1940 to 1942. During the period of the "phony war" (September 1939 to May 1940), there was a distinct trend favoring Britain and France, critical of Germany and Italy. In 1941 the distance grew wider; and by February of 1942 (after the attack on Pearl Harbor), the Axis nations were seen as completely "bad," the Allies as "good." In an investigation of industrial conflict, Stagner and Eflal (1982) found that union members' perceptions of the "big three" automakers were virtually identical. However, when the Ford workers went on strike, their perceptions of Ford as an employer became far more hostile; workers in General Motors and Chrysler showed no change in their attitudes toward their employers. (The Ford average dropped back to the average of all United Auto Workers' members six months after the strike ended.)

Polarization blocks peaceful solutions because it denies the possibility of compromise. It operates as a filter, screening out intermediate positions about the conflict, so that the participants see no possible outcome except for victory of one side or the other. Polarization also results in persecution of ingroup members; those who advocate compromise are labeled "traitors" because the polarized attitude permits absolutely no deviation from the extremist position.

A proposed third dimension of conflict—that some conflicts are realistic while others are in part neurotic—is more debatable, but it seems to me to be valid and important. The position is that we have a gradation from instances in which obvious physical or economic injury has been inflicted on a group to instances in which myth and legend are the principal components. A realistic conflict, in this sense, would be one between Native Americans and the European immigrants who seized their land, killed off the game on which they lived, and fenced them off in reservations of undesirable land. A case in which realistic factors were minimal is that of the controversy between Chile and Argentina over the islands off Tierra del Fuego. While "national sovereignty" was at stake, no economic or military advantages were involved. With realistic values negligible, it was not difficult for the parties to accept the mediation of the Pope and settle the argument without violence.

Some industrial conflicts have been treated on this theory. Muench (1960) has described a union-management controversy that had become so heated that neither side would speak to the other except in the presence of witnesses and even then the conversation consisted mostly of name-calling. By working with people from both sides, Muench succeeded in reopening communication and introducing several years of labor peace.

The domestication of conflict (lowering the level of emotional intensity and reducing polarized thinking) is hindered by what may be called cultural schizophrenia. (Be it understood that I am speaking metaphorically and not fantasizing the operation of a group mind.) Cultural schizophrenia is manifested by the tendency of ethnic groups to seek mutually exclusive goals. For example, Jews in America want to be seen as loyal Americans, not as foreigners, but they also want to preserve group identity and a distinctive culture. Blacks want to be hired into well-paid jobs and join the mainstream of economic life, but they also want to protect a unique lifestyle, an idiomatic language, and other behaviors that may hinder their employability. Vietnamese immigrants want to be fully accepted as Americans but they ask to be educated in their own language and to retain their own customs with regard to food and living patterns.

Most Western intellectuals agree that cultural diversity is desirable, but few have reflected on the difficulties involved. The most successful accommodations in the United States appear to have involved virtual merger of the once-distinctive ethnic group into the majority population; thus while recent immigrants cluster together, their children move to the suburbs and abandon the parental identification with "the old country." This solution may not be optimal, but it is clear that cultural fragmentation provides ample opportunities for conflict and violence to ensue.

There is, unfortunately, no statute of limitations on group conflict. The northern Irish Catholics are still violent opponents of British rule, a conflict dating back at least to Oliver Cromwell. Hindus and Muslims in India have been feuding for a comparable time. Hostile stereotypes are passed on from parent to child, and violent solutions are advocated with emotional intensity. Leaders like Mohandas Gandhi, who preach mutual brotherhood and cooperation, are assassinated by fanatics within their own group.

And yet the only source from which a solution may come is the individual. Groups cannot think. Thinking is a process irrevocably confined within a single human being. Thus—despite the fate of Gandhi and many other advocates of peaceful settlement of disputes—we must still hope that individuals will actively seek solutions and propose them to the public at large.

The most promising of such developments seems to be the search for superordinate goals (Sherif, 1958). Hostile groups can learn to cooperate when a goal urgently needed by both cannot be obtained by either group acting alone. Thus ethnic groups collaborate when a natural disaster strikes. Unfortunately, the cooperative posture often ends as soon as the emergency is over.

The form of a superordinate goal is that of cooperation against a common enemy. This is likely to involve displacement of aggression from an ethnic enemy inside the nation to an external enemy. Like the natural disaster, this cooperation often ends when the enemy outside has been defeated.

Debates about solving intranational conflicts have often argued the issue of changing attitudes versus changing behavior. Recent American history seems to indicate that legal steps may change behavior, and attitudes are modified subsequently. But such legal changes often wait upon the occurrence of violence. Black-White relationships in the United States did not improve until the protests and sit-ins of the 1960s created enough discomfort to motivate change. The advances that have been made in India in the conflicts between castes were not introduced until protests became overt and violent. Thus there is a parallel with parent-child relationships in which overt rebellion may be a precondition to the separation of the adolescent from tight parental control. If the parents can accept the offspring as an independent being, peace and cooperation become possible.

The other aspect of this analogy—and it is no more than an analogy at this point—is that excessive conflicts destroy the human personality, and malignant conflicts can destroy a society. Majority groups in any culture may prefer to live by Freud's pleasure principle, seeking immediate gratification, rather than undergo the painful adjustment involved in maximizing long-term gains as the reality principle dictates. And belief in the use of force as the only solution to conflicts is held tenaciously. Everybody agrees that the arms race between the U.S. and the U.S.S.R. is wasteful and potentially suicidal, but the refusal to seek common goals and to abandon mutually destructive tactics (on both sides) maintains high levels of emotional intensity and neurotic obsession with violence.

It is trite to say that any specific problem calls for more research if we are to evolve a mutually acceptable solution to a group conflict. However, the alarming possibilities for mutually assured destruction make it urgent that we pursue the study of group conflict at all levels. It is, quite literally, a matter of life and death.

References

Muench, G.A. (1960). A clinical psychologist's treatment of labor-management conflict. *Personnel Psychology, 13,* 165-172.

Osgood, C.E. (1962). *An alternative to war or surrender.* Urbana: University of Illinois Press.

Sherif, M. (1958). Superordinate goals in the reduction of intergroup conflicts. *American Journal of Sociology, 63,* 349-356.

Stagner, R. (1967) *Dimensions of human conflict.* Detroit: Wayne State University Press.

Stagner, R., & Eflal, B. (1982). Internal union dynamics during a strike: A quasi-experimental study. *Journal of Applied Psychology, 67,* 37-44.

Stagner, R., & Osgood, C.E. (1946). Impact of war on a nationalistic frame of reference. *Journal of Social Psychology, 24,* 187-215.

Acknowledgments

It is a triviality to say that no work is the product of a single mind. Being a triviality does not make the statement any less true. The present work is no exception. The planning and managing of an international conference is not an easy task; we were fortunate to have the talents of many East-West Center staff to whom the vagaries of visas, plane schedules, accommodations, food preferences, and so forth are challenges to be handled. Gayle Awaya and Liz DeCova performed far beyond the call of duty. Since the conference involved much interplay between the participants, extensive notes of the colloquies were necessary. These notes were used by the editors to clarify points and linguistic obscurities (often due to our less than perfect command of the language). We thank Bobbie Sullivan, Jeanne Eldman, Susan Goldstein, and Joanne Harper for their extensive and accurate recordings. Susan Goldstein also prepared the summaries that appear at the beginning of each chapter. The preparation of some of the chapter drafts—through many revisions—was completed, with good cheer, in Oxford by Debbie Harris, who long ago learned how to handle a boss who should have been caged and fed through a window. We thank the East-West Center for providing the majority of the funding and the facilities for the conference.

We give a special acknowledgment to Dr. Peter E. Wagner, who while serving as Academic Vice Chancellor at the University of Mississippi showed his commitment to interethnic understanding by providing funds to cosponsor the conference. Dr. Wagner's belief that a great university is, by definition, controversial made his tenure in Oxford, though short, memorable to those who share high academic and social goals.

—Jerry D. Boucher, Dan Landis, and Karen Arnold Clark
Honolulu, Hawaii and Oxford, Mississippi

1

Themes and Models of Conflict

DAN LANDIS and JERRY BOUCHER

During the fall of 1985, while this volume was being edited, the press reported that the house and property of a Black family was destroyed by White neighbors in Philadelphia ("the city of brotherly love"). Buses containing the football team and fans from a predominately "Haole" school were stoned by fans from a predominately "Local" school in Hawaii. Locals fought colonials in New Caledonia; Christians battled Muslims in Lebanon, and Muslims battled Christians in the Philippines; overt anti-Semitism was reported in the Soviet Union; anti-Arab acts were reported from Israel; anti-Israeli acts were reported from North Africa; North Africans demonstrated for civil rights in Paris; immigrants rioted in Britain, and the "troubles" continued in Ulster.

Conflict between language, religion, physical appearance, beliefs, and customs of people from different ethnic groups has been—and probably will continue to be—a primary source of unrest in the world. In response to this condition, an international conference on interethnic conflict was convened at the East-West Center in Honolulu during March, 1985. The chapters in this volume are revised and edited from papers prepared for and discussed at the conference. While we recognize that there is a vast literature on the issue of conflict and conflict resolution, we hoped for a fresh approach to these issues at the conference and in this volume. Accordingly, the participants were selected not because they were necessarily experts in the study of conflict (although some were) but, rather, because they were scholars from different countries and academic disciplines who had firsthand experience and/or knowledge of a specific conflict situation. Practical considerations limited the number of participants at the conference. Therefore, this volume contains research on a sample of interethnic conflicts that we hope are of sufficient generality so as to be useful to persons considering the antecedents and dynamics of the many conflicts that infest our world.

We deliberately did not invoke a strict definition of the term *ethnicity* or limit this effort based on any given definition. While most of the participants in the present group do have academic concern for accurate use of the term *ethnicity,* it is apparent from these chapters that while ethnicity is a pervasive issue in these conflicts, there is also an intertwinement of other important classificatory concepts, such as political and national boundaries, religion, language, and race or phenotype. For example, Trimble observes that the term "Indian" is an imposed gloss for hundreds of distinct nations and cultures. He is also able to present a coherent picture of conflict between "Indians" and the majority population of America. Likewise, the position of Blacks in the United States is too important to ignore in this context—even though Bailey discusses this issue as race rather than ethnicity.

Common Themes of Interethnic Conflict

At the conference, the participants examined each conflict in detail, deriving a list of themes that seemed to generalize across all the conflicts. These themes were not mutually exclusive categories but were descriptors to be used as organizing principles. The participants used these themes—to varying degrees of effect—in preparing the chapters in this volume. Seven of the more general themes are considered below, with examples drawn from the chapters and from discussions at the conference of these conflicts.

Perceived Differences Between
Groups, Stereotypes, and Ethnic Identity

A common denominator of so many of the present and historical conflicts—including many of those represented in this volume—is between-group differences, with race or phenotypes, or physical attributes, being dominant. Bailey's chapter on American Blacks and Trimble's chapter on American Indians show race to be a major component of these conflicts, and Ramirez and Sullivan write that race is a component of the Basque conflict. Furthermore, the addition of the racial issue often changes the quality of a particular ethnic encounter. For example, Ginorio points out in her chapter that skin color is a small concern among Puerto Ricans in Puerto Rico, but becomes a major concern of Puerto Ricans who move to New York. Armstrong's chapter suggests that a partial explanation of the vast differences between the historical situations of New Zealand and Australia is the respect shown to the Polynesian Maori as opposed to the contempt shown to the darker-skinned Melanisian Aborigines of Australia. Going beyond Kirkpatrick's chapter, there is the glaring case of racism regarding Japanese-Americans during World War II: Relatively little effort was expended in "protecting" the domestic scene against immigrant Germans. However, shortly after Pearl Harbor, the United States began a massive campaign to incarcerate immigrant Japanese and Americans of Japanese ancestry. This took place despite considerable evidence of more sympathy to the Axis Powers within the German-American community than within the Japanese-American community.

Land Tenure and Homeland Issues, and
Immigrant versus Native Status

The relationship of people to their land is pervasive throughout the conflicts represented in this volume. The American Indian, Maori, and native Hawaiians were dispossessed from their traditional lands. The Basque and Philippine Moro conflicts, and part of the Puerto Rican conflicts, involve a striving for independence from an encroaching political system. The Tamils, originally immigrants to Sri Lanka, now seek a division of the island to give them independence from the Sinhala majority, but the Sinhalas see the Tamils as encroaching on their territory. The Malay-Thai conflict involves artificial boundaries that do not account for the geographic dispersion of the people, and thus there is a two-way tension regarding identity with traditional homelands. Papua New Guinea is a new country encompassing hundreds of cultures and ethnic groups. The tensions there are, in part, the result of traditional homelands (as well as cultures) being subordinated to the national government. The minority groups of China—in a situation similar to that of Papua New Guinea—are threatened by the dominant culture and political system of the majority Han people.

Involvement of Outsiders

To a greater or lesser extent, all of the conflict situations surveyed here have antecedents involving colonization by a foreign power. While this colonial legacy perhaps has had its greatest impact on the land and homeland issues discussed above, the roots of present-day conflicts are often actions and policies established in colonial days, even though the colonial power may no longer be a direct party to the conflict. For example, part of the present-day conflict between Malays and Chinese began when the British imported Chinese laborers to Malaysia, was exacerbated by British support of Chinese guerrillas during World War II, and reached a peak during the "emergency" period when the British and predominantly Malay forces fought against a predominantly Chinese Communist insurgency. The legacy of British colonialism is likewise felt in the present conflict between the Tamils and the Sinhalese in Sri Lanka. Going beyond the colonial issue, Casiño notes that in the Philippines, the Moros have gone to Muslim groups outside the country to seek legitimacy and support for their cause, while the actions of the Philippine government are affected by pressures from other governments—particularly the United States. Bond's chapter on Hong Kong, while emphasizing the lack of conflict, does note the tension of the present status of Hong Kong as a colony, and its imminent absorption into China.

Disparate Allocation of Power and Resources

The frequency with which interethnic conflict involves a difference in allocation of resources between the groups in conflict makes it tempting to suggest that interethnic *contact* becomes interethnic *conflict* when such an imbalance occurs. While this is too simplistic a suggestion, it does point to the importance of this theme. The conflicts involving the American Blacks, Indians, and Puerto Ricans are prime examples of vast differences in wealth and status between groups. From the conflicts discussed in this volume it appears that the issue of allocation of resources is a more important source of conflict when the parties to the conflict occupy the same territory. Thus, for example, while there is a difference in wealth between the Basque provinces and the rest of Spain, and between the Moros and the rest of the Philippines, the issues of ethnic identity appear to outweigh the economic problems. Malaysia is an example of a double imbalance: a major component of the Malay-Chinese conflict is a perceived preponderance of economic power in the hands of the Chinese and political power in the hands of the Malays.

Effects of Language and Language Policy

Language, as a basic component of ethnicity, is a common theme in interethnic conflict. Major conflicts over language usage have occurred in Belgium, Canada, and India. Within the conflicts represented in this volume, the Basque and Malaysian situations have probably been most strongly affected by national policies on language. During much of the Franco period of Spain, government prohibitions against use of any language other than Castillian caused considerable resentment and turmoil in the Basque provinces (and other areas of Spain, such as Catalonia). In Malaysia the government's concern for developing a "national culture," which included instituting Malay as the national language, has resulted in problems for the Chinese and contributed to increased tensions between Malays and Chinese. Thus the issue of language can be a multiple-bind problem: Conflict can arise when an ethnic group's right to speak its own language is threatened. Conflict can also occur as a result of decreased communication between groups.

Process of Conflict Resolution

The chapters by Zhang and Wu and by Bond both stress the institutionalization of modes of conflict resolution within the Chinese culture. Zhang and Wu also emphasize the effects of legal structures in the Chinese government that aim to forestall interethnic conflict by assuring the rights of the minority cultures. At the opposite extreme, Kuschel reports that there is a temporary resolution of conflict on Bellona following an act of violence—at least until such time as it becomes again necessary to take vengeance for the previous act. Armstrong discusses the enduring effects of the Treaty of Waitangi in minimizing conflict between the Maori and Pakeha, although it would appear that present conditions are leading to increasing tensions.

Religion

Differences in religious beliefs and attitudes have historically been a source of conflict between groups. These differences can be the primary source of the conflict, or can exacerbate a conflict that arises from other conditions. The Tamil-Sinhalese conflict has been heightened because the Tamils are Hindu and the Sinhalese are Buddhist. The Moro conflict involves Muslim versus Christian considerations. The Malaysian condition is heavily influenced by Muslim Malay attitudes toward the non-Muslim Chinese. And going beyond the conflicts discussed in this book, the troubles in northern Ireland and in the Middle East have a major religious component.

As interesting as the above themes are, they form nothing more than a set of descriptors. Without some sort of model, predictions as to the when and where of conflict cannot be made. The development of conflict models has a long and respectable history. We now turn, therefore, to a brief sketch of the major theoretical models.

Notes on Models of Conflict

Conflict remains a ubiquitous concept in psychological and sociological theory. Within many major systems of psychology (e.g., those of Freud and of Piaget) the clash of opposing forces provides the motivation and rationale for system growth. This Hegelian-like formulation even appears in Heider's (1958) cognitive calculus and in the Foas' (1974) resource exchange model. The formulation is attractive, we suspect, since it provides a method of calculating a resultant that is different from the constituent parts. So, in the Freudian framework, conflict of the child's desire to possess the mother and father's prior claim produces mutually incompatible goals unless both can be satisfied by an advance into representational thought (to borrow from Piaget). Perhaps the most articulated version of this approach when applied to social conflict is the analysis provided by Rummell (1976). We will return to Rummell's conflict helix later.

Within sociological and other macro-oriented social sciences, the analysis of conflict rarely proceeds with a level of precision common to micro-level theories (e.g., Brown, 1957). Here we find the analysis of conflict either breathtakingly simplified (as in the distinction between horizontal and vertical discrimination) or buried in a blizzard of statistics. For example, one analysis of the genesis of recent Tamil-Sinhalese conflict in Sri Lanka seems to place a great deal of weight on policies that restricted Tamil entry into universities (de Silva, 1984). One could argue—and with considerable justification—that such policies were the result, not the cause, of differences in important psychological characteristics between individuals who are self-identified as Tamil or Sinhalese.

Clearly, the understanding of interethnic conflict will require some agreement not only on the meaning of terms but on a consequent model development that transcends many levels of analysis. It is, however, an article of faith—not to mention logic—that such an analysis must begin at the individual level, with one's perceptions of oneself and others. For unless an individual perceives that his or her interests are in conflict with the interest of others, communal opposition cannot occur.

Curiously, a psychologist, John Berry (1980, 1984) uses a sociological, group-level kind of analysis. He suggests that the behavior of ethnic groups can be divided into four classes as a function of the answers to two questions, Is cultural identity and customs of value, and to be retained? and, Are positive relations with the larger society of value, and to be sought? The possible yes and no answers provide the resultants of *integration, assimilation, segregation-separation, and deculturation.* We call this a group-level analysis since the type of relations are descriptive, not explanatory. We need to know not the questions that may be asked of people in a group, but how those questions come to be the most important ones posed. Further, we must analyze the intensity of the questions. Questions that are not held with high levels of intensity may not lead to conflict but only to disinterest. Berry's analysis, while interesting in that it directs survey researchers to ask certain questions, is too gross to permit much prediction of the course of ethnic relations.

A second model, often favored by social psychologists, is a group-level analysis, but phrased in propositional calculus (e.g., Landis, Campos, Goodman, & Osato, 1983; LeVine & Campbell, 1972; Mack & Snyder, 1957; Williams, 1947). The most articulate and complete example of this approach is given in Mack and Snyder (1957). These authors distill over 100 propositions from many authors into 50 statements, each of which is phrased in the form of an "if-then" hypothesis. All of the 50 deal with aspects of conflict ranging all the way to major international confrontations. Almost all (except for 2) of the propositions are at the group level; for example,

Proposition 4: The more compartmentalized and restricted are the claims of a particular faith to define and regulate religious values, the less likely is religious group membership to be a division (Williams, 1956, cited in Mack & Snyder, 1957).

and

Proposition 21: Social conflict is normally accompanied by a felt or actual discrepancy in the power relations of the parties (Mack & Snyder, 1957).

The few dealing at the individual level are rather general:

Proposition 2: Certain personality characteristics germane to particular national groups are conflict-instigating (Klineberg, 1950, cited in Mack & Snyder);

Proposition 38: Persons with character disorders have predilection for public positions, and the public has a predilection for electing such persons (Cooper, 1955, cited in Mack & Snyder);

Proposition 39: Intrapersonal conflict between aggressive impulses and socially sanctioned moral norms of behavior leads to projection of aggression on external groups (Mack & Snyder).

To the extent that the Mack and Snyder formulations are representative, we see a strong influence of Freudian theory in the study of conflict. But the critical intrapsychic transition to group action is lacking. We know little about how people with "character disorders" influence others and direct their behaviors. Nor can we note with much precision or even formulation how that process occurs.

A much more intrapsychic point of view, but without the Freudian overlay, was presented by Stagner (1961). Stagner adapted homeostatic theory, as he did elsewhere, to personality theory and thence to the study of conflict. For Stagner, the human being *creates* a stable environment so that events can be predicted. This is done by distorting "sensory inputs" as necessary so that the result is a percept that is most probable.

> The specific application of this thesis . . . is that man comes to value his nation, or other social group, as an essential part of his environment, and mobilizes energy to protect it. Further, as part of this process, he distorts the input of information in such a fashion as to protect valued aspects of his social environment, and these distortions contribute in no small degree to the intensity and bitterness of social conflicts (Stagner, 1961).

The critical, and interesting, aspect of Stagner's approach is the role of basic perceptual mechanisms, such as the filtration and construction of percepts. This strategy brings to bear a well-developed research literature on perception that allows us to see social conflict as quite rational, when taken from the viewpoint of the person. It places the individuals in a much more active role as constructors of their views of their social groups, with behavior following as one logical proposition follows from another. Even more important, social conflict is not an aberration to be seen as part of the abnormal psychology, but a problem in the construction of the social world. The assumption, then, is that once a percept of another social group is formed that is inimical to the perceiver, attempts will be made to convince others of the validity of the percept. Such attempts may require that one individual control the information available to the other, thus leading the normal perceptual selection down certain predetermined paths. As more and more people come to share the same world view, a consensual validation develops which applauds consistent actions. These actions may start as the behaviors of a few people but, if the world view is widely shared, lead to greater levels of actions and even civil war.

We find Stagner's view most intriguing. Unlike most social psychologists, he recognizes the essential unity of the human being. The functions of learning, perceiving, emoting, and behaving are all occurring in the same person. An even more detailed model (which in its elements has a number of similarities to Stagner's) is presented by Rummell.

Rummell (1976), a political scientist, has taken a distinctly individualistic and psychological point of view. His analysis postulates a fivefold process that leads to constant change through conflict. The bending back on itself leads Rummell to call the model a "helix." Although the description of the phases is often obscure and needlessly muddy, from an introspective point of view there is a kind of intuitive sense. Conflict, which in Rummell's view is universal and necessary for life, starts with "transformation of sociocultural conflict space into opposing interests." This first stage is simply that differences in attitudes and other subjective attributes are perceived as being sufficiently distinct as to set up a desire for making some sort of change. So, awareness of differences is the first requisite for conflict. But no conflict yet exists—it is merely a cognitive exercise, in Rummell's view.

The next stage occurs when the person (which he calls the "will") chooses to initiate conflict by seeing the attitudinal differences as in need of a resolution. That is, the person decides that the differences cannot be allowed to continue and therefore accepts a level of uncertainty about the outcome of the conflict. Some sort of "trigger" is necessary to provide the move from the first to the second stage. The discussion (Rummell, 1976, p. 370) of such triggers sounds like psychologically familiar conditioned stimuli. That is, the trigger leads to a state of uncertainty (perhaps anxiety) that has been conditioned to a search for dimensions along which differences exist. So, two groups may have many attitudinal differences that do not lead to conflict until some event increases anxiety in members of one group. The affective state then leads to a search for a source of the anxiety and the development of a rationale for its reduction (e.g., "they are very different from us").

The uncertainity that results from the trigger into the second stage is probably an uncomfortable cognitive state. We have suggested that one of the reasons that anxiety results from intercultural training is that attributional categories come to have lower probabilities (Landis, Brislin, & Hulgus, 1985). A similar process may underlie Rummell's second stage.

The uncertainty that results from the opposition of two or more attitudinal vectors and those oppositions being judged to be important leads to attempts to recapture the balance, maybe an internal balance. The third stage, then, is the process of regaining balance and involves some three major subphases: testing to see if past cognitions can be used to resolve the uncertainty; if so, then an accommodation reestablishing the old balance; if not, then an analysis of available power to see if it can be brought to bear to achieve balance.

Now if the power brought by one person can be accepted as legitimate or noncoercive, then a new accommodation can be reached. Conversely, if no acceptable noncoercive power can be used, coercive power (force or threats) becomes the instrument of choice. But still there is no overt conflict—we are still in the realm of potentialities or psychological weighing of possibilities. In any case, the fourth stage—balance of power—is entered.

The balance of power stage, since it leads to a new set of expectations and attributions, is a fundamental change in the cognitive structure. The attributions about the likely behavior of others may now be quite negative and may include violence or other socially destructive behaviors. A random, triggering event that appears to confirm the new expectations leads to not only a recycling of the processes but also to overt behaviors. The assassination of Mrs. Gandhi (which confirmed expectations about the Sikhs) and the move of Sinhalese to restrict university placements in Sri Lanka (which confirmed expectations of Tamils about Sinhalese) are such triggering events.

As interesting as Rummell's analysis is (and we confess it is more fascinating than most models used by psychologists), we still lack the "maguffin"—the rule for transitioning from individual to group conflict. Interethnic conflict is not just the prejudice of one person (e.g., a White) against another (a Black) but also involves the tacit agreement among many "ones" that they share common views about the others. It also involves shared expectations about the others' behaviors—particularly those that involve the first group.

We suggest that the answer lies in the nature of the perceived dimensions of differences—Rummell's first stage. It would seem reasonable to note that not all dimensions are equally important. As Triandis (1972) noted, dimensions (he called them "concepts") vary in their level of abstraction. At the lowest level are categories of perceptual experience (e.g., hues, sounds). At the highest (and with the most affective component) are values (e.g., religiosity, relationship to elders, seeking after pleasure). It seems as though differences at the lowest levels of abstraction produce the least conflict. It is hard to imagine a lasting group conflict over the color of a piece of cloth. The reason may lie in the individual differences in perception—that is, while two people may disagree on a percept, it is unlikely that large numbers of others would be in agreement with the two protagonists. More to the point, even if there were large numbers of like-minded individuals, that fact would be uncorrelated with any aspect of group membership.

Values, on the other hand, seem to be the most susceptible to large-scale agreement and thus conflict. There are two important aspects here: First, values have large affective components. People become emotional about their country, their church, and their family. Second, values, because of their level of abstraction, serve as organizing principles for most other concepts. There is little that cannot be seen as an exemplar of a particular value. One could then postulate that when differences in values are made salient, the stage is set for interethnic conflict; when the differences are confined at lower levels of abstraction (e.g., visual stimuli, behaviors, stereotypes) their use as antecedents to larger conflicts is minimized.

When salience occurs, predicting the occurrence of a critical mass is still a significant problem. Social identity theory outlined by Tajfel (1978) attempts to provide a mechanism. Brewer and Miller (1984) describe the central proposition of social identity theory as the belief that "an individual's personal identity is highly differentiated and based in part on membership in significant social categories, along with the value and emotional significance attached to that membership" (p. 281). Thus when a particular membership is very important, the tendency is to respond to others as if they were members of an outgroup. There is, consequently, a depersonalization of the people in the out-group; that is, they no longer are individuals but exemplars of their group. Individual variation is lost and the assumption is that there is identity within the group. Once the process begins there is, presumably, a need for justification, which cannot exist if the ingroup and outgroup are both equally and positively valued. So, features of the ingroup that are positively related to a *positive self-identity* (Turner, 1975) are enhanced and the members of the outgroup are found wanting. Contrast effects would predict that the discontinuity between ingroup and outgroup would increase until there is virtually no overlap possible between the two groups. While attractive, there are too many undefined terms (e.g., "significant") to make this approach predictive of the transition from intraindividual to intergroup conflict. Tajfel's (1978) explanation for extreme social categorization (i.e., interethnic conflicts of the type covered in this book) is to point to the existence of the societal conflict and the accompanying beliefs about boundaries that are "sharply drawn and immutable." Such an explanation is little more than a tautology and certainly begs the question.

Our aim in this section has been to summarize the main theoretical approaches to conflict. It would seem that the most vexing problem is the transition from intrapsychic to intergroup conflict. The propositions of Mack and Snyder and others fairly well serve to predict behavior at the group level, but do not really provide explanations that reflect the fact that groups are made up of individuals. On the other hand, the approaches of the Freudians and, to some extent, Rummell, fail to explain how the conflicts of a person become the behavior of a group. Stagner's hypotheses are a step in this direction but need to be supplemented with perceptual research that shows how one person controls the sensory input of another. We think this can be done and is certainly being accomplished every day by parents and leaders of every type.

The desire to control not only our own percepts but those of others is a pervasive part of our lives. From Hitler's burning of books, to the Soviet's revising of history, to the religious fundamentalists' outrages on television programming—the examples are legion. It is our belief that here, in a simple psychological mechanism, lies the structure for understanding conflict.

References

Berry, J. (1980) Acculturation as varieties of adaptation. In A. Padilla (Ed.), *Acculturation: Theory, models and some new findings* Washington, DC: AAAS.

Berry, J. (1984). Cultural relations in plural societies: Alternatives to segregation and their sociopsychological implications. In N. Miller & M. B. Brewer (Eds.), *Groups in contact: The psychology of desegregation* (pp. 11-27). Orlando: Academic Press.

Brewer, M. B. & Miller, N. (1984). Beyond the contact hypothesis: Theoretical perspectives on desegregation. In N. Miller & M. B. Brewer (Eds.), *Groups in contact: The psychology of desegregation* (pp. 281-302). Orlando: Academic Press.

Brown, J. S. (1957). Principles of intrapersonal conflict. *Journal of Conflict Resolution, 1,* 135-153.

Cooper, J. B. (1955). Psychological literature on the prevention of war. *Bulletin of the Research Exchange on the Prevention of War, III,* No. 17.

de Silva, K. M. (1984). University admissions and ethnic tension in Sri Lanka: 1977-82. In R. B. Goldmann & A. J. Wilson (Eds.), *From independence to statehood,* (pp. 97-110). New York: St. Martins.

Foa, U. G. & Foa, E. (1974). *Societal structures of the mind.* Springfield, Ill.: Charles C. Thomas.

Heider, F. (1958). *The psychology of interpersonal relations.* New York: Wiley.

Klineberg, O. (1950). *Tensions affecting international understanding.* New York: Social Science Research Council.

Landis, D., Brislin, R. W., & Hulgus, J. (1985). The effects of two types of acculturative training: A laboratory study. *Journal of Applied Social Psychology, 15,* 466-482.

Landis, D., Campos, P. E., Goodman, N., & Osato, S. (1983). *Thoughts on the effects of heterogeneity: Predictions and research models* (ONR Tech. Rep. No. 83-4.) Indianapolis: Indiana University-Purdue University Center for Applied Research and Evaluation.

LeVine, R. & Campbell, D. (1972). *Ethnocentricism: Theories of conflict, ethnic attitudes, and group behavior.* New York: John Wiley.

Mack, R. W., & Snyder, R. C. (1957). The analysis of social conflict—toward an overview and synthesis. *Journal of Conflict Resolution, 1,* 212-248.

Rummell, R. J. (1976). *Understanding conflict and war.* New York: John Wiley.

Stagner, R. (1961). Personality dynamics and social conflict. *Journal of Social Issues, 17,* 28-44.

Tajfel, H. (1978). Social categorization, social identity, and social comparisons. In H. Tajfel (Ed.), *Differentiation between social groups* (pp. 661-676). London: Academic Press.

Triandis, H. C. (1972). *The analysis of subjective culture.* New York: John Wiley.

Turner, J. C. (1975). Social comparison and social identity: some prospects for social behavior. *European Journal of Social Psychology, 5,* 5-34.

Williams, R. M., Jr. (1947). *The reduction of intergroup tensions.* New York: Social Science Research Council.

Chapter Summary

Sinnapah Arasaratnam's discussion of "Sinhala-Tamil relations in modern Sri Lanka (Ceylon)" begins with an argument that what is commonly believed to be a conflict-laden history of Sinhala-Tamil relations may be less a product of fact and more the result of Buddhist rewritings of history. The author suggests that because of the accessibility of Sri Lanka by the Dravidian people, most nonreligious aspects of its culture have strong Dravidian (Tamil) influence. Thus Buddhism has been emphasized as distinguishing the Sinhalese and Tamil.

Arasaratnam states that the precolonial spatial separation between Sinhalese and Tamil was upset by the British introduction of Tamils as plantation labor in the central highlands. This, in addition to the increasing urbanization, began increased interethnic contact and thus increased economic and social competition. Changes in Sinhala-Tamil relations accompanying the political evolution of Sri Lanka are also discussed.

The author points out that Sinhala activism began as primarily an anti-Christian and anti-West movement resulting from the low status accorded to the Sinhalese language and the Buddhist religion in the period after independence. Arasaratnam discusses how various grievances gradually took a political form and became targeted against the Tamils; eventually the emphasis of the Sinhala movement became presenting the Tamil as their traditional enemy.

Events that further led the Tamils to rally behind a single political party are reviewed, including government colonization of Tamil land. The transformation of government agencies, such as the armed forces, to Sinhala power is described as is the discrimination against Tamils in public jobs and education. Such discrimination became institutionalized as ethnic, language, and regional requirements became law.

Arasaratnam explains how in the 1970s many Tamils, whom he describes as "unemployed, under-employed, and dissatisfied," left their villages in search of greater opportunities only to find that what had traditionally been Tamil land had been colonized by the Sinhalese. The author suggests that such events, in conjunction with the anti-Tamil riots of 1977, increased the geographical and psychological solidarity of the Tamil people. He asserts that Sinhala politicians could not make concessions without the strong negative reactions of their constituents, and that this polarization led to a reorganization of Tamil resistance, politicizing large segments of the Tamil population. The author reviews the actions taken by various Tamil activist groups, including the Tamil United Liberation Front, who increasingly sought an independent Tamil state.

Arasaratnam describes the escalation of Sinhala-Tamil violence and the resulting internationalization of the conflict, including strengthening ties between Tamil of India and Tamil of Sri Lanka. He states that in 1983 India volunteered to mediate the conflict, further incurring the distrust of the Sinhalese.

Arasaratnam maintains that Sinhala-Tamil conciliation can only come through increasing international pressure and a recognition of the interest of both ethnic groups.

—Susan Goldstein

2

Sinhala-Tamil Relations in Modern Sri Lanka (Ceylon)

SINNAPPAH ARASARATNAM

Contemporary events in Sri Lanka, reinforced by the strident propaganda on all sides of the island's multiethnic policy, may give the
impression that Sinhala-Tamil relations have always been characterized by hostility and violence. That this is not the case is made
clear when one looks at the reality of the social configuration of
these two language-culture groups at present and in its historical
dimension. Over a period of two millennia, the two communities
have settled on the island as migrants from the neighboring sub-
continent. They have been known to exist in close proximity to
each other as well as spatially separated from each other, and in
both these forms they have coexisted for centuries. Both adjacent
and segregated settlement continue in Sri Lanka today.

This is not to say that the "enmity" model of relations does not
also have a long history in people's perceptions. In the precolonial
periods the Tamils were portrayed as hostile invaders in some of the
traditional ideologies of the Sinhala literati. These ideologies issued
from the established Buddhist monasteries of particular sects that
sought to entrench their legitimacy through direct linkage with the
ruling house. This ruling house itself was legitimized by ascribing
direct descent from an eponymous founder of the Sinhala race, a
mythical first settler, and a first fleet. As these Buddhist monks
dominated the emergence of a historical tradition, the political his-

tory of the island—with its continuing saga of internecine wars, foreign invasions, and migrations—was rewritten as a great apocalyptic clash between the Sinhalese, who possessed the island, and the Tamils (Dravidas), who came seeking to dispossess them (Geiger, 1950, 1953).

As opposed to perceived history and distorted history, reality was polycentric and multiform. Relations between Indo-Aryan speaking peoples who settled in waves in the island from about the sixth century B.C. and Dravidian language speakers (chief of whom were the Tamils) have followed a course dictated by a variety of determinant causes and needs. The simplest but most poignant is the fact that the island is separate from India by eight miles of shallow water at its narrowest and less than two days journey in the larger sailing ships between the deep water ports. Across this narrow waterway have come in historic times not only invaders but, in greater abundance, artisans, merchants, Buddhist and Hindu scholars and priests, bringing with them technologies, philosophies, architectural and sculptural styles, and literary texts. The consequence of all this has been that Sinhala is the Indo-Aryan language most influenced by Dravidian languages; the social structure of the Sinhalese has many Dravidian elements; the art and architecture of the island is permeated with the major south Indian styles; and Buddhism, the one phenomenon that is held to distinguish the Sinhalese from the Tamils, is riddled with Saivite and folk Hinduism (Bandaranayake, 1984; Goonatilake, 1984; Gunawardena, 1984).

Colonial Rule and Elite Accommodation

As happened in plural societies elsewhere in the Asian and African continents, Sinhala-Tamil relations, which developed in a situation of dynamism and flux in the precolonial period, became frozen at the level they were when the first colonial power conquered the maritime areas. At that time a spatial separation of the two ethnic groups had come about with a broad stretch of jungle spreading as a no-man's-land between them. Tamil settlements were concentrated in the northern third of the island and in another strip southwards in the eastern part. The remainder of the island was occupied by the Sinhalese. This demographic map is an important feature in understanding subsequent developments in ideas and aspirations. The British contribution to upset this demography was to introduce into the central highlands as plantation labor a new wave of migrants from the Tamil districts of South India. Thus at independence there were an equal number of the post-nineteenth-century migrant Tamils as there were Tamils of earlier settlement.

The imposition of colonial rule had the effect, in the short term, of freezing the pluralism in society at the level it had then reached. In the long term, it pushed in the direction of greater interaction between communities, especially from the nineteenth century onwards. From this time, the Tamils, who had been spatially separated from the Sinhalese, were brought, by the force of economic factors, to more direct contact and hence competition with them in the market place, in the public services, and in educational institutions. The growth of incipient capitalism and of a bureaucracy in the public and private sectors created conditions of growth in employment of which all communities took advantage. With the growth of the urban metropolis of Colombo, Sinhalese and Tamils faced each other in situations of work, residence, and recreation. This picture of communal interaction was reproduced, on a smaller scale, in other administrative and commercial growth centers in other parts of the country.

These developments were taking place at the level of the elites of all communities. The stages for their interplay were British institutions, whether of government, commerce, or education. The vital tools that brought them together were a common facility in servicing these institutions, and this was expressed through the acquisition of English education at various levels. At the base, the respective traditional societies were unaffected. They merely produced recruits to the British raj, creamed off in various ways and differentially motivated. This elite was the first integrated national social "class" that began to think in terms of territorial loyalty to an all-island polity which they hoped, with increasing enthusiasm, to inherit from the British colonists. The two major communities that constituted this first Ceylonese elite—Sinhalese and Tamils—uneasily worked together in the first political associations, though even in the early stages each was conscious of appropriating its communal share of the total.

In this stage of political evolution, when the political process was limited to a narrow social class of urban elite, communal relations were a matter of horsetrading between members of this class. The early divisions were primarily over allocation of seats in legislatures, executive councils, and local bodies. With the broadening of representative government and the early stages of devolution of power, the dominance of the numerically superior Sinhalese was established, and this in turn aroused the fears of the Tamil political leaders. When negotiations were carried on between Sinhalese political leaders and the colonial government over the transfer of power, these divisions were papered over. Unlike the Indian struggle for independence, Ceylon's progress to dominion status was through discussion held behind closed doors and the deliberations of a constitutional commission appointed by the British government. Though there was some attempt by a Tamil political leader to raise issues of communal division and the necessity for minority safeguards, these were not aired throughout the country and the commissioners decided that Ceylon had reached a stage of nationhood at which such safeguards were unnecessary.

The politics of communal consensus went on into the period after independence. Governments of this time were constituted of the elite, cutting across ethnic divisions; but what the elite achieved through horizontal integration they lacked in vertical penetration. The vast subelite mass, whether Sinhalese or Tamil, was not brought actively into the political process, except for their votes during general elections. This form of consensus government necessarily meant a continuation of the cultural milieu of the colonial period and left those outside the elite dissatisfied and disgruntled. This dissatisfaction was seen in the lowly position accorded to the two dynamic elements of Sinhalese culture, the Sinhala language and Buddhism (Buddhist Committee of Inquiry, 1956). The convergence of these two elements in the 1950s produced a catalyst of revolutionary proportions that was to determine the course of Ceylonese politics for the next three decades.

Language and Religion as Definers
of Sinhala Identity

At first the Sinhalese language and Buddhism movement was not overly anti-Tamil. It was more anti-West and anti-Christian. In this stage of its growth, the Sinhala movement saw as its enemy not the

Tamils but the westernized elite and the Christians. Somewhere along the line, its hostility was broadened to embrace the Tamils of the island. A number of factors are responsible for this broadening of hostility. The legitimate grievances of Sinhala-educated and Buddhist rural intelligentsia—the outsiders in the power structure which paraded itself as a democracy—formed the solid foundations of the movement. This was matched by the arrogance and assertiveness of the westernized elite, a self-perpetuating oligarchy of about 7 per cent of the population.[1] Under the guise of neutrality, the state perpetuated unequal growth of religious institutions and denominations, with the Buddhist monasteries and clergy very much the underclass. When, as a natural outgrowth of the political process, the ruling elite was factionalized in 1951, these issues were brought into the arena of political conflict and became grist to the mill of political mobilization. It only needed the emergence of a Bandaranaike to give political form to these forces and articulate them on national platforms.[2]

In 1956, with the downfall of the political structure of elite consensus, Ceylon entered a new era in which the establishment of Sinhala hegemony was followed by Tamil resistance. This new force has been referred to by a number of analysts as a second wave of Sinhala nationalism, to contrast it with the elite nationalism of the first phase before and immediately after independence. While such periodization is convenient, it could obscure the fact that the so-called second-wave nationalism had deep roots in the past and was always present in the years when the first wave was dominant. Further, it is doubtful whether the Sinhala elite had developed an ideology of nationalism in the manner that the Indian elite had. What really seems to have happened is that a section of the Sinhala elite, in its drive for power, seized on issues of Sinhala communal identity and unsatisfied aspirations to mobilize mass support among the Sinhalese. The drive to mobilize Sinhala nationalism and keep it in a state of constant mobilization developed its own momentum.

The ideology of Sinhala nationalism looked naturally to the past—an idealized past of glorious Sinhala kingdoms, extensive political power, and high cultural achievements. It was a past when the state and church were in a symbiotic relationship, each fostering, legitimizing, and strengthening the other. In the search for an ideological essence or soul for the Sinhala nation, the answer was found in the *Buddha Dhamma,* the faith which was implanted in the island by the mythical visits of the Buddha himself and then reinforced by missionary activity of the great Mauryan Buddhist Emperor Asoka. The Sinhala race thus became custodians of the *dhamma* and the island of Ceylon its special home.

In the first phase of Sinhala hegemony, the state became an instrument for remedial legislation, redressing centuries-old grievances the Sinhalese had suffered. Thus they had a plausible democratic and even socialist underpinning and attracted wide support and sympathy. But right from the outset the movement met with resistance from the Tamils who were, at this stage, only reacting to Sinhala initiatives. It was thus that the Sinhala movement, which was at first a cultural movement of assertion against westernization and Christianization, now saw the Tamils as the main enemy. This helped add another plank to the ideological platform; there was emphasis now on presenting the Tamils as the traditional enemy of the Sinhalese. There was any amount of plausible historical evidence to be presented to support this view, including an epic battle that had become part of the Sinhala folklore between a Sinhala and a Tamil king for dominance in the island in the second century B.C. Moreover, over a thousand-year period, from the fifth to the fifteenth centuries A.D., the island had been subject to invasions by south Indian Dravidian kingdoms. These invasions had been a contributory factor behind the decline of the Sinhala kingdoms of the dry zone and their hydraulic civilization.

Though these ideologies began to permeate deep into Sinhala society, in the first phase of communal tensions they were only weapons used by the old Sinhala westernized elite and the emerging Sinhala-educated elite to mobilize support for their own particular concerns. These concerns were to seize state power, to use this power in the interests of furthering educational and employment opportunities for Sinhala-educated youth, and to widen commercial opportunities for an emerging class of small-scale Sinhala entrepreneurs. In all these avenues, Tamils were seen to be the major obstacle. Tamil opposition to making Sinhala alone the official language and the consequent preference of Sinhalese in employment served to harden Sinhala attitudes. Likewise, Sinhala educationists saw the Tamils having undue advantages in the availability of education of a high standard through the operation of larger numbers of Christian denominational schools. Measures were taken to neutralize this advantage by the nationalization of all schools. The conversion of the medium of instruction in schools and university to the child's mother tongue removed the disadvantages suffered by many Sinhalese students of competing in the English medium for higher education places and for employment.

Rise of the Sinhala Hegemonist State

The process of Sinhala ascendancy, achieved through the ballot and control of the state, could not be reversed, and Sinhalese dominance became entrenched. Untrammeled by the need to accommodate Tamil opinion, Ceylonese governments became increasingly Sinhala and the state itself became transformed from a truly national entity, standing above separate communities, into an instrument of communal Sinhala power. This transformation was effected more rapidly under Mrs. Bandaranaike who took power in 1960 after her husband's assassination. It was effected through a number of steps. One of the most important agencies of the state to be so transformed was the armed forces. Earlier these had reflected a genuinely intercommunal and supracommunal ethos. Particularly the officer corps had absorbed from the British Army the ideologies of an army subordinate to the state and carrying on its wishes with impartiality.

In 1962 an ill-thought-out and poorly planned attempt at a coup against the state by officers of the armed forces, police, and senior bureaucrats was nipped in the bud. A number of serving officers were dismissed or resigned and the government had an opportunity to transform the ethos and ideology of the army. The officers and new recruits were sympathetic to the new forces of Sinhala communalism and hegemony; by the 1970s, with hardly any Tamils being recruited, the army became predominately Sinhala (Horowitz, 1980, pp. 53-75, 193-216). The situation in the police force was not as bad, as here there were still Tamil officers who had been recruited under the open competitive system continuing in senior positions. However, new recruitments were heavily weighted in favor of Sinhalese, who were the products of the new Sinhala communal wave. In the bureaucracy the situation was much worse for the Tamils. It is true that under the system of open recruitment Tamils had entered public service at various grades in numbers considerably more than their proportion in the population. This was particularly noticeable in technical and professional services such as engineering, accounting, medicine, and veterinary sciences. The initial positive discrimination to redress the imbalance of the Sinhalese became a habit and by the 1980s the overall proportion of Tamils in public service had been reduced. Among new recruits they had a ratio much lower then their proportion in the population (Abeysekera, 1984).

With the growth of state control over the economy brought about under the two administrations of Mrs. Bandaranaike (1960-65 and 1970-77), the Sinhala dominance over avenues of state power was complete. With the proliferation of state corporations managing many sectors of the economy—transport, port, petroleum, wholesale trade, a number of industries, plantations—the capacity of the state to extend this domination was limitless. It was in these corporations, where political jobbery was rife due to the absence of the controls of a public services commission, that the Tamils were most disadvantaged.

Finally, Sinhala interests launched an attack on the country's tertiary institutions, again reversing the criterion of merit that had so far been used for admission to the universities of the country. Admission criteria were changed to take in ethnic and district considerations; and when these were applied from 1971 onward they resulted in a substantial change in the racial mix of the undergraduate population. Using these criteria in admissions to the prestigious medical, engineering, agricultural, and physical science faculties, the ratio of Tamils in these faculties was substantially reduced. This was yet another measure, introduced on the principle of egalitarianism, to satisfy Sinhala grievances but felt by the Tamils to be grossly unfair to them. It had the further effect of denying higher education to a large group of students who had achieved high grades in the high school certificate examination (De Silva, 1974, 1978). These students were thus let loose on society with a deep antagonism to communal discrimination and the desire to do something about it.

Thus over a period of over two decades, Sinhala pressure groups could call the tune in the use of state power to assert their hegemony. The Sinhalese, constituting 74 per cent of the population, were the undisputed majority community, yet had the complex and the fears of a minority need to be buttressed by state power. This power they had in abundance, as the role of the minorities in the political process was reduced to a cypher. Sinhala groups were in the position of determining the extent of positive action to redress past grievances and imbalances and were unable to draw the line at what was feasible, prudent, and just in a multiethnic society.‘This unrestrained exercise of power was given ideological justification by reference to that element of Sinhala tradition portraying them as the original inhabitants and owners of the entire land. Buddhism was destined to find its home in the whole island and had to be defended against threats from whatever quarter. The threat that earlier was believed to have come from the West in the form of Christianity and imperialism was in the 1970s identified as coming from northern Sri Lanka where the Tamils were and further across the Palk Straits. This fear of cultural extinction, which was played upon by political opportunists, kept alive the demand for communal hegemony and fostered a minority complex with the power of a majority community.

Tamil Response:
Identity, Language Rights, Land Colonization

Tamil political attitudes in Sri Lanka had until 1953 been reactive rather than innovative. Tamil communities in the island were isolated from each other and their concerns had been largely parochial. The Tamils of the Jaffna peninsula struggled along to sustain life in the difficult physical conditions there and migrated southward as well as overseas in large numbers. On the northern part of the mainland were Tamils engaged in agriculture of a different pattern from those in the peninsula. These two groups were in turn totally isolated from those in the east, who were themselves separated into the Trincomalee, Mullaithivu settlements and those of the Batticaloa coastlands. There was, of course, the big divide between all these and the Tamils of the plantation hill country. English-educated Tamil leaders sought to unify the Tamils largely as a political power-base for themselves in their dealings with the parties of the south. Bandaranaike's victory of 1956 had ended this form of Sinhala-Tamil elite accommodation and a process of mass mobilization belatedly took place among the Tamils.

For the Tamils, the first phase of Sinhala hegemonism presented challenges but was not as yet fundamentally destructive of their interests. The official language legislation was, for the time being at least, more of an emotive issue rather than of material concern. The employment situation was not as yet critical nor were educational opportunities adversely affected till the end of the 1960s. Other issues were, however, beginning to make their appearance. The most important of these was land colonization, a policy that had been initiated by government to open virgin land to relieve the pressure of population in the south and west of the island. These colonization schemes were beginning to encroach on land in the Tamil-occupied areas of the country. But even here, there was as yet no land hunger among the Tamils and no competition for the newly opened land. Tamil leaders were thinking ahead of their time and trying to devise permanent solutions to secure long-term interests. Besides leading campaigns against the official language policy, Tamil leaders were propagating ideas of autonomy and decentralization of power to secure a measure of self-management of their affairs for the Tamils. But there is no evidence that such radical constitutional measures were understood or appreciated by Tamil public opinion, though Tamils began politically to rally behind the one party that propagated these ideas—the Federal Party.

The Federal Party sought to achieve a conservatively led communal solidarity among the Tamils. The solidarity was articulated in muted fashion by the traditional social hierarchy of leaders of the community. The political, economic, and cultural reforms of the 1960s and 1970s were producing major changes among Tamils in respect to their political influence, economic mobility, and social relations. The language issue, which had begun as an emotive issue involving claims to equal rights in the island's polity, broadened into one with economic implications as it extended into the employment and educational spheres. Large groups of young, potentially upwardly mobile people from lower-middle-class and peasant families of the north and the east found these avenues closed to them. Those who already had a foot in the public services had the grievance of blocked further promotions. Unemployed, underemployed, and dissatisfied Tamils were the constituents whom their leaders now faced.

The issue of land colonization also acquired a new intensity in the 1970s. As noted above, there had been no great demographic push from the nuclear Tamil areas of Jaffna, Trincomalee, and Batticaloa to the outer fringes where the new colonization schemes were. But with the shrinkage of employment opportunities, more of these Tamils left their natal villages in unsponsored private migrations to occupy land in the Vavuniya, Mullaithivu districts and in the outer districts of Trincomalee and Batticaloa. They found that here Sinhalese were beginning to be settled in large numbers in the state-sponsored schemes. The demography of Trincomalee district, for example, had changed markedly in favor of the Sinhalese in twenty years. Some districts west of Batticaloa had been transformed in this time to Sinhala majority areas. And there was a continuing push in the Vavuniya district. The Tamils felt that they were being discriminated against in land allotments in colonization schemes in traditionally Tamil districts.

The land issue was further complicated by a new element that emerged after 1972. The nationalization of the plantations undertaken from 1972-74, combined with the downturn in world prices for tea and rubber, had seriously destabilized the plantation industry. There was heavy unemployment among Tamil labor in the plantations and many of them were displaced and evicted from housing they had occupied within the plantations for generations. At first these displaced families gravitated to urban centers of the hill country, but these towns could not provide them a livelihood. During this time, the first voluntary welfare groups emerged among the Tamils trying to provide homes in the unoccupied lands of the Tamil districts of the north and the east for these destitute Tamils. Within a few years a number of such settlements had grown up where Tamils lived and worked in relative contentment. This process was speeded up with the first anti-Tamil civil riots that broke out in the highland towns and plantation centers in 1977. Thereafter these continued with regularity whenever racial violence was perpetrated against Tamils in the rest of the country. After such violence, there was an exodus of families to the settlements of the north and the east. At first the government did not interfere with this dispersal, but as it accelerated government attitude turned hostile. On some occasions when Tamils squatted on state land, they were evicted. To the Tamils the attitude of the state toward sponsored colonization of Sinhalese contrasted glaringly with its treatment of Tamil settlements (Tamil United Front of Ceylon, 1973).

Growth of Political Activism

While issues touching Tamil interests were being transformed and broadened in their mass impact, the leadership of the community continued to operate in the old mold. Their tentative essays into civil disobedience brought on them the wrath of the state and the Sinhala mob. As early as May 1958, in response to the first attempts by Tamil political leaders to launch a campaign of resistance to the Sinhala Only Act, an organized movement of terror and violence was let loose on Tamil communities living in Sinhala areas. Worst affected were the capital city of Colombo, other urban centers along the south-western coast, and the new colonization settlements of the east and north-central dry zone. After this experience, Tamil leaders were understandably wary about the extent of their resistance. Civil disobedience campaigns were launched as new issues arose, but the incidents were isolated to the Tamil majority districts and were quickly suppressed by the force of state power.

Hesitant and reluctant to move in the direction of mass resistance, Tamil leaders were inclined to take the paths of accommodation and compromise, whenever such were open to them. In 1957 the prime minister entered into negotiations with the Tamil leader and an agreement known as the Bandaranaike-Chelvanayakam Pact, which went some way toward conceding Tamil demands, was signed. No sooner was the ink dry on the signatures than extreme Sinhala elements led by influential Buddhist clergy began a counter-movement of protest and the prime minister gave in and repudiated the pact. Likewise, in 1965, the United Nationals Party (UNP) leader entered into an agreement with the leaders of the Tamil Federal Party to legislate for the redress of some Tamil grievances. When the government sought to give effect to this agreement, a mass Sinhala communal outburst was raised against the provisions and again the government abandoned its efforts.

Thus Sinhala-Tamil relations became locked into a system in which when one party of Sinhala leaders decided to solve the Tamil problem by making some concessions they faced a massive and often hysterical outcry from those in opposition and with the support of extremist groups. The major Sinhala political parties were vying with each other in the hardness of their position toward the Tamils, especially during election campaigns. This is clearly demonstrated in the shift in position on communal questions by the parties of the Marxist left. These parties felt they had to move from support of minority rights to a capitulation to the demands for Sinhala hegemony in order to escape electoral slaughter. This political polarization was complete by 1970 and led to a reconsideration of strategy by Tamil politicians and by Tamil interests in general. It was recognized that it was no longer possible for Tamils to win concessions by supporting one Sinhala political grouping against another. Whatever one party might promise, it could never deliver in government.

The spread of discontent with state policies and the widespread effect of these policies on several sectors of the Tamil population took the mobilization of Tamil public opinion a step further and politicized large segments of Tamils in dispersed areas of the island. It was a degree of politicization and awareness that could not be contained by the older political parties and their leadership. This process of politicization was accelerated by more rigorous measures of repression and even terror initiated by the security organs of the state. A number of incidents in the 1970s, each worse in its impact than the preceding one, left the Tamils with a feeling of insecurity and helplessness when faced with state repression. In so far as it is possible to identify a starting point, it could be the January 1974 incidents in Jaffna, when the police rushed a crowd of participants at a public meeting organized during the Fourth International Conference of Tamil Studies. Eleven persons of ages from 14 to 52 were killed in this outrage and it was followed by days of police terror and brutality on innocent civilians in the city of Jaffna (Inthu Ilainjan, 1974). Subsequent acts of police and army brutality have been well documented by local and foreign press and by national and international civil rights groups (Amnesty International, 1983; Hyndman, 1984; Moore, 1984).

By 1974 the parameters of political activity and the ground rules of political participation had changed so fundamentally that it was necessary for the existing political leaders and their parties to take account of these changes or themselves be rendered irrelevant and worthless. They responded to the challenge by moving in the direction of a separate Tamil identity in the island and underlining the claims of self-determination for the Tamils in Sri Lanka. The major Tamil party, the Federal Party, had so far been wedded to the concept of a unified polity within which it was seeking a greater devolution of power through a federal constitution. In 1975, it reconstituted itself into the Tamil United Liberation Front (TULF), bringing together a number of splinter groups and individuals and demanding, in the Front's session of 1976, the right of self-determination for the Tamils. It asserted the claim of a separate Tamil nationhood in Sri Lanka, to which nation was given the name Eelam, an old Tamil name for the island of Ceylon (Ponnambalam, 1983).[3] By adopting this extreme position, the old leadership succeeded, at least temporarily, in continuing in the vanguard of the Tamil struggle and retained its electoral popularity.

Emergence of Tamil Youth Militancy

The TULF was merely responding to the radicalization of opinion and the birth of militancy, especially among Tamil youth. Shortly after the abortive Marxist insurrection of Sinhala youth in April 1971, there appears to have arisen among the Tamil youth of the north various splinter groups that explored alternative ways of carrying on the struggle of the Tamils. A few of these were Marxist-inspired and used the language of Leninist and Maoist doctrines in their analyses and their propaganda. Others were founded on the basis of an ethnic-linguistic identity. All of them had the common aim of an armed struggle to preserve Tamil identity against what they saw as Sinhala domination and all were fed by economic grievances. By 1980, it was estimated that over 40 per cent of holders of the Advanced Level of the General Certificate of Education (GCE) among Tamils were unemployed. In addition to economic and ethnic factors, the romanticism of clandestine revolutionary activity attracted a number of the able and educated youth of the Jaffna peninsula. Through the 1970s these groups consolidated their organizational machinery and prepared themselves for armed insurrection. At first they considered themselves a militant wing of the political movement of the Tamils represented by the TULF. Increasingly, as succeeding Sinhala governments hardened their attitude to the TULF, the youth militants distanced themselves from the TULF and began to work out independent strategies to achieve a sovereign state of Eelam for the Tamils. With the election of the UNP government of Jayawardena in 1977, they came out in the open to challenge this government in an armed insurrection. They are generally known by the term one of the groups called itself—the Tigers.

These developments, namely the transformation of the Federal Party into the TULF and the rise of the Tiger militancy, form an important stage in the evolution of Tamil political consciousness and are of profound significance to Sinhala-Tamil relations. Up to 1980, the strength of Sinhala communal-consciousness had been the vanguard political force in Sri Lanka and had shaped the course of politics and social reform. Tamils had, as seen above, merely acted reactively to this phenomenon and the mass of the community had not been bestirred to any remedial action. Now the changes came like an avalanche, first among the youth and soon to be followed by their elders. The Sri Lankan Tamil community achieved, for the first time, a genuine solidarity that brought together Tamils from the spatially separate regions. The Tamils of the Jaffna peninsula were naturally the leaders but were soon followed by those of the Vanni, of Mannar and Mullaithivu, and of Trincomalee and Batticaloa. In these areas outside Jaffna peninsula it was the issue of colonization that roused them and brought them into the growing Tamil unity.

The rise of Tamil separatism and the growth of extremism created problems for Tamil solidarity among the diverse socioeconomic and spatially separated groups. There was first the different interests of the old Tamil settlers and the migrants of the colonial period. The Tamils of the plantations of the central highlands had different problems and expectations. They were neither directly affected by the Sinhala-only language policy nor were they greatly concerned with higher echelons of employment. But when their basic interests in the plantation economy were affected from 1972 and even more when their security was jeopardized by attacks on them by Sinhala mobs, they began to look northward to the older Tamil settlers. A state of Eelam compromising the north and east was no solution to their problems, though they identified themselves with the Tamil struggle. This incongruity was reflected in the fact that the leader of the plantation Tamils was a member of the UNP government of 1977, a government against which the Tigers and the TULF were fighting with different methods. Nonetheless the rise of Sinhala hegemony after 1956 achieved what was once thought impossible—the unity of Tamils of all regions and every economic group into the realization of a common ethnic and linguistic identity.

Additionally, there was the problem of the Tamil-speaking Muslims. The Muslims of Mannar and Batticaloa have much affinity with the Hindu Tamils amidst whom they live. Tamil Muslims were beginning to be affected adversely by state policies, and the favored treatment they had once received had come to an end. Muslim communities were being subjected to Sinhala attacks. All these factors brought Hindu and Muslim Tamils closer, and the latter are seen to be involved even in the extremist insurrectionary groups. But the Islamic identity that united Tamil Muslims to Muslims in the south was also present, and Sinhalese leaders were able to play on this to cast doubts on the Tamil Muslims' identification with the Tamil cause. In 1985, these inner tensions broke out in Hindu-Muslim riots in the Batticaloa district and there was widespread suspicion of incitement by the state and *agent-provacateurs* from the south.

Outbreak of Armed Insurgency

With the appearance of an armed challenge to the Sinhala-dominated Sri Lankan state, it was now up to the government and Sinhala community leadership to redefine their attitudes and devise new policies toward the Tamils. Until this point, governments had followed the familiar pattern of giving too little too late. After years of agitation and tension, some official recognition had been given to the Tamil language in 1965. This recognition was evidenced in the constitution in 1978. Again in 1981 some measure of devolution of power was attempted, but it was largely ineffective. In all these cases what was granted was a shadow of what had been asked, which left neither party satisfied. Powerful Sinhala interests were opposed to every one of these concessions while Tamil representatives felt they went nowhere near the heart of their grievances. In the important exercises of the formation of new constitutions in 1971-72 and 1977-78, Tamil representatives took no part and did not accept the final product. Right up to the promulgation of the 1978 constitution, Sri Lankan governments and Sinhala community leaders could ignore Tamil political opinion. They had overwhelming majorities in the legislatures and could pass laws and amend constitutions as they wished without reference to the wishes of the Tamils or any other minority.

Armed insurrection begun in 1978 changed all this. The government was now faced with two opponents, the TULF on the political and parliamentary front and the Tigers on the military front. On

the political front the government moved to engage the TULF leaders in discussions and even to offer concessions. But the time when
these concessions were sufficient had passed. The TULF were not
amenable to compromise settlements as they saw the Tamil militants over their shoulders. They increasingly talked the extremist
language of separation and an independent Tamil state. They would
certainly not settle for anything less than substantial devolution
of power. The government had behind them the forces of Sinhala
extremism that had secured a new lease on life by this new challenge to Sinhala hegemony. The cry for a division of the island raised
all the old fears and recreated the old alliance of Buddhist priests,
Sinhala literati, entrepreneurs, unemployed, and hoodlums. Even
within the government were factions that were allied to the extremist and racist elements outside it. Thus the government was faced
with a growing militancy and more extreme separatist political
demands from the Tamil opposition. Behind it was a hardening Sinhala public opinion opposed to every concession and watching every
sign of compromise by the government.

Facing armed insurrection was the first priority. The government
was ill-prepared to do this. The army and the navy had never seen
combat and, apart from the brief encounter with the left-wing insurgency of April 1971, had no experience of such warfare. The armed
forces, and to a lesser extent the police, were overwhelmingly Sinhalese and had, after 1961, been impregnated with the Sinhala hege-
monistic ideologies that succeeding administrations had espoused.
They went into the campaign, not as a professional army fighting a
war on behalf of a supracommunal state, but as an army asserting
the interests of the Sinhalese against Tamils. This, compounded by
the deterioration in standards of training and discipline, was responsible for the widespread terror perpetrated by the armed forces and
the police in the Tamil areas. Losses suffered by the army in an
encounter with the insurgents would be followed by extensive reprisals, arson, and assault on civil populations in the vicinity. Very
often the government has been embarrassed by this army and police
rampage (see, e.g., Moore, 1984, pp. 21-27).[4]

The effect of these actions on the Tamils was to alienate them
totally from the state and indeed from the Sinhalese, on whose
behalf they felt the state was acting. What had once been a mild
interest in the path of armed resistance as an option to achieve their
aims was now turned into a belief in it as the only way to force con-

cessions from the state. The insurgents operate in a climate of total support from the Tamil population, making the task of the security forces doubly difficult. This convinced the security forces that they were fighting the entire Tamil population. Thus armed insurrection became the main, indeed the only, strategy of the Tamils, and fighting insurrection became the main response of the state. In August 1983, the constitution was amended to outlaw parties supporting separation. Members of parliament and officers of state were required to take an oath of allegiance to the constitution and eschewal of separation. TULF members of parliament refused to take the mandatory oath and lost their membership in the legislature. Thus the Tamils were unrepresented in the country's parliament, apart from a few members of the governing party from the eastern provinces and the highlands.

Internationalization of the Tamil Problem

This escalation in relations between Sinhalese and Tamils has contributed to the internationalization of what had been an internal problem of communal politics. In one aspect the Tamil problem had external implications from the outset. This was the status of Indian immigrants under British rule, a question in which the Republic of India had an understandable interest. Indian and Ceylonese prime ministers and senior officials had met off and on to solve this problem. In 1964 the Indian government had made a major concession in recognizing the principle of repatriation, and had entered into an agreement on providing citizenship to a proportion of Indian immigrants and repatriation of others. The Tamils themselves, though maintaining religious, linguistic, and educational ties with southern India, never entertained any ideas of political linkage or affiliation. Two broad trends converged to change all this. On the one hand, across the Palk Straits was the rising tide of Tamil nationalism under a Dravidian cultural identity, mobilizing all Tamil speakers into a recognition of their unity and common interests within the Indian nation-state. Parties espousing this identity soon became dominant and seized power in the state of Madras (renamed Tamil Nadu). The Indian central government had to recognize this Tamil nationalism and come to terms with it, which it did successfully under the leadership of Prime Minister Indira Gandhi. The counterpart of this trend in south India was the unfolding struggle of the Tamils in Sri Lanka against Sinhala domination. Tamil leaders of Sri Lanka found in the more radical Dravidian leaders of south India allies and supporters in their struggle. Thus links were forged between the exponents of armed insurrection and extremist groups in south India, just as they were between the more moderate TULF and the leadership of Dravidian political parties in government and opposition in Tamil Nadu.

With political alliances strengthening cultural and emotional ties between Tamil India and Tamil Sri Lanka, the Indian government now came into the picture and had to define its attitudes toward the problem of the Tamils of Sri Lanka. In doing this, it had to take account of the depth of feeling generated in the state of Tamil Nadu as accounts of mob violence (such as in July 1983) and army brutality directed against the Tamils were disseminated in the Indian press. More important, it had to take account of the political instability on its southern frontiers and the consequent dangers of intervention by powers from outside the region. After July 1983, India began to take a more direct interest in the Sinhala-Tamil conflict, even to the point of coming forward as a mediator and urging the Sri Lankan government to curb the excesses of its security forces. This Indian intervention triggered off the latent distrust and fear of India that had existed for some time among influential sections of the Sinhala elite. To counter this Indian intervention, the government looked elsewhere and chiefly among its western allies, the United States and Britain, for more overt expressions of support. But these powers, conscious of the global implications of great power intervention and to some extent wary of the moral dimensions of the conflict, show no signs of offering such support.

Conclusion

The dynamic transformation of Sinhala-Tamil relations from competitive coexistence to intense conflict and even racial warfare is a part of the process of the search for national identity and of the complex interaction between tradition and modernity. While the precolonial heritage had elements that pointed to conciliation and coexistence as well as to competition and conflict, the colonial experience left deep scars especially on the Sinhalese, particularly in respect to their Buddhist cultural personality. In the process of redressing the legitimate grievances of the colonial era, Sinhala public opinion overreached itself; and there were no leaders of statesmanship to hold back the forces they had unleashed. Sinhala populism took over and established a Sinhala hegemonial state where the Tamil position was increasingly devalued. Tamil response was slow and ineffective until a delayed process of politicization took place in the 1970s. As resistance to the Sinhala state intensified, its leaders took up more and more extreme positions to safeguard Tamil interests. A military solution through armed insurgency was conceived by the youth, and preparations were made for armed struggle. The Sri Lankan government responded with extensive anti-insurgency measures including widespread retaliation on large sections of the Tamil population. This made the insurgents popular and widened the gulf between the Tamils and the Sinhala state. Bridging this gulf can only come through international pressure as well as a realistic appreciation of what the interests are of the two ethnic groups.

NOTES

1. This is the proportion of the population that was English-educated. An even smaller proportion controlled the higher echelons of power and the economy.
2. The split in the governing party led to the resignation of S.W.R.D. Bandaranaike from the government. He went into the opposition, formed a new party, and became the focal point of a nationalist elite alternative to the government.
3. This was the famous Vaddukoddai resolution taken on May 14, 1976.
4. Reports of army atrocities have appeared widely in the world press. From 1984, the Sri Lankan government has severely restricted access to overseas reporters and has, with some success, controlled the flow of news. Evidence from refugees suggests, however, that there has been no change in the pattern of army behavior.

REFERENCES

Abeysekera, C. (1984). Ethnic representation in the higher state service. In *Ethnicity and social change in Sri Lanka* (pp.179-195). Colombo: Social Science Association.

Amnesty International. (1983). *Report of an Amnesty International Mission to Sri Lanka 31 January - 9 February 1982*. London: Amnesty International.

Bandaranayake, S. (1984). The peopling of Sri Lanka: The national question and some problems. History and ethnicity. In *Ethnicity and social change in Sri Lanka* (pp. Ai - ixx). Colombo: Social Science Association.

Buddhist Committee of Inquiry. (1956). *The betrayal of Buddhism*. Balangoda.

De Silva, C.R. (1974). Weightage in university admissions: Standardization district quotas in Sri Lanka. *Modern Ceylon Studies, 5*(2), 152-178.

De Silva, C.R. (1978) The politics of university admissions. *Sri Lanka Journal of the Social Sciences, 1*(2), 85-123.

Geiger, W. (Ed.). (1950). *The Mahavamsa*. Colombo: Ceylon Government Information Department.

Geiger, W. (Ed.). (1953). *The Culavamsa* (Vols. 1-2). Colombo: Ceylon Government Information Department.

Goonatilake, S. (1984). The formation of Sri Lankan culture. In *Ethnicity and social change in Sri Lanka* (pp. i-xxiii). Colombo: Social Science Association.

Gunawardena, R.A.L.H. (1984). The people of the lion: Sinhala consciousness in history and historiography. In *Ethnicity and social change in Sri Lanka* (pp. 1-53). Colombo: Social Science Association.

Horowitz, D. L. (1980). *Coup theories and officers' motives: Sri Lanka in comparative perspective*. Princeton, NJ: Princeton University Press.

Hyndman, P. (1984). *The communal violence in Sri Lanka, July 1983*. Sydney: The Law Association for Asia and the Western Pacific.

Inthu Ilainjan. (1974). Colombo.

Moore, T. J. (1984, February). *Ethnic and communal violence: The independence of the judiciary; protection of "Fundamental Rights" and the rule of law in Sri Lanka—fragile freedoms?* Sydney: International Commission of Jurists.

Ponnambalam, S. (1983). *Sri Lanka, the national question and the Tamil liberation struggle*. London: Zed Books.

Tamil United Front of Ceylon. (1973). *Memorandum on discrimination*. [Submitted to the International Commission of Jurists September 4, 1973.] Jaffna.

Chapter Summary

Michael Harris Bond examines intergroup relations in Hong Kong and proposes an explanation of why these relations have generally been without conflict despite Hong Kong's rapid economic and social transformation and the accompanying initial poverty.

Bond reviews the historical context of Chinese-British relations preceding Britain's leasing of Hong Kong for 99 years in 1898, including the Opium War, and the British acquisition of Kowloon following its defeat of the Chinese in 1860. Patterns of immigration to Hong Kong are examined. The author points to three main sources of immigration: foreign merchants seeking a base for trade; mainland Chinese brought in as part of the needed labor force in Hong Kong; and persons fleeing China following such political changes as the Japanese invasion, the fall of the Kuomintang, and the Taiping movement. Bond explains that although the status of Hong Kong as a colony was never officially recognized, it was tolerated primarily as an interface for Western goods necessary for China's modernization. The British-Chinese negotiations in 1982 for the future of Hong Kong are also reviewed.

The author asserts that there is a general view that Hong Kong is exceptionally free from civil unrest, despite characteristics present in Hong Kong—such as a high population density and a large proportion of recent immigrants—that are often associated with conflict elsewhere. He describes both sociopolitical factors and psychological factors that support the social order in Hong Kong.

Bond presents four sociopolitical factors that prevent conflict: (1) China's need for a Western interface, and the recognition by both Hong Kong and China that China will not tolerate activities that threaten the stability or prosperity of Hong Kong; (2) the introduction of government reforms and the increase in public expenditures to meet the needs of Hong Kong's masses in such areas as health, education, and housing, and thus undercut potential intergroup conflict; (3) the government cooption of potential leaders, primarily by involving industrial and commercial leaders in the drafting of policy; and (4) Hong Kong's irreplaceable role in the international situation. Psychological factors that Bond sees as diminishing intergroup conflict include: (1) the general avoidance of extrafamilial associations; (2) an attitude, which the author terms "minus-sum," that conflict should be avoided since it is harmful to all involved; (3) a perception that opportunity is not tied to group membership; and (4) the ability to value ingroup members without devaluing outgroup members.

Finally, Bond speculates on the possible future situation of Hong Kong after 1997, when he predicts even greater incentive for the maintenance of smooth intergroup relations and social stability.

—Susan Goldstein

3

Intergroup Relations in Hong Kong

The Tao of Stability

MICHAEL HARRIS BOND

> It is better to be a dog in times of peace,
> than a man in times of conflict.
> —*traditional Chinese proverb*

Hong Kong is an extraordinary place. Barely 1000 square kilometers of infertile, resourceless land, it has been transformed since the end of World War II from a colonial backwater into a thriving metropolis. Its roughly 6 million inhabitants have labored to make tiny Hong Kong the world's seventeenth most productive economy, outstripping countries such as Argentina, Greece, Spain, and Israel in per capita GNP. Hong Kong is a charter member of an elite club called the Five Dragons, whose annual growth rate in gross domestic product has consistently outperformed the rest of the world for the last two decades.

This "economic miracle" (Hicks & Redding, 1983) has been wrought by refugees from China who flooded into an unprepared Hong Kong from diverse parts of China after 1945. There, they labored under a British colonial administration that fostered an economic policy of "laissez-faire capitalism" while ensuring a basic level of social services and political stability.

Despite initial poverty, despite both ethnic and racial differences, despite turmoil in the colossus to the north, this transformation of a rocky outpost into the world's third largest financial center has been achieved without intergroup conflict or social unrest. The purpose of this chapter is to discuss some of the major themes in this success story, paying particular attention to its psychological underpinnings. It is a fascinating story in its own right, but especially important as social science has perhaps been too enamored with failures in intergroup relations, and too indifferent to the successes.

The Historical Context

Hong Kong is a child born of the unhappy relations between China and Britain in the nineteenth century. With the political transformation of both the People's Republic of China and the United Kingdom following World War II, the character of this association has changed. During this period, their offspring has grown and prospered, but the lines of its development have always been informed by the delicate state of affairs between its parents. Intergroup relations in Hong Kong must therefore be examined against the backdrop of Chinese-British history.

The Imperial Assault

In the nineteenth century, Britain truly ruled the waves and commanded the largest colonial empire ever brought under one flag (Morris, 1968). This empire was sustained by the wealth amassed from imperial trading practices. China represented a vast potential market then, as it still does now, and a source of materials, especially tea and silk. With silver in short supply, Britain began paying for its purchases with opium. This "coin of the realm" soon became unacceptable to the Chinese, however, and the Emperor forbade trading in the drug. Queen Victoria was not amused.

This act of Chinese defiance resulted in the first Opium War of 1840-41, when gunboat diplomacy was used to breach the barriers of the Ching Dynasty (Hookham, 1969). By force of arms, five ports were opened to foreign trade. In 1842, missionaries were reluctantly granted readmission on the coattails of the China traders, and the full panoply of Western influences was soon in its resented place.

The British acquisition of Hong Kong. Following her victory in the Opium War, Britain wrested Victoria Island from Chinese control under the provisions of the 1842 Nanking Treaty. A small part of the China mainland facing the island, called Kowloon, was later extracted from the Manchus by the Peking Convention, which followed China's second defeat by Britain in 1860. These acquisitions gave the British control of a superb natural harbor and thereby a base for the expansion of their trade into southern China.

A larger land mass adjacent to Kowloon was later leased by Britain from China for 99 years, beginning in 1898. Many nearby islands were also included in this lease. Together, these new territories constituted about 95 percent of the total area in the British Crown Colony of Hong Kong, and provided room for possible relocation of its expanding population (see also Endacott, 1964).

Patterns of immigration. Once Victoria Island was secured under the British flag, the outpost began to attract many foreign merchants needing a base for trade. This economic magnet thereafter exerted a consistent pull on the Chinese from the mainland to meet the growing demands for labor. As a consequence, Hong Kong's population surged from a paltry 5,650 in 1841 to 23,817 as reported in the Registration Ordinance of 1845 (Wang, 1982).

The steady upward climb of population continued, and was fueled by political vicissitudes in China. So, for example, the Taiping Movement of the 1850s created unstable conditions in the south of China, with the result that population increased by an estimated 82.5 percent between 1848 and 1853. The Japanese invasion of China in 1937, the fall of the Kuomintang in 1949, and the famine of the Great Leap Forward in 1962 all produced similar quantum jumps in the mass of people crowded into tiny Hong Kong. Hsungsing Wang analyzed a cross-section of this population as it appeared recently:

> At the end of 1978, the total estimated population was 4,720,200 [sic] comprising 2,427,900 males and 2,212,300 females. More than 98% of these can be described as Chinese on the basis of their language and place of origin. In fact, whether young or old, they identify their *heung-ha,* place of origin, in a village of a province of China, though about 59% of the population are Hong Kong-born. Most of these are Cantonese, the next largest group are the Sze Yap, followed by the Teochew. . . . The remaining Chinese population is

made up of Hakka, Shanghainese, Tanka (boat people) and others. (1982, p. 183)

Illegal immigration has been drastically reduced since the "touchbase" policy was abrogated in 1980. Nevertheless, 50 legal immigrants a day enter the colony from China. The most recent government census in 1981 puts the population of Hong Kong at 5.1 million, although this figure is now more realistically believed to exceed 6 million. Despite the recent development of new towns in the New Territories, most of this mass of people is concentrated in that part of Kowloon originally ceded to the British. In the urban areas of Mong Kok, Yau Ma Tei, and Hung Hom, there are more than 100,000 people per square kilometer (Sit, 1981, p. 141), the highest population density in the world (Lee, 1981).

The reversion to China. The status of Hong Kong as a colony has never been officially accepted by China. In March of 1972 this long-standing position was formally conveyed to a special committee of the United Nations concerned with the independence of colonial territories. Hong Kong had been exacted as a partial price for resolving conflicts between a then-mighty Britain and a then-faltering dynasty. As such, the Chinese have always proclaimed the treaties to have been unfair and unequal. Nevertheless, the existence of Hong Kong was tolerated on practical grounds: It was a useful dumping ground for malcontents, a source of hard currency (nearly 40 percent of China's total in 1983), and a geographic interface for Western things needed by China in its modernization program.

Eventually, however, the forthcoming expiry of the New Territories lease in July 1997 was bound to force China's hand. In addition, Hong Kong's position as an international center of finance dictated that Britain and China negotiate an early accord, so that investors could make long-range plans. Although Britain opened with Mrs. Thatcher's truculent assertion in October 1982 that the original treaties were "legal and binding," the sovereignty issue was quickly resolved in China's favor. The whole territory, including that in the original treaties, will revert to Chinese control when the lease expires.

The only concession that Britain managed to extract from the Chinese was a publication of its guidelines for the territory's future in more detail than the Chinese originally proposed. Under Deng Xiaoping's conception of "one country, two systems," the legal, social, and economic fabric of Hong Kong will be retained for at least 50 years after 1997. Hong Kong will become a "special administrative region," enjoying an unexpected level of local autonomy.

Hong Kong has traditionally granted its citizens much freedom, but little democracy. With the advent of 1997, however, electoral reforms are being introduced to ensure some degree of self-government before the change in sovereignty. In a proposal introduced in July of 1984, the government initiated arrangements to make 24 of the 50 seats on the formerly appointed Legislative Council subject to election. Of these seats 12 were decided by *indirect* vote, 12 by direct voting from the Functional Constituencies (teachers, lawyers, social workers, etc.). Campaigning was low key and the elections in October 1985 proceeded smoothly with a turnout of about 50 percent of the registered electorate.

Social disturbance in Hong Kong. Commentators agree in their assessment of Hong Kong as remarkably free from civil unrest (England & Rear, 1975, pp. 278-287; Young, 1981). Their surprise appears to be derived from the fact that they find in Hong Kong many of the social conditions often blamed for instability and conflict elsewhere. These conditions include the following:

(1) the high density of population (Lee, 1981);
(2) the concentration of immigrants and recent arrivals;
(3) the colonial structure of government and an alien legal system;
(4) the magnitude of income differentials—"The Gini coefficient which measures income inequality in the population [was] 0.43 in 1971. This was still considerably higher than what was observed in . . . Taiwan and Korea (0.30) and Singapore (0.40)" (Lee, 1982, p. 25);
(5) a massive relocation scheme that has seen the population of the New Territories expand from 300,000 to 1,500,000 inhabitants between 1970 and 1985. The thorny issue of acquiring the necessary land for the new towns from its traditional landowners has been fraught with difficulties elsewhere (Chau & Lau, 1982);
(6) the strongly held political orientations among local Chinese, ranging from extreme right-wing support of Taiwan to extreme left-wing support of the People's Republic of China (Lau, 1982).

The most significant episode of social unrest in the last 25 years was undoubtedly the so-called riots of 1966-67 (see Kowloon Disturbances, 1967). To quote extensively from Kuan's (1979) analysis of this watershed in Hong Kong history,

In April 1966, a riot spontaneously broke out as a result of a peaceful demonstration against an increase in ferry fares. Before the dust could settle, wage disputes in a textile industry in May 1967 escalated into riots of much more violence, encouraged by the Cultural Revolution in China and organized by local communists.

In as much as the participants in the disturbances were comparatively poorly educated, poorly housed and poorly employed youth, the protest was believed to be a manifestation of an undercurrent of suppressed frustrations and resentment and in this sense not a protest against the increase of ferry fares so much as a protest of the Government handling of public affairs generally. (p. 153)

These outbreaks terminated in about six weeks, with no apparent aftershocks. The majority of the community was not galvanized. The government moved quickly to undertake legal-political reforms and policy changes that made the administration more responsive to the needs of local people. These events reflected what Kuan has called a crisis of trust; they constituted a "watershed" because thereafter the government has implicitly acknowledged its duty to serve all of the people in Hong Kong, not just the social elite (see Davies, 1977).

The only disturbance since 1967 was the looting in early 1984. For three days in January, taxi drivers had been protesting a proposed increase in licensing fees. They coordinated their efforts to blockade certain key roads, thereby paralyzing traffic flow in much of Hong Kong. On one evening before the end of the strike, youths in Kowloon overturned a bus and began ransacking businesses in the area. The police moved in, arrested many looters, and restored order quickly. There was no recurrence, the taxi drivers returned to work the next day, and it was "business as usual" throughout Hong Kong.

Two such episodes in 25 years, one of minor scale, is a remarkable record for any city the size of Hong Kong, particularly when considering its particular circumstances, discussed before. How are we to account for the social harmony in Hong Kong and what are its social-psychological manifestations?

Sociopolitical Factors Promoting Harmony

China's Need for a Western Interface

Hong Kong is indefensible. Recent reports indicate that the British themselves realized the obvious and were unwilling to defend their colony against possible Chinese invasion in 1949. The Communists did not cross the border, however, and Hong Kong remained part of the British empire.

In the normal course of events, it would have joined other colonies in the process of decolonization that followed World War II. China, however, was unwilling to countenance an independent Hong Kong along its border. So, the British, tied to Hong Kong for economic, strategic, and moral reasons (see Miners, 1975, pp. 3-13), have remained. Although nominally under British control, the territory has an unprecedented degree of financial and legislative autonomy from the "mother country" (Hicks, 1985a; Kuan, 1979, pp. 149-151). As a consequence,

> Hong Kong is a member of that class of cities and territories whose *de jure* status is irrelevant in comparison to their *de facto* functions. Such places often occupy niches adjacent to larger nations or groups of nations, and they come into being to accomplish important tasks or to relieve significant pressures that their larger neighbors find useful but that their legal rigidities or ideological pretensions prevent them from acknowledging. (Johnson, 1984, p. 889)

Why has China not pressed Britain for an early termination of the 1898 lease and abrogation of the treaties? The answer, intimated by Johnson (1984) above, is that Hong Kong in its present form serves Chinese needs superbly. To understand this reasoning, we must return to the nineteenth century.

The impact of westernization. When British gunboats sailed up the Yellow River, they breached more than the fortress walls of Canton. They also breached Chinese complacency. The legacy of 4,000 years of recorded civilization was the belief that China stood at the center of the earth and was, indeed, the "middle kingdom." It was accepted by the Chinese that their culture bequeathed upon its descendants an innate superiority over all other peoples. These other peoples were innocently called "barbarians" and were tolerated as long as they subscribed to the natural order of things, with China, of course, in a regnant position. This concept of international affairs has been labeled "Sinocentrism" by Yang (1968), and has been described by numerous observers using a variety of labels (Ho, nd., has called it "Chinese culturocentrism"; Yin, 1966, the "Imperial *Weltanschauung*").

It became harder and harder to sustain this self-satisfied world view in the face of the rapid capitulations of the Ching Dynasty to Western firepower. Complacency was replaced by intense self-examination, focused on the issue of how best to absorb the technical mastery and scientific knowledge commanded by the West (see Bond & King, in press, for an outline of these developments). A lasting theme that has emerged from this continuing debate is embodied in Chang Chih-tung's phrase, "Chinese learning for essentials; Western learning for practicalities." In short, the essence of Chinese culture should be protected, as Western technology is being incorporated.

Implications for Hong Kong. One time-honored strategy for protecting the heart of the Dragon is to confine the interface between China and the West geographically. The potential virus to Chinese culture, sometimes called "spiritual pollution," is thereby isolated and contained. Hong Kong fulfills this role perfectly. It is a major international center for finance, communications, and trade (Hicks, 1985b, pp. 41-48). Further, it is a training ground for people of Chinese origin to learn these skills and later transmit their expertise to those in the People's Republic of China. In short, Hong Kong is a funnel, a conduit regarded as useful by China in its pursuit of the Four Modernizations. It is precisely for this reason that Hong Kong's legal, economic, and social system has been guaranteed existence beyond 1997 by the Chinese authorities.

Of course, there are limits to what can be tolerated by Beijing. Open challenges to its ultimate authority over Hong Kong is one. Consequently, Britain's representatives in Hong Kong have deemed it prudent since World War II to moderate their imperialistic stance and avoid acts considered provocative or detrimental to China's political overlordship. Similarly, the recent "one country, two systems" concept for Hong Kong's future can be understood in the same vein: It is a piece of political *legerdemain* that publicly asserts ultimate Chinese authority over Hong Kong in the absence of many of the sociopolitical trappings normally associated with that authority.

Regardless of what happens in practice, China must be acknowledged by all parties to rule Hong Kong.

Any internal disorder that threatens the stability and prosperity of Hong Kong is a second limit. Should civil unrest rear its head, the international community would quickly lose confidence in Hong Kong. Its delicate economic infrastructure would collapse and with it the networks of technology, communication, and personnel that are so useful for China in its interface with the Western world (see Hicks, 1985b; Postiglione & Femminella, nd.).

Should Hong Kong prove no longer able to play this mediating role for China, there would be no reason for Beijing to maintain its legal, social and economic system past 1997. Hong Kong Chinese would then face a complete disruption of the material and political basis of the society they have worked so hard to secure. Could any possible gain resulting from any group action justify the downside potential that might arise from taking that action?

For Britain's part, reversion of the territory under such chaotic circumstances would constitute a diplomatic and moral humiliation as well as a betrayal of the trust many of its international allies have evidenced by their heavy investment in Hong Kong. London is consequently proceeding with great circumspection, consulting continuously with Beijing as it moves to assuage local concerns by implementing more democratic institutions (Williams, 1985).

The three major actors in this unfolding historical drama thus share a preemptive superordinate goal—the need to maintain order. The existence of just such a shared goal has been consistently shown to undercut intergroup conflict (Hewstone & Giles, 1984), pushing all parties toward alternative strategies for resolving problematic differences.

Government Reforms and Policy Re-orientation

Kuan (1979) has argued that the nature of colonial government in Hong Kong has been transformed since the Korean War. Essentially, there has been a steady development of local autonomy from Britain. Miners (1975) summarized this state of relative self-governance in the following terms:

In constitutional law, the administration of Hong Kong is completely subordinate to the Crown—that is, to the government at present holding office in Britain; but in practice the Colony is very largely autonomous, particularly in internal matters, and discussions between London and Hong Kong are sometimes much more like diplomatic negotiations between two sovereign states than the compliant obedience by an inferior to orders from above. (p. 203)

This increase in local control should function to undercut social movements directed to overthrowing foreign control and fears of exploitation. It will only do so, however, if external authority is replaced by responsive internal government. The riots of 1966-67 seem to have achieved precisely this outcome. As Kuan (1979) maintains, these disturbances indicated that a new generation of Hong Kong youth was emerging. It was realized that their dissatisfaction at not having their interests heard could ignite with astonishing speed. To short-circuit this incendiary potential, the government recognized it would have to become more responsive to the needs of the man on the street.

In some detail, Kuan (1979) outlines the actions that were taken. A City District Officer Scheme was developed, a Government Information Service was established, Chinese was legalized as a language of government in 1974, and the unofficial members of the Executive and Legislative Councils revitalized a government-supported office for receiving public complaints.[1] "[These] legal-constitutional reforms [are] designed to bring the Government and the people closer to each other by a greater degree of centralization of administration and by an improvement in communication structures" (p. 156).

This specific focus of reforms was part of a broader shift in the role of the government from laissez-faire detachment to "discrete guidance" (Hong Kong, 1976, p. 9). The direction of this shift was indicated in the annual report of 1970 (Hong Kong, 1971) which asserted that "the task that lies ahead now is to ensure that the efforts of both the community and the Government are used in the properly planned and common objective of raising the social benefits and standards of living for all and of making Hong Kong a better place in which to live" (p. 20). As a consequence of this new concern of the administration, substantial increases have been made in public expenditures—education, health, housing, and social welfare. Legislation and institutions were created to protect the labor force and to stamp out corrupt practices in both businesses and the public sector. In short, the administration began paying more concrete attention to the needs of Hong Kong's masses, thereby defusing many potential sources of social unrest.

Government Cooption of Potential Leaders

The above policy reorientation had important implications for stability since it implicitly recognized the legitimacy of the claims advanced by the less advantaged sectors of Hong Kong. The Chinese elite, however, had always been served. A number of observers (e.g., Davies, 1977; King, 1975) have described a pattern of political integration that was achieved in Hong Kong by involving commercial and industrial leaders in the drafting of policy. Intellectuals have also been similarly involved (Lee, 1982, p. 26). King labeled this undertaking, "the administrative absorption of politics," defined as "a process by which the Government co-opts political forces, often represented by elite groups, into an administrative decision-making body, thus achieving some level of elite integration; as a consequence, the governing authority is made legitimate" (p. 424).

The support thus accorded to a colonial administration is considerable, and serves to stabilize the polity. The process also erodes the supply of powerful, educated leadership to champion the needs of the people. The dissatisfaction of the nonelite masses would thus have to be articulated by a grassroots leadership. With scarce resources and undeveloped institutions at their disposal, such individuals would face a daunting task (see also Clammer, in press, for a discussion of this cooption strategy for diffusing ethnic tension in Singapore).

The International Dimension

Developments in Hong Kong are of considerable moment to other countries. Its other major trading partners, the United States and Japan, are vitally concerned about the security of their prospective, long-term investments. The territory's infrastructure, communications network, and geographical position are unique in the East Asian Basin and would be difficult to replace (Hicks, 1985b). It is thus probable that considerable outside pressure would be brought to bear on any of the major actors in the Hong Kong drama should they threaten its stability.

Hong Kong is also a goldfish bowl for the longstanding problem of China's reunification with Taiwan. In its overtures to the government of Taipei, Beijing has vowed to guarantee Taiwan's right to retain its basic institutions following a return to the fold. Given the obvious parallel between this guarantee and that concerning Hong Kong's social and economic freedoms post-1997, many observers regard the fate of Hong Kong as a test case of China's sincerity (Kwok, 1984). Beijing is clearly aware of this widely held perception and must address itself to Hong Kong using a broader perspective.

As mentioned earlier, the British managed to extract from their negotiations with China an agreement of much greater detail and concreteness than Beijing probably wished. The obvious advantage for the departing power is that world opinion can thereby more easily judge whether China is honoring its treaty after 1997. This agreement was registered with the United Nations by both governments on June 13, 1985, and provides further ballast against impetuous shifts in China's policy toward its then Special Economic Region.

Psychological Dimensions Supporting Social Order

The foregoing has been a selective discussion of themes in Hong Kong's historical background and present situation as they relate to intergroup relations. I have been guided in my selection of facts and issues by assessments of those factors widely believed as conducive to social harmony or conflict. In a sense, I have imposed a theory upon the flux of external events, extracting and interpreting accordingly.

I am uncomfortable with an exclusive reliance upon this *ex cathedra* approach because it totally ignores the perspective of the actors in this human drama. It is, after all, individuals who act in ways to promote group civility or violence (see also Stagner, this volume). The external factors that I have isolated to account for Hong Kong's social order must be represented at the individual level in some ways if they are to influence individual behavior.

So, for example, one could well ask if the Chinese masses consider that their needs have been served by the policy reorientations mentioned before. If not, these changes hardly constitute an explanation for Hong Kong's stability. Even if one grants that people perceive their needs to have been met, one wonders why this accommodation by the government has not been met with a spiraling of expectations. The result would then be more, rather than less, conflict.

Perhaps it is therefore necessary to supplement the above with a consideration of the motivations and perspectives distinguishing the chief actors in present-day Hong Kong (see also Lau, 1981, pp. 195-200 for a statement of this necessity). Four broad issues seem worthy of consideration from a psychological perspective: the weakness of broad group identifications, the passion for stability, the perception of opportunity, and stereotypes in Hong Kong. These issues are probably not independent of one another, nor are they unrelated to the external factors mentioned before. Their discussion does justify a psychologist's salary, however, and may suggest alternative approaches to changing the character of intergroup relations. It should be pointed out that there are only sparse data to support these speculations, so perhaps this will serve to stimulate work on these issues.

The Weakness of Broad Group Identifications

In trying to account for the political stability of Hong Kong, S.K. Lau (1981) isolated an explanatory mechanism he labeled "utilitarianistic familism":

> Briefly, utilitarianistic familism can be defined as a normative and behavioural tendency of an individual to place his familial interests above the interests of society or any of its component individuals and groups, and to structure his relationships with other individuals and groups in such a fashion that the furtherance of his familial interests is the primary consideration. (p. 201)

An important component of this constellation involves the relationship between the individual and family to other social and political groups. In essence, Lau asserts that Hong Kong Chinese generally avoid extrafamilial associations, keep those they have to a minimal level of involvement, and only maintain their membership if the association furthers their material aspirations without promoting social conflict.

This inward-looking tendency is combined with a belief that they are politically impotent in affecting government policy anyway. As the maintenance of stability is seen as the prime duty of government, there is no need to influence policy in any case, since Hong Kong suffers no social unrest. This narrow view of government's functional role is buttressed by the frequent provision by the family of the social welfare package often regarded elsewhere as government's duty.

This analysis is remarkably similar to that of Clammer's (1983), derived from reflections on the political scene in Singapore:

> Most Chinese, except those involved in the political institutions themselves and who have a high degree of ideological motivation, are a-political. They are uninterested in government except as it directly impinges on them and uninterested in political ideas; their idea of the good life politically is to be left alone as much as possible and to avoid unnecessary contacts with the bureaucracy. But this is not strictly to be defined as 'apathy.' It is a cultural response with deep historical roots, and which is also closely linked to Chinese social structure in which loyalties to family and clan are strong and functional, transcending abstract loyalties to the state. In any case to most Chinese even the state itself is not seen in political terms; to be Chinese is not to owe allegiance to a political unit, but to a cultural one. (p. 280)

This relative indifference to issues in the political arena is, of course, based on political theory that assigns political issues to the stewardship of a moral-intellectual elite (see e.g., Geiger & Geiger, 1975, chap. 2). Social truth does not arise from the open clash of contending opinions, but is delivered by conscientious leaders after careful consideration of the issues. A grateful citizenry plays its role by repaying the efforts of the leadership with loyalty and acceptance. A peaceful society is thereby ensured (see also King & Bond, in press). The response of the Hong Kong Chinese to their government appears to be cast in this same cultural mold.

The net result of these beliefs and behaviors is the difficulty of organizing and maintaining any social organizations that might be the basis of concerted social action. As Lau (1981) concludes,

> the lack of organization among the socially isolated familial groups prevents their easy mobilization by demagogues or other interested

parties even if they had the intention to do so, and this accounts for the relative sparseness of issue-oriented social and political movements in the last several decades. (p. 213)

This explanation provided by utilitarianistic familism dovetails neatly with that based on the cooption of potential leaders by the government. The latter prevents many matches from igniting; the former starves any potential fire spot of fuel to sustain the blaze.

The Passion for Stability

An arresting Chinese proverb states, "It is a step toward chaos when a quarrel begins." The implication is that conflict should be avoided because it will quickly escalate to the disadvantage of all the participants. In essence, everybody loses. This reasoning differs from the logic of construing conflict in zero-sum terms. The latter conceptualization makes it reasonable to engage in conflict, since there is a chance of winning; a "minus-sum" belief about such encounters does not. Where everyone must lose, no one will contend. This micro-level concern is paralleled and reinforced by the structural analysis of the minus-sum reward structure at the macro-level mentioned before.

Recent research on intergroup behavior has begun paying more attention to wider values concerning the need for harmony (see e.g., Hewstone, Bond, & Wan, 1983). In part this growing interest arises from a number of psychological studies comparing a variety of Chinese-Western differences in social behaviors (see Bond & Hwang, in press, for a review). A basic explanatory construct seems capable of summarizing many of these diverse findings, namely, conflict suppression versus conflict enhancement. In the area of procedural justice, for example, Americans show a stronger preference for adversarial compared to nonadversarial modes of conflict resolution than do Hong Kong Chinese (Leung & Lind, in press). In collectivistic cultures (Hofstede, 1980), the concern for equity may be tempered by a preemptive concern about possible escalation. This escalation is believed to undermine group life and make future relationships between the contending parties fraught with incendiary potential. In short, conflict is seen as much more costly in such cultural contexts.

Reinforcing the passion for stability is the nonideological orientation of the Chinese. In a provocative paper, Bloom (1977) has used Hong Kong Chinese in a cross-cultural study of social principledness. As argued by Bloom,

> A low level along such a dimension—low social principledness—would be marked by a capacity for understanding the abstract notion of sociopolitical responsibility at the societal level, but be limited to the view that sociopolitical responsibility consists in unanalytic adherence to the demands of existing political authority, i.e., in placing obedience to that authority above any individual intuition as to what might constitute proper action. By contrast, a high level along such a dimension—high social principledness—would be marked by the development of a personal, analytically derived conception of what values a sociopolitical system should seek to maximize and by a continuing critical evaluation of the degree to which the institutions and policies of the existing system are successful in realizing that goal. An individual who is high on this dimension will then, by contrast to his low-principled counterpart, consistently differentiate between the social and legal definitions of correct action and what he believes to be a morally correct stance. He will consistently reject an unquestioned acceptance of conventionally defined values, an unanalytic response to conventional authority, in favor of becoming his own moral arbiter, responsible for determining whether a demand of the society should or should not be obeyed, whether a position adopted by the polity should or should not be supported. In those situations in which the value claims for disobedience seem to him to outweigh the claims for obedience, he will consider it right to disobey. (pp. 69-70)

The relationship of social principledness to group action aimed at redressing perceived inequity is obvious. Mobilization of those low on this dimension would be difficult, and on Bloom's scale the Hong Kong Chinese were dramatically lower than comparable French or American samples.

Other lines of evidence suggest that Hong Kong residents place a high value on stability. Lau (1981) reported on the results of the extensive biomedical survey undertaken in the early 1970s. Of the more than 500 respondents, 82.2 percent indicated that they would avoid conflict with outsiders even if doing so would incur damage to themselves and their family. The majority of respondents likewise indicated that they would not approve of others should they put even their family's interests above the preservation of social order. In a similar vein, 87.3 percent indicated a preference for social stability over economic prosperity. In fact, 48.1 percent would remain in a socially unjust society as long as it was socially stable. Taken as a whole, these responses emphasize the strength of the general goal of sidestepping trouble with others at almost any price.

More recently, Bond and Hewstone (1986) have been sampling the attitudes of British and Chinese youth in Hong Kong in an effort to illuminate intergroup relations during the recent negotiations. One question asks high school respondents, "How important do you feel it is to maintain harmony between [the British and the Chinese] in Hong Kong?" On a five-point scale ranging from "not at all" (1) to "extremely" (5), the Chinese average 4.3; the British, 3.9. Responses to other questions in the survey were rarely as extreme as these, an outcome underscoring the strength of the shared desire by two of the main parties in Hong Kong to avoid conflict.

The centripetal focus of these disparate types of evidence is what I have labeled "the passion for stability," an overriding concern by local Chinese for preserving the fabric of social order by actively avoiding confrontation. There is no instrument currently available for measuring its strength in various cultures around the world, although Triandis's (1972) antecedent-consequent technique for assessing concept implications is tantalizing in this regard. Nor do we know its origin. One can speculate about the impact of directly experiencing violence, as have so many Hong Kong refugees, about Confucian social philosophy (Bond & Wang, 1983; Solomon, 1971), or about Chinese socialization practices surrounding the control of aggression (Ho, in press). Regardless of its origin, however, the passion for stability does not encourage the attitudes and behaviors that pollinate intergroup conflict.

The Perception of Opportunity

One of the best known theories of intergroup conflict has been labeled "realistic group conflict theory" (Sherif, 1958). According to this position, intergroup hostility arises because opposing groups are competing for a scarce external resource and group action is instrumental in winning this zero-sum contest. This theory is obviously applicable to situations where one group is acting to deny another group access to valued resources and commandering these resources for its own group members.

Such intergroup conflict will not arise if individuals in a society do not see such discriminatory practices in operation. The press for joining forces to engage in realistic group conflict is undercut if people see that opportunities exist for them individually to compete for these resources despite their group memberships.

Wealth is one obvious and basic resource. Many conflicts about political representation, access to education, and control of land derive, of course, from the potential of these resources for generating wealth. If people then believe that the access to wealth is open, one could well assume that the fundamental support for realistic group conflict is undermined.

Furnham and Bond (1985) have examined the explanations given by university students in Hong Kong for becoming wealthy. Subjects were first interviewed to solicit their explanations for why people became wealthy; these explanations were combined with those used in studies elsewhere. A representative sample from the two universities was then given the opportunity to endorse individually oriented explanations (e.g., good business sense) as well as externally oriented explanations (e.g., governmental policies favor certain parties). What is striking about the results is the general pattern of high endorsement of the internal explanations as opposed to the external. Compared to respondents in other cultures, Hong Kong students believe that their future wealth or poverty is very strongly the result of their own skill, effort, creativity, and timing. It is most certainly not the preserve of certain social groups acting to deny them access to a fair competition.

Likewise, Lee (1982) concluded that Hong Kong Chinese perceive an openness in the social structure. He reports on the results of a survey he conducted in which 70 percent of his respondents agreed that "there is always the chance of improving one's status if one has the ability and initiative and if one works hard enough." He summarizes,

> Family background, race, sex and other ascriptive factors are no longer as important as they were in the past, in deciding a person's achievement. Technical competence has become the central criterion for appointment and promotion in most industrial and administrative bureaucracies. Achievement in competitive examinations testifies in objective terms to a person's ability and qualifies him for a job. In this way, the bureaucracies level off social differences and break down barriers to social mobility. (pp. 25-26)

Clearly, Hong Kong Chinese appear to share an ideology of meritocracy. Clammer (1984, p. 16) has discussed the importance of such an ideology in buttressing ethnic harmony in Singapore, one of the world's remarkable success stories in intergroup relations (see also Clammer, 1982). Where one can rise economically and socially through individual effort, there is no need to mobilize social power blocks as a way of destroying obstacles to fair access.

Stereotypes in Hong Kong

A fundamental tenet of Tajfel's (1974, 1978) social identity theory is that people strive to achieve a positive view of themselves in part through their group memberships. They do so by differentiating their own groups from their relevant groups along valued dimensions, such as wealth, power, culturedness, and so forth. The outcome of this social comparison is, of course, constrained by the actual position of the relevant groups on these various dimensions. Where this outcome fails to secure an adequate social identity, the individual will strive for a change that can redress the shortfall. Tajfel identified three strategies—individual mobility, social creativity, and social competition—that could be undertaken to effect such a change.

The examination of social stereotypes can provide some information about whether group memberships are providing a positive social identity. In this respect, a number of studies indicate clearly that Hong Kong Chinese evaluate themselves as higher than Westerners in general (Gibbons, 1983; Lyczak, Fu, & Ho, 1976), British (Bond, 1985) or Americans (Bond, 1982) in particular, on the basic dimension of morality-goodnaturedness. These studies also indicate, however, that Hong Kong Chinese see themselves as lower than these Western groups along the competence dimension, a finding consistent with the historical legacy discussed earlier.

Further enhancing a positive social identity, however, is the emerging distinction between the Hong Kong Chinese and the mainland Chinese. A number of writers (Baker, 1983; Bond & King, in press; Young, 1984) have commented on the apparent development of a Hong Kong Chinese identity. This identity is set in opposition to that of Chinese in the People's Republic of China along the dimension of modernity in areas of technical and organizational competence. So, locals may acknowledge some subordination in matters of competence to Westerners, but not with respect to a group of considerable future relevance, their brothers in mainland China.

So, there seems to be an adequate basis for a positive social identity derivable from these group characterizations. Two additional points should be made, however, to complete the picture. First, the ratings of one's own group and the Western groups both tend to be high, regardless of which is higher. Ingroup enhancement without outgroup denigration facilitates both positive group identity and positive intergroup relations. Second, the structure of the ratings appears to be well differentiated. In many cases (Bond, 1982, in press), three or four factors emerge as bases of comparison among groups. This articulation provides a greater chance of achieving an adequately positive identity and may be a necessary psychological condition for a harmonious multiethnic society (see also Kalin, 1984).

The Future

In his conclusion to the Raj quartet, Paul Scott (1977) writes a fictional editorial for the *Ranpur Gazette*. It includes the portentious observation that

> the Viceroy . . . has found himself in the unenviable position of opening Pandora's Box and letting out all the evils that have afflicted this country probably since time began but which have been imprisoned, under a lid shut and locked by the single rule of British Power and British Law, evils which have not died of asphyxiation, but multiplied. (p. 525)

Hong Kong in 1985 is a far cry from India of 1947. Religious cleavages, reinforced by profound differences in lifestyles, do not exist in the indigenous population; a long buildup toward the transfer of sovereignty is anticipated; the stability of institutions up to and for 50 years after transfer has been guaranteed by treaty; and little economic specialization or ascendency by Chinese ethnic groups has become evident. Most important, however, is the spectre of full-scale Chinese intervention should intergroup conflict flare up in Hong Kong. The "one country, two systems" approach has only been deeded in trust to the people of Hong Kong. Should they fail to maintain the order necessary to foster prosperity, the experiment will be terminated by Beijing. This downside potential will add considerable weight to the traditional Chinese concern with maintaining social stability (Bond & Wang, 1983) and defuse intergroup conflict before it gathers momentum.

Nevertheless, anything is possible in this contingent world— China may turn its back on its headlong pursuit of modernity when Deng Xiaoping passes into history, a worldwide depression may strangle international trade, an exodus of talent before 1997 may undermine Hong Kong's competitive edge in the eyes of other countries, including the People's Republic of China. Some commentators (e.g., Lau, 1984) believe that internal cleavages are in fact already established and will become manifest with the approach of 1997.

Amidst all these speculations, one is reminded of the Chinese proverb, "Man has a thousand ways of calculating; heaven has but one." My analysis leads me to be optimistic about the prospects for future stability in Hong Kong; 4000 years of recorded Chinese history supports the sentiment of another Chinese proverb, however: "Man's goodwill is thin as paper and world events are like a chess game, changing with every move." I await the year 2000 with interest.

NOTE

1. Localization of the civil service is proceeding apace, with virtually complete Sinicization expected before 1997.

References

Baker, H.D.R. (1983). Life in the cities: The emergence of Hong Kong man. *China Quarterly, 95*, 469-479.

Bloom, A. H. (1977). A cognitive dimension of social control: The Hong Kong Chinese in cross-cultural perspective. In A. A. Wilson, S. L. Greenblatt, & R.W. Wilson (Eds.), *Deviance and social control in Chinese society* (pp. 67-81). New York: Praeger.

Bond, M. H. (1982). *Chinese students' perceptions of Chinese and American traits.* Unpublished manuscript, The Chinese University of Hong Kong.

Bond, M. H. (1985). Language as a carrier of ethnic stereotypes in Hong Kong. *Journal of Social Psychology, 125*, 53-62.

Bond, M. H. (in press). Mutual stereotypes and the facilitation of interaction across cultural lines. *International Journal of Intercultural Relations.*

Bond, M. H. & Hewstone, M. (1986). *Social identity theory and the perception of intergroup relations in Hong Kong.* Manuscript submitted for publication.

Bond, M. H., & Hwang, K. K. (in press). The social psychology of Chinese people. In M.H. Bond (Ed.), *The psychology of the Chinese people.* Hong Kong: Oxford University Press.

Bond, M. H., & King, A.Y.C. (in press). Coping with the threat of Westernization in Hong Kong. *International Journal of Intercultural Relations.*

Bond, M. H., & Wang, S. H. (1983). Aggressive behavior in Chinese society: The problem of maintaining order and harmony. In A.P. Goldstein & M. Segall (Eds.), *Global perspectives on aggression* (pp. 58-74). New York: Pergamon.

Chau, L. Y., & Lau, S. K. (1982). Development, colonial rule, and intergroup conflict in a Chinese village in Hong Kong. *Human Organization, 41,* 139-146.

Clammer, J. (1982). The institutionalization of ethnicity: The culture of ethnicity in Singapore. *Ethnic and Racial Studies, 5,* 127-139.

Clammer, J. (1983). Chinese ethnicity and political culture in Singapore. In L.A.P. Gosling & L.Y.C. Lim (Eds.), *The Chinese in Southeast Asia* (Vol. 2, pp. 266-284). Singapore: Maruzen Asia.

Clammer, J. (in press). Ethnicity and the classification of social differences in plural societies: A perspective from Singapore. *Journal of Asian and African Studies.*

Davies, S.N.G. (1977). One brand of politics rekindled. *Hong Kong Law Journal, 7,* 44-80.

Endacott, G. B. (1964). *Government and people in Hong Kong 1841-1962: A constitutional history.* Hong Kong: Hong Kong University Press.

England, J., & Rear, J. (1975) *Chinese labour under British rule.* Hong Kong: Oxford University Press.

Furnham, A., & Bond, M. H. (1985). *Hong Kong Chinese explanations for wealth.* Unpublished manuscript, University of London.

Geiger, J., & Geiger, F. (1975). *The development progress of Hong Kong and Singapore.* London: Macmillan.

Gibbons, J. (1983). Attitudes towards languages and code-mixing in Hong Kong. *Journal of Multilingual and Multicultural Development, 4,* 129-148.

Hewstone, M., Bond, M. H., & Wan, K. D. (1983). Social facts and social attributions: The explanation of intergroup differences in Hong Kong. *Social Cognition, 2,* 142-157.

Hewstone, M., & Giles, H. (1984). Intergroup conflict. In A. Gale & A. J. Chapman (Eds.), *Psychology and social problems* (pp. 275-295). London: John Wiley.

Hicks, G. L. (1985a). *Hong Kong: The role of illusions.* Unpublished manuscript.

Hicks, G. L. (1985b, April). *Hong Kong on the eve of communist rule.* Paper presented at the meeting of the Western Social Science Association, Fort Worth, Texas.

Hicks, G., & Redding, S. G. (1983). The story of the East Asian economic miracle. 1. Economic theory be damned. *Euro-Asia Business Review, 2,* 24-32.

Ho, D.Y.F. (in press). Chinese patterns of socialization: A critical review. In M.H. Bond (Ed.), *The psychology of the Chinese people.* Hong Kong: Oxford University Press.

Ho, D.Y.F. (nd.). *Prejudice, colonialism, and interethnic relations: A East-West dialogue.* Unpublished manuscript, University of Hong Kong.

Hofstede, G. (1980). *Culture's consequences: International differences in work-related values.* Newbury Park, CA: Sage.

Hong Kong. (1971). *Report for the year 1970.* Hong Kong: Government Printer.

Hong Kong. (1976). *Report for the year 1975.* Hong Kong: Government Printer.

Hookham, H. (1969). *A short history of China.* New York: New American Library.

Johnson, C. (1984). The mousetrapping of Hong Kong: A game in which nobody wins. *Asian Survey, 24,* 887-909.

Kalin, R. (1984, August). *Models of tolerance in multicultural and assimilationist societies.* Paper presented at the 7th International Congress of Cross-Cultural Psychology, Acapulco, Mexico.

King, A.Y.C. (1975). Administrative absorption of politics in Hong Kong: Emphasis on the grass roots level. *Asian Survey, 15,* 422-439.

King, A.Y.C., & Bond, M. H. (in press). The Confucian paradigm of men: A sociological view. In W. S. Tseng & D.Y.H. Wu (Eds.), *Chinese culture and mental health: An overview.* New York: Academic Press.

Kowloon Disturbances. (1967). *Report of the Commission of Enquiry.* Hong Kong: Acting Government Printer.

Kuan, H. C. (1979). Political stability and change in Hong Kong. In T. B. Lin, R.P.L. Lee, & U. E. Simonis (Eds.), *Hong Kong: Economic, social and political studies in development* (pp. 145-166). New York: M.E. Sharpe.

Kwok, S. T. (1984). Reflections on Hong Kong. *Chinese Fortuna,* no. 10, 12-17 (in Chinese).

Lau, S. K. (1981). Utilitarianistic familism: The basis of political stability. In A.Y.C. King & R.P.L. Lee (Eds.), *Social life and development in Hong Kong* (pp. 195-216). Hong Kong: Chinese University Press.

Lau, S. K. (1982). *Society and politics in Hong Kong.* Hong Kong: Chinese University Press.

Lau, S. K. (1984, December). *Political reform and political development in Hong Kong: Dilemmas and choices.* Paper presented at the Conference on Hong Kong and 1997: Strategies for the future, Hong Kong.

Lee, M. K. (1982). Emerging patterns of social conflict in Hong Kong society. In J.Y.S. Cheng (Ed.), *Hong Kong in the 1980's* (pp. 23-31). Hong Kong: Summerson Eastern Publishers.

Lee, R.P.L. (1981). High density effects in urban areas: What do we know and what should we do? In A.Y.C. King & R.P.L. Lee (Eds.), *Social life and development in Hong Kong.* Hong Kong: Chinese University Press.

Leung, K., & Lind, E. A. (in press). Procedural justice and culture: Effects of culture, gender, and investigator status on procedural preferences. *Journal of Personality and Social Psychology.*

Lyczak, R., Fu, G. S., & Ho, A. (1976). Attitudes of Hong Kong bilinguals towards English and Chinese speakers. *Journal of Cross-Cultural Psychology, 7,* 425-438.

Miners, N. J. (1975). *The government and politics of Hong Kong.* Hong Kong: Oxford University Press.

Morris, J. (1968). *Pax Britannica: The climax of an empire.* London: Faber and Faber.

Postiglione, G. A., & Femminella, F. X. (Eds.). (nd.). *Ethnic ideological themes across generations of ethnic Chinese living in Hong Kong.* Unpublished manuscript, University of Hong Kong.

Scott, P. (1977). *A division of the spoils.* London: Granada Publishing.

Sherif, M. (1958). Superordinate goals in the reduction of intergroup conflicts. *American Journal of Sociology, 63,* 349-356.

Sit, F. S. (1981). Post-war population and its spatial dynamics. In F. S. Sit (Ed.), *Urban Hong Kong* (pp. 2-25). Hong Kong: Summerson Eastern Publishers.

Solomon, R. H. (1971). *Mao's revolution and the Chinese political culture.* Berkeley: University of California Press.

Tajfel, H. (1974). Social identity and inter-group behavior. *Social Science Information, 13,* 65-93.

Tajfel, H. (Ed.). (1978). *Differentiation between social groups: Studies in intergroup behavior.* London: Academic Press.

Triandis, H. C. (1972). *The analysis of subjective culture.* New York: John Wiley.

Wang, H. S. (1982). Ethnic communities in Cheung Chau, Hong Kong. In D.Y.H. Wu (Ed.), *Ethnicity and interpersonal interaction: A cross-cultural study* (pp. 181-198). Singapore: Maruzen Asia.

Williams, P. (1985, October 2). Hong Kong: The way ahead. *South China Morning Post,* p. 2.

Yang, L. S. (1968). Historical notes on the Chinese world order. In J. K. Fairbank (Ed.), *The Chinese world order* (pp. 20-33). Cambridge, MA: Harvard University Press.

Yin, H. K. (1966). *The prospect of Chinese civilization.* Taipei: Wenshing Book Store.

Young, J. D. (1981). China's role in two Hong Kong disturbances: A scenario for the future? *Journal of Oriental Studies, 19,* 158-174.

Young, J. D. (1984, December). *Socialism vs. capitalism: Towards a Hong Kong strategy for absorption without integration.* Paper presented at the Conference on Hong Kong and 1997: Strategies for the Future, Hong Kong.

Chapter Summary

Zhang Shifu and David Y. H. Wu focus on factors contributing to smooth interpersonal relations among four Chinese ethnic minorities: the Kemu, Jinuo, Lahu, and Hani of Xishuangbanna on the southern border of Yunnan, China. The authors explain that although each of these four groups has its own culture and language, they have common values of altruism and respect for elders and children. Zhang and Wu describe these communities as relatively free from child abuse, quarrels, violence, or crime. Sanctions for not adhering to behavioral or interpersonal norms consist primarily of condemnation and criticism by other villagers. The effectiveness of such sanctions is explained in terms of the importance of group membership for survival in these communities. According to the authors, ballads, folktales, and songs convey this need for group cooperation. Songs also serve as a method of socializing children, an outlet for emotional expression, a form of communication in the absence of a written language, and most commonly, as a method of social discipline.

Zhang and Wu detail five main factors leading to the low levels of conflict among the Kemu, Jinuo, Lahu, and Hani. First, imitative learning and reinforcement stressing socialization is emphasized as a common task of all village members. Second, organizations of young people led by elders function to teach group loyalty and other social norms. Third, public opinion, both positive and negative, is highly respected. Fourth, the Kemu, Jinuo, Lahu, and Hani are well educated in terms of morality and discipline. Finally, the policies of China promote unity and equality. These policies provide that the administrative head of an autonomous region must be a citizen of the nationality of that region; the congress of a region decides the proportion of deputies exercising regional autonomy belonging to that region's ethnic group; and an effort is made to include ethnic minorities in the government on the national level.

—Susan Goldstein

4

Ethnic Conflict Management in Yunnan, China

ZHANG SHIFU and DAVID Y. H. WU

This chapter deals with ethnic relations and conflict between the Han Chinese and other ethnic minorities as well as relations among the other minorities in China. China has 55 minority groups, totaling some 60,000,000 people, or 0.6 percent of China's total population of 1 billion. These nationalities are distributed on 60 percent of China's land mass and occupy strategically significant territories along the Chinese borders. Interethnic relations between the numerically dominating Han Chinese and the strategically important minority groups are extremely important to China, both historically as well as at present.

The four minorities to be discussed here—the Hani, the Lahu, the Jinuo, and the Kemu, inhabiting the southern border of the Yunnan Province of southwest China—are good examples of minorities in China. Studies of ethnic relations in China, especially for the region under discussion, are scarce. Our observations and tentative assessments are based on brief field trips for the study of psychological and ethnological aspects of the Yunnan minorities.[1] Any generalizations or conclusions drawn in this chapter should be regarded as preliminary and subject to further investigation.

The theoretical point we wish to present is an argument that we believe would help to explain interethnic relations and conflict from a different perspective. Like many social scientists, we believe ethnic conflict or harmony is contingent upon complicated factors, both external and internal to a group, including such aspects as political, economic, cultural, or a combined ecological environment. But, we argue, given that these factors are controlled (e.g., if between groups obvious political oppression, economic exploitation, and forced cultural assimilation do not exist), then the ways in which the group members manage interpersonal and intergroup conflict play an important role in determining the state of conflict or harmony among groups.

On the basis of the first author's study of moral development among the mentioned peoples (Zhang, 1984), we argue that moral socialization, family education, and social sanction work in combination to play an important role in minimizing intra- and interethnic conflict. Of course, managing conflict or minimizing aggression works when the people desire harmonious relations with the outside groups and the dominating majority power. In this regard we should consider the history of ethnic relations in the region and the ways in which implementation of the minority policy of the People's Republic of China affects group relations.

Han-Minority Relations and Contemporary Policy on Nationalities

Interethnic conflict, armed rivalries, or large-scale warfare between ethnic groups have been constants in Chinese history. Yunnan is particularly renowned for such conflicts as it has been the crossroads for migration and intervention of diverse peoples. For example, the Han Chinese, since the establishment of the Han Empire around the Christian era, tried to gain influence, if not control, of this region. However, the Han Chinese bureaucracy did not actually enter Yunnan until after the Mongols conquered the area in the thirteenth century, and the Chinese political power did not penetrate down to the minority villages until after the 1950s (Ma, 1983). The four minority groups discussed here have in the past centuries been subject to the reign of a feudal political system of the ethnic Thai ("Dai" in official classification) rather than the ethnic Han Chinese. They all share a common ethnohistory. According to the legends of these groups, and to Chinese historical texts, they are not original inhabitants of southern Yunnan, but are migrants from the north who settled in this region some two to four centuries ago. They must have shared a common ancestral stock, as they speak languages classified under the same Tibetan-Burmese family, with a close relationship with the Yi language branch. (The Yi is now a separately defined ethnic group of 5.5 million who are dispersed among Sichuan, Yunnan, Guizhou, and Guangxi provinces.)

Historically, armed feuds between different ethnic groups, or even between villages of the same group, were common practice. This is because of competition for resources, customary practices of collective responsibility in blood retaliation, and religious beliefs. Furthermore, in the past 300 years, many large-scale armed conflicts or battles were fought between the minorities and the ruling ethnic Han and Thai authorities in southern Yunnan. For instance, during the 1850s, the Muslim uprising in many parts of Yunnan caused the massacre of thousands of Muslims, Han Chinese, and other minorities. And several times the Muslim militia leaders were able to temporarily capture the capitol city of Kunming and drive away the Quing officials (Ma, 1983). In 1917, after the establishment of the Republic, several large-scale armed uprisings broke out against the ruling Chinese and Thai authorities at local administrative centers and the fighting spread to hundreds of villages, involving the Hani, Lahu, and Jinuo who aligned with the larger groups of Yi, Miao, and sometimes Thai (Guo-ja, 1981).

The latest armed conflict occurred in 1941, when the Jinuo people, united with the Hani and the Han in the region, fought against the ruling force, by whom these people felt they were being politically oppressed and economically exploited. The fighting lasted for several months. However, there has since been no more fighting among the ethnic minorities in Xishuangbanna.

In the view of the first author, during the several thousand years of feudal rule in China, various ethnic groups have discriminated against one another, oppressing one another, killing one another, and letting different nationalities become entrenched in their miserable ethnic conflict. We may conclude, therefore, that harmony in ethnic relations in the region is a very recent phenomena.

One may argue that recent stability of interethnic relationships among groups in the region is due at least in part to the national policy governing the minorities, especially the implementation of the policy to provide autonomous status of a minority administration and culture. Since the early days of the Chinese Communist

Party, emphasis on equal and autonomous status has been guaranteed the minorities in China, and the point was reiterated in the first constitution of the People's Republic. However, many studies have pointed out a changing course of policy implementation in the minority regions (see Dryer, 1976; Grunfeld, 1985; Hsieh, 1984). The "great Han Chauvinism"—that is, local officials' view of encouraging assimilation to the Han culture and placing local ethnic interest secondary to the interests of the state (e.g., the issues of religion)—has been an obstacle to good ethnic relations. But the modernization of China has also improved aspects of making and implementing minority policy. From the provincial to the village level, the minorities now enjoy a higher degree of self-government; and the minority cultures have gained more respect from the Han authorities.

The Law on Regional Autonomy for Minority Nationalities, issued in May 1984, addressed the correct handling of relations among ethnic groups and the promotion of national unity and group equality. It stipulates that China shall have 5 autonomous regions (equivalent in size to a province), 31 autonomous prefectures, and 80 autonomous counties. The law specifies an autonomous administration: (1) The administrative head of an autonomous region, prefecture or county shall be a citizen of the nationality exercising regional autonomy in the area concerned. The chairmanship or vice-chairmanships of the standing committee of the people's congress of an autonomous region, prefecture, or county shall include a citizen or citizens of the nationality or nationalities exercising regional autonomy in the area concerned. (2) The number or proportion of deputies belonging to the minority that exercises regional autonomy is decided by the standing committee of the regional or provincial people's congress. Due consideration should be given to the national minorities with a smaller population when distributing the number of deputies. (3) Efforts should be made to include minorities in the people's governments of the national autonomous areas.

We note with interest that even in some provinces, such as Yunnan and Qinghai, which are not autonomous minority administrations but which have a high proportion of minority population and lower level autonomous administrations in the area, a minority person has been appointed as the governor or deputy governor. The law provides the basis for strengthening friendly relations among various nationalities in that it stipulates that the governing bodies of national autonomous areas and the higher state departments must ensure political equality and unity among nationalities. It calls for the development of economic and cultural exchanges and cooperation between autonomous areas to educate all the people in patriotism, morality, and the state's national policy. The law points out that Han nationality and local nationality chauvinism should each be strongly opposed. Emotions and attitudes evolved from these ideas, says the law, are harmful to the unity of the people of all nationalities. Conflict among the people should be solved through democratic discussion, criticism, and self-criticism, which, according to the law, are methods consistent with the Chinese ways of solving problems and differences.

The reality of the political situation in this region is such that government authorities did not penetrate down to the village level until the mid-1950s. At that time government "work teams" entered the villages to implement land reform, to destroy the feudal systems of political power, and to promote economic and agriculture development. In the 1950s, autonomous regional governments were established at the Zhou (larger than a county), county, district, and even the village level (e.g., the Jinuo Commune). Young minority students were educated by the hundreds at the secondary and tertiary level of cadre schools, and they later became leaders in their home regions or villages. It was observed that self-government was functioning at the village level as minority peasants formed administrative and public work committees. And village mayors and other officials who may not even be party members were elected by the villagers. In recent years priority in budget, economic aids, and construction were offered to the minority regions at all levels of administrative units. The effect of these decisions leading to educational and public health facilities could be clearly seen on the first author's field trip even though it is true that the minority regions have traditionally lagged behind in other areas.

Background of the Four Minority Groups

Table 4.1 gives the basic information about the four groups discussed in this chapter. Among the 55 officially recognized minority nationality groups, 25 are found in the Yunnan Province alone.

TABLE 4.1:   Four Minority Groups in Xishuangbanna

Group Name	Population	Language	Distribution	Place Studied
Hani	1,058,836[a]	Tibetan-Burmese	In many counties of southwestern Yunnan coinhabit with Yi and Thai, at the borders of Vietnam and Laos.	Monghai county
Lahu	304,174[a]	Tibetan-Burmese	Monglien, Lancang, and other autonomous counties at the Burmese borders	Monghai county
Jinuo	11,974[a]	Tibetan-Burmese	Jinghong county of Dai Autonomous Zhou	Jinghon county
Kemu	1,700[b]	Hmong-Kmer	Mongla and Jinghong counties of Dai Autonomous Zhou	Mongla county

a. According to the 1982 national census (Exhibition Hall, 1984).
b. According to the 1982 national census (Yunnan-Sheng, 1983, p. 415).

There are, in addition, two peoples—Kemu and Kucung—who have not gained the official status of a "nationality" but are no doubt separate ethnic minority groups. Among the high mountains and deep river valleys, settlements of certain minorities are found to be occupying different ecological niches, in a vertical pattern of distribution. Namely, the Han Chinese and Thais inhabit the lowlands and river valleys; the four minority groups along with the Yi settle on the hills; while the Lisu and Nu peoples live on mountain tops.

According to ethnographical studies (see Guo-ja, 1981), these four peoples share many common characteristics in migration history, settlement pattern, kinship, traditional political organization, traditional means of production, and religious life. They live in villages of extended families or dominating clans, or sometimes in small hamlets of a few families. Despite traceable clues of a matrilineal kinship structure and marriage practices, and of collective, communal productivities, all of these peoples have for centuries undergone assimilation with the dominating Thai and Han Chinese. For instance, many of them are bilingual or trilingual, speaking Thai and Chinese in addition to their mother tongue. There is also a clear influence of Mahayana Buddhism and of agricultural skills for paddy rice cultivation. (Hani and Lahu are known for their terraced paddy fields on the hills.) More recently, the effects of outside influences are seen in cash crops, light industries, and many schools at both the primary and secondary level. They were originally hunters, gatherers, and horticulturalists practicing slash-and-burn agriculture on the hills, with rice, corn, and hemp as their main crops. Today, paddy rice terraces for wet rice cultivation and cash crops such as tea and tobacco have replaced traditional hunting and gathering.

Means of Group Conflict Management and Individual Control of Interpersonal Aggression

We shall now describe customs observed among the Kemu, Jinuo, Lahu, and Hani people that help to promote friendly social relations and to prevent expression of hostility among individuals, both within and between ethnic groups. There is an emphasis on etiquette and behaving in conformity to moral standards that may serve to regulate group tension. By means of child socialization, public education in many forms, social sanction, and use of folk songs, the minority people educate members to value nonviolence and to promote harmonious interpersonal and group relations.

Socialization and the Teaching of Social Norms

Violence is not part of the child socialization experience among these people. Parents rarely physically discipline their children. The parents consider it shameful to have to resort to beating or cursing a child, and any child beating would result in public criticism by others. The adults are rarely seen quarreling or fighting, while the elders' words are respected by the young. Thus the adults provide behavioral examples for the young.

The custom of youth clubs for educating the young is still popular among these four minority peoples. On Jinuo Mountain, for instance, when boys and girls reach the age of 15, a ceremony to mark their adulthood is performed, and the parents ceremonially offer the child who came of age tools and instruments to symbolize their ability to live an independent life. Hereafter, a boy goes to live in a man's house called *raolan,* and a girl joins a *mikao.* The youths in these organizations go through education and training, and they perform duties such as guarding the forests, entertaining visitors, and organizing night parties. Disciplinary measures for the club members include open criticism of any inappropriate or antisocial behavior. The village elders serve as club leaders or supervisors who set up standards, by exemplary behavior, for the young to emulate. Participating in these organizations gives the young members the feeling of belonging, sense of group, loyalty to the club, and devotion to the community. Moral teaching of proper conduct and discipline of social discord are carried out in routine daily activities of the youth club.

Young people are trained in and required to observe good manners. The young, for example, are asked to show respect for an elder, or a visitor, by bowing and saying "pardon me" at each meeting. A visitor is offered a place to sit by the fireplace of a house (a bamboo pavilion), and the young people sit in a certain posture of modesty in front of a visitor or an elder. When visiting others, the young people learn to sit a little distance away from the fireplace—a place of honor in the house—and to never show eagerness when offered food.

Traditional Organization and Social Sanction

Despite increased contact with the outside in recent years, traditional social organization is still intact at the family and community levels. For instance, it is observed among the Lahuna (black Lahu) on the Mengsong or mountain, that the family head, or *yexiepa*, is always a female who is in charge of family finance, food provisions, child rearing and education, and wedding and funeral ceremonies. The rest of the family members are expected to respect her status.

Among the Hani (or Aini) of the Nannun Mountain, every village has a traditional chief, known as a *jiuma*. The jiuma has the authority to settle disputes as well as to organize village festivals or ceremonies. Each year, for example, the jiuma leads a planting ceremony by sowing the first seed in the village field before villagers begin ploughing the land to prepare it for new planting. Communal sharing by all members of a village is still practiced for game or fish procured through hunting and fishing. The fish and game, no matter how large or small, must be divided in equal shares and distributed to all members of the village. A newborn baby, a dying old man, or even a visitor will receive an equal share. Sharing of hunting and fishing is a symbolic gesture which demonstrates that they value generosity to others.

Gossip is another method of social sanction. A frequently discussed subject for Kemu, Jinuo, Lahu, and Hani people is the behavior of others. At night, by the fireplace, people gather to gossip, expressing opinions about someone, praising, criticizing, or accusing the person. On many occasions, in public meetings or ceremonies, the elders praise the young for their generosity, empathy, or kindness to others. However, criticism is seldom offered in formal, public gatherings. Rather, people gossip about wrongdoings or express disapproval of someone's conduct in private gatherings. The expression of public opinion through gossip is a real weapon that is used to discipline social deviants. A person who violates the social norm will be punished by the entire community. The most serious form of punishment, known to the Jinuo as *dudaozao* and the Lahu as *maizha,* is an action in which the villagers may eat up all the food the person possesses, distribute all the person's belongings, and send him or her into exile. Expulsion from a community (not unknown) is the most serious form of public punishment.

Songs to Educate

Songs and dances are important parts of the life of the Kemu, Jinuo, Lahu, and Hani, helping to emphasize the value of peaceful social relations. Sometimes sung and danced spontaneously, other times performed during festivals, the songs serve many individual and social purposes. Songs have well-defined roles: (1) to educate the group, (2) to communicate between two individuals (as in love songs) and between members of two ethnic groups, (3) to settle disputes, and (4) as a means of social sanction.

Songs may be sung as a means of disciplining an individual who has violated the social norms. A singer, in this case, may compose a song to describe a person's behavior, and then the person is praised or condemned with the song. During fieldwork in a Jinuo village, it was observed that a group of Jinuo and Hani people were involved in a dispute over the use of land and water. They resolved their differences by songs. Many disputes were resolved in this fashion before they developed into quarrels or physical violence. In general, when dealing with other groups, these minority people refrain from physical violence as tensions appear to mount and often manage to avoid open hostility.

The Hani people distinguish their songs into two types: *agiku,* spontaneous songs, including many love songs; and the *habare,* songs of legends and ballads of moral teachings. The latter have fixed texts, are handed down by singers from generation to generation, and are usually sung while drinking at festivals and ceremonies. Old singers sing *habares* to young people in order to recite moral teachings on how to maintain social order and good social relations. Once we saw an old Hani man of 70 sing ballads for an entire evening. And a Jinuo man of over 60 once sang for 7 days consecutively to tell the epoch legends of the Jinuo people. Especially at weddings, people sing and dance, and young people listen to elders singing ballads throughout the night. The songs often serve to emphasize social harmony, personal accord, respect of social norms, and avoidance of conflict with outsiders.

Conclusion

This chapter briefly reviews the situation of four minority groups—Kemu, Jinuo, Lahu, and Hani—in Yunnan, China. We have also discussed the ethnohistory and current policy on nationalities in China in order to explain the changes that have occurred in the minority administration and in their sociocultural activities. Due to the relatively small population, especially for the Kemu and Jinuo, and the nature of the multiethnic environment, these groups are the minority among the minorities. In order to minimize open hostility among individuals and to manage potential conflict between groups, they emphasize peaceful ways of conflict resolution. The ways in which they educate their children and youth, for instance, place a high value on group harmony and conformity to social norms. The maintenance of traditional social organization contributes to an orderly society that resolves disputes through the unique medium of folk songs. Although we recognize the complex nature of interethnic relations, which can be studied from many levels of analysis, we have attempted in this chapter to show examples of minority group customs for conflict management. As we mentioned earlier, however, in our opinion, any true amicable relationship among ethnic groups must be built on the basis of true equality, nonexploitation, and mutual cooperation between groups. That is the prerequisite of group unity and conflict management among the minorities.

NOTE

1. Zhang visited the Jinuo and Kemu peoples in the Xishuangbanna region in 1981. He also did a psychological study of moral development in the same region among the Lahu and Hani peoples in 1982. Wu visited Yunnan for the first time in 1984 and, in 1985, he spent the summer conducting ethnographic field work in a Bai minority village in Yunnan.

References

Dryer, J. T. (1976). *China's forty millions.* Cambridge, MA: Harvard University Press.

Exhibition Hall, The Cultural Palace of Nationalities (1984). *China's nationalities.* Beijing.

Grunfeld, A. (1985). In search of equality: Relations between China's ethnic minorities and the majority Han. *Bulletin of Concerned Asian Scholars, 17*(1), 54-67.

Guo-ja Min-wei Min-zu Wen-ti Wu-zhong Cung-shu Bein-ji Wei-yuan-hui "Zhong-Kuo Shao-shu Min-Zu" Ban-xie-zu [Editorial section for the "Chinese Minority Nationalities" of the Editorial Committee of the National Commission of Nationality Affairs' Five Series of the Nationality Problem Books]. (1981). *Zhong-Kuo-Shao-shu Min-zu* [Chinese Minority Nationalities]. Beijing: Ren-min [People's Press].

Hsieh, Jiann. (1984). *China's policy toward the minority nationalities: An anthropological perspective.* Unpublished manuscript.

Ma, Yao. (1983). *Yun-nan Jien-shi* [A Short History of Yunan]. Kunming: Yunnan Ren-min Chu-ban-she [Yunnan's People's Press].

Yunnan-Sheng Li-shi Yen-jiu-so [Yunnan Provincial Research Institute of History]. (1983). *Yun-nan Shao-shu Min-zu* (Minority nationalities of Yunnan.) Kunming: Yun-nan Ren-min Chu-ban-she [Yunnan's People's Press].

Zhang, Shifu. (1984). Yun-nan-sheng Xi-shuang-ban-na Dai-zu Zi-zhi-zhou La-hu-zu he Ha-ni-zu Qing-shao-nian Pin-te Xing-ching, de Dao-cha Yen-ju [Study of the Formation of Morality Among the Lahu and Hani Youths in Dai Nationality Autonomous Zhou, Xishuangbanna, Yunan]. In Zhong-quo Xin-li Xue-hui Di-wu-jei Quan-guo Xue-shu Hui-yi Wen-ze Xuan-ji [A collection of papers presented at the Fifth National Conference, Chinese Association of Psychology] (pp. 175-177). Beijing: Ke-xue [Science Press].

Chapter Summary

Anthropologist Ronald Provencher discusses the unique situation of the Chinese, Malays, and Thais of the Malay peninsula in which each of these three ethnic groups experiences both majority and minority status in relation to one or both of the other groups.

Provencher begins his chapter with a discussion of the geographical and historical factors involved in the development of the ethnic diversity of this region. Attention is given to the economic and political changes that led to an influx of immigrants (primarily Chinese) and the factors involved in the varying degrees to which these immigrant groups were assimilated into Malay and Thai society. Provencher also traces and analyzes the development of a Chinese association with commerce and a Malay and Thai association with agriculture, fishing, and government employment, emphasizing actions of the British which, he suggests, strengthened these structural differences.

In a section on ethnicity and race, Provencher points out that although scientific study has failed to find racial differences between Chinese, Thai, and Malay peoples, a common view persists among these groups that physical differences do exist and that these differences are associated with differences of an intellectual or moral nature. In specific discussions of Malay, Chinese, and Thai ethnicity, Provencher looks at how the consequences of identifying with each of these groups has changed over time and related to this, changes in the degree of flexibility in what constitutes membership in each of these ethnic groups.

Finally, the author presents a detailed discussion of the nature and possible antecedents of conflict between the Malay and Chinese and between the Malay and Thai. In both cases much attention is given to the stereotypes each group holds of the other. With regard to the Malay-Chinese situation, Provencher concentrates on the situation in which the Malays are given an advantage in terms of the political system and government services by their constitution in order to offset the perceived economic advantage of the Chinese. Both groups' interpretation of these circumstances are explored. Provencher comments on the economic and political reality of the situation. The Malay-Thai conflict, on the other hand, is described as having a primarily historical basis in a struggle of Malays against Thai Buddhists, who dominated the political realm. Distinctions among groups of Malays in their views of Thais are explained in terms of educational and regional differences.

Provencher emphasizes the need for research on the role of ethnic stereotyping in conflict and advocates that this research be of an emic orientation which is systematically conducted across time and structural context.

—Susan Goldstein

5

Interethnic Conflict
in the Malay Peninsula

RONALD PROVENCHER

Historical Background

The Malayan peninsula extends southward from the mainland of Southeast Asia for more than 600 miles, presenting a strategic obstacle to the long-distance sea trade between India and China that has existed for two or three millennia (Hall & Whitmore, 1976; Taylor, 1976; Wolters, 1970). This circumstance led to the development of the earliest states in the area, and attracted many kinds of foreigners—Indian, Sumatran, Javanese, Thai, Cham (Vietnamese), Chinese, Persian, Arab, Buginese (Sulawesi), Portuguese, Dutch, and English.

A number of very different ethnic groups continue to reside in the Malayan peninsula. Only three are discussed here because they are the dominant ethnic groups of the peninsula, they are the main protagonists in the major instances of ethnic conflict, and each experiences both majority and minority status vis-à-vis one or both of the other groups. Each is the ethnic core of a modern nation state: the Chinese of Singapore, the Malays of Malaysia, and the Thais of Thailand. And each is an economically or politically underprivileged minority in one or both of the other two states. Moreover, the cultural world of each ethnic community extends well beyond the Malayan peninsula: The various subethnic varieties of Chinese have long dominated the whole eastern mainland of Asia and constitute a most important urban element in virtually every nation of Southeast Asia; speakers of Tai language, of which Thai (Siamese) is but one dialect, dominate the central core of mainland Southeast Asia, especially Thailand and Laos, and are an important element of the populations of Burma (Shan), Vietnam (Tai), and southern China (Dai); and the Malay world extends deeply into the island world of Indonesia, including the southern and most of the coastal areas of Sumatra, and many coastal enclaves of Java and Borneo [Kalimantan]. Indeed, from before the Portuguese arrival in 1509 until 50 years ago, Malay was the major trade language spoken in ports and coastal areas throughout Southeast Asia, and the Johore-Riau dialect of Malay was the base from which Indonesian and Malaysian were developed as national languages in the twentieth century (Alisjahbana, 1962; Teeuw, 1959). It is important to add that this broad Malay world was not and is not culturally homogeneous. That is, there were and are many different kinds of Malays (Provencher, 1975, pp. 84-90; Wu, 1982, p. 39). And the same may be said of Thais and Chinese. Finally, each group is culturally chauvinistic, holding its own particular views of the centuries-long association of these three ethnic groups in the Malayan peninsula. Interpretations and even the facts are in dispute. Some examples follow.

Ethnic Perspectives of History

South of the Kra isthmus, from earliest times until the southward intrusion of Thais in the thirteenth century, the native states of the peninsula were Malay. Less certainly, so were the states north of the Kra isthmus; but, in any case, the majority of the population, north and south, was Malay. This interpretation is based upon well-established facts from the perspective of Western history. But, more important, these "facts" are variously true or false from Malay, Thai, or Chinese perspectives. Each view establishes the historical precedence of a particular ethnic community.

Some present-day Thais maintain that the fabled trading empire of Sri Vijaya, which controlled much of the long-distance trade that passed through Southeast Asia from the fifth to the thirteenth centuries A.D., was located in Thailand and was dominated by Thais. Royal Malay tradition, like modern Western scholarship, locates

Sri Vijaya in Sumatra, another part of the Malay world, but further insists that Melaka, the most powerful of the Malay states in the peninsula at the time of the Portuguese arrival in 1509, was not only the direct heir of all of the Sri Vijayan empire but was founded by a member of a family of Java-based emperors who for a time ruled the famous mainland empires of Funan and Angkor, centered in present-day Kampuchea (Cambodia). Finally, although many of the "facts" in modern Western scholarship regarding ancient states in Southeast Asia are based on ancient Chinese records, some present-day Chinese insist that there were no real native states, Malay or Thai, in the peninsula until the arrival of regular Chinese commercial and political interest in the fifteenth century A.D.

These Thai-centric, Malay-centric, and Chinese-centric views are not without basis from the view of Western scholarship. As noted above, the Thais began to intrude seriously into the northern reaches of the Malay world in the thirteenth century, about the time that the Sumatran capital of the Malay empire of Srivijaya was con-quered by the Javanese empire of Majapahit. Just as individual Thais had entered the Malay world before that time, so had indi-vidual Chinese. But after the fall of Srivijaya, Thais (Ayutthaya) claimed suzerainty over all states in the Malay peninsula, the Chi-nese (Ming) interceded in behalf of the Malays (Melaka), and com-munities of Chinese began to assume greater importance in Malay ports.

Outsiders and the History of Ethnic Relations

It would be easy, but not accurate, to view all present-day eth-nic conflict in the Malayan peninsula as mere extensions of this centuries-old competition for domination of the region. Much of the present ethnic conflict, although referenced within the various accepted versions of this history, relates more directly to fairly recent competition within the framework of a radical economic system—modern capitalism—introduced by Europeans after the Melakan period. Some English historians and social scientists have been loath to admit that much of the current ethnic strife is a direct result of colonial policies, but the evidence is fairly clear (Provencher, 1985).

The Melakan period, which from the Western (but not the Malay) perspective ended in A.D. 1511 with the Portuguese conquest, did not last very long, but it began a period of increasing involvement in regional and world trade, which eventually required development of massive local and regional supplies of staple food as well as luxury goods such as spices and tin ore. It was the beginning of a long period of economic change that affected not only Southeast Asia but also the world beyond, and that witnessed the eventual transformation of a relatively low volume trade in luxury goods into a very high volume trade in common goods (van Leur, 1955).

One aspect of this transformation was the need for more and more human beings to be engaged as laborers, small-scale entrepreneurs, and customers for enterprises that profited European corporations. From Melakan times onward this increasing need was filled mostly by immigrants, especially Chinese and Indians but also hundreds of thousands of Malays from the now Indonesian islands of Sumatra and Java. This massive immigration was especially marked after the English, having previously dislodged the Dutch from the peninsula in 1824, interceded in the Tin Wars of 1874 and took effective control of the political economy of the Malay states of the peninsula. At that time the English began to assume direct control of the economy, displacing the Malay chiefs who had until then administered the extraction of economic resources for the European trade, declaring all Malays to be agricultural peasants, and fostering Chinese control of the lower and middle levels of commerce (Provencher, 1985). This, more than the natural propensities of Malays and Chinese, marked the beginning of their current stereotypes as peasants on the one hand and business persons on the other.

Before the English took control, Malays and Chinese were often at least allies, if not friends. This was true in the Melakan period during which China guaranteed Melakan independence from Thai suzerainty, and also in the Tin Wars, when interethnic alliances of English merchants, Malay royalty and chiefs, and Chinese miners fought other interethnic alliances of similar ethnic diversity (Cowan, 1962).

Problems of Chinese assimilation of Malay culture also date from the period of direct British control. Earlier Chinese immigrants, such as the founders of the "Straits Chinese" or "Baba Chinese"

communities, who immigrated during the Melakan period or during subsequent periods of limited Portuguese and Dutch control,
seem to have assimilated Malay culture rather more easily and
thoroughly than did those who arrived later. This probably reflects
greater economic and political dependence of Chinese immigrants
on Malays before the period of British control. Additionally, it may
reflect the fact that the later immigrants arrived in greater numbers, and sometimes with wives and children, so that it was easier
to establish greater cultural autonomy. And it may also reflect
an increasing Islamic orthodoxy in the Malay community, which
began at the end of the nineteenth century in response to the economic, political, and cultural inroads of modern capitalism into the
Islamic world. The increase in Islamic orthodoxy began to lead to
rejection of close social ties with non-Muslims. This new religious
orthodoxy in the peninsula was closely related to the massive injec-
tion of Indonesian immigrants into the Malay community that eventually protected the majority position of Malays.

The importance of native control of political and economic institutions as a factor contributing to rapid assimilation of immigrants
may be seen also in the relative ease of Chinese assimilation to Thai
ethnic identity. Specifically, a series of events giving rise to the
Chakri Dynasty of modern Thailand (following the destruction of
Ayutthaya by the Burmese in 1767) insured a strong positive relationship between Thai royalty and a particular segment of the Chinese business community of Bangkok and thereby helped to insure
a favored position for Chinese merchants. An important part of
these circumstances was the undisputed authority of Thai royalty
over the Chinese, resulting in the transfer of power from a part-
Chinese general who saved the kingdom and even ruled for a time,
but who nonetheless gave way not to his own heirs but to the heirs
of Thai royalty. The Chinese were favored but never more favored
than Thais; and in the subsequent history of the Chakri Dynasty
Chinese have been given strong negative and positive incentives to
acquire the appearances of Thai ethnicity in order to succeed in
commerce. Present-day Chinese in Thailand are hardly distinguishable from Thais except through self-identification. In Malaysia, where British colonial policy removed for many decades the
authority of Malays over Chinese in economic matters, very little
assimilation occurred. It may be argued that the Chinese were culturally much less similar to Malays than to Thais, and that this

accounts for much of the difference in assimilation; but the case of
the Straits Chinese suggests that a greater part of the difference lies
in the degree of native control of the political economy.

The Japanese, in their brief occupation of the Malayan peninsula during World War II, certainly widened the distance between
Malays and Chinese and to a lesser extent between Thais and Chinese. Concerned with the Japanese conquest of China, many more
Chinese than Malays joined the organized resistance to the Japanese occupation of the Malayan peninsula. While Chinese were
more or less continuously harassed by Japanese authorities, Malays
were only occasionally bothered, and many close personal relationships developed between Malay and Japanese individuals. Malay
clerks and entrepreneurs were placed in charge of the distribution
of food and other supplies in the towns. Malays were allowed to
join the Japanese armed services, and received basic educational
and occupational training. As the war became more hopeless, Japanese authorities encouraged Malays to think of an independent
Malaya ruled by Malays. Although some Malays protected their
Chinese acquaintances during the occupation, and a few joined the
resistance movement against the Japanese, the very different treatment of Chinese and Malays by the Japanese served to further separate them, encouraging the Malays to distance themselves from
difficulties suffered by the Chinese and embittering the Chinese
against the Malays who received better treatment. Among themselves, many elderly Malays reminisce about the Japanese occupation as a period when they gained a new self-confidence concerning
their political and economic rights. Many elderly Chinese remember the period as one in which the Malays collaborated with the
enemy.

Tensions between Malays and Chinese reached the breaking
point, briefly, in the interim between the Japanese surrender and
the reoccupation by the British. Deadly conflicts between Chinese
and Malays took place. Some conflict may have concerned personal grievances, but some was more broadly based on ethnic
hatred and bigotry.

The British, mindful of technically having only an advisor's role
in the governance of the Federated Malay States they had just reoc-
cupied, foolishly promulgated a new constitution that transferred
the sovereignty of the Malay kings to the British crown and placed
residents of the Federated Malay States, whatever their ethnicity, on

an equal political footing as citizens of a new polity—the Malayan Union. Commoner Malays objected to the loss of their kings' sovereignty and to giving non-Malays full political equality; the British government relented; and many of the Chinese and Indian residents of the FMS joined a 12-year rebellion, which was led by the Malayan Communist Party.

The rebellion, called "the emergency," increased the level of ill feeling between Malays and Chinese. Government propaganda branded the Chinese community as the main source of support for the rebels by attributing planning and leadership of the rebellion to the Communist Party of the People's Republic of China. The irony of an ethnic group noted for its fierce entrepreneural involvement in capitalist enterprises being accused of communist sympathies was matched only by the partial truth of the accusation. Rural Chinese communities were transformed by the government into "new villages" with central kitchens and surrounded by barbed wire fences guarded by British and Malay soldiers to prevent the Chinese villagers from provisioning the rebel forces. Most Chinese who sympathized with the rebellion did so on the principle of ethnic equality. Most Malays opposed the rebellion on the basis that it was communist led.

When the emergency eased and the British granted independence to the Federation of Malaya in 1957, the constitution of the new country granted clear political advantages to Malays: less stringent rules for claiming citizenship, claim to more (80 percent) of the higher civil service positions, and sovereignty of the states and nation in the hands of Malay kings. But Chinese, in spite of their suspected communist sympathies, continued to dominate the lower and middle levels of the economy. Real communist rebels, mostly Chinese, retreated into southern Thailand.

At first the Federation of Malaya, which became the Federation of Malaysia in 1963 through the addition of Singapore and the north Bornean states of Sarawak and Sabah, seemed to provide a context within which both Malay and Chinese ambitions might be satisfied. A political coalition of conservative Malay (United Malay Nationalist Organization—UMNO), Chinese (Malaysian Chinese Association—MCA), and Indian (Malaysian Indian Congress—MIC) parties, known as the Alliance, ruled parliament without significant opposition. Moreover, the Malay party was easily the strongest partner in the Alliance.

The basic source of Alliance strength, the common interest of Malay and Chinese and Indian elites, was also its greatest weakness. Wealthy Chinese had acquiesced to Malay political dominance in exchange for business as usual, which they dominated. But a new Chinese political force became active in the peninsula with the establishment of Malaysia—Singapore's Lee Kuan Yew and his Peoples Action Party (PAP). PAP made no deal with UMNO or the Alliance; PAP sought political domination of the peninsula. Moreover, poor and middle-class Malays became aware of the fact that most of the native inhabitants *(bumiputera)* of Sabah and Sarawak were not really Malays or even Muslims. In the end (1965), rather than risk possible electoral defeat at the hands of the wiley Lee Kuan Yew, UMNO and the Alliance pushed Singapore out of the Federation of Malaysia and avoided the specter of Chinese political control, which surely would have resulted in Malay uprisings.

In the meanwhile, more of the poor and lower-middle-class Chinese and Indians, who realized that a political change might better their economic status, acquired citizenship and the right to vote, increasing the electoral base of old and newly formed socialistic parties and diluting the power of the conservative MCA and MIC. Poor Malays, too, were tempted to desert UMNO because of its mediocre performance in increasing the Malay share in the economy and because of its protective stance vis-à-vis the wealthy Chinese. These festering problems, only temporarily and superficially soothed by the exit of Singapore from the federation in 1965, came to a head following the elections of 1969, in which the margin of the Alliance's majority was greatly reduced and a number of "safe" contests were lost. UMNO did reasonably well; but its Chinese and Indian partners failed, provoking a feeling of betrayal among Malays. Ethnic riots, in which Malays attacked Chinese, began when opposition parties, mostly Chinese, celebrated their victories near and even within Malay communities. These were the most bloody riots ever, and although they continued for some time and in a number of places, they are generally referred to by Malaysians as the "May 13th Incident" (Goh, 1971).

This incident, along with the weak electoral showing of the Alliance, marked the beginning of a revolutionary effort by the government to reduce Chinese domination of the domestically owned part of the economy while attempting to retain and even strengthen the Malay domination of government. The key to this effort is the New

Economic Policy (NEP), which in its various manifestations is intended to insure that Malays claim the lion's share of the economic growth that has been fueled by foreign investment and national development projects, so that only additional economic opportunity rather than capital is to be taken away from the Chinese business community.

Malay cultural chauvinism has been strengthened by these and other government efforts. English, spoken by more Chinese and Indians than Malays, lost its status as a coofficial language; and Malay language *(bahasa melayu)*, now called "Malaysian language" *(bahasa malaysia)*, has become the language for all official business. As Malaysians of all ethnic communities have shifted to Malay language, Islam has become a much more salient dimension of Malay ethnicity, supporting the development and acceptance of a fundamentalist *dakwah* movement to purify Malay culture of its non-Islamic elements and providing a context in which the holy places of other religions have been desecrated by a few Malays. The fundamentalist movement has pressured the modernists who control the government to be more Islam-centric (Nagata, 1984). The strength of Islamic fundamentalism in Malaysia has been strengthened by outside pressures, such as anti-Western reactions of Malay students who have studied in Western countries, fundamentalist Islamic missionaries from other parts of the Islamic world, and the friendly persuasion of Arab capital.

North and south of the Malaysian portion of the peninsula, in southern Thailand and in Singapore, political and economic circumstances of the modernization following World War II differed. Although the economic development of Thailand barely touched Malay communities of the south, political and educational modernization did lead to a strong effort to increase literacy in the national language and teach national governmental structure to all citizens. Inevitably, the lessons in Thai language and national government describe the fundamentals of Theravada Buddhist belief, and Malays have resisted these efforts as an attempt to weaken Malay ethnicity through recruitment of their children into the Thai ethnic community. Malay separatists and bandits raid Thai government and Chinese commercial facilities, and retreat into isolated rural areas or across the border into Malaysia. But the most aggressive activists on behalf of poor Chinese in Malaysia (the Malayan

Communist Party) and poor Malays in Thailand (the Malay separatist movement) reside in the same area, the Thailand-Malaysian
border, without fighting each other.

Singapore has enjoyed interethnic peace in the years since 1965,
when it separated from Malaysia. The Chinese constitute an overwhelming majority and have uncontested control of the government and the economy. They have maintained Malay as well as
English as official languages, and have maintained a nominal Malay
sovereign. Many Malaysians, mostly Malay, cross the causeway
to work in Singapore, where they as well as Malay Singaporeans
earn better wages than they would in Malaysia. The government's
approach to ethnic relations has been to insure "collaborative and
benevolent specialization" of the several ethnic groups, the quoted
phrase being one used by a well-known authority in the balmy days
of the late 1950s and early 1960s to characterize ethnic relations in
Malaysia (Freedman, 1960). Recently, as he has aged, Prime Minister Lee Kuan Yew has come to emphasize Confucian values and
has attempted to replace other Chinese dialects with Mandarin, but
he has so far successfully avoided any serious difficulty with Malay
Singaporeans.

Finally, many outside influences have contributed to ethnic
conflict in the history of the Malayan peninsula, but no outsiders
deserve more credit for the present state of ethnic relations in
Malaysia, Thailand, and Singapore than the British colonialists. In
the nineteenth and the twentieth centuries the British were fore-
most among the prime movers of events that (1) established Singapore with a strong Chinese majority population and a sizable Malay
minority; (2) removed several hundred thousand Malays from the
suzerainty of Thailand, while leaving more hundreds of thousands
of Malays under Thai suzerainty; (3) placed thousands of Thais
in the position of a powerless minority under the local authority of
a Malay majority and Malay rulers; and (4) established a Malaysian state with a bare Malay majority and a strong Chinese minority.
These historical circumstances, together with others that strengthened Chinese involvement in commerce and Malay and Thai involvement in small-scale agriculture and fishing and government
employment, have remained as the major structural factors in present-
day relations between Chinese, Malay, and Thai ethnic communities of the Malay peninsula.

Structural Themes of Conflict

However lengthy it seems, this thumbnail sketch of the histories of relations between these three ethnic groups has been too brief to be entirely accurate. Nonetheless, it is hoped that it may provide a context in which to consider the various themes of interethnic conflict among the three groups.

Political, Economic, and Social Conditions

Relationships between these three ethnic groups may be seen as functional, and may be stated oversimply as follows: In the northern portion of the Malayan peninsula that is part of Thailand, Thais are government workers, Chinese are in commerce, and Malays and Thais are small-scale agriculturalists and fishermen; and in the southern portion of the peninsula that is part of Malaysia, Malays are government workers, Chinese are in commerce, and Malays (and Thais near the Thai border) are rural agriculturalists and fishermen. The functional pattern of ethnicity in Singapore differs superficially from that of the Thai and Malaysian portions of the Peninsula because of the overwhelming urban character of the island. It is similar in that the national ethnic majority (in this instance Chinese, rather than Thai or Malay) dominate the government sector, and the Chinese, as usual, dominate the commercial sector. There are, of course, no rural areas of Singapore sufficiently large to support a peasantry. However, the unskilled and semiskilled labor sector, in which a large proportion of the workers are Malay (and a few are Thai), may be seen broadly as the "moral equivalent" of the rural peasant sectors of Malaysia and Thailand.

At worst, these relationships may be seen as the result of certain ethnic or racial prejudices, which in effect deny individuals of different ethnic communities equal participation in political and economic systems. The usual statement of this view is even more simplistic. Briefly, the Malays and the Thais are viewed as politically privileged (except in each other's countries and Singapore) and economically deprived, while the Chinese are seen as politically deprived (except in Singapore) and economically privileged.

Chinese domination of the Malaysian economy is more apparent than real in the sense that it is much less absolute than it is relative. In 1970, foreigners were dominant in the corporate sector, owning

63.3 percent of the equity capital; Chinese owned only 27.2 percent of the equity capital in the corporate sector (Tan, 1982). However, Malay interests owned only 2.4 percent, less than one-tenth the level of Chinese ownership. Another factor that adds to the image of Chinese as capitalists is their common involvement in very small-scale enterprises, as middlemen dealing directly with rural Malays, and as managers of foreign-owned enterprises. In southern Thailand, many more Malays than Chinese, in absolute numbers, are engaged in business. Chavivun Prachuabmoh (1982) notes, for example, that in the fresh food markets on special market days in Pattani town there may be close to 1,000 Malay traders (mostly women), whereas the number of Chinese shops is only 266. But the Chinese shops are much larger-scale businesses and represent much more capital. The extent of Chinese involvement in the economy of Thailand is estimated by everyone to be considerable, but it is not certainly calculable because many of the Chinese of Thailand are virtually Thai (Punyodyana, 1971).

Homelands, Immigrants, and Land Rights

No informed person seriously doubts that Malays came to the peninsula before Thais or Chinese. Each of the three governments explicitly recognizes, in its own way, that the peninsula is a Malay homeland. The Malaysian government makes the most of this, labeling the Malays along with other aboriginal peoples as *bumiputera* ("princes of the soil"—a Sanskrit word only recently adopted into everyday Malay language) and guaranteeing the sovereignty of the Malay rulers. The Singapore government has admitted it through designation of a Malay ruler. And the present Thai government is cognizant that Thailand once recognized the independent status of the Malay kingdom of Pattani, which once ruled the southern-most part of present-day Thailand.

Nonetheless, as previously noted, many of the Malays of the peninsula are themselves immigrants or the children or grandchildren of immigrants from the Indonesian islands during this century, while some of the Chinese are descendants of immigrants who arrived in the peninsula more than a century ago. Individual Thais, too, may or may not be recent immigrants to the peninsula. This seems an important issue, from a Western perspective.

Chinese perspectives are concerned primarily with political

equality and only to a minor extent with the question of birthplace. This is clear in the example of Singapore. Very different, the central issue from the traditional Malay perspective has been that the peninsula is a homeland of Malays because Malay kingdoms predate the polities of other ethnic groups. In this perspective, Malays derive their special political status not from place of birth but from the fact that they are the "true" subjects of Malay kings who are charged with the preservation of Islam, Malay language, and Malay customary law. According to this logic, residents of Malay kingdoms who are not Muslims, do not habitually speak Malay, and do not follow Malay traditional law are seen as less than "true" subjects. That the traditional Thai view is similar, except for the substitution of Thai religion, language, and customs, can be seen in the strong incentives (negative in the sense of favoring Thais absolutely over other ethnic groups; positive in the sense of accepting other ethnic groups into Thai ethnicity) provided by the Thai government for other ethnic groups within their kingdom to assimilate. That Chinese Singaporeans perhaps do not fully appreciate the traditional Malay perspective is clear in their own acceptance of a Malay ruler (although there has been no Malay kingdom on Singapore island since before the time of Melaka) as part of the ceremonial trappings of a British-style parliamentary democracy.

The right to land by particular ethnic groups is not an issue except in Malaysia with respect to Malays. Since independence the federal government and several state governments have sponsored the opening of lands through time-payment schemes that provide land, housing, tools, and other needs at minimal cost to the landless poor. Although virtually all ethnic groups are represented in these schemes, Malays have benefited most. Traditionally, of course, royalty held ultimate title to land; and in even in colonial law all land belonged ultimately to the state, which leased it at prescribed tax rates to individuals or corporations. Quite naturally, much of the richest timber lands and mineral deposits are owned by members of Malay royalty. The easy claim to land by Malays, poor and rich, is a source of ethnic conflict.

Language Policy

Thai has always been the national language of Thailand. Thais have insisted that members of other ethnic groups learn Thai. This policy has seriously eroded the ethnic identity of most non-Thai groups, particularly those who share religious beliefs the same or similar to those of Thais. Malays of southern Thailand, as the descendant population of an indigenous Malay state, as a majority population in their own provinces, and as adherents to a different religion, have been much less inclined to accept linguistic assimilation. Indeed, the teaching of Thai language in the Malay provinces is an important issue related to the separatist movement.

Singapore has four national languages (English, Chinese, Malay, and Tamil). Interestingly, linguistic chauvinism has been apparent only with respect to the Chinese languages and has taken a "rational" form. Mandarin has been proclaimed the official Chinese language because of its status as a "world language" such as English, Russian, or Spanish (which are the media or codes for vast and growing accumulations of human knowledge). This policy has caused some unhappiness among Chinese Singaporeans, but it has not affected the official status of Malay, Tamil, or English as official languages.

Malaysia began with the same array of official languages as Singapore, but Malay has finally become the national language. The language issue has been a major source of ethnic conflict. Some Chinese and Indian Malaysians have resisted this change—as much to retain English as to retain Tamil and Cantonese—but to no avail. Malays in Malaysia, like Thais in Thailand, have subscribed to a very strong policy of linguistic assimilation of all ethnic groups to the national language.

Religion and National Integration

Islam is the national religion of Malaysia, just as Theravada Buddhism is the national religion of Thailand. Singapore is a secular state. But even in Singapore, it might be said that Confucianism is the national religion. As in the case of official language policy, it is not the Malays or Indians of Singapore who are distressed; it is the Chinese, many of whom are Christian or secular in their ideology. But the distress of Chinese Singaporeans is not as great as that of non-Muslims in Malaysia or of non-Buddhists, particularly Muslims, in Thailand.

In Malaysia and Thailand, the legitimacy of the royal head of state is defined in terms of the national religious ideology. Moreover, in the federal constitution of Malaysia, being a Muslim is a requirement in law for any individual who claims to be Malay, and it is illegal to attempt to convert a Malay to another religion. Thai ethnicity does not bind individuals to the national religion. Some Thais are Christians and others are Muslims, although the overwhelming majority are Theravada Buddhists.

Racial and Ethnic Stereotypes

It is worth noting at the beginning of this section that physical anthropologists, even those few who continue to struggle with distinctions between geographical and micro-races, do not find that the physiological differences between southern Chinese, Thais, and Malays are sufficiently great to warrant distinguishing them as separate races (see "Southeast Asiatic" in Dobzhansky, 1962, pp. 263-264). Moreover, scientific specialists in human biology have found that the concept of race is not especially useful in research on genetically based behavioral differences between human populations (Coon, Garn, & Birdsell, 1950; Garn, 1961; Dobzhansky, 1962). But this has not prevented politicians and others in the Malay peninsula and elsewhere from speculating on the relationship of intellectual and moral capacity to skin color, hair form, and facial features (see Mahathir, 1970).

Malay population and ethnicity. Malays constituted about 55 percent, or about 7 million, of the 13 million people living in peninsula Malaysia in 1985. This estimate is based on the 1980 Census Report of 11,426,600 people and a population growth rate of 2.2 percent in peninsular Malaysia (Jabatan Penangkaan Malaysia, 1983). This is not a very secure majority of the population, and it is even less certain in the total population of Malaysia of about 15 million, because the percentage of Malays in the population of Sabah and Sarawak is so small (respectively 18.69 percent and 2.8 percent). The problem of maintaining a majority in order to maintain political control in a democracy adds intensity to Malay feelings about other ethnic communities. And some scholars believe there is little doubt that the government tends to overstate the number of Malays in the population. David Wu (1982, p. 39), for example, notes the inclusion of non-Malay aborigines *(orang asli)* in the "Malay" category in government census reports. The government's aggressive population policy—a planned expansion to 70 million by the beginning of the next century—seems to imply a hope that the Malays will capture more than an even share of the expanding population, paralleling their hoped-for increased share in an expanding economy. Malays are clearly a small minority in the total population of Thailand, numbering no more than 2 million persons in a nation of 50 million, perhaps 85 percent of whom are Thai; but they constitute a clear majority in the five most southern provinces of Thailand, where many of them are sympathetic to a separatist movement. Of Singapore's 2.5 million, only about 15 percent are Malays; and their relations with the Chinese, who have a firm majority of 76 percent of the population, are good.

From Malay points of view, there are many kinds of Malay. Their native word for Malay is *melayu,* which itself has had many meanings attributed to it. Only three of these will be considered here. First, Melayu is an ancient place, near present-day Jambi in Sumatra, which was the center of Malay trading empires at various times between the fifth and thirteenth centuries (Wolters, 1970). Second, melayu is the name of one of the major matrilineages *(suku)* of the Minangkabau, a people closely allied to the Malays in all but the part of customary law *(adat)* that refers to inheritance (Provencher, 1982, p. 142). And third, melayu may once have referred to the act of inking the formal seals that were stamped on letters of authority held by local chiefs from kings of the old trade empires (Siegal, 1979, pp. 23-31). Each of these explanations of the meaning of melayu—as a central place, as a corporate unit within a larger society, and as a label of formal membership in a central polity— illustrates the strongly political character of Malay identity in the distant past. In the more recent past and present the political character of Malay ethnic identity, especially regarding its inclusion of many other ethnic identities, is even more clear.

A number of scholars have noted that over the years the official census reports have become less precise in distinguishing between "Malays" and "other Malays." Perhaps Judith Nagata's is the most concise statement of this phenomenon:

> In 1901, the census of the Straits Settlements separately enumerated the peninsular Malays and Sumatrans from the Javanese, Bugis [Buginese], Boyanese, Acehnese, Dayaks, and Filipinos. . . . From 1911 onward, the sub-count only recognizes the separate existence of these groups, but for most official purposes the final count merely

distinguishes between "Malays" and "other Malays." In 1911 and 1921, a "true" Malay was judged to include some Sumatrans, for example, Minangkabau and Rawa, but not the Acehnese, Batak, Buginese, or Boyanese. By 1947 and in 1957, all the latter were aggregated with the peninsular Malays as "Malaysians," but now that "Malaysian" refers to any citizen of the Federation, regardless of sub-national or ethnic affiliation, the old term "Malay" has been resurrected for the 1970 census. (Nagata, 1979, p. 44)

This gradual change toward a more inclusionist definition of "Malay" in the census may appear to reflect a gradual reawakening of Malay political interests or a gradual awakening of government awareness of such interests (Roff, 1967). More certainly, it reflects a forgetting (perhaps even a forgiving) of once important conflicts with Javanese, Acehnese, and Buginese polities; and an awareness that some otherwise similar people, such as the Batak, have customary laws and religious beliefs that are not compatible with those of other Malays.

That the ethnic identities sometimes included within Malay identity survive is clear, nonetheless. Even in urban Malay communities, where contrasts between Malays and non-Malays assume more constant and immediate significance and Malay identity is thereby made more salient, individuals regularly comment upon their own particular subethnic identities and those of their neighbors. In rural areas, particularly in states such as Negri Sembilan, Selangor, and Perak, whose Malay populations are drawn from almost every corner of the Malay world, comment on the subethnic identity of other Malays in the community is an everyday matter. Moreover, many individuals can claim more than one subethnic identity through consanguineal or even affinal relationships, and know the customary law (adat) and dialect associated with each. It is also true that following the riots associated with the elections of 1969 and the consequent institution of economic reforms favoring Malays, there is a much stronger awareness of Malay ethnicity among those who can claim it as their own.

Until the early 1970s when this strengthened awareness and the concomitant benefits of being Malay began, it was relatively easy to become a Malay. Malay identity, in customary law as well as in the formal constitution of Malaysia, required only behavioral conformity. That is, a Malay was defined as anyone who is a Muslim, habitually speaks Malay language, and follows Malay customary law. Over the years, some Indians, Chinese, and Aborigines, and even a few Europeans met the rules of behavioral conformity as a result of marriage or informal adoption. They were gracefully incorporated, if not entirely assimilated, into Malay communities. Their children were entirely assimilated into Malay identity. And the fact of ethnic transition was usually forgotten within several generations. After 1969, an interest in biological conformity, as manifested in the need to have "pure" *(melayu jati)* Malay parents, began to grow within Malay communities. This represents a rather dramatic change from the old days of open assimilation, before 1969, when anyone could convert to Islam and thereby "join the Malays" or *masuk melayu* (Nagata, 1979, 1984).

Chinese ethnicity. Chinese ethnicity is more complex than Malay ethnicity. As an identity it includes a wider range of linguistic and other cultural differences. Many of the dialects are so different from each other as to be separate, although closely related, languages. Moreover, religion is not a critical dimension of Chinese identity (as it is in the case of Malay identity), and Chinese identity traditionally involves a notion of biological race.

The traditional Chinese notion that theirs is a singular race has served at times to weaken the status of Baba or Straits Chinese in the view of the "pure" *(sinkheh)* Chinese community because the founders of the Baba community were the children of native women (Clammer, 1980, p. 46). Moreover, the Baba founders assimilated most of the habits of their mothers' culture, including Malay language and excluding only Islam. From the perspective of some of the "pure" Chinese, they are both racially and culturally "not quite Chinese." But behavioral definitions of Chinese identity have been weakened by the fact that such a large proportion of the Chinese population in the peninsula is urban and middle class, and thereby subject to strong Western and other cosmopolitan cultural influences.

In Malaysia, subethnic Chinese identities, in total constituting about 35 percent of the population of peninsular Malaysia, have remained sufficiently strong so that virtually all Chinese individuals are like the Malays in being able to identify their own particular subethnic identity. It may be easier in some sense to retain subethnic identities in Chinese than in Malay communities because of the greater differences between Chinese "dialects" than between dialects of Malay. Perhaps even more than the Malays, the Chinese have a deep sense of belonging to their broader identity as Chinese and are impressed with the grandeur and long history of accomplishment associated with Chinese ethnicity. Neither subethnic identity nor identity as Chinese appears to be as important in Thailand as in Malaysia. Possible reasons for this include (1) the greater similarity of Chinese culture to Thai culture than to Malay culture, including religious beliefs; (2) the much smaller percentage of Chinese in the total population of Thailand—5 to 15 percent, compared to 35 percent in the total population of Malaysia; and (3) the more powerful negative and positive sanctions imposed by the Thai government than by the Malaysian government on Chinese individuals to assimilate to the majority ethnic identity.

Subethnic Chinese identity in Singapore is strongly developed, as might be expected in a society where the overwhelming majority of people (76 percent) are Chinese. The Singapore government has avoided identification with Taiwan or mainland China and has greatly emphasized the use of English as the major common and official language, while admitting subsidiary official use of Malay, Tamil, and Mandarin, and common use of other Chinese languages. Emphasis on the use of English has seemed to be an effort toward developing a modern syncretic culture for all Singaporeans, regardless of their cultural origins. However, since 1980 the government has seemed to turn more to the problem of coalescing the many Chinese subethnic identities. To this end, the government has decreed that Mandarin (the national language of both Taiwan and mainland China, but one of the least commonly spoken Chinese languages in Singapore) is to be learned by all Singapore Chinese, and the government has begun to emphasize the importance of traditional Confucian values. These are not especially popular measures among the Chinese of Singapore; and to the extent that Chinese ethnicity is coalesced by such measures, Malay and Indian Singaporeans are somewhat ill at ease.

Thai ethnicity. Thai ethnicity is as complex a matter as Malay ethnicity. Within Thailand there are a number of regional varieties of Thais—Lanna Thai in the north, Issan in the northeast, Siamese or Central Thai in the center, and Pak Thai in the south. Of these, Siamese or Central Thai has the highest prestige, and Issan the lowest. Perhaps Lanna Thai is second highest and Pak Thai next lowest in prestige. Issan has low prestige because of the poverty of the northeast and because of the great similarity of their dialect to Lao, a dialect or language closely related to Thai. There are some Shan in the north, an extension of the Shan population of Burma into Thailand, and several groups of hill Tai in the north and northeast, such as the Tai Dam, whose populations extend into Laos, Vietnam, and China. The Shan and Tai, like the Lao, speak dialects/ languages that are very closely related to Thai. Because of the difference of their dialects from Central Thai (the standard national dialect) and the association of these people with the uplands, their prestige (from the perspective of Bangkok) is lowest and their identity as Thai least secure. Nonetheless, in some circumstances they are Thai. The same is true of other people who have assimilated to Thai identity, such as most Mon residing in Thailand, the Vietnamese who settled long ago in central Thailand (as opposed to those who more recently have moved into northeastern Thailand as refugees), and the Chinese. In fact, the Thai identity of these latter people, who are culturally more closely assimilated to the Central Thai standard, may be more secure than that of the uplanders.

The Thai government regards the Malays of southern Thailand as Thai-Muslims who happen to speak Malay language. But ordinary Thais see them as they are: Malays. They have not been assimilated, as have most of the Chinese, into an identity as "virtually-Thai." Their distinction from Thais is clear from the presence of Pak Thai in these same provinces (Thomas, 1982).

However, at least some of the Pak Thais may be descendants of Malays who converted to Buddhism rather than descendants of immigrants from the north. Perhaps more intriguing is the presence of several thousands of Pak Thai (*samsam* in Malay), who are more numerous than other non-Malays in the rural areas of the northern states of peninsular Malaysia—Perlis, Kedah, Kelantan— bordering on Thailand. These states and Trengganu were part of Siam (Thailand) until after 1909, and it is conceivable that the ancestors of some of these Pak Thai were Malays who converted to Buddhism. Mostly bilingual, they live in rural villages and they are hospitably tolerated by bilingual Malays in neighboring villages. They are sometimes perceived as bumiputera (native inhabitants) if not Malay (Golomb, 1978).

In spite of the Thai-Muslim case, it is clear that Thai ethnic identity in present-day Thailand is more open, more like Malay ethnic identity in the past than like Malay or Chinese ethnic identity in present-day Malaysia.

Malay-Thai conflict and ethnic stereotypes. There have been many incidents of conflict between Malays and Thais, and between Malays and Chinese in recent decades, but it is important to recall that Malay-Thai conflict dates back at least to the fourteenth century when the founder of Melaka, Parameswara, was expelled from the island of Singapore by a Thai expedition (Winstedt, 1962, p. 42). By warfare and an alliance with China, in the fifteenth century Melaka regained control of the peninsula north to the kingdom of Pattani (which included what is now Pattani, Yala, and Narathiwat provinces of Thailand) and perhaps beyond. After the fall of the city of Melaka to the Portuguese in 1511, Thailand reclaimed sovereignty over the Malay states of Pattani, Perlis, Kelantan, and Trengganu. Major rebellions occurred in 1767 and 1790. In 1821 the Thais conquered Kedah, provoking rebellions in all of the Malay states under Thai control, which were suppressed by an army sent from Bangkok in 1831. In 1837, Malays placed Songkhla under siege, and the siege was raised by an army of 5,000 Thai soldiers from Bangkok (Tugby & Tugby, 1973, pp. 274-275).

Thereafter, the British, first from their position in the Straits Settlements (Singapore, Melaka, Province Wellesley, Penang) and later from their position in the Federated Malay States, exerted pressure on the Thai government to cease further southward expansion into the Malay states. The Anglo-Siamese treaty of 1909 transferred control of Kelantan, Trengganu, Kedah, and Perlis from Thailand to Great Britain, although the actual transfers did not occur until later—Kelantan and Trengganu in 1910, Kedah in 1925, and Perlis in 1930 (Winstedt, 1962, p. 237).

The Malay states in Pattani, Yala, Narathiwat, and Satun provinces remained under Thai control. Since that time, violent conflicts have flared up from time to time (rebellions in 1947, 1950, and 1954, and since 1969 the government has declared it a terrorist area) primarily in response to Thai national policy and the aspirations of local Malay nationalist leaders (Tugby & Tugby, 1973, p. 276). Obviously, Malay-Thai conflict has been and continues to be largely a matter of competing polities.

There has been very little research published on Malay and Thai stereotypes of each other in southern Thailand (see White & Prachuabmoh, 1983). Malay stereotypes of Thais are made ambiguous by differences in the attitudes of those who are Thai-educated and those who are *pono (pondok)*, or Malay-educated. Thai-educated

Malays tend to have more positive images of Thais, and say of them that they are polite, helpful, and friendly. Conversely, Thais are said to be insincere. Pono-educated Malays are more likely to have negative stereotypes of Thais, and note such traits as arrogance, untrustworthiness, and spiritual pollution (White & Prachuab-moh, 1983, pp. 12-13). Most Malays say that Thais are not very religious. Most agree that many Thais are pleasant in physical appearance. Stereotypes held by Malays of Thais in the northern Malaysian states, where Thais constitute about 1 percent of the population, are different. For example, Thais are seen as having strong community spirit and unity, and as being charitable, very trustworthy, ignorant, and poor. But they agree in their assessment of Thais as spiritually polluted heathens (Golomb, 1978, pp. 51-52). Throughout the peninsula, Thais have a strong reputation for being powerful magicians, especially with regard to what might be called "affective magic."

Thais in southern Thailand regularly refer to Malays as *khaek,* which is applied to people with dark skin or to Muslims, and which probably has the connotation of "barbarian." Overall, the Thai stereotypes of Malays are negative. Many Malays are seen as having an unpleasant physical appearance and character because they have "dark skin, oily or dirty hair, [and are] overdressed, . . . [too] religious, . . . ethnocentric, unfriendly, selfish, lazy, untrustworthy, poor, and lusty" (White & Prachuabmoh, 1983, p. 13). Thais in northern Malaysian states have positive stereotypes of Malays except that they are fearful of circumcision and feel that Malays are overly curious about the affairs of others. They do not see Malays as especially religious, because many of the Malays they know personally are "free-thinkers" or "backsliders" who enjoy visiting Thais in order to escape temporarily the religious constraints of their own society. Just as the Malays view the Thais as magically powerful, so the Thais view Malays.

Malay-Chinese conflict and ethnic stereotypes. Malay-Chinese conflict does not date back so far; and in the beginning, Malay-Chinese relationships were not characterized by ethnic conflict. This is clear from the history of fourteenth and fifteenth century Melaka and the Tin Wars of the late nineteenth century (Provencher, 1985). Nonetheless, even then, the potential for violent conflict, phrased partly in terms of ethnic stereotypes, must have existed. But violent ethnic conflict hardly occurred until after World War

II, when it became almost commonplace: 1945 and 1946 in Batu Phat; 1946 in Batu Malim, Raub, and in Batu Kikir; 1958 in Penang; 1959 in Pangkor; 1967 in Bukit Mertajam; 1969 in Kuala Lumpur; and communal clashes of smaller scale since then (S. Husin Ali, 1981, p. 119).

Malay stereotypes of the Chinese are not entirely negative. Particular Chinese women, partly because of their relatively light skin color, are considered to be beautiful. Chinese men are thought to be clever and thrifty businessmen, skilled craftsmen, and industrious workers, if not handsome. There are minor negative views of Chinese appearance, especially regarding the inner epicanthic folds that are somewhat more frequent and pronounced among Chinese than Malays and which give an undesirable "half-closed" or "slit" *(sepet* or *sipit)* appearance to eyes. And the Malays, like the Thais, have a saying that "normal conversation in Chinese sounds like a quarrel in our language." Moreover, the virtues of cleverness, thrift, and industry may be alternatively viewed as the vices of cheating, stinginess, and materialism. Baba stereotypes of the sinkheh or "pure" Chinese are very similar: "competitive, brusque, materialistic" (Clammer, 1980, p. 134). Also, many Malays feel that Chinese are dirty, mostly in the sense of being spiritually unclean because they eat pork and keep dogs. This part of the negative stereotype of the Chinese is, of course, heightened by the fundamentalist Muslim notion that a plate touched by food that is not *halal* ("ritually pure") can never be cleaned sufficiently to contain halal food, and that a single non-halal kitchen endangers the ritual purity of the whole community.

Malaysian Chinese stereotypes of Malays are not entirely negative. Particular Malay women are considered to be beautiful, for example, and particular men handsome; but Malays, on average, have somewhat darker skin than Chinese, and dark skin is viewed by the Chinese (and Malays) as less attractive and refined than light skin. Malays are said to be easy-going and generous. Conversely, they may be seen as stupid and lazy spendthrifts. Charles Hirschman (1979) has noted that the latter stereotype has found its way, unexamined and in more subtle words, into social science literature on differences between Malay and Chinese economic aspirations and efficiency. Babas stereotype Malays in just this fashion, and are themselves stereotyped by sinkheh Chinese as "soft . . . exhibiting a non-competitive attitude to life" (Clammer, 1980,

p. 119). Oddly enough, in recent years many Singapore Chinese businessmen have come to view Malays as especially industrious and careful workers, preferring to hire them rather than Singapore Chinese.

Probable Causes and Possible Resolutions of Conflict

It is important to keep in mind that stereotypes do not necessarily force ethnic groups into conflict with each other. Stereotypes do keep people from fully interacting. Also, stereotypes may reinforce participation in aggressive behavior motivated by other factors, such as economic or political competition. Surely this has been the case with respect to competition between Malay and Thai polities, and with regard to economic and political competition between Malay and Chinese social strata within the Malaysian state. Obviously the problem is as much a matter of managing competition as it is one of managing ethnic conflict.

Conflict has occurred precisely in those instances when competition has been possible—when the less powerful ethnic group had resources almost equal to those of the more powerful group. Singapore may be peaceful because the Chinese constitute a huge majority of the population, control the government without effective opposition from other ethnic groups, and control the economy. Malaysia has not been peaceful because Malays have political power and Chinese have economic power, and each kind of power can be transformed into the other. Thailand is overwhelmingly Thai, except in the southern provinces, where Malays have a sizable majority and see an opportunity to compete successfully for political power in that particular region. And Malays in the northern Malaysian states treat the tiny Thai minority hospitably, and are in turn liked by the Thais, just as Malays are treated hospitably and seem satisfied in Singapore.

In sorting through the literature on the three major ethnic groups in different societies of the Malay peninsula, it is clear that some portions of ethnic stereotypes are closely related to factors that create friction between groups. Some aspects of Malay stereotypes of Thais vary, and Thai stereotypes of Malays vary more according to structural rather than cultural variables. That stereotypes of Chinese are relatively consistent, except perhaps in the case of Baba versus sinkheh Chinese, may simply reflect the strong position of Chinese in commerce—a structural feature that may outweigh political and demographic variables. Malays too may be said to have the structural stereotype of the poor, who throughout the world are said to be lazy and stupid spendthrifts. But why are the Thais of northern Malaysia, who are poorer than their Malay neighbors, not seen as lazy and stupid spendthrifts by the Malays? And why are Malays ugly in Thai eyes and occasionally beautiful in Chinese eyes? The question of the relationships between factors of culture, competition, and stereotypes require much more careful research.

The literature does not provide enough data to develop really trustworthy and detailed explanations of why particular structural variables are most or least important in ethnic stereotypes and ethnic conflict. Moreover, there are no reliable data on situational variation in stereotypes. There are nonetheless indications that some features of ethnic stereotypes may be quite volatile. It is possible to do better and more research on ethnic stereotypes and on the way that stereotypes affect the course of conflict between ethnic groups. Such research should be conducted from the cultural or emic perspectives of the groups involved, so that the traits listed in stereotypes can be thoroughly understood. And such research must systematically sample stereotypes over time and in different structural contexts, some of which include different types of active competition and conflict. If the answers to our questions do not light the way to understanding and resolving the problem of ethnic conflict, maybe we need to discover new, better questions. Governments in the Third World have not supported this kind of research, seeming to fear involvement of scholars; but it would be in their best interests to do so, because of the inevitable structural disruptions associated with economic development. In the meanwhile, some of the most careful economic planning may contain the seeds of more ethnic competition and conflict.

References

Alisjahbana, S. T. (1962). *Indonesian language and literature: Two essays* (Cultural Report Series No. 11). New Haven: Yale University, Southeast Asia Studies.

Clammer, J. R. (1980). *Straits Chinese society.* Singapore: Singapore University Press.

Coon, C. S., Garn, S. M., Birdsell, J. B. (1950). *Races*. Springfield, IL: Charles C. Thomas.

Cowan, C. D. (1962). *Nineteenth century Malaya*. London: Oxford University Press.

Dobzhansky, T. (1962). *Mankind evolving*. New Haven, CT: Yale University Press.

Freedman, M. (1960). The growth of a plural society in Malaya. *Pacific Affairs, 33*, 158-168.

Garn, S. M. (1961). *Human races*. Springfield, IL: Charles C. Thomas.

Goh, Chenk Teik (1971). *The May thirteenth incident and democracy in Malaysia*. London: Oxford University Press.

Golomb, L. (1978). *Brokers of morality: Thai ethnic adaptation in a rural Malaysian setting* (Asian Studies at Hawaii No. 23). Honolulu: University Press of Hawaii.

Hall, K. R. & Whitmore, J. K. (1976). Southeast Asian trade and the isthmian struggle. In K. R. Hall & J. K. Whitmore (Eds.), *Explorations in the early Southeast Asian history: The origins of Southeast Asian statecraft* (Monograph No. 11). Ann Arbor: Center for South and Southeast Asian Studies, University of Michigan.

Hirschman, C. (1979). Sociology. In J. A. Lent (Ed.), *Malaysian studies: Present knowledge and research trends* (Occasional Paper No. 7). DeKalb: Center for Southeast Asian Studies, Northern Illinois University.

Jabatan Perangkaan Malaysia [Department of Statistics Malaysia] (1983). *Laporan am banchi penduduk* [General report of the population census] (Vol. 1). Kuala Lumpur: Author.

Mahathir, M. (1970). *The Malay dilemma*. Singapore: Donald Moore Press.

Nagata, J. (1979). *Malaysian mosaic: Perspectives from a poly-ethnic society*. Vancouver: University of British Columbia Press.

Nagata, J. (1984). *The reflowering of Malaysian Islam: Modern religious radicals and their roots*. Vancouver: University of British Columbia Press.

Prachuabmoh, C. (1982). Ethnic relations among Thai, Thai Muslim and Chinese in south Thailand. In D.Y. H. Wu (Ed.), *Ethnicity and interpersonal interaction: A cross cultural study* (pp. 63-83). Singapore: Maruzen Asia.

Provencher, R. (1975). "Groups" in Malay society. *Rice University Studies, 61* (2), 79-110.

Provencher, R. (1982). Islam in Malaysia and Thailand. In R. Israeli (Ed.), *The crescent in the east: Islam in Asia Major* (pp. 140-155). London: Curzon Press.

Provencher, R. (1985). National culture and ethnicity in Kuala Lumpur. In G. H. Krausse (Ed.), *Southeast Asian cities: Cultural and political issues*. Hong Kong: Asian Research Service.

Punyodyana, B. (1971). *Chinese-Thai differential assimilation in Bangkok: An exploratory study* (Data Paper No. 11). Ithaca, NY: Cornell University.

Roff, W. R. (1967). *The origins of Malay nationalism*. New Haven: Yale University Press.

S. Husin Ali (1981). *The Malays: Their problem and future*. Kuala Lumpur: Heinemann Asia.

Siegal, J. (1979). *Shadow and sound: The historical thought of a Sumatran people*. Chicago & London: University of Chicago Press.

Tan, Chee-Beng (1982). Ethnic relations in Malaysia. In D.Y.H. Wu (Ed.), *Ethnicity and interpersonal interaction: A cross cultural study* (pp. 37-61). Singapore: Maruzen Asia.

Taylor, K. (1976). Madagascar in the ancient Malayo-Polynesian myths. In K. R. Hall & J. K. Whitmore (Eds.), *Explorations in the early Southeast Asian history: The origins of Southeast Asian statecraft* (Monograph No. 11). Ann Arbor: Center for South and Southeast Asian Studies, University of Michigan.

Teeuw, A. (1959). The history of the Malay language. *Bijdragen tot de taal, land en volkenkunde, 115,* 138-156.

Thomas, M. L. (1982). The Thai muslims. In R. Israeli (Ed.), *The crescent in the east: Islam in Asia Major* (pp. 156-179). London: Curzon Press.

Tugby, E. & Tugby, D. (1973). Inter-cultural mediation in south Thailand. In R. Ho & E. C. Chapman (Eds.), *Studies of contemporary Thailand* (Publication HG/8) (pp. 273-293). Canberra: Research School of Pacific Studies, Australian National University.

van Leur, J. C. (1955). *Indonesian trade and society.* The Hague, Bandung: W. van Hoeve Ltd.

White, G. M. & Prachuabmoh, C. (1983). The cognitive organization of ethnic images. *Ethos, 11* (1/2), 2-32.

Winstedt, R. O. (1962). *A history of Malaya* (rev. ed.). Singapore: Marican & Sons. (First published as Part I, Vol. XIII, March 1935, of *The Journal of the Malayan Branch of the Royal Asiatic Society*)

Wolters. O. W. (1970). *The fall of Srivijaya in Malay history.* Kuala Lumpur & Singapore: Oxford University Press.

Wu, D.Y.H. (1982). Ethnic relations and ethnicity in a city-state: Singapore. In D.Y.H. Wu (Ed.), *Ethnicity and interpersonal interaction: A cross cultural study* (pp. 13-36). Singapore: Maruzen Asia.

Chapter Summary

Ramirez and Sullivan discuss the past and present situation of the Basque people, whose country lies on both sides of the Spanish-French border. The basis for the Basque cultural identity is examined in terms of its linguistic, religious, racial, and historical aspects. A historical review traces the emergence and reemergence of the issue of Basque autonomy and the related changes in Basque-Spanish relations.

Emphasis is given in this chapter to the role of political and terrorist groups, with particular attention to the ETA, a group known for its violent tactics. The goals and organization of the ETA and other terrorist groups are presented. Ramirez and Sullivan also address changing policy regarding treatment of terrorists and laws concerning their extradition.

With regard to the present situation in the Basque region, Ramirez and Sullivan see autonomy and economic issues as the most pertinent. They explain that most Basques favor some form of autonomy, but differ greatly in their view of the urgency of the situation and the methods that should be used. These differences are the basis for the formation of various Basque political parties.

The authors explain that the economy of the Basque region, once considered a model of industrial success, has greatly deteriorated over the past decade, increasing the frequency of labor disputes with racial overtones. Ramirez and Sullivan express the view that improvement in economic conditions would counter the general instability of the region. Problems of a social nature are also addressed, including the prevalence of terrorist acts and an extremely high rate of drug addiction. Ramirez and Sullivan are of the opinion that the Basques must take a more moderate stand and abandon their separatist goals if they are to reach an understanding with the Spanish government.

—Susan Goldstein

6

The Basque Conflict

J. MARTÍN RAMIREZ and BOBBIE SULLIVAN

This chapter intends to review, in as unbiased a way as possible, the explosive situation in the Basque country and its possible antecedents. Our wish is to facilitate a more thorough awareness of the conditions and dimensions of the actual problems, inasmuch as there is little hope for resolving a problem that is not well understood.

In one sense, the general problems of the Basques are similar to other conflict situations elsewhere around the world. On the surface, the situation in the Basque region seems to have an array of psychological, social, economic, and cultural causes and symptoms common to most other interethnic conflicts. Nevertheless, factors that appear in this way to be generically the same from one situation to another actually do vary, not only in regard to specific character, which is usually peculiar to each country, but also in terms of their relative weight in importance from setting to setting. So, when we speak of the Basque problems, we are often referring to a generic kind of problem, condition, or event, but with an overlay of characteristics or qualities informed by cultural and historical mechanisms unique to the Basques and their position in the world. Therefore, "idem sed alter," as the classics would say.

The rugged, heavily forested Basque country, called *Euskadi* by the Basques, straddles the Pyrenees Mountains along part of the Spanish-French border. Historically, two rivers have served as its borders—the Garona on the north and the Ebro on the south. Today

Euskadi is divided in two by the political border between Spain and France. The southern section, inhabited by some 2,100,000, consists of three Spanish provinces: Vizcaya, Guipuzcoa, and Alava. The adjacent province of Navarra, with its half million inhabitants, is also looked upon by some as part of South Euskadi, an issue yet to be settled officially. On the French side of the border are the three Basque provinces of Bas Navarra, Laburdi, and Zuberoa, collectively known as North Euskadi, or *Iparralde* to the Basques. Administratively included in the French department of the Atlantic Pyrenees, Iparralde is inhabited by about 250,000 Basques. Thus about one-eighth of the Basques are French nationals, while the rest are Spanish.

The geography of the mountainous Basque region has been important in shaping and maintaining the Basque cultural identity. Owing to scanty recorded information, details of the historical origins of the Basques are uncertain, or at best imprecise. Their original forebears were probably Indoeuropeans, descendents of ancient Iberians who managed to keep their identity in their remote valleys. While the Iberian peninsula has seen wave after wave of invaders over the centuries, the relative inaccessibility of the Basque settlements largely spared them from domination. The Romans, Visigoths, and Moors in turn failed to bring the Basques completely into their spheres of influence. Coupled with tribal values and traditions, this geographical isolation led to a propensity for endogamous marriage. An outcome of this maintenance of a relatively homogeneous gene pool over the generations is that the Basques are distinguished from other Europeans genetically, linguistically, and culturally.

The Basques share a distinct set of biological traits. Although Spanish Basques are usually shorter than French Basques, both groups have a similar body build, elongated facial structure, similar hair and eye coloring, and a high incidence of Rh negative and O blood groups. These relatively uniform structural features, combined with their linguistic and cultural characteristics, add up to something akin to racial homogeneity which, unfortunately, sometimes carries with it certain racist overtones. While in actuality having nothing to do with supposed superiorities or inferiorities, the fact that the Basques form a relatively distinct biological group is held out by some as a symbol of "racial" independence. The

Basque "race" is idealized by some insiders as the basis for their supposedly superior moral integrity.

An important reinforcing agent of Basque consciousness and identity is the existence of its own language, called Euskera. In the words of the late Basque Premier, Lehendakari Garaikoetxea, the language is "the most intimate trait of the Basque people and testimony to their national identity." There is no body of original literature written in Euskera, which has always been a rural, colloquial language. The Basque tongue is virtually incomprehensible to speakers of other languages. Certain features of Euskera resemble the Iberian idiom of earlier times, and it has some elements in common with the Caucasian languages. Still, the true origins of Euskera are unknown, and its precise relationship to other modern languages remains in question.

From the sixteenth century onward, Euskera gradually fell into disuse. It is spoken today, in a variety of dialects, as a minority language throughout the region, yet only about 20 percent of Basques know how to speak their language, and barely 12 percent can read and write it. Since so few Basques know Euskera well enough to use it widely, and since a large proportion of the population in the region today is non-Basque, Castillian is used for everyday conversation. Nevertheless, being able to speak Euskera, or at least to understand it, is regarded by many as a symbol of Basque solidarity. The Basque autonomous government recently has been promoting a resurgence in the use of Euskera, and present-day activists favor songs and sayings in Euskera for ceremonies and at political rallies. Caro Baroja, a prestigious Basque anthropologist, warns that this practice carries the danger of further isolating the Basques from the community at large. While the language is often held out as a pillar of Basque uniqueness, clearly setting them apart from "barbarians" who do not speak it, many also understand that a common language does not always insure unity. Language can separate as well as it can unite.

Religion, in the form of devout Catholicism, is an important aspect of Basque cultural identity. Known since time immemorial for a profound religious sentiment, the collective reputation of the Basques as a people of integrity and high principles is undoubtedly rooted in their devoutness. The Church has always been a focal institution in Basque history and tradition, and its role extended to matters beyond the spiritual. Until recent times, there were no secular universities in the region; the Church, through its seminaries, educated generations of Basque youth. These men were the predecessors, and in many cases the teachers, of present-day Basque activists. Hence one could say that the Church played a central role in spawning the Basque nationalist movement. The Church did not specifically encourage the establishment of nationalistic organizations; rather, it is linked to the movement by virtue of the fact that, in the absence of a secular alternative, most of the Basque intelligentsia, including the first leaders of the Basque nationalist underground, happened to be seminary educated.

Basque Economic and Social History

The Basques have always held strong convictions regarding self-sufficiency. The predominantly rural life of the early Basques was built upon a pastoral and agricultural economy, but without the vast property holdings and agrarian feudalism seen elsewhere. Instead, rural populations traditionally were grouped together in *caserios* spread about the mountainsides. These *caserios* consisted of homes for the families, and barns for livestock, around which were orchards and fields worked directly by their owners. Cattle, dairying, beets, and corn were the mainstays. More recently, due to a progressive "deruralization," the focus has shifted to forestry and lumbering rather than on cultivated fields and grazing meadows.

The sea has figured strongly in the Basque economy. The Basques have a long history as fishermen and whalers, and have also gained a reputation as navigators, having had a role in the discovery and colonization of the Americas and Asia. Their forests provided good hardwoods for shipbuilding, and their skill at this craft was famous. Nearly half of all commercial shipyards in Spain today are Basques, and substantial numbers of Basques continue to make their living as seafarers.

Industrialization came to the Basque region in the late nineteenth century, followed closely by an economic boom bringing real prosperity to the region. Bilbao, traditionally important as a major port, also developed into a large, industrialized city as the nearby iron deposits were exploited.

Industrialization also brought about a large growth in population, particularly in the urban centers. The massive influx of people from other parts of Spain, attracted by the demand for labor, balanced the population deficit caused by the emigration of many indigenous Basques to the Americas. The majority of the present population is not native to the region, and is predominately young (43 percent are younger than 25 years of age).

Today, 70 percent of Guipuzcoa's population live in cities of over 10,000. This province covers only 1.4 percent of Spanish territory; but according to 1970 figures, it was inhabited by 5 percent of the population of Spain and accounted for 9 percent of the total of Spanish production, putting it in first place among the provinces in terms of per capita income at that time.

The Basque region was hailed as a veritable model of the economic prosperity, brought about in the 1960s with the opening by Franco's government of a more realistic trade and industrial policy. In addition to mining, it was involved in the production of steel, machinery and tools, automobiles, petrochemicals, fertilizers, and so on. The iron mines and related industries, such as the production of heavy machinery and equipment, are still the primary focus of the region. Sadly, the worldwide market for such goods has been depressed in recent years.

The powerful Basque economy has begun to erode over the past decade. The GNP has decreased by 18 points since 1973. It is estimated that two-thirds of Basque business enterprises are presently in financial trouble. The region's unemployment rate of 16.8 percent is not only higher than Spain's national average, but is surpassed only by that of the traditional, underdeveloped regions of the country, such ask Andalucia and the Canary Islands. Guipuzcoa has been lowered to ninth place, and Vizcaya to fifteenth, in rank among the provinces for per capita income.

This decline is attributed in part to the global economic crisis of recent times and in part to depletion of resources and tough outside competition. Foreign investors have withdrawn capital, discouraging further private investment. There has been an exodus of Basque entrepreneurs, largely due to the civil unrest and the plague of terrorist demands for "revolutionary taxes." Labor relations have deteriorated, disputes have cropped up, and some of these have carried racial overtones. Violence has been frequent enough to further disrupt the region's already unsettled sociopolitical climate.

Basque morale has deteriorated along with the economy. The

standard of living in the region is in decline, bringing about a mood of pessimism and discouragement. Reactions range from apathy to desperation. Activists, taking advantage of the climate of dissatisfaction, agitate for violent social and political upheaval. The gravity of the present economic situation is high on the list of causes contributing to the continuing political unrest.

Historically throughout the world, violence and economic decline have repeatedly been linked. The linkage often evolves to a vicious cycle. Poor economic conditions provide a platform for political and social agitation. Such agitation, particularly when it results in violence, disrupts the economy further: Labor disputes and production slowdowns reduce industrial output, resulting in smaller profits, diminished confidence in the marketplace, and, ultimately, the flight of capital. These losses only worsen the economic situation to the point of chaos, thereby strengthening the position of the activists and facilitating their efforts to incite upheaval by radical means. Without substantial, coordinated intervention, such situations continue to disintegrate in a self-reinforcing downward spiral toward catastrophe.

Thus a significant improvement in the economic conditions of the Basque region would go a long way toward relieving the generally unstable situation there. Without some convincing changes to the status quo, it does not seem likely that the Basque region will be able to embark on a successful economic recovery. Industrial diversification away from the present monolithic focus on iron and steel, and technological renewal are desperately needed to restore the Basque economy to its earlier prosperity. This cannot be accomplished without a substantial infusion of new capital. Unfortunately, all of the factors cited above have worked together to create an aura of such uncertainty about the future that there is great reluctance on the part of potential investors to supply the capital so urgently needed. Beyond recapitalization, additional requirements include greater labor flexibility, better forecasting in order to adjust production capacity to existing market conditions, and development of the service sector.

Basque Political History

The early Basques constantly warred with the Visigoths in the South and the Franks to the North. Late in the sixth century they invaded southwest France, pushing their frontier with the Franks to the Garona River. Compelled to swear allegiance to the Frankish king in the mid-seventh century, they were thereafter governed by French dukes and Basque functionaries. The area became a part of the duchy of Aquitania, which was in turn incorporated into the kingdom of France. The Iparralde Basques attempted to become independent, but Charlemagne obliged them to lay down their arms and integrate permanently with France. They did so, and they remain under French sovereignty today.

The southern Basques had frequent encounters with Castilla and Navarra throughout the Middle Ages. This led to their being incorporated under the crown of Castilla by late in the fourteenth century. The Basques insisted that the terms of their incorporation into the Castillian kingdom be set forth as a pact between equals, acknowledging their right to autonomy and affirming the legitimacy of the *Fueros*—the ancient Basque laws. Accordingly, the Castillian king, or his representative, met once every two years in Guernica with an assembly of Basque men. In a ceremony that traditionally took place under a certain oak tree, the king swore to respect the Fueros in return for Basque allegiance. Maintained until the nineteenth century, this pact guaranteed the continuance of the Fueros and the Basque identity.

Early in the last century, the "Basque problem" reappeared. During the Carlist Wars (1833-36), the power of the liberals favoring Queen Isabel II was rooted in the support of the urban bourgeoisie. The support of the rural population, including most Basques, went to the conservatives who favored Isabel's brother, Carlos. Most of the battles actually took place in Basque territory. When the Carlists were defeated, the Basques themselves felt defeated, and an army of "foreign invaders" occupied their territory.

Angry at having their autonomy curtailed by the ruling Isabelists, a new Basque consciousness began to emerge. Grounded on conservative Carlist ideals and traditional Basque values, a renewed sense of collective identity and consciousness surfaced, consolidating to the point of a nationalist movement by the close of the nineteenth century.

Industrialization of the region was proceeding rapidly, centering on development of the mining and steel industries. The working class grew in size as immigrants seeking jobs poured in from other regions of Spain. Along with the mines, mills, and immigrants, the incipient socialist workers' movement also arrived, somewhat displacing the Basque nationalist movement as the focus of political attention. Frequent confrontations between the Basques and the socialists ensued.

In 1894, Sabino de Arana, son of a Carlist shipowner, founded the Basque Nationalist Party (PNV) under the motto "For God and for Our Ancient Laws," with the aim of achieving independence for Euskadi. He and his mostly middle-class separatist followers envisioned a state based on "the fundamental links that unite the Basques," namely, the Catholic religion and "the race."

In 1898, certain Vizcaya bourgeoisie with a conservative political stance formed a combined group with PNV. They enjoyed popular support, but had little practical power. In 1931, the PNV proclaimed that they would not oppose the Second Spanish Republic so long as the Basques were allowed to govern themselves. The PNV and the Carlists joined in an active right-wing coalition, obtaining some administrative autonomy and grants of fiscal concessions. Discussions concerning a Basque state were initiated, but the idea was rejected by the Assembly of Councils of Navarra on June 19, 1932.

The PNV ran alone in the December 1933 elections. Right-wing parties triumphed throughout Spain, subsequently staying in power until February 1936. The Basques saw certain new laws during this period as threatening to economic concessions they had gained earlier. This perceived threat, coupled with a general disillusionment with the Spanish right wing, led to a rekindling of agitation for Basque autonomy.

In search of new patrons for their cause after falling out with the Spanish right wing, Basque activists approached socialists and other leftists. In their fervor to gain support for statutory autonomy, the traditionally conservative, religious Basques joined in what has come to be viewed as an irrational alliance with the Popular Front, the revolutionary Spanish left.

In 1936, at the outset of the Spanish Civil War, Alava province joined the rebellion on the side of Franco. Meanwhile, Vizcaya and Guipuzcoa led in a general voluntary mobilization on the Republic side, hoping to insure the continuity of the middle-class social order. On October 7, 1936, a Basque Statute was signed forming a Basque government. On June 19, 1937, however, the experiment of the "Republic of Euskadi" was terminated when Bilbao fell to

Franco's army. While Alava and Navarra were allowed to retain fiscal and administrative autonomy in reward for their alliance with Franco, it was decreed that Vizcaya and Guipuzcoa would be subject to the same standards as the rest of Spain, thus removing the last vestiges of their autonomy.

Most defeated PNV militants went into exile, emigrating mainly to Latin America where many became quite influential. But in the 1950s exiled militants regrouped, joined with new recruits, and reorganized the PNV. Then in 1959 one group separated itself from the PNV, adopting the name *Euskadi ta Askatasuna* (Fatherland and Freedom; ETA).

The appearance of ETA sparked a revival of Basque nationalism in Spain during the 1960s. Formation of an independent Basque State to embrace the present French and Spanish Basque provinces, plus Navarra, has been the main goal of ETA. They proposed political, economic, and armed struggle as means for attaining this end. A great number of Marxists, Maoists, and Trotskyites were attracted to ETA by its promise of Basque social liberation through armed conflict. Their priorities turned out to be somewhat different than those of ETA, however, resulting in the first fissures in the organization around 1965. The newcomers left ETA to join other leftist organizations.

ETA is largely youthful, made up primarily of workers, students, and seminarians. Their methods include kidnapping and the demanding of so-called "revolutionary taxes" and other extortions on threat of death. A "settling of accounts" among members, reminiscent of the *vendetta,* is a part of their code, which also features *omerta* or the "complicity of silence."

Initially, ETA was organized around several fronts: military, political, cultural, and worker. In the mid-1970s, ETA split into two branches: the "mili" and the "poli-mili." This seemed to result from disparities in prestige among the fronts in the aftermath of terrorism carried out by the more extremist elements in the military front, especially following the 1973 assassination of the president of the Spanish government, Admiral Carrero. The military front of ETA (the "milis") gained prestige in certain circles, with a consequent reduction in the prestige of the other ETA fronts. Thereafter, the milis saw the other three as hindering the progress of ETA.

The "poli-milis" objected to the creation of a popular army without prior and intense mass action, a point of contention with the milis. In essence, the milis were promulgating the ideas learned through the French experience of May 1968 and subsequently adopted by the Red Brigades in Italy. The strategy was to avoid any sympathizer not in favor of armed violence. They envisioned mass actions carried out by independent organizations but under the control and direction of ETA militants.

A variety of events led the milis to form *Herri Batasuna* (Popular Unity; HB), a political coalition gathered around the HASI (Social Revolutionary Basque Party) over which they maintain iron-fisted control. HB, backed by about 10 percent of the Basque electorate, has about 50 activists directly involved in terrorist activities, according to police estimates.

The poli-mili branch has a more limited operative capacity, in part because they are fewer in number and in part because the organization has been subjected more frequently to deportations and to shutdowns by police. Nevertheless, their actions are well noticed and have a major political echo: bombing tourist facilities, airports, and railway stations; kidnapping diplomats and political figures; and selective assassinations.

Politically, the poli-milis were integrated into the EE (*Euskadiko Ezquerra,* or Basque left), a coalition for which mass action takes precedence over armed combat. The EE adds socialism to nationalism and enjoys the support of about 5 percent of the electorate.

In 1981, the Spanish government offered amnesty to ETA members not guilty of blood crimes who would abandon the notion of armed struggle. About 250 *etarras* of the seventh poli-mili assembly accepted the offer. The assembly dissolved itself on September 30, 1982, acknowledging that the sociopolitical conditions of years past had now changed. Given present-day conditions, they concluded that use of the democratic process would be a better strategy than taking up arms for defending the rights of their people.

The Franco-Spanish Convention of 1887 and the Law of 1927 strictly prohibit extraditions of political detainees between the two countries. This may explain why the French government allowed its territory to be used with impunity by the etarras for a long while as a sanctuary and as a staging area for attacks launched against Spanish territory. However, the French view of the ETA's activities seems to have changed, as suggested by more recent events. On several occasions, beginning in 1984, France agreed to extradite etarras to Spain. The French have deported some ETA members to South America and Africa, and have resettled others in French provinces far from the Spanish border. These measures have been interpreted as an acknowledgment by the French of the essentially criminal nature of the activities of the etarras. According to minutes of the French Conseil d'Etat, the extraditions had to do with "infractions of common law which cannot be considered of a political character or linked to a political crime." French Prime Minister Fabius added, "The end does not justify the means, and France is not a sanctuary for those who commit such crimes of violence" (September 26, 1984). These events necessitated a change in ETA strategy to either of two alternatives: transferring to locations inside the Spanish border, thus risking severe repression by the police; or installing itself in some geographically more distant country, thus reducing its operative capacity.

In sum, despite recurring internal problems, ETA has demonstrated staying power and relative consistency in regard to ideology and strategy. Its ideology is one of nonnegotiable radical independence. Its strategy of violence is directed not at any particular form of government but rather against the national unity of Spain as manifested in the Spanish state. Its opposition to national unity explains why its armed fight against the Spanish democracy continues even today.

Several other radical organizations operate in the Basque region alongside, or in opposition to, ETA. *Iparretarrak* might be described as the French version of ETA. However, compared with the Spanish ETA, it is less hostile. The CCAA (Autonomous Anticapitalistic Commands) has some ties with the ETA mili, but their ideology puts them more correctly in the international proletarian movement rather than with the Basque separatist movement per se. Weaker than ETA, with far fewer resources and less operative capacity, they espouse an ideologically based view of elections as "dangerous" and they customarily attempt to interfere at polling places. They are a potentially destabilizing force, given that the terrorism they do engage in is carried out indiscriminately.

The GAL (Antiterrorist Groups of Liberation) made themselves known in 1983 with the kidnapping of a Spanish Basque residing in France, freeing him 10 days later. This group is in opposition to ETA, but has never operated on Spanish territory. Instead it directs its actions against ETA members and other Basques in France, using ETA's own methods. At least a dozen assassinations have been attributed to GAL, all of them reprisals against ETA. Theirs is a counterterrorist tactic: They launch their reprisals in immediate response to terrorism by ETA. Some who mount these counter-terrorist attacks are believed to be mercenaries. Others are thought to be connected with extremists of the French right. In some quarters it is claimed that the GAL are connected to the Spanish police. For all the speculation, however, it is not known who actually controls this group.

Today, there are five active political parties in the Basque region. One is a coalition of the nonnationalist right, with about 10 percent of the vote. Largely representing the immigrant workforce, and of great historical importance, is the socialist party (PSOE), which carries 25 percent of the vote. Both of these parties are active in other areas of Spain as well. In addition are the three Basque nationalist parties—the EE, HB, and the PNV. The EE and the HB are two small leftist parties that carry between them about 10 percent of the vote; the PNV, with its conservative stance, appeals to traditionalist Basques and enjoys the favor of nearly half the electorate in the region.

Given its relative majority, the PNV has been in virtual control of the Basque region since the beginning of autonomy in 1979. Within the PNV are two different approaches to nationalism, each equally influential relative to the other. On the one hand is the "foralist" approach, best described as Christian-democratic. Citing historical reasons for maintaining decentralized control in the various provinces or "historical territories," they argue that the Basque region never has been a territorial entity with a central government. This historically based point of view reflects a basic tenet of traditional Basque nationalism: To change historical traditions is dangerous for the continuity of the Basque identity. The "technocrats," on the other hand, espouse a social-democratic approach. They favor greater centralized power and are advocates for a strong executive in the Basque country. The power struggle between the proponents of these two positions was made evident as the Basque Parliament met to consider the project of an internal constitution for the Basque country. The Law for the Historical Territories, a foralist formulation, was presented on March 19, 1981. The dispute culminated in December 1984 with the dismissal of the Basque Premier, Lehendakari Garaikoetxea, a partisan of the technocrats, and the nomination of Ardanza, a foralist.

Euskadiko Ezquerra (Basque Left for Socialism), or the EE, has as its goal an independent Basque country, arguing that "Euskal Herria is a country, and as such it has the nonnegotiable right to be a self-governing nation." Its ideology is Marxist, appealing to the working class. EE sets itself forth as an alternative to socialism, favoring a "struggle for national liberation" by means of action among the working class instead of the armed action promulgated by the ETA mili. Considered a separatist version of the communists, its stance is close to certain positions of the former poli-mili.

A coalition was formed in April 1978 by "all Basque political parties of the left whose strategy for the liberation of Euskadi and the installation of socialism is established within the frame of Basque nationalism." This is *Herri Batasuna* (Popular Unity), or HB, a coalition of five parties: (1) HASI (Popular Socialist Revolutionary Party), a Marxist group evolving from ETA, founded and run by Santiago Brouard until his assassination in September 1984; (2) LAIA (Revolutionary Party of Basque Workers); (3) National Basque Action, a group that split from the PNV at the beginning of this century; (4) ESB (Basque Socialist Convergence); and (5) Popular Organization, a group promoting amnesty, antinuclear committees, and so on. In 1980, LAIA and ESB left the HB coalition. The latter eventually ceased to exist as an entity.

The coalition represents about 10 percent of the Basque population, including those who, in other regions, would vote for the parties of the extreme left. HB is viewed as the political arm of the ETA mili to which it offers protection. Members recognize neither the Spanish constitution nor the Basque Statutes. Consequently, they do not participate in institutions of the establishment nor do they occupy parliamentary seats. The aims of HB are encompassed by a five-point program: (1) amnesty—liberation of all Basque prisoners; (2) democratic liberties—legalization of all Basque political parties, including independent ones; (3) expulsion of state security forces (i.e., police and civil guard) from the Basque region; (4) integration of Navarra into the Basque country; (5) an autonomy statute recognizing the national sovereignty of the Basques, their right to self-determination, and their right to create an independent state (with ties to French Euskadi), with armed forces under the sole control of the Basque government.

A new Spanish constitution was brought forth in 1978, after Franco's death, and in 1979 all of the Basque parties except HB signed a new statute of autonomy known as the Statute of Guernica. It was hoped that this would serve as a panacea for the unrest that had plagued the Basque country for so long. Lehendakari Garaikoetxea referred to it as a "formula for peace and concordance"; instead it became a point of discord. Each faction seems to have interpreted the statute in its own way, to serve its own needs. The Spanish parties see it as an adequate framework for coexistence with the Basques; the PNV, EE, and others consider it to be merely a starting point, a "statute of minimums" as it were, which should lead to further negotiations; still others—namely, ETA and HB— look upon it as just so much wasted paper.

Most Basques favor some form of autonomy, and the parties, exhibiting considerable solidarity in their feelings of belonging to a common Basque nation, all have some form of autonomy as the goal toward which they strive. While the Spanish parties tend to be partisans of centralization or of a limited autonomy, the Basque parties defend either a more complete autonomy or the establishment of an independent Basque State, to include Navarra and Iparralde. Some, such as the PNV and the EE, trust that the movement will gradually mature and that the goals will be realized little by little. HB, ETA, and other radicals wish to pursue independence immediately, by means of armed combat if necessary. Thus the parties disagree not so much in their principal objective as in the urgency and methods for realizing that objective. This results in alternations between pragmatic moderation and a tendency to negotiate, on the one side, and a rigid, extremist intransigence on the other, affecting not only the setting of objectives but also the strategies and methods for attaining them.

The Present Situation in the Basque Region

The situation in the Basque country today is confused and anything but tranquil. The serious economic deterioration is reflected in a mood of discouragement and impotence and in the presence of social problems such as depersonalization and the weakening of the family, which often accompany industrialization and economic crisis. Such problems are not unique to the Basque region nor do they arise from one source, although there is a tendency among the Basque to place the blame for these things on the Spanish state.

The permanent state of tension between the pro-Basque activists and the officials of the Spanish state frequently erupts in violence, infusing the atmosphere with fear. Terrorism began to hit the newspaper headlines with greater frequency in the mid-1970s. The number of assassinations, beginning with that of a police inspector in 1968, has now surpassed 600. Included among the victims are 50 high-level military officials, all killed since democracy was reinstated in 1977. The Spanish Ministry of the Interior reports that 156 terrorists have been killed during the same period—75 in the Basque region of Spain, 21 in France, and the rest elsewhere.

Public opinion regarding what should be done to resolve the situation varies widely. Some take extreme positions on the issue, advocating severe punishments for captured terrorists. Regardless of what punishment is imposed, many think the authorities should be absolutely unrelenting in their pursuit of the terrorists until they are eliminated completely. Others sympathize with the terrorists, offering them at least passive support, and sometimes providing them with help in the way of food and lodging.

This attitude of sympathy for ETA is understandable to some extent: The ETA ideology of independence for the region is appealing to the Basques who resent the power wielded over them by the central government and who blame Madrid for the economic ruin and social decay in their region. Many Basques may feel that the strategies and tactics of ETA are ill advised and even wrong. Nevertheless, they also tend to believe that ETA wants to make a "better world," based on their own ideals and traditions. Madrid seems determined to dissuade them by means of systematic persecution, exemplified by recent jailings of nearly half a thousand HB militants and ETA sympathizers. Thus the Basques exist in a subjective atmosphere of repression.

It must be said that the central government is not exempt from blame for its lack of tact in dealing with the local people or for the apparent failure of its chaotic police system in combating terrorism. Often given to excess, methods for dealing with captured terrorists have included physical and psychological torture, confirmed by a report of Amnesty International (1984). Given the nature of the terrorists' methods, it would be nothing short of miraculous if the police were not at times moved to severe methods in return, including those which infringe on ordinary rules of respect for human rights. Perhaps, in this light, an understanding of the excesses committed by the Spanish state through its police may be possible; still, torture in any form is never justifiable, and such behavior remains reprehensible. It only serves to further alienate the people, damaging the image of the Civil Government and ultimately being counterproductive.

Historically, many Basques have looked upon the Spaniards who live in their region as "foreigners." The presence of so many non-native people in their midst makes them feel invaded and occupied by outsiders. Some Basques, fortunately a minority, seem unable to view the Spanish police as normal, human individuals. Instead they are seen as a group caricature: aliens armed with helmets and visors, riding in armored vehicles, ready for action. This view, if not wholly justified, is at least somewhat understandable given that so many interactions between the police and the local people occur in the midst of some unpleasantness. In their own right, many of the police, having joined the ranks simply for economic reasons, do not have a very pleasant existence. Posted in a region culturally quite different from their own, and not daring to have their families accompany them for fear of reprisals, they live an almost monastic life. They leave their barracks only in groups to exercise their official duties, such as putting down demonstrations.

A drug abuse problem of phenomenal proportions is another serious and pervasive social problem in the Basque region, particularly among its disaffected youth. The statistics are startling. The Basque region reportedly has the highest drug addiction rate in Europe; the town of San Sebastian has the highest rate of heroin consumption per capita in the world. Over 11,000 young people are heroin addicts. Up to 17 percent of those aged 13 to 17 reportedly smoke marijuana; and even in this age group, 0.5 percent are addicted to heroin. The problem is pervasive across the sociopolitical spectrum.

The various factions, far from working together to alleviate the drug problem, seem instead to be aggravating it, promoting drug use directly or indirectly for their own reasons. The Basque bishops, in a pastoral letter dated September 20, 1984, accused the terrorists of trafficking in drugs as means of getting funds to purchase weapons, and accused the police of providing drugs to informers in order to get them to cooperate. This problem, perhaps more than any other, is symptomatic of the extent to which the moral order and social stability of the Basque region have broken down and is an example of the social repercussions that have been felt acutely and widely throughout the Basque region.

Given their turbulent and stubborn spirit, Basques have always lived by continuously turning their backs on one another. The community is essentially divided into two sides, always in confrontation. Common phenomena in the Basque nationalist movement, therefore, are frequent schisms, lack of coordination between factions, and dispersion of resources. This does not change much over time, as evidenced by the recent desperate complaint of a politician who said "We Basques do not agree on a thing!" Apparently, in fact, they do not even agree on the model of society and state that they want, as the recent PNV crisis has shown.

Another characteristic, the "irrational factor," is present throughout Basque history. During the Carlist wars in the last century, irrationality took the form of absolutism, racism, and separatism. This was followed by the irrational alliance between right-wing Basques and the leftist Popular Front during the civil war. At present is the irrationality of terrorism that is literally demolishing the economy of the Basque region. This irrational component is important for understanding the present Basque problem.

If separatism is wrongly based on dogmatic claims that all central power is useless, then centralism may breed another no less grave mistake in confusing centralism with patriotism. Castilla, the core of Spanish unity, has not asked other regions for help in its task of unifying the country "as if only Castillian heads would have adequate organs for perceiving and resolving the great problem of the Integral Spain," as Ortega says in his *Invertebrate Spain*. Therefore, even though the Basque country has a privileged situation in that it is economically more developed than other regions, its subjective feeling of "oppression" by the Spanish government is understandable. The Castillians and the Basques look differently upon the region. Consequently, Madrid's ministrations are perceived differently by each side, resulting in a kind of background incompatibility.

Madrid's ignorance of the problems and idiosyncrasies of Basque culture leads to oversimplifications, unnecessarily irritating the Basques further. Major mistakes made out of ignorance can have far-reaching negative effects, easily fomenting feelings of discontent and oppression. An interesting question is why Basque nationalism was not born in rural Ipparalde but in industrial Vizcaya, where Euskera was hardly spoken. Several reasons come to mind that may help to explain this. First, France has allowed external signs of "Basqueness" to be expressed, such as folklore and customs. Consequently, Basques in France had no repression to fight against. More important is the French policy of promoting agriculture and tourism rather than industry in French Basque territory; it is in urban industrial environments where radical political notions seem to germinate. Finally, nationalism finds more sympathy and support when fought against a totalitarian regime such as Franco's rather than a democracy like the French Republic.

Rational agreement with Madrid will not be attainable while the separatists persist. Some of their conditions are completely unacceptable, and they well know it. Both sides must admit at the outset that the Basque region has no possible future as an independent state. Successful negotiation requires moderation on both sides and a willingness to at least consider rational compromise. Autonomous spheres are permitted by the Spanish constitution, so long as they do not destabilize Spain. Using the Statute of Guernica as a negotiating frame, the Basques could conceivably obtain a condition of inclusion in the Spanish state based on terms satisfactory to all parties. Some present-day Basques, mostly those who live in rural areas, hold to traditional notions of nationalism, resisting all outside influence and defending their language, customs, and ancient laws. Other Basques, especially those who live in urban centers, are rather more interested in problems of the economy and of class, whether from a Marxist, conservative, liberal, or even independent point of view. The point is that they are all Basques; their main hope is to integrate, respect one another, and cooperate. There is no culturally and ethnically monolithic Basque society as some nationalists myopically pretend; rather, the region is peopled by a plural and polymorphous society in which different cultures and interests must coexist. Such recognition can be a starting point for rectifying old mistakes, ultimately improving prospects for coexistence, and, as Ortega said, "living in harmony as part of an all and not all apart.

References

Amnesty International. (1984, April). *1984 Amnesty International Report on Torture.* London: Amnesty International.

Arana, S. de. (1890). *Cuatro Glorias Patrias.* Bilbao.

Caro Baroja, J. (1984). *El Laberinto Vasco.* San Sebastian: Txertoa.

Chamber of Commerce of Bilbao. (1980). *Los Vascos somos Así.* Bilbao: Cámara Oficial de Comercio, Industria y Navegación.

Emopública. (1984, December). [Poll conducted with 1200 people]. Unpublished raw data.

Genovés, S. (1980). *La Violencia en el Pais Vasco y en sus relaciones con España.* U.N.A.M.: Mexico.

Madariaga, S. de. (1928). *Englishmen, Frenchmen and Spaniards.* Oxford: Oxford University Press.

Madariaga, S. de. (1969). *Bosquejo de Europa.* Buenos Aires: Editorial Sudamericana.

Mendoza, D. L., & Ramirez, J. M. (1985). Aggression and cohesion in Spanish and Mexican children. In J. M. Ramirez & P. F. Brain (Eds.), *Aggression: Functions and causes* (pp. 152-163). Sevilla: Seville University Press.

Orueta, J. de. (1934). Fueros y Autonomía: El Proceso del Estatuto Vasco.

Chapter Summary

Ronald Bailey's chapter "Black-White Relations in Mississippi" focuses on understanding Black-White conflict, with specific reference to Mississippi. The author rejects the assumption made by many race relations scholars that the Black experience is merely a reaction to the behavior of the White majority. Bailey also emphasizes the need for attention to structural aspects of race relations (i.e., those based on the economic and political power distribution) rather than solely ideological (i.e., moralistic) aspects.

In his discussion of race conflict, the author concentrates on demographic issues and examines the hypothesis that a high proportion of a racial group in the population is associated with higher levels of racial conflict. In an examination of class issues, Bailey points out that this high proportion of Blacks in the South has not been associated with commensurate representation in politics, occupations, income level, or ownership of land or businesses.

The author suggests that it is the level of nationality in which the greatest racial conflicts are manifested and where race relations theory is most flawed. Bailey advocates greater emphasis on nationality in both internal and external contexts. He proposes that internally, nationality consolidates and transmits a sense of common identity and purpose and, thus, the motivation for self-development. Externally, Black-White conflict is based on efforts to deny Blacks equal access and opportunity and to limit expressions of Black culture. Bailey's central focus is on the example of Mississippi, tracing racialist thinking across several stages of history and giving special attention to issues of politics and government.

—Susan Goldstein

7

Black-White Relations
in Mississippi

RONALD BAILEY

Scholars and observers have long recognized the centrality of "race relations" and Black-White ("racial") conflict and have commented on it widely.[1] In 1903, W.E.B. DuBois, considered the father of Afro-American Studies, declared that "the problem of the twentieth century is the problem of color line—the relation of the darker to the lighter races of men in Asia and Africa, in America and the islands of the sea" (DuBois, 1903, p. 23). Later he added the fact "that so many civilized persons are willing to live in comfort even if the price of this is poverty, ignorance and disease of the majority of their fellow men"—the class problem—"both obscures and implements" the color or race problem (DuBois, 1940, p. xiii). In 1928, the White historian U.B. Phillips characterized the South as inhabited by "a people with a common resolve indomitably maintained—that it shall remain a white man's country" and asserted that belief in this view was "the cardinal test of a Southerner and the central theme of Southern history." (Quoted in Woodward, 1966, p. 8)

As a central theme in the history of the United States, the study of Black-White conflict and race relations has been itself as strife-ridden and tumultuous as the reality of conflict it purports to investigate and understand (see Drake, 1969). Gunnar Myrdal's widely heralded *American Dilemma* (1942) illustrates the difficulties involved in studying race relations (see Lynd, 1944, p. 5 for a representative review).[2]

Among the then-contemporaneous criticisms of Myrdal, two stand out as important for this chapter. The first was Myrdal's conception of Black people as "creations" of White society with no independent and determining capacity for social action: "All our attempts to reach scientific explanations of why the Negroes are what they are and why they live as they do have regularly led to determinants on the white side of the race line" (Myrdal, 1942, p. lxxv). The second was Myrdal's conception of the nature of and the relationship among economic, social, political, cultural, and other aspects of life as they impinge on race relations. This led him to characterize "the American Negro problem [as] a problem in the heart of the American" (p. lxxi). Myrdal defined the "American Dilemma" as a "moral dilemma," "an ever-ranging conflict" between the "American Creed" which emphasizes national interest and Christian principles and more narrow values that stress personal interests and social jealousies. (Ellison, 1953 and Cox, 1948 elaborate these two points, respectively.[3])

Many insightful contributions to the study of race relations theory fall short for these two reasons: (1) They fail to posit the internal, cohesive integrity and logic of the Black experience as it has developed over time and in interaction with other races and nationalities; (2) they fail to treat adequately the structural roots of race conflict, often overemphasizing narrower moral or psychological predispositions, the realm of ideas. I will argue that race relations in Mississippi and the South are both ideological (i.e., rooted in Myrdal's moral dilemma, and leading to Blacks being treated differently because of ideas about their "racial" inferiority) and structural (i.e., rooted in the distribution of economic and political power, and in the racial-class exclusionary operations of institutional and cultural forces). The tension between the *ideological* and the *structural,* and the tension between the *internal* corpus of Black life and the *external* reality of a race-conscious (or racism-conscious) society, provide the dynamic context and the source of complexity in exploring and understanding Black-White relations in Mississippi, in the South, and in the United States.

I will seek to demonstrate this point with an assessment of the Civil Rights movement—certainly among the most intense and significant periods of Black-White conflict and transformation—and a brief examination of the kinds of issues that set the agenda for race relations in Mississippi and the South for the remainder of the decade and the century. This is a particularly timely assessment since we are in the midst of a round of nostalgic reminiscences and commemorations of 20- and 25-year anniversaries of significant events (e.g., James Meredith's admission to the University of Mississippi in 1962, the Civil Rights Act and the Mississippi Summer Project of 1964, the Mississippi Freedom Democratic Party challenge of 1964 and 1965, the Voting Rights Act of 1965, etc.). And in light of mounting evidence that there has been a marked improvement in attitudes toward greater racial tolerance among Whites but a less than satisfactory transformation of social, political, and economic conditions among the masses of Black people, such an examination is warranted.

Studying the Black Experience
and Racial Conflict:
A Framework and Historical Overview

A full analysis of this topic would require an approach to the Black experience that is both comprehensive and historical. A recently published book, Abdul Alkalimat and Associates' *Introduction to Afro-American Studies: A Peoples College Primer* (1984), grapples effectively with the long-standing question of an overall framework for the study of the Black experience.[4] It proposes what it calls, using the language of Thomas Kuhn (1964) in *The Structure of Scientific Revolutions,* "a paradigm of unity in Afro-American Studies," an analytical tool that "defines a logical space for the entire field of Afro-American Studies." (The following summary is based on Alkalimat and Associates, 1984, pp. 22-27. For a recent summary of issues, see especially McWorter & Bailey, 1984. See also, Robinson, Foster, & Ogilvie, 1969; Blassingame, 1971; and Ford, 1973. Alternative approaches are presented in Harris, 1982, 1985; Karenga, 1982; and Willie, 1983.) Essentially, the paradigm suggests answers to two fundamental questions about the Black experience and thereby helps clarify the intellectual turf for the field of Afro-American Studies: What is the Black experience? How does the Black experience change?

The paradigm posits that there are four levels, or "fundamental entities," of human reality that should be taken into account in studying the experiences of any people—biology, political economy, society, consciousness. Each level has a particular manifestation for Black people—race, class, nationality, ideology. The sum total of these entities defines what is meant by the "Black experience."

On the biological level, the key variable is race (and secondarily, gender and age), traits controlled by a genetic code inherited from one's biological parents (e.g., sexual organs for gender, and skin color for race; Miller & Dreger, 1973). On the level of political economy, the central concept suggested is class; class is defined as "a historical relationship between groups of people. It is a relationship of power that determines who works, what they get from it, and what impact they can have on the society at large."

There are two major aspects of nationality on the level called society: culture and social institutions. "Culture refers to values and life style, whereas social institutions refer to roles and collective forms of social interaction. These are permanent features of a society that are reproduced and transmitted across generations." Nationality (sometimes called ethnicity) "is the particular identity of a group based on its culture and social institutions." (See Drake, 1965, for a discussion of nationality in an urban context.)

"Consciousness" addresses the way in which these three aspects of the human experience—race, class, and nationality—are known, thought about, and discussed. Ideology is "the most formal organization of one's consciousness . . . a set of beliefs that serve to define physical, social, mental, and spiritual reality." (Newby, 1968, for example, traces the development of segregationist ideology.)

The Black experience has undergone several centuries of historical change and transformation. Several overlapping stages are specified: traditional Africa; the slave trade; slavery; emancipation; rural life; migration; and urban life.[5]

Combining these two dimensions—the four levels or entities and historical periodization—constitutes the paradigm of unity for Afro-American studies (see Figure 7.1). With this analytical tool, it is possible to have a holistic conception of the Afro-American experience and the field of Afro-American studies. It enables us to identify and codify existing research, as well as to chart the path for additional new research (Merton, 1957).

This paradigmatic conception of the Afro-American experience provides new handles on understanding race relations and racial conflict. The South, because it was the main stage for the drama of slavery—the *raison d'etre* of the forced migration of Africans to the United States—has obviously been an important region in the unfolding of Black-White relations, and Mississippi is an especially important state for this investigation since its Black population constituted a majority of the state from 1840 to 1940. The full historical overview is only hinted at in the discussion that follows. I want to argue that there are several specific bases for what we label *racial conflict:* the struggle for physical space, the struggle for economic resources, a social dimension rooted in contending institutional and cultural realities, and ideological disputes (reflecting competing values and beliefs about racial equality and related issues)—all of which can be mapped over historical time. This is the framework that will be applied in brief to a historical overview of Mississippi and the South, and to more recent developments in Mississippi. (Useful historical overviews can be found in Bailey, 1986; Loewen & Sallis, 1982; McLemore, 1973; Sansing, 1981).

The Black Experience and Black-White Conflict

Demography, "the systematic study of population phenomena" (Petersen, 1969, p. 1), is useful in the study of race. In the United States, the percentage of Black people has decreased from a high of 19.3 percent in 1790 to a low of 9.7 percent between 1930 and 1950. The 1790 percentage equalled 757,208 Blacks, a number that had grown to 26.5 million Black people in 1980 (calculated from U.S. Bureau of the Census, 1975, 1982). The South, because it was the main stage for the drama of slavery, has obviously been an important region in the unfolding of Black-White relations. The percentage of Black people in 11 Southern states exceeded 70 percent for each decade from 1790 to 1930, ranging as high as 82 percent. These same 11 states accounted for about 45 percent of the 1980 Black population. Black people constituted 35 percent of the South's population in 1870 and about 20 percent in 1980, as the Census Bureau defines the South (U.S. Bureau of the Census, 1975, p. 22; 1982).

The significance of these statistics to Black-White relations can be made more precise if we focus on the concentration of Black

Figure 7.1 Toward a Paradigm of Unity in Afro-American Studies

LOGIC OF CHANGE	Social Cohesion — Social Disruption	Traditional Africa —	Slave Trade —	Slavery —	Emanci-pation —	Rural Life —	Migrations —	Urban Life —
UNITS OF ANALYSIS	Ideology	A1	B1	C1	D1	E1	F1	G1
	Nationality	A2	B2	C2	D2	E2	F2	G2
	Class	A3	B3	C3	D3	E3	F3	G3
	Race	A4	B4	C4	D4	E4	F4	G4

SOURCE: Alkalimat & Associates (1984). PERMISSION ? ?

people in the "Black Belt," a crescent shaped region of rich, dark soil stretching from Virginia through the deep South to the Mississippi River Valley, and on to the state of Mississippi (Frazier, 1957a, pp. 187-190; U.S. Bureau of the Census, 1918, 1935, pp. 70-77). In 1900, the number of Black people living in Black majority counties in the South reached its peak at 4.1 million living in 286 such counties. This represented 41 percent of all Black people in the United States and 46 percent of Blacks in the South. For Mississippi, these demographic trends are even more pronounced. Mississippi's Black population ranged from 39.4 percent (1790) to 58.7 percent (1900). Its 1980 population was 35.9 percent Black, making it the state with the highest proportion of Black people in the United States. Perhaps most surprising is this fact: From 1840 to 1940—a full century—Black people constituted a majority of the state's population.[6] There were a significant number of majority Black counties and a significant number of Black Mississippians living in these counties. In 1900, 46 percent of Mississippi's 82 counties were majority Black, and 77 percent of the state's Black citizens resided in these counties (down from over 80 percent during the two previous decades), most of them clustered in an area of contiguous counties in the cotton-rich Delta along the Mississippi River.

These figures are important because they point to a source of potential conflict. Blalock (1957, p. 187) and others have argued that there should be a positive relationship between minority percentage and discrimination, or "as the percent Black grows, so does occupational discrimination against them but at a decelerating rate" (Semyanov, Moshe, & Scott, 1983, p. 242). Thus the higher the proportion of a racial group in the population the more likely it is that racial conflict will occur (Kousser, 1974). Black people have often been present in numbers far exceeding Whites, especially in Mississippi and the South.

Additionally, the preponderance of Black people and their historical concentration in such large numbers over such a long period of time are the bases on which Black cultural and institutional expression have been most intense. These realities have helped to condition Black-White relations in significant ways, and continue to do so, especially in undergirding Black resistance, as we shall argue below. A consideration of demographic factors is thus a necessary first step in unraveling the patterns of Black-White relations.

In considering the economic dimension of the Black experience, we will focus on only three indicators—occupation, income, and ownership of land and businesses. The pattern that emerges clearly is the persistence of economic exploitation, inequality and poverty through the three stages of the Black experience: slavery, rural life, and urban life.

Ransom and Sutch's (1977) important study used a sampling of five cotton states and concluded that only about 6 percent of adult male slaves held occupations above those of agricultural worker, unskilled labor, or house servant. On the other hand, 24.5 percent of free White males were employed as skilled artisans or professionals, or worked in commercial or managerial activity. Almost 55 percent were classified as farm operators as compared to only 11.6 as field hands (p. 15). In 1860, only 6 percent of the U.S. Black population was free, as compared to 5 percent in 1790 (U.S. Bureau of the Census, 1979, p. 11). In Mississippi, however, the percentage of free Blacks in 1860 was less than 0.2 percent (Mississippi Power, 1983). The central role occupied by cotton in the U.S. economy explains this fact and the increase in the U.S. Black population cited above, and the fact that only a few Blacks escaped the class of slaves, especially in Mississippi. Between 1791 and 1815, cotton production increased from 189,000 pounds to 83 million pounds, with the big increase after the cotton gin's invention and spread from 1793 to 1795. Between 1815 and 1860, the total value of U.S. exports increased 379 percent and cotton exports climbed from roughly 30 percent to 58 percent of the total during this period (Bruchey, 1967, pp. 7-40). The fact that Mississippi was the leading cotton-growing state should come as no surprise: It ranked first in 1839 and 1859, suffering an "atypical" decline to third in 1849 (Scarborough, 1973, pp. 322-323). Thus cotton was clearly on the throne and this economic fact did more than anything else to shape the work experience of Black people during slavery.

For the rural period, the first census data on occupation by race became available in 1890 and a clear picture of the occupational status of Blacks—80 percent who lived in rural areas and 90 percent in the South—can be gained. Ransom and Sutch (1977) list occupations according to the percentage of Blacks in each class and then construct a "racial balance index," which indicates the extent to which racial discrimination prevents Blacks from equal participation in any occupation. The "black occupations" for men included servants, agricultural laborers, laborers, porters, barbers, and teamsters; and

> all the skilled occupations other than masonry were predominately white. (Printer, machinist, and seamstress were almost exclusively white.) All, or nearly all, of the professional, mercantile, and commercial occupations effectively excluded blacks. (p. 38)

The transition from rural life to urban life represented a significant shift for Blacks. While 80 percent of all Blacks lived in rural areas in 1890, this figure had dropped to 19 percent in 1970. In 1890, 90 percent of Black men were concentrated in agriculture and 90 percent of Black women were in agriculture and domestic service. By 1970, only 5 percent of Black men worked in agriculture while 77 percent worked as blue-collar and service workers; and only 19 percent of Black women worked in agriculture and service while about 50 percent worked in clerical, sales, and service occupations (Reich, 1981, p. 23).

Freeman (1976, p. 5) utilizes an index that compares these shifts in Black occupations in relationship to simultaneous shifts among Whites. In his assessment, the index indicates that "no relative progress for Blacks occurred between 1890 and 1940, but there has been a modicum of improvement in recent decades" (Reich, 1981, p. 25). Between 1945 and 1977, the ratio of median incomes for non-White families has fluctuated between a low of .51 and a high of .65 and has averaged about .57, with an average of .71 for females and .56 for males (Reich, 1977, p. 31, tab. 2.3).

In the ownership of wealth, the number of Black property owners in the South during slavery was minimal since 94 percent of Blacks were owned as property (U.S. Bureau of the Census, 1979). In 1830, free Blacks owned about 32,000 acres of land valued at $184,184, and both value and acreage doubled by 1860. Almost half of these farms contained 25 acres or less and Frazier argued that they were used "for subsistence rather than for commercial enterprises" (cited in Alkalimat and Associates, 1984, p. 148). In the rural period, when the ownership of land was essential to economic well-being, Ransom and Sutch (1977, p. 83) suggest that "even as late as 1880, only 9.8 percent of the acreage which was actually cultivated in crops was owned and operated by Blacks, who nevertheless represented more than one-half of the agricultural population." When total acreage was considered, a more dismal picture emerged.

The same trends continue in the urban period. Between 1954 and 1969, the number of Black full-time landowners dropped from 125,831 to 51,757—a decline of 58.9 percent—while the number of Black part-time owners declined from 49,555 to 15,058—a decline of 69.6 percent. The South is significant since Black-owned farms have been concentrated there. Mississippi alone accounted for almost one-quarter of the Black farm landowners in the region; and Alabama, Mississippi, North Carolina, and South Carolina accounted for almost 60 percent of all Black landowners and 52 percent of all Black-controlled land in 1969 (Salamon, 1976, pp. 3-4).

A similar picture emerges from a study of Black business ownership: "The narrative of Black business activity after 1890 is filled with very rugged, very inspiring but also very sparsely scattered success stories—and many more unsuccess stories" (Bailey, 1971, p. 6; Harris, 1936). The number of Black-owned businesses increased from 2,000 in 1863 to 17,000 in 1883, and to 40,000 in 1913. There was a dramatic increase as Blacks moved into the cities, but the relative size and wealth of these businesses are still small, despite government emphasis in past years on "Black capitalism." From 1969 to 1982, there was a 119 percent increase in the number of businesses, and a 278 percent increase in gross sales. But such gross sales represent a very small portion of the total U.S. sales—2 percent in 1977. Most Black businesses operate with no full-time staff and even the largest are comparatively small. For example, if the total sales of $2.6 billion of the largest 100 Black businesses on the *Black Enterprise* 1985 listing were combined as one business, they would have placed just below the 145th corporation among the Fortune 500 of that year. The Black 100 had 17,760 employees and $2 trillion in sales (*Black Enterprise* "Annual Report," June 1985, p. 87 ff.; Bailey, 1971; *Fortune* "The Directory," May 1985; Ofari, 1970).

It is in the consideration of nationality that the most important shortcomings are found in race relations theory. The failure to consider both the internal reality of the Black community as well as its external context has distorted our understanding of Black-White relations.

Internally, a sense of nationality rooted in a common culture and shared institutional experiences constitute "the ties that bind," the social glue that helps to mold Black individuals into a nationlike entity, or nationality, with a sense of peoplehood and a sense of community. The most important contribution that nationality makes is that it is the main means by which a sense of common identity and purpose is nourished, crystallized, refined, and transmitted across generations. And it is on the basis of this common identity and through the mediation of social institutions such as the church, school, and the family that Black people are mobilized for self-development and collective action, and learn to respond to perceived external threats to their mutual self-interest.

The development of nationality among Black people has been influenced by their African heritage (Ferris, 1983; Herskovits, 1941; Thompson, 1983; Turner, 1949) and has characterized all historical periods—slave life, rural life, and urban life. But it was in the period of rural life in the South, especially between about 1870 and 1940, that Afro-American nationality fully blossomed (Alkalimat and Associates, 1984, chaps. 5 and 9). This reflected the new conditions of relative freedom after the demise of slavery and the historical concentration of the Black population, both of which spurred the development of Black social institutions. Sutch and Ransom (1978, p. 57; Ransom & Sutch, 1977, app. C) calculate that ex-slaves reduced the amount of time they worked between 28 and 37 percent, a major portion attributed to the withdrawal of Black women from fieldwork. It is not difficult to imagine how this additional time was utilized in consolidating families, organizing churches and lodges, building schools, and other social development initiatives.

There is ample evidence to support this contention regarding the flowering of Black nationality in the emancipation and rural life periods. As a rough indicator of early consolidation of the Black family after the Civil War, DuBois (1935, p. 447) observed that the number of marriage licenses among Blacks in Mississippi increased from 564 in 1865 to 3,427 in 1870 as compared to an almost 20 percent decrease among Whites, and that the number of churches built in those same years increased from 105 to 283. In 1872, five associations formed the General Missionary Baptist Association with 226 churches and 21,000 members at its first meeting, and had 47,200 members by 1890 (Wharton, 1947, p. 259). In 1890, this association merged with another to form the General Baptist Missionary Convention of Mississippi, which brought together 900 churches with a membership of almost 80,000. Mississippians were also active in the formation of the Colored Methodist Episcopal Church in 1870 in Jackson, Tennessee. All of this reflected a national trend: By 1906, there were 36,563 Black churches in the United States with a membership of almost 3.7 million people (U.S. Bureau of the Census, 1935, p. 55).

The most important Black leaders in Mississippi were those intimately involved in the development of Black social institutions. A notable example is Dr. Thomas W. Stringer, a native of Maryland who came to Mississippi from Ohio following the Civil War. A medical doctor, Stringer introduced Masonry to Blacks in Mississippi and organized lodges at Vicksburg, Jackson, and Natchez. In 1868, a number of churches organized by Stringer in his capacity as presiding elder formed the Mississippi conference of the African Methodist Episcopal Church. He was also elected to the state legislature in 1870 and helped organize Campbell College in 1890 (Harrison, 1977; Holtzclaw, 1984, pp. 9-10; Wharton, 1965, p. 149).

Between 1870 and 1920, the illiteracy rate among Blacks decreased from 80 percent to 23 percent, as compared to a decrease from 11.5 percent to 4 percent for Whites (U.S. Bureau of the Census, 1975, p. 382). By 1890, 75 of the 123 predominately Black colleges in operation in the 1960s were already in existence (Bullock, 1971, p. 581). In Mississippi, several colleges, many of which are still in operation, were launched during this period: Rust, 1866; Tougaloo, 1869; Alcorn, 1871; Jackson State, 1876; Natchez College, 1885; and Mary Holmes College, 1892 (Wilson, 1947). Several scholars have identified the struggle over the control of Black education as an early and key arena for the expression of Black Power (see Woods, 1986).

Similarly, the Black press experienced a rapid growth in the era immediately following the Civil War. There were 10 Black journals in 1870, 31 in 1880, and by 1890 there were 154 (Myrdal, 1942, p. 913). In 1880 there were such journals in 19 states and in 28 states by 1890. Thompson (1986) suggests that in Mississippi, 5 Black newspapers were published in the 1870s, 17 in the 1880s, and 45 in the 1890s. Myrdal observed that "the development of the Negro press follows closely two interrelated trends: the rising Negro protest and the increase in Negro literacy" (p. 913).

Externally, the efforts to limit or negate the expression of Black nationality—to denigrate Black culture, to hamper the development of Black institutions, or to otherwise deny the full and equal access of Black people to the mainstream of U.S. society—has been and continues to be the basis of substantial "racial," or Black-White, conflict.

Conversely, these developments (churches, businesses, newspapers, lodges, schools and colleges, etc.) are important institutional resources that undergird the Afro-American struggle for equality, "structural forces . . . that can serve as the basis for building a powerful united front" (King, 1967, p. 124; McAdam, 1982). Their existence and development alone has and continues to generate one powerful basis for potential racial conflict in a social context that is racist, or intolerant of cultural and national diversity, and that deprives nationality groups of power (economic, political, social, cultural, etc.) commensurate with their numbers in the population. (Cruse, 1967 and YTPTCOI, 1974 discuss the cultural arena and the mass media.) Black Power or "Black self-determination" are two important summary expressions for focusing the implications of nationality for Black-White relations (Franklin, 1984). More generally, it is within nationality—and more specifically within social institutions, perhaps because these constitute the core of social life most accessible to people—that we find most often the arena of sharpest racial conflict (e.g., school and housing desegregation).

Ideology was defined above as set of beliefs that serve to define physical, social, mental, and spiritual reality. In the arena of Black-White relations, I would argue that the central ideological tension and conflict revolves around racism, or the belief and practice of White racial superiority on the one hand versus the insistence on absolute racial equality on the other. I will not try to trace the development of racialist thinking, especially since it has been done so thoroughly by others (Fields, 1982; Fredrickson, 1977, 1983; Jordan, 1968). Mississippi provides a good example of racialist thinking throughout several stages of history. The field slave was described by one Mississippian as "the last and lowest link in the chain of the human species" (quoted in Sydnor, 1933). After slavery, the sentiment hardly mellowed: "A white man in a white man's place. A black man in a black man's place. Each according to the eternal fitness of things." God was often viewed as legitimizing this racial hierarchy (see Wharton, 1941, p. 367). It is important to note how the role of the "inferior" is rationalized and assigned an essential economic role, a point argued by many scholars as one of the key functions of ideological racism—to rationalize an existing racial hierarchy from which the "superior" group derives economic benefits (Bunche, 1936; Frazier, 1955, 1957b).

We get some sense of how violence was effectively used in Black-White relations during this period by looking at the average number of lynchings for five-year periods beginning in 1885 (Work, 1937-1938), a period that laid a basis for the removal of Blacks from full political representation and participation.

1885-89:	91
1890-94:	122
1895-99:	100
1900-04:	91
1905-09:	84
1910-15:	58

It is thus not surprising that with disenfranchising measures like the poll tax, literacy tests, the civic understanding test, and the grandfather clause—and in the face of widespread lynching and other attacks—Blacks were driven from electoral politics. In Louisiana, one of the few states for which data is available, in 1896 there were 130,344 Black people registered in the state, constituting a majority in 26 parishes. By 1900, two years after a new disenfranchising constitution, only 5,320 Black people were registered—a drop of 96 percent (Lewinson, 1932). Indeed, for this period, it is difficult not to agree with the characterization of the Handsboro, Mississippi, *Democrat* that Mississippi and the South was essentially "a white man's government, by white men, for the benefit of white men" (quoted from the Yazoo City *Banner* in Wharton, 1947, p. 184). But it is only by grasping the inherent integrity of the Afro-American experience that we can appreciate the words of George H. White of North Carolina, the last Black member of Congress from any state until 1929 and from the South until 1973. In his final speech to Congress in 1901 he said,

This, Mr. Chairman, is perhaps the Negro's temporary farewell to the American Congress; but let me say, Phoenix-like, he will rise up some day and come again. These parting words are in behalf of an outraged heart-broken, bruised and bleeding but God-fearing people, faithful, industrial and loyal people—full of potential force. (quoted in Gosnell, 1935, p. 78)

The existence of this "force," this will to resist, does as much in continuing to shape Black-White relations as any other factor.

The Civil Rights Era: An Assessment

The Civil Rights movement has been heralded as a watershed in race relations in Mississippi and the South. There was the "Negro Revolution," and legislation such as the 1964 Civil Rights Act and the 1965 Voting Rights Act was passed and signed into law, described by President Lyndon B. Johnson as intending to "strike away the last major shackle . . ., the ancient bond" that contradicted the view that all persons are created equal and as citizens are guaranteed equal protection of the law. He declared that "we will not delay or will we hesitate, or will not turn aside until Americans of every race and color and origin in this country have the same rights as all others to share in the progress of democracy" (quoted in Scher & Button, 1984, p. 20; Lawson, 1976, p. 329).

Given the presence of Black people in such great numbers and with poverty, disenfranchisement, and oppression so intense, it should have come as no surprise that Mississippi became a key arena in the Civil Rights struggle. It is not possible here to even encapsulate the history of the Civil Rights movement in Mississippi. The younger militants of the Congress of Racial Equality (CORE) and the Student Non-Violent Coordinating Committee (SNCC) joined such organizations as the NAACP, which had been active in Mississippi since its start in 1918, and the Regional Council of Negro Leadership, organized in 1950 by Dr. T.R.M. Howard (McMillen, 1973). They entered the state as freedom riders; in 1961 SNCC opened offices in Jackson, Greenwood, and Greenville, and proceeded to launch projects throughout Mississippi (see, e.g., Carson, 1981; Evers & Peters, 1967; Greenberg, 1969; Moody, 1968; Raines, 1977; and Wirt, 1970). A key event during this period was James Meredith's success in entering the University of

Mississippi in 1962, amidst great turmoil and resistance (Barrett, 1965; Lord, 1965; Silver, 1963).

The Conference of Federated Organizations, or COFO, emerged in 1961 and became a focal point for creating a united front for all civil rights groups operating in Mississippi. Campaigns were launched in McComb, Jackson, and several Delta towns such as Clarksdale, and included voter registration drives, boycotts, and mock "freedom" elections to protest being barred from regular elections. In 1964, much of this energy was focused on the Mississippi Freedom Summer Project through which COFO brought hundreds of Northern sympathizers to Mississippi (Belfrage, 1965; Holt, 1965). The Mississippi Freedom Democratic Party started in April of 1964 and proceeded to challenge the legitimacy of the "regular" all-White Democratic Party at the national party convention in Atlantic City and later in the U.S. Congress (Walton, 1972).

The responses of Whites in Mississippi to these initiatives of the Black community were equally as intense. The many acts of violence, orchestrated especially by the Ku Klux Klan and the White Citizens Council (McMillen, 1973; Sitkoff, 1981; Whitehead, 1970), reflect the legacy of racism outlined above, though more ferocious in the face of challenge. The most violent responses were the many reported and countless unreported murders of Black citizens and civil rights activists. Less obvious but usually effective were the many acts of economic intimidation and threats of violence (see, for example, U.S. Commission on Civil Rights 1965a, 1965b; and Carter, 1965—a collection of 57 notorized affidavits in a lawsuit filed by COFO).

In light of the intensity of the Civil Rights movement and in addressing the future of race relations in Mississippi, it is necessary to ask: What did the Civil Rights movement accomplish? Did it bring about the kinds of changes that were necessary to assure the rights that Black people and their allies sought so valiantly? Its successes, failures, and unrealized agenda will provide one clue to the likely course of future events.[7]

In the social arena, it cannot be disputed that many of the more obvious and blatant forms of racist discrimination have been removed. The general conclusion reached some years ago should still stand, modified by the overall conservative shift of opinion all over the United States:

> While all major segments of the white population have intensified
> their pro-integration stance, the change has been most noticeable
> among groups formerly the most hostile: those who are rural, poorly
> educated, unskilled, and southern. (Karnig & Welch, 1980, pp.
> 9-10)

But significant problems still remain in this area, for example in
public school segregation. A recent study reported that 37 percent
of Black students in Mississippi are in schools that are 90 to 100
percent minority—a higher percentage than in any other southern
state. There are still many predominantly and almost totally Black
schools and districts in the state. (Moreover, 35 percent of all
White students in the South are in schools that are 90 to 100 percent
White.) The study concluded that "the school statistics show that,
as the United States becomes an increasingly multiracial society,
racial segregation remains the prevailing pattern in most regions
with significant minority populations" (Orfield, 1982, p. 65).

The movement of the 1960s and 1970s had its greatest impact
on voting rights, entirely expected since "the vote" and electoral
politics were critical weapons in the battle for justice. In Mississippi, provisions of the Voting Rights Act of 1965 had a substantial
impact—such as suspending literacy tests and federalizing the voter
registration process in counties in which the test had been used and
where less than 50 percent of the voting age population was registered (Scher & Button, 1984).Consider these facts (taken mainly
from news articles in the *Jackson Clarion-Ledger*):

(1) In 1964, only 6.7 percent of Black Mississippians who were eligi-
    ble were registered to vote (as compared to 70.2 percent of Whites).
    In 1984, 77 percent of Blacks were registered, almost identical to
    the figure the Census Bureau claimed for White registration in
    1980 (Treyens, 1985, November 3).
(2) Voter turnout among Blacks in Mississippi remains low, though it
    exceeds the national totals. The Census Bureau reports that only
    50.8 percent of Black Mississippians voted in the 1982 congres-
    sional elections, as compared to 52.4 percent of the Whites. For
    the United States overall, the rate for Whites was 49.9 percent and
    43.0 percent for Blacks.

(3) The overall result is a larger number of Blacks elected. In Mississippi, the number of Black elected officials has grown from 6 in 1964 to 444 in 1985, placing the state second only to Louisiana with 475 (Joint Center for Political Studies, 1985; Treyens, 1985, November 3).

But if democracy is government "of the people, by the people and for the people," then it is clear that there are tremendous shortfalls in the democratic representation of Black Mississippians. Mississippi is 35 percent Black, yet less than 12 percent of the state's elective offices are held by Blacks; only 11.4 percent of the state legislature is Black (20); and 50 of the 410 country supervisors (12.2 percent, counting the newest one elected on November 5, 1985); and not a single Black person served in Mississippi's U.S. congressional delegation between 1873 and 1986, despite the fact that the state's population reached as high as 57 percent Black. Of the 91 municipalities in Mississippi that have Black populations over 50 percent, only 19 (or 20.9 percent) have Black mayors—and all of these have Black populations of at least seventy percent of the total population.

Industry

There have been substantial shifts in Black employment by industry. While in 1950 over one-half of Black Mississippians worked in agriculture (as compared to 31.3 percent of Whites), this decreased to 5.3 percent (and 3.6 percent for Whites). In 1980, 30.7 percent of all Black people worked in industry, a percentage higher than that of Whites. (Black people were more industrialized than Whites in 1950 as well.)

The service industry employed the largest share of Black workers, though in 1980 only 4.2 percent did private household work (as compared to 11.4 percent in 1950). The third highest percentage after industry and services was that of elementary and secondary education—12.8 percent.

Thus there was the precipitous decline—almost disappearance—of agricultural workers in an industry in which the total number of workers dropped from 302,086 in 1950 to 38,102 in 1980; and an increase of industrial workers, where the total number of jobs reached 228,840 or almost 25 percent of the Mississippi labor force.

Occupations

In 1940, 52.6 percent of all Black men in Mississippi were employed as "farmers," 10.3 percent as paid farm laborers, and another 12.6 percent as unpaid (family) farm laborers. Less than 1 percent (.83 percent) were classified as professional. In 1980, 13.2 percent were classified as professionals, 26.8 percent as factory operatives, 19.2 percent in service occupations (excluding domestic), and 10.1 percent as craftsmen. About 5 percent were classified in farm occupations.

For Black women in 1940, 37.7 percent were classified as domestic laborers, 32.4 percent were classified as unpaid family farm laborers, and 12.2 percent as farmers and farm managers. Only 3.2 percent were professionals (as compared to 18.9 percent for Whites). In 1980, 27.5 percent were service workers (excluding domestics), 26.5 percent were operatives, and 17.8 percent were professionals.

Income

In 1950, the family income of Black people in Mississippi was $601 per year, as compared with $1,614 for Whites. In 1980, the income for Blacks was $9,013, and $17,264 for Whites—an increase in income for Blacks of 181 percent as compared to 92 percent for Whites. However, by 1980, the median income for Black families equalled only about one-half that of Whites—52.2 percent, up from 37.2 percent in 1950, 34.3 percent in 1960, and 42.3 percent in 1970.

In 1980, still over one-quarter (26.1 percent) of Mississippi Black families were living on incomes of less than $5,000 per year, as compared to 8.3 percent for Whites. Thus Black people still find themselves on the lowest rungs of the occupation ladder in the hardest-working, dirtiest, and generally lowest-paying occupations; and still in 1980 Blacks earned only about one-half what the average White family earned.

Ownership

Land ownership continued to decrease during the Civil Rights era. Between 1950 and 1978, the number of acres owned by Blacks declined from 2.1 million to 662,130 acres, a loss of 68.5 percent (as compared to a 9 percent decline for Whites, Funchess, 1984, p. 22). While before and after figures are not available, the current status of Black business ownership (based on the most recent figures) suggests what must have been the case in the 1950s: In 1977, there were 5,220 minority-owned businesses in Mississippi, generating gross receipts of $217 million. These firms comprised 12.4 percent of all Mississippi businesses, but only 1.6 percent of the gross sales and less than one-half of 1 percent of the total payroll in the state (Stringfellow, 1985, p. 8A).

Education

This has been another area of definite improvement. The median years of school completed has almost doubled, from 5.1 years in 1950 to 9.4 years in 1980. Blacks still lag 3 years behind Whites in this area. The increase in college graduates is even more dramatic. Whereas the number of White college graduates has increased almost 2.5 times—from 6.1 to 14.4 percent, there was a twelvefold increase in the percentage of Black graduates—from 0.6 percent to 7.1 percent.

This increase in the number of Black college graduates and those found in professional occupations is a definite achievement, but only serves to underscore the plight of the vast majority of Black people in Mississippi—the group that is being widely called the "underclass" (e.g., Auletta, 1982; Cottingham, 1982; King, 1967). The most disturbing summary statistic and a compelling reminder of the Civil Rights movement's unrealized goal of racial equality, is the fact that in Mississippi in 1980 39.1 percent of all Black families (as compared to 10.1 percent for Whites) lived beneath the poverty line, defined by the Census Bureau as an income of $7,412 for a family of four.

In discussing politics, Katznelson and Kesselman (1979) suggest that we must distinguish between "procedural democracy" and "substantive democracy." The former focuses on the democratization of *political process*—whether Blacks can register, vote or run for office—while the latter stresses the democratization of *the resulting outcomes.* Given the vastly increased numbers of Black people who now participate in electoral politics in Mississippi and the South since the Civil Rights gains of the 1960s, and given the persistence of fundamental problems such as poverty, we must

carefully consider whether the gains were more symbolic or procedural than substantive—vitally necessary in the immediate period,
but quite insufficient for addressing all the real causes of what ailed
the Black community, and which exist for the broader society.

It is clear that the relationship between Black people and White
people in Mississippi, the South, and the United States will be
shaped by the deepening concern of larger numbers of people with
issues of increasing wealth and increasing poverty—and their coexistence—and the seeming failure of electoral politics to provide
effective solutions. Given the tenor of recent writings and discussions, it is also clear that this concern will have a new intensity and
the added insight of decades of struggle that exceeds the terms of its
previous treatment on the Civil Rights agenda.

Future of Black-White Relations in Mississippi: A Scenario

What does the future hold for Black-White relations conflict in
Mississippi, and by implication the South? The obvious trend in
terms of living standards and quality of life is one of persisting
economic inequality that has plagued Black people since slavery,
despite significant gains in political participation, access to public facilities, and even in the attitudes of many Whites. But rough
waters could lie ahead, especially because of the fundamental
impact that economic inequality and living standards have had in
the history of Black-White relations. I would argue that the future
of race relations hinges on the manner in which two dynamic realities unfold and interact:

(1) the intensity of Black peoples' struggles to resolve the persisting
     patterns of racial/class inequality, and to confront apparently deteri-
     orating conditions in almost all aspects of their lives; and the
     extent to which Black people continue to exhibit their historical
     openness to building working coalitions across racial lines to con-
     front problems of mutual self-interest to Blacks and Whites (and
     to other nationalities).

(2) the extent to which there is exhibited among Whites a conscious-
     ness of the fact that Whites have competing and conflicting self-
     interests—economic, especially—and a demonstrated willingness

to join with Black people to confront and solve problems of mutual self-interest.[8]

While these points may appear self-evident to many, they have often not guided social science, policy, or movement prognosis in this area. Let me discuss three likely arenas of turbulent times and conflict in Black-White relations and a case that manifests many of the prevailing difficulties and trends—higher education, politics and political power, economic well-being, and the case of Tunica County, Mississippi.

Higher Education

Education has generally been an important sector of life in the United States, arising to meet the needs of training and transforming new generations and of promoting social cohesion and continuity. Education has historically been viewed as a prime vehicle for upward mobility, and this has been especially true for Black people. It should not be surprising that higher education has been a key arena for Black-White conflict, and is likely to remain so. (See, for example, essays on Black student and community protest in Avorn, Crane, & Staff of the Columbia Daily Spectator, 1970; Becker, 1970; Foster & Long, 1970; Kahn, 1970; and Weinberg, 1977, 1981.)

First, historically Black institutions continue to educate a significant though declining number of Black students. In 1982, only 16.1 percent of all Black students attended such schools. In 1982, over 70 percent of Black students attended predominately White schools in the 17 (mainly southern) states covered by the Adams desegregation case, as compared with 1952 when no Black students attended such schools (Wilson & Melendez, 1985). But there is evidence that these colleges and universities—now fewer than 90 in number and enrolling only a small percentage of all U.S. students—continue to play a role far greater than their size or numbers indicate. In 1981, 84 traditionally Black institutions awarded about half the 40,000 degrees awarded to Blacks, while the other half were awarded by 673 nontraditionally Black institutions (Wilson, 1985, p. 18).

Second, Black colleges and universities are important forces and repositories in the broader cultural and institutional development of the Black community (campus organizations, leadership skills and opportunities, personal and preprofessional relationships, ideological orientation, etc.). Third, these institutions continue to serve as one of the main sources of employment for Black professionals, especially important given recent policies dismantling many of the programs that have provided jobs for the Black middle class. In 1976, for example, over 51 percent of Black men and 72 percent of Black women worked for some level of government (Freeman, 1976).

There is growing controversy over the future of public higher education in Mississippi, which consists of three historically Black institutions—Jackson State, Alcorn A & M, and Mississippi Valley State—and five historically white institutions—University of Mississippi, Mississippi State University, University of Southern Mississippi, Delta State, and Mississippi University of Women.

There are at least four areas of conflict. The first involves a possible decision to close one or more of the Black colleges, especially Mississippi Valley (Kanengiser, 1984). A new bill mandating closure was introduced in the first session of the State Legislature in 1986, and was the finding most anticipated in a recent study commissioned by the Board of Trustees (Foster, 1985). On January 15, 1986—the first national observance of Dr. Martin Luther King, Jr.'s birthday—the Board of Trustees voted to close Mississippi Valley State as one of six resolutions (Davis, 1986, p. 1). The second issue concerns the level at which Black institutions are funded, especially Jackson State, which is ideally situated in the state capitol and has been given the "urban university" designation by the Board. A third issue concerns the disproportionately negative impact of newly adopted entrance requirements on already declining enrollments at Black institutions. These requirements include higher scores on standardized tests, and changes in the number of units required in English, Math, and Science. These are special concerns for Blacks since poorer districts where Blacks are most often concentrated do not have sufficient funds to offer sections of the required courses, and where Black students are often counselled into vocational programs and away from college preparatory classes. There is also evidence that suggests racial, class, and cultural biases in standardized tests, which are not the most adequate predictors of subsequent academic performance for Black students

(Astin, 1982; Wigdor & Garner, 1982, especially articles by Skager and Gardner).

In general, the issue is one of equality of access and equality of results. Black people constitute over 35 percent of the state's population, and over 35 percent of the students enrolled in higher education (ranking it first in the United States in both categories). But the percentage of Black students at the three largest state universities averages under 10 percent, and even fewer graduate. To phrase the question as it is often heard, "If Black colleges are closed, underfunded, or otherwise undermined, what assurance do we have that Black people will have equal educational opportunities, given the dismal record of historically White institutions in Mississippi in recruiting, retaining, and graduating Black students?"

The federal courts are likely to be the scene of the next major installment in this continuing drama. Enforcement of higher education desegregation was halted by the Nixon administration from 1970-1973, until it was subsequently ordered to solicit desegregation plans in 1973. In 1974, Mississippi was referred to the Justice Department because of its lack of a plan (Ayres, 1984). A court case that parallels similar higher education desegregation cases in other states—*Ayers v. Allain et al. (1987)*—was filed in January 1975 and remains an active case on the docket of the federal court in Oxford, Mississippi. The *Jackson Advocate* (Tisdale, 1985) has recently decried the 11-year delay as "justice delayed, justice denied," stating that "no rulings have been made public despite rumors that a 17 million dollar settlement in favor of Black schools was handed down by Judge Keady three years ago." It charged that "the College Board . . . continues to rush pell mell toward restricting courses at Black colleges and universities while targetting Mississippi Valley State University for extinction," contrary to Judge Keady's ruling. The case will be heard in April, 1987.

The legacy of racial discrimination and persisting inequalities will fuel Black-White conflict regarding higher education in the future. This is amply demonstrated in the December 1985 decision of (Black) federal judge U.W. Clemon in Alabama, which concluded, "the state of Alabama has indeed operated a dual system of higher education; that in certain aspects, the dual system yet exists, and that in other respects the 'root and branches' have not been destroyed" (for the complete text of the ruling, see Clemon, 1985).[9]

Electoral Politics

Despite impressive gains in the political arena—in voter registration, voter turnout, and the election of public officials—governmental units in Mississippi at no level reflect the democratic representation of Blacks commensurate with their 35 percent representation in the state's population, and this extends to the national and local levels of government as well (Bailey, 1980). This reality is almost certain to spur intensified drives for the full realization of Black political power in the electoral arena in the years ahead, a potential point of Black-White conflict.

The course of such developments, however, is not obvious. The mass protest politics of the 1960s have not only been replaced by legal and electoral tactics, but these methods are often disparaged as being outmoded and unworthy of consideration. But it is very likely that conditions in Mississippi will lead again to the reemergence of the politics of social movements.

As we have discussed elsewhere (McWorter, Gills, & Bailey, 1987), Harold Washington's election as Mayor of Chicago was a very important event, with implications far beyond that city. Most important,

> it was a case of successful political protest rather than merely conventional institutional political behavior. The Washington campaign became a crusade in the Black community, and there, its implications for the future has as much to do with the development of the Black liberation movement as it does with the routine organization of behavior within the established political system.

A social movement paradigm that "focuses on the social behavior of an aggregate of individuals mobilized outside of formal political institutions to use resources to make a change in the social situation" is the most productive approach to understanding the politics of Harold Washington's election and Jesse Jackson's run for the presidency.

Only by using this approach can we explain the significant differences by which voter registration and voter turnout for Blacks in Chicago exceeded that of Whites in the general elections of 1982 and 1983, and the 1983 primary, overcoming an 8 percent deficit in registration and a 16.1 percent deficit in turnout in 1979. Alkalimat and Gills (1984) describe the dynamic of how local struggles over "a series of welfare and substantive issues targeted City Hall and the mayor's office . . . as the focal point to attack deteriorating conditions faced by Blacks, Latinos, and poor whites in Chicago"— issues including jobs, housing, education, health care, political representation, business development, and others. Comparing Mississippi with Chicago, the missing ingredient is certainly not "deteriorating conditions" but rather an effective network and organizational focus to mobilize and crystallize grassroots political activity into a social movement.

The relevance of the Chicago example to Mississippi is thus two-fold. First, it is in the context of social movements that Black political energies have been most effectively mobilized. Currently in Mississippi there are more registered White voters than Blacks, though in many political units this is not the case. But these potential voters have not been drawn to the polls, as illustrated in the 1984 campaign of State Senator Robert Clark to become the first Black member of Congress from Mississippi since the 1880s. After the 1982 election, the Second Congressional District was redrawn to create a more secure majority-Black district. The district had a Black population of 53.8 percent and a Black voting age population of 48 percent in 1982, when Clark lost to Webb Franklin by a vote of 73,588 to 71,335 (or 2,253 votes). The federal court reapportioned the district so that in 1984, its population is 58.3 percent Black, and its voting age population was 52.8 percent. In 1984, Clark again lost to Franklin by some 3,000 votes. (Blacks argued that this was not an effective majority since it has been shown that the age composition, education, income, and occupational status of Blacks tends to lower voter registration and turnout rates. See O'Hare, 1982.)

Despite serious irregularities, including the distribution of a bogus ballot that linked national and state Democratic candidates with the Republican candidate Webb Franklin, the key to Clark's defeat lies in voter turnout (Henderson, 1983). In Bolivar County, for example, with 15,560 Blacks of voting age in 1982, Clark polled only 7,058 votes as compared to 5,979 by Franklin. More generally, with 157,200 Blacks of voting age in 1982, Clark's 1984 vote totaled only 71,489, or 45.5 percent (or perhaps even lower considering Whites who voted for him). When one compares these figures with the 89.1 percent registration and the 73.0 percent turnout among Blacks in Chicago in 1983, and in more politically active periods of the Civil Rights movement, the validity of the social movement approach as a model for understanding Black political struggles and for mobilizing effective electoral challenges becomes clearest.

The second implication of the Chicago election relates to the capacity to field effective Black candidates independent of the established political parties. In Mississippi, this could very well take the form of an independent political party in Mississippi with strong Black involvement, if not Black-initiated or Black-led. One of the major concerns and criticisms of the Jesse Jackson campaign was that it was too focused on national "big-time" politics, and did not lead to the development of local organizations that could be sustained as bases for a new level of consciousness raising and long-term struggle (Peoples College, 1984).

This possibility of independent political involvement by Blacks has not been lost on astute observers. In one poll, almost 60 percent of those Blacks interviewed—a potential 6 million voters—said they would have supported Jesse Jackson as an independent, damaging to the Democrats who usually win with a slim margin provided by Black voters (Broder, 1985). The test is likely to come in the 1986 congressional race in Mississippi's second district. White Democrats appear ready to support White candidates against Black candidates, believing that Blacks cannot win after two unsuccessful tries by Robert Clark. A broad range of Black political activists feel strongly that the district should be represented by a Black member of Congress and vow to mount an independent campaign if necessary. This could very well be a dress rehearsal for considerable sentiment that the 1988 presidential bid by Jackson—or that of another Black candidate selected to be the standard bearer—should be mounted as an independent candidacy and then be used to build a more solid infrastructure for local political education and mobilization.[10]

The courts, again, will be a key arena for struggle in this area. In November 1985, there were more than 20 lawsuits challenging at-large elections in Mississippi cities, and more planned. Lawsuits have also been filed challenging the use of multimember districts for the election of circuit, chancery, and county court judges (Treyers 1985, November 7).

Economic Well-Being

With 39 percent of all Black families living under the poverty line in 1980, and with a median income of only 52.2 percent of that of White Mississippians, the economic conditions of Black Mississippians will remain on the agenda as a potential flash point for decades to come.

Another disturbing trend discussed nationally is also present in Mississippi. Called "the feminization of poverty," it should be seen more accurately as reflecting the intersection of class, race, and gender, or the "triple oppression" of Black women (Beal, 1975; Williams, 1980). In 1970, 32.7 percent of Black families in Mississippi living beneath the poverty level were female-headed households; and that figure has grown to 47.5 percent in 1980. Where only 27.9 percent of these families had children under 18 in 1970, the 1980 figure is 42.4 percent. (In comparison, only 21.2 percent of White families in poverty were female headed in 1980, up from 17.9 percent in 1970. The figures for White, female-headed, poverty-stricken families with children under 18 was 13.2 percent in 1970 and 16.9 percent in 1980.) Thus in Mississippi, as throughout the United States, Black women are bearing the brunt of the current crisis, and the increasing number of children in these poverty-stricken households has made this matter of greater concern. Unfortunately, much of the commentary and policy discussions place the blame on the victim—Black women—and not on poverty and associated problems.

Black people bear a disproportionate share of unemployment, poverty, low incomes, and low-status jobs. Because of this, there is still a substantial amount of discussion and some activity aimed at improving the economic conditions of Black people in Mississippi. There are still a number of Black community development corporations and projects. In addition, activity is aimed at developing the business enterprises of individual Blacks, similar to the Black Capitalism programs of Richard Nixon. But there is little evidence of a "poor people's campaign," of the kind envisioned by Dr. Martin Luther King, which rallied many Black Mississippians in 1968 when a large delegation took a mule train to protest poverty at the Washington Monument and "Resurrection City" (King, 1967).

While I have presented data on the impact of racial discrimination that disproportionately disadvantages Blacks, there is a basis for joint efforts between Blacks and Whites to improve their mutual economic well-being. Mississippi ranks fifty-first in per capita income. For Mississippi Whites, per capita income in 1980 was only $6,484, or 68 percent of the U.S. figure of $9,522. Further, employed Whites in most industries have the same relationship to the overall U.S. workforce that Black Mississippians have had to White Mississippians. In 1981, the $236 average weekly earnings of production workers in manufacturing industries in Mississippi is higher only than North Carolina, and it is only 74% of the U.S. average (U.S. Bureau of the Census, 1982). Mississippi, with 16.3 percent of its workforce unionized, joins other states in the southern region having the lowest percentage of union members: South Carolina, 7.8 percent; North Carolina, 9.6 percent; Texas, 11.4 percent; Florida, 11.7 percent; Georgia, 15.0 percent; and Arkansas, 16.0 percent. Thus while a focus on the poverty and discrimination plaguing Blacks will continue, attention to the common structural impediments to improving the economic lot of poor and working Black and White people is likely to build unity and joint action across racial lines where only antagonism and conflict once existed.

The Case of Tunica County, Mississippi

One recent case clearly illustrates how race relations are likely to unfold in Mississippi for the years to come, and reveals the confluence of race, class, nationality, and ideological forces discussed above. Tunica County, Mississippi, is situated at the northern tip of the Mississippi Delta, about 35 miles southwest of Memphis, Tennessee. Its population is almost 75 percent Black. The population of its largest significant town, Tunica, is only 35 percent Black.

The economic, political, and social conditions of Tunica County are reminiscent of an earlier period. In 1980, the average family income there was $6,014, lowest of all the counties in the United States, one-third the U.S. average. Almost 70 percent of the residents live below the poverty line (1979). The unemployment rate among Blacks was 25.1 percent in 1980, as compared to 4.2 percent for Whites. Though the percentage of the gross state product made up of farm products has declined from 30 percent in 1950 to 3.9 percent in 1984, Tunica County still depends on farming for

40 percent of its incomes. And while the Mississippi agricultural workforce has declined from 57.7 percent to 3.3 percent today, in Tunica County 30 percent of the people rely on agriculture and only 12 percent are in manufacturing.

There are only four White doctors and no general practitioner. Infant mortality among Blacks was 34.3 per thousand (three times the U.S. average), as compared to 15.6 for White residents. One-half of the housing occupied by Blacks lacks indoor plumbing, and only 35.7 percent of Black housing is owner occupied, as compared to 64 percent for Whites. Seventy percent of Black residents have an eighth-grade education or less, and only 14.4 percent are high-school graduates. Almost all White students attend an all-white academy, created in the 1960s to avoid desegregation. However, the superintendent and the majority of the public school board are White (and their children attend the academy).

Tunica has been the subject of recent national media attention. Reverend Jesse Jackson and Operation PUSH held several sessions of its national convention in this small Mississippi community in August 1985. "Sugar Ditch," an area inhabited by Blacks near the middle of town, was the subject of much criticism because of its open stream of raw sewage and dilapidated rental units without indoor plumbing, several of which were owned by city council members.

Recent efforts to attack these problems demonstrate how such efforts focus on mere manifestations and not causes, how the victims are often further victimized, and how further conflict is inevitable. To solve the immediate crisis of poor housing, Black residents are being moved into trailers in various county locations because no city land was made available by local landowners. This will dilute Black voting strength in the city, already the focus of a lawsuit alleging that at-large elections violate the rights of the Black community. It will also conveniently dilute a political rapport and militancy that has developed. Further, community residents decry their lack of input into local planning and the fact that the local Black community will not benefit from the millions of dollars being spent on housing construction (or from the rental of trailers).

The flurry of national press attention and the intervention of national civil rights groups has brought needed attention and some minimal immediate assistance. But, similar to many campaigns during the Civil Rights movements of the 1960s, it has also hampered the developing organizational capacity of local residents to set their own priorities and to mobilize and educate local citizens for the long haul of self-initiated and self-directed development. Since glaring poverty will remain long after "Sugar Ditch" has been razed and replaced by gleaming new trailers, the agenda of Black people in Tunica County will undoubtedly include the development of an independent political organization that can spearhead the election of more Blacks to the county government and building organizations which can undertake community economic and social development. Tunica County will thus reveal much about Black-White relations in the decades ahead.

Conclusion

The history and current reality of the Black community have been and will continue to be a sufficient basis for Black-White conflict in a society where full and genuine political, social, and economic democracy does not exist. The development of social movements among Blacks and the response this generates among Whites is a key lynchpin in determining future Black-White relations. On each of the levels of human reality presented in the discussion above—race, class, nationality, and ideology—there is in the 1980s a general persistence of barriers that hamper the attainment of full equality for the masses of Black people, fully evident in the United States and even more manifest in Mississippi and the South.

This persisting inequality and the inevitable struggle of Black people to resolve these difficulties will continue to generate Black-White conflict until fundamental changes in these conditions occur. Even with a reported shift of attitudes toward increased "racial" tolerance, "racial" or nationality conflicts are being exacerbated by structural impediments—job migration overseas, increased forced immigration from underdeveloped and plundered Third World nations, increasing unemployment due to the use of high technology, and other factors that will worsen income, employment, educational, and housing disparities—and result in an increase of racist intolerance among certain segments of the population. Anderson (1984) grasps the central complexity that continues to confuse many analysts who seek to understand the implications of the profound and important changes that have transpired in the New South since the 1950s (or the Civil War, for that matter):

> The fact that economic benefactors in the South have greater racial tolerance than did their predecessors is no reason to believe that they will relinquish their own material rewards for the sake of racial equality. So, although prejudice may not be as rampant in the South as it was in the past, we should not fool ourselves in thinking that the South is now on the verge of racial tranquility. (p. 261)

Grasping the nature of the changes required to address the distribution of "material rewards" and mobilizing sufficient resources to institutionalize them remain the pivotal problems. Dr. Martin Luther King in *Where Do We Go from Here: Chaos or Community?* (1967, p. 3-4) discussed a theme that was widespread in the movement and that has been increasingly echoed by academics and analysts. He described the Civil Rights movement as consisting of two stages: first, "a struggle to treat the Negro with a degree of decency, not of equality" which he says ended "with Selma and the Voting Rights Act" in 1965. The second phase sought "the realization of equality," and here lies the difficulty. The rights of individuals have been well recognized by the economic, political, social, and ideological status quo in the United States. Thus the achievement and upward mobility even of Blacks as individuals could be tolerated, eventually and not without considerable struggle, and encouraged and aided by numerous public and private policy interventions. Only rarely and grudgingly have group concerns—such as ending poverty for almost 40 percent of Mississippi's Black families—been the focus of serious "official" attention, and usually only under conditions of severe social turmoil.

For these reasons, issues of strategy and tactics have emerged rather sharply in recent years in considerations of the impact of the Civil Rights movement and the present status and future direction of the Black liberation struggle. Why was the Civil Rights movement not sufficient to address the fundamental needs of that vast number of people who needed changes in their economic status to enjoy the fruits of desegregation? The discussion has revolved around (1) a consideration of race and class, and their relative positions in causing the problems that face Black people; and (2) the alternatives of reformist and revolutionary strategies—"the ballot or the bullet," in the words of Malcom X (1965)—as the most appropriate and effective means to meet this complex condition. It is clear that this continuing theoretical discussion and resulting practical action will continue to shape the dynamics in Black-White relations in the future.

We have not yet fully grasped the modern-day legacy from the previous historical periods and practices of slavery, sharecropping, peonage, disenfranchisement, lynching, dislocations of migrations, exploitation, poverty, unemployment, racism, social degradation, and cultural oppression, nor the tremendous resilience and tenacity that has characterized and sustained the Black community through more than three centuries in the United States. But DuBois' (1898, p. 23) is as relevant a challenge as we approach the twenty-first century as it was just before the beginning of the twentieth: "It is these problems that we are today somewhat helplessly—not to say carelessly—facing, forgetful that they are living, growing social questions whose progeny will survive to curse the nation, unless we grapple with them manfully and intelligently."

NOTES

1. The very use of the terms "race," "race relations," and "racial conflict" have important implications, a discussion of which would constitute another paper. The issues revolve around the definition of "race" and the relationship of race to other concepts describing social realities, notably "nationality" or (ethnicity) and "class." This note must suffice as a reminder of the need for much discussion in lieu of using quotation marks each time "race" appears in the chapter. For an insightful discussion see Fields, 1982; see also George, 1984; Geshwender, 1978; Jordan, 1968; Kuper, 1975; Willhelm, 1983; and Wilson, 1978. The analysis in this chapter is presented essentially along the lines that "race" is widely used precisely because it is one empirical category by which we can appropriate concrete social relations that embody a variety of other equally important relationships, especially class and nationality.

2. The Myrdal study is particularly intriguing because of the number of leading Black intellectuals who contributed a voluminous body of research memoranda (pp. llv-lvi) for Myrdal's use; almost all of it, with the notable exception of Bunche (1936) is still largely unpublished. But it is more immediately interesting because of a current controversy raging around the criticism by Black scholars of a multiyear study of the status of Black Americans recently launched by the

National Research Council and funded by major foundations.

3. On the first point, Ralph Ellison (1953) queried pointedly:

> But can a people (its faith in an idealized American Creed notwithstanding) live and develop for over three hundred years simply by *reacting*? Are American Negroes simply the creation of white men, or have they at least helped to create themselves out of what they found around them? (p. 301)

Ellison goes on to argue that Black people created a culture "of great value, of richness" that would "help create a more human America."

On the second point, the noted Black sociologist Oliver C. Cox in his (1948) classic *Caste, Class, and Race* characterized the book as "the mystical approach to the study of race relations." In a decidedly caustic critique, he chastised Myrdal for developing a theory of race relations without looking "to the economic policies of the ruling class and not to mere abstract depravity among poor whites" (pp. 524-525). He castigated Myrdal for failing to pursue his own finding that, quoting Myrdal, "discrimination against Negroes is . . . rooted in this tradition of economic exploitation."

4. Using the paradigm, the fuller version of this chapter includes a detailed historical treatment of the Black Experience and Black-White conflict in the South, with a special emphasis on Mississippi. Useful historical overviews can be found in Bailey, 1986; Loewen and Sallis, 1982; McLemore, 1973; and Sansing, 1981. For a discussion of several aspects of race and demography, see the cited volumes of the U.S. census for population data, and Bailey, 1986 (especially articles by Alkalimat, Hill, & Bailey on census undercount); Blalock, 1957; Frazier, 1957a, pp. 187-190; Kousser, 1974; and Semyanov and Scott, 1983, p. 242. Economic life is treated in Bailey, 1971; Bruchey, 1967; Freeman, 1976; Ofari, 1970; Ransom & Sutch, 1977; Reich, 1981; Salamon, 1976; Scarborough, 1973; and Sutch & Ransom, 1978. Considerations of nationality— culture and social institutions—are in the following: Alkalimat and Associates, 1984, especially chapters 5 and 9; Ferris, 1983; Herskovits, 1941; Thompson, 1983; and Turner, 1949. The blossoming of Afro-American nationality in the rural period is discussed in Bullock, 1971; DuBois, 1935, p. 447; Harrison, 1977; Holtzclaw, 1984; King, 1967; McAdam, 1982; Myrdal, 1942; Wharton, 1947, p. 259; Wilson, 1947; and Woods, 1986; all support the contention that these were important institutional resources. Ideological matters—both the development of racism and ideas about "freedom" and "liberation"—are discussed in Bunche, 1936; DuBois, 1935; Fields, 1982; Frazier, 1955; Fredrickson, 1971; Sydnor, 1933; and Wharton, 1941. The general context and development of the various "liberation ideologies" among Blacks is treated in Alkalimat and Associates, 1984.

5. The importance and implications of historical periodization for the study of the Black experience has not yet been fully elaborated. Alkalimat and Associates (1984) is the best discussion available. Harris (1982, 1985) is the most explicit alternative proposal. One might compare the divergent conceptions of historical periods found in Alkalimat and Associates (1984) and Karenga (1982). Both Wilson (1978) and Karenga (1982) fail to give adequate attention to the

period of rural life in their overviews of the Afro-American experience.

6. The Census Bureau actually reported a Black population of 49.3 percent of Mississippi's total population in 1940. However, there is documented evidence of a considerable undercount. For 1940, the undercount of Black males is placed at 15 percent; and this figure when combined with an undercount of Black women and youth would put the Black population over 50 percent. See Bailey, 1980, especially the articles by Gerald McWorter, Robert Hill, Henry Kirksey, and Ronald Bailey.

7. Many of the recent data reported in this chapter have been drawn from state and federal government sources and usefully reported in a series of special supplements and articles appearing in the Jackson *Clarion-Ledger*. See, for example, "Freedom Summer: A Generation Later," July 1, 1984; "The Fight to Vote: 20 Years After the Voting Rights Act," week of November 1, 1985; "The State We're In," week of December 7, 1985; and special reports on the twentieth anniversaries of the admission of James Meredith to the University of Mississippi (September 1982) and thirtieth anniversary of the murder of Emmett Till, a Black youth visiting the state from Chicago (July 1985). Peden (1983) contains useful statistical data.

8. This view regarding the simultaneous relationship of building Black unity while building Black-White coalitions at the same time has long been discussed, especially among Black intellectuals, and reveals itself in the practice of many Black organizations. See, for example, the discussion of the Reconstruction, the Depression, and organizations like the Negro American Labor Council and the National Negro Labor Council in Foner (1974); "The Power of Negro Action" in Robeson (1958); and "Where are We Going" in King (1967).

9. A similar argument can be made for secondary education as an arena of racial conflict. Over the past year, significant protests involving the public schools have occurred in Indianola, Hattiesburg, Wier, Canton, Oxford, Senatobia and other communities. The most significant was a 31 day boycott of schools and businesses in Indianola (Sunflower County), a school district with a 95 percent Black student body. The protest led to a group of White business leaders spending almost $100,000 to buy out the contract of a White school superintendent installed over the objections of the Black community and two Black representatives on a majority White school board. A Black school superintendent has since been appointed.

10. Since this article was prepared, a newcomer to electoral politics—former Assistant Attorney General Mike Espy of Yazoo City—was elected in November 1986 as the first Black congressman from Mississippi since the 1880s. In the Democratic primary, Espy narrowly defeated two sons of the Mississippi White establishment—Pete Johnson and Hiram Eastland—by 84 votes of the near 60,000 cast. In the general election, Espy defeated conservative incumbent Webb Franklin with 51.7 percent of the total vote. Despite his victory, however, the issues raised in the article—mobilizing the Black community, coalition building, and independent politics—are still relevant. The Democratic Party was generally lukewarm to Espy's campaign and there was no broad base of support among White voters. Details of this election will be reported in a forthcoming documentary history produced by the author and the Afro-American Studies Program at the University of Mississippi.

References

Alkalimat, A. & Associates. (1984). *Introduction to Afro-American Studies: A Peoples College primer.* Chicago: 21st Century Books and Publications (P. O. Box 803351, Chicago, IL 60680).

Alkalimat, A., & Gills, D. (1984). Black power vs. racism: Harold Washington becomes mayor. In R. Bush (Ed.), *The new Black vote* (pp. 55-159). San Francisco: Synthesis Publications.

Anderson, M. L. (1984). Race beliefs in the new South: From caste to class. In M. Black & J. S. Reed (Eds.), *Perspectives on the American South* (Vol. 2, pp. 251-264). Chapel Hill: University of North Carolina Press.

Astin, A. (1982). *Minorities in higher education.* San Francisco: Jossey-Bass.

Auletta, K. (1982). *The underclass.* New York: Random House.

Avorn, J. L., Crane, A., & Staff of the Columbia Daily Spectator. (1970). *Up against the ivy wall: A history of the Columbia crisis.* New York: Atheneum.

Ayers, Jake et al. vs. William Allain (current governor of Mississippi) et al. (1987). Senior College Desegregation Suit, GC-75-9-NB. U.S. District Court, Northern District of Mississippi (Greenville Division).

Ayres, Q. W. (1984). Racial desegregation in higher education. In C. Bullock & C. Lamb (Eds.), *Implementation of civil rights policy* (pp. 118-147). Wadsworth, CA: Brooks/Cole.

Bailey, R. W. (Ed.). (1971). *Black business enterprise.* New York: Basic Books.

Bailey, R. W. (1980). *Black people and the 1980 census: Proceedings from a conference on the population undercount.* Chicago: Chicago Center for Afro-American Studies.

Bailey, R. W. (Ed.) (1986). *The experience of Black Mississippians: 1986 research conference proceedings.* University of Mississippi, Afro-American Studies Program.

Barrett, R. H. (1965). *Integration at Ole Miss.* Chicago: Quadrangle Books.

Beal, F. (1975). Slave of a slave no more. *Black Scholar, 6,* 3-10.

Becker, H. S. (Ed.). (1970). *Campus power struggle.* Hawthorne, NY: Aldine.

Belfrage, S. (1965). *Freedom summer.* Greenwich, CT: Fawcett/Crest.

Blalock, H. M. (1957). Percent non-White and discrimination in the South. *American Sociological Review, 22,* 677-682.

Blassingame, J. W. (Ed.). (1971). *New perspectives on Black studies.* Urbana: University of Illinois Press.

Broder, D. (1985, September 12). As the Democrats fiddle, Black discontent rises. *International Herald-Tribune.*

Bruchey, S. (1967). *Cotton and the American economy.* New York: Harcourt Brace Jovanovich.

Bullock, H. A. (1971). The Black colleges and the new awareness. *Daedalus, 100,* 573-602.

Bunche, R. (1936). *A world view of race.* New York: Kennikat Press.

Carson, C. (1981). *In struggle: SNCC and the Black awakening of the 1960s.* Cambridge: Harvard University Press.

Carter, H. (1965). *Mississippi Black paper* (57 notarized statements from legal cases initiated by the COFO). New York: Random House.

Clemon, U.W. (1985, December). A special report on the Alabama desegregation suit ruling (complete text of Clemon's order). *Advertiser* (Montgomery,
AL), p. 11A.

Cottingham, C. (1982) *Race, poverty and the urban underclass.* New York: Lex-
ington Books.

Cox, O. C. (1948). *Caste, class, and race: A study in social dynamics.* Garden
City, NY: Doubleday.

Cruse, H. (1967). *Crisis of the Negro intellectual.* New York: William Morrow.

Davis,D. (1986, January). Budget woes are cited in panel's proposal. *Clarion-
Ledger,* p. 1.

Drake, S. C. (1969). *Black studies: Toward an intellectual framework.* Unpublished speech, Brooklyn College, New York.

DuBois, W.E.B. (1898, January). The study of Negro problems. *Annals of the
American Academy of Political and Social Science,* pp. 1-23.

DuBois, W.E.B. (1935). *Black reconstruction.* New York: Atheneum.

DuBois, W.E.B. (1940). *The souls of Black folk.* Greenwich: Fawcett. (Original
work published 1903)

Ellison, R. (1953). An American Dilemma: A review. In R. Ellison, *Shadow and
act* (pp. 290-302). New York: Signet Books.

Evers, M., & Peters, W. (1967). *For us, the living.* Garden City, NY: Doubleday.

Ferris, W. (Ed.). (1983). *Afro-American folk art and crafts.* Boston: G. K. Hall.

Fields, B. (1982). Ideology and race in American history. In J. Kousser & J.
McPherson (Eds.), *Region, race and reconstruction: Essays in honor of
C. Vann Woodward* (pp. 143-177). New York: Oxford University Press.

Foner, P. S. (1974). *Organized labor and the Black worker 1619-1973.* New
York: Praeger.

Ford, N. A. (1973). *Black studies—threat or challenge.* Port Washington: Kennikat Press.

Foster, J. D. (1985). *Restructuring higher education: Choice and analysis for
Mississippi.* Jackson, MS: Board of Trustees (Higher Education).

Foster, J., & Long, D. (Eds.). (1970). *Protest! Student activism in America.* New
York: William Morrow.

Frazier, E. F. (1955). Racial problems in world society. In F. G. Edwards,
E. Franklin Frazier on race relations (pp. 103-116). Chicago: University of
Chicago Press.

Frazier, E. F. (1957a). *The Negro in the United States.* New York: Macmillan.

Frazier, E. F. (1957b). *Race and culture contacts in the modern world.* Boston:
Beacon Press.

Fredrickson, G. M. (1977). *The Black image in the White mind.* New York:
Harper & Row. (Original work published 1971)

Fredrickson, G. M. (1981). *White supremacy: A comparative study in American
and South African history.* New York: Oxford University Press.

Freeman, R. (1976). *The Black elite: The new market for highly qualified Black
Americans.* New York: McGraw-Hill.

Funchess, C. (1984). *The decline in Black-owned land in Mississippi.* Unpublished seminar paper, University of Mississippi.

George, H. (1984). *American race relations theory—a review of four models.*
Lanham, MD: University Press of America.

Geshwender, J. (1978). *Racial stratification in America.* DuBuque: William C. Brown.

Greenberg, P. (1969). *The devil has slippery shoes.* London: Macmillan.

Harris, A. L. (1936). *The Negro as capitalist.* Philadelphia: American Academy of Political and Social Science.

Harris, R. L. (1982). The coming of age of Afro-American historiography. *Journal of Negro History, 67,* 107-121.

Harris, R. L. (1985). *Teaching Afro-American history.* Washington, DC: American Historical Association.

Harrison, A. (1977). *A history of the most worshipful Stringer Grand Lodge: Our history is our challenge.* Jackson: Stringer Grand Lodge.

Henderson, G. G. (1983). *An analysis of voting behavior in elections for the Mississippi Second Congressional District in 1982.* Unpublished manuscript.

Herskovits, M. J. (1941). *The myth of the Negro past.* Boston: Beacon Press.

Holt, L. (1965). *The summer that didn't end.* New York: William Morrow.

Holtzclaw, R. F. (1984). *Black magnolias: A brief history of the Afro-Mississippian, 1865-1980.* Shaker Heights, OH: Keeble Press.

Joint Center for Political Studies. (1985). *1985 roster of Black elected officials.* Washington, DC: Author.

Jordan, W. (1968). *White over Black: American attitudes toward the Negro, 1550-1812.* Chapel Hill: University of North Carolina Press.

Kahn, R. (1970). *The battle for Morningside Heights: Why students rebel.* New York: William Morrow.

Kanengiser, A. (1984, July). Historically Black universities feel threatened. *Clarion-Ledger/Jackson Daily News,* p. 11H.

Karenga, M. R. (1982). *Introduction to Black Studies.* Los Angeles: Kawaida Publications.

Karnig, A. D., & Welch, S. (1980). *Black representation and urban policy.* Chicago: University of Chicago Press.

Katznelson, I., & Kesselman, M. (1979). *The politics of power: A critical introduction to American government.* New York: Harcourt Brace Jovanovich.

King, M. L. (1967). *Where do we go from here: Chaos or community?* Boston: Beacon Press.

Kousser, J. M. (1974). *The shaping of southern politics suffrage restriction and the establishment of the one-party South, 1880-1910.* New Haven, CT: Yale University Press.

Kuhn, T. (1964). *The structure of scientific revolutions.* Chicago: University of Chicago Press.

Kuper, L. (Ed.). (1975). *Race, science and society.* Paris: UNESCO Press.

Lawson, S. F. (1976). *Black ballots: Voting rights in the South, 1944-1969.* New York: Columbia University Press.

Lewinson, P. (1932). *Race, class and party: A history of Negro suffrage and White politics in the South.* New York: Grosset & Dunlap.

Loewen, J., & Sallis, C. (1982). *Mississippi: Conflict and change.* New York: Pantheon.

Lord, W. (1965). *The past that wouldn't die.* New York: Harper & Row.

Lynd, R. S. (1944). Review of Gunnar Myrdal's American Dilemma. *Saturday Review of Literature, 27,* 5-6.

Malcolm X. (1965). *Malcom X speaks: Selected speeches and statements.* New York: Merit Publishers.

McAdam, D. (1982). *Political process and the development of Black insurgency 1930-1970.* Chicago: University of Chicago Press.

McLemore, R. A. (Ed.). (1973) *A history of Mississippi* (Vols. 1-2). Jackson: University and College Press of Mississippi.

McMillen, N. (1971). *The White citizens council.* Urbana: University of Illinois Press.

McMillen, N. R. (1973). Development of civil rights, 1956-1970. In R. A. McLemore (Ed.), *A history of Mississippi* (pp. 154-176). Jackson: University and College Press of Mississippi.

McWorter, F., Gills, D., & Bailey, R. (1987). Black politics as social movement: Leadership in the campaign to elect Washington mayor of Chicago. In S. Gove & L. Masotti (Eds.), *Chicago politics in transition.* Urbana: University of Illinois Press.

Merton, R. (1957). *Social theory and social structure.* New York: Free Press.

Miller, K. S., & Dreger, R. (Eds.). (1973). *Comparative studies of Blacks and Whites in the United States.* New York: Seminar Press.

Mississippi Power and Light Company. (1983). *Mississippi statistical summary of population, 1800-1980.* Jackson: Author.

Moody, A. (1968). *Coming of age in Mississippi.* New York: Dial Press.

Myrdal, G. (1942). *An American dilemma.* New York: Harper & Row.

Newby, I. A. (Ed.). (1968). *The development of segregationist thought.* Homewood, IL: Dorsey Press.

O'Hare, W. (1982). *Racial Differences in Socioeconomic Status and Political Participation in the 2nd Congressional District of Mississippi.* Unpublished manuscript.

Orfield, G. (1982). *Desegregation of Black and Hispanic students from 1968-1980.* Washington, DC: Joint Center for Political Studies.

Peden, G. T. (1983). *1983 Mississippi statistical abstract.* Starkville: Mississippi State University.

Peoples College. (1984). Black people and presidential politics. *In Peoples College, 1984 Black Liberation Month news.* Chicago: Peoples College.

Peterson, W. (1969). *Population.* London: Macmillan.

Raines, H. (1977). *My soul is rested.* New York: Penguin.

Ransom, R., & Sutch, R. (1977). *One kind of freedom: The economic consequences of emancipation.* Cambridge: Cambridge University Press.

Reich, M. (1981). *Racial inequality: A political-economic analysis.* Princeton, NJ: Princeton University Press.

Robeson, P. (1958). *Here I stand.* Boston: Beacon Press.

Robinson, A., Foster, C. C., & Ogilvie, D. (Eds.). (1969). *Black studies in the university.* New Haven: Yale University Press.

Salamon, L. M. (1976). *Land and minority enterprises: The crisis and the opportunity.* Washington, DC: Department of Commerce

Sansing, D. G. (1981). *Mississippi: Its people and culture.* Minneapolis, T. S. Denison & Company.

Scarborough, W. K. (1973). Heartland of the cotton kingdom. In R. McLemore,

A history of Mississippi (pp. 310-351). Jackson: University and College Press of Mississippi.

Scher, R., & Button, J. (1984). Voting Rights Act: Implementation and impact. In C. Bullock & C. Lamb (Eds.), *Implementation of civil rights policy* (pp. 20-54). Belmont, CA: Brooks/Cole.

Semyanov, M., Scott, R. (1983). Percent Black, community characteristics and race-linked occupational differences in the rural South. *Rural Sociology, 48*(2), 240-252.

Silver, J. (1963). *Mississippi: The closed society.* New York: Harcourt Brace Jovanovich.

Sitkoff, H. (1981). *The struggle for Black equality 1954-1980.* New York: Hill & Wang.

Stringfellow, E. (1985, December 10). Blacks: In ourselves the future lies. *Clarion-Ledger,* p. 1.

Sutch, R., & Ransom, R. (1978). Sharecropping: Market response or mechanism of race control? In D. G. Sansing, *What was freedom's price?* (pp. 51-70). Jackson: University Press of Mississippi.

Sydnor, C. S. (1933). *Slavery in Mississippi.* Gloucester, MA: Peter Smith.

Thompson, R. F. (1983). *Flash of the spirit.* New York: Vintage.

Tisdale, C. (1985, December 19-25). Tisdale's topics. *Jackson Advocate,* p. 1.

Treyens, C. (1985, November 3) Landmark voting act sets tone for generation. *Clarion-Ledger/Jackson Daily News,* p. 1.

Treyens, C. (1985, November 7). Blacks see lawsuits as springboards. *Clarion-Ledger,* p. 1.

Turner, L. (1949). *Africanisms in the Gullah dialect.* Chicago: University of Chicago Press.

U.S. Bureau of the Census. (1918) *Negro population, 1790-1915.* Washington, DC: Department of Commerce.

U.S. Bureau of the Census. (1935). *The Negro in the United States, 1920-1932.* Washington, DC: Department of Commerce.

U.S. Bureau of the Census. (1975). *Historical statistics of the United States.* Washington, DC: Department of Commerce.

U.S. Bureau of the Census. (1979). *The social and economic status of the Black population in the U.S.* Washington, DC: Department of Commerce.

U.S. Commission on Civil Rights. (1965a). *Hearings in Jackson, Mississippi—February 16-20, 1965: Voting* (Vol. 1) and *Administration of Justice* (Vol. 2). Washington, DC: Government Printing Office.

U.S. Commission on Civil Rights. (1965b). *Voting in Mississippi.* Washington, DC: Government Printing Office.

Walton, H. (1972). *Black political parties: A historical and political analysis.* New York: Free Press.

Weinberg, M. (1977). *Minority students: A research appraisal.* Washington, DC: Government Printing Office.

Weinberg, M. (1981). *The education of poor and minority children: A world bibliography* (Vols. 1-2). Westport, CT: Greenwood.

Wharton, V. L. (1941). The race issue in the overthrow of reconstruction in Mississippi. *Phylon,* 362-378.

Wharton, V. L. (1965). *The Negro in Mississippi*. New York: Harper & Row. (Original work published 1947)

Whitehead, D. (1970). *Attack on terror: The FBI against the Ku Klux Klan in Mississippi*. New York: Funk & Wagnalls.

Wigdor, A. K., & Garner, W. R. (Eds.). (1982). *Ability testing: Uses, consequences, and controversies* (Vols. 1-2). Washington, DC: National Academy Press.

Willhelm, S. M. (1983). *Black in a White America*. Cambridge, MA: Schenkman.

Williams, L. (1980). Census data in research, teaching, and studying the conditions of Black women. In R. W. Bailey (Ed.), *Black people and the 1980 census: Proceedings from a conference on the population undercount* (p. 601). Chicago: Chicago Center for Afro-American Studies.

Willie, C. V. (1983). *Race, ethnicity, and socioeconomic status: A theoretical analysis of their interrelationship*. Bayside, NY: General Hall.

Wilson, C. H., Sr. (1947). *Education for Negroes in Mississippi since 1910*. Newton, MA: Crofton Publishing Corporation.

Wilson, R., & Melendez, S. E. (1985). *Minorities in higher education*. Washington, DC: American Council on Education.

Wilson, W. J. (1978). *The declining significance of race*. Chicago: University of Chicago Press.

Wirt, F. M. (1970). *Politics of southern equality: Law and social change in a Mississippi county (Panola)*. Chicago: Aldine.

Woods, W. (1986). White missionary goals and Black power responses in Black education in Mississippi, 1862-1869. In R. W. Bailey (Ed.), *The experience of Black Mississippians: 1985 Research Conference Proceedings*. University of Mississippi, Afro-American Studies Program.

Woodward, C. V. (1966). *The strange career of Jim Crow*. New York: Oxford University Press.

Work, M. (1938). *Negro year book, 1937-1938*. Tuskagee, AL: Tuskagee Institute.

YTPTCOI [Year To Pull The Covers Off Imperialism project]. (1974). Imperialism and the Black media. *Black Scholar, 6*, 48-57.

Chapter Summary

Angela B. Ginorio presents an analysis of Puerto Rican ethnic relations concerning conflict both within Puerto Rican society and between Puerto Ricans and other groups such as Cubans, Black Americans, and Puerto Ricans living in New York City. Ginorio's chapter opens with a brief review of the post-Columbian history of Puerto Rico, which provides a basis for understanding of the Puerto Rican culture of today—a mixture of the descendents of Tainos, Spaniards, West Africans, and a number of nineteenth-century immigrant groups. The author emphasizes the importance of one's political preference for Puerto Rican autonomy, statehood, or independence in the formation of one's identity and attitudes toward others. The relationship of political status preference to outgroup attitudes and other issues central to this chapter are explored primarily through the use of social distance measures, with attention given to the variables of race, religion, socioeconomic status, place of birth, and language dominance.

Ginorio also discusses a number of ethnic identity issues such as the ethnic status of Puerto Ricans living in New York City from the perspective of those living in Puerto Rico. The Puerto Ricans in New York, especially those who no longer speak Spanish and who are more acculturated are often said to be non-Puerto Ricans. Unlike the Puerto Ricans of Puerto Rico, the Puerto Ricans of New York were found to have lowest social distance scores for other minorities of color rather than for persons of culturally similar ethnic groups. Such differences in social distance data and ethnic identity between these two groups are viewed in light of the behavior necessary for Puerto Ricans in New York to survive in a situation of scarce resources and minority status.

The author also points out differences in the system of categorization of racial type in these two settings and the implications of these differences for ethnic identity and social distance attitude formation. Ginorio proposes that racial definitions in the U.S. mainland are discrete whereas in Puerto Rico they are more of a continuum. This, she suggests, is due to the large range of racial phenotypes in Puerto Rico, which results in a system that considers nonracial factors, such as socioeconomic status, in racial labeling.

The relationships between Puerto Ricans and Blacks, and Puerto Ricans and Chicanos are explored, and an example is given of how this relationship has manifested itself in terms of education in New York City.

Finally, Ginorio discusses the situation of Puerto Ricans who return to Puerto Rico having lived on the mainland, concentrating on value differences regarding racial definitions, gender roles, and cultural themes.

—Susan Goldstein

8

Puerto Rican Ethnicity and Conflict

ANGELA B. GINORIO

Historical Overview

In 1493 Christopher Columbus arrived at the island called Borinquen by the native Tainos. On November 8, 1511—18 years later—Ferdinand II and his daughter Juana, king and queen of Castille, gave the island of San Juan its great seal with a lamb as the central symbol. Although devoid of the fabulous riches of Peru and Mexico, San Juan was noted for its strategic location in the Caribbean as well as for a natural harbor of such quality that the city at its entrance was called Puerto Rico (rich port). The development of the island in the sixteenth century centered mostly on beginning the fortification of the capital city and establishing the governmental structures considered basic by the Spanish Crown.

As the first major land mass encountered when coming from Europe, the island—which eventually came to be known as Puerto Rico and its main city as San Juan—was considered the frontline of defense for the Spanish empire in the Americas, with elaborate fortifications built around the capital city. Three forts and the walls that protected San Juan still stand as mute evidence of the architectural genius of the Spaniards and of the military past of the island. Puerto Rico became a prime target for attacks by ships bent on conquest—some openly representing their countries of origin, as with the English and Dutch attacks of 1595, 1598, and 1625; and some attacking for commercial adventurism, as with the pirate attacks against ships arriving to or leaving the island during the 1600s and the town of San Germán from 1528-38. During the seventeenth century Puerto Rico suffered eight attacks, all of which were eventually repelled by the Spanish garrison or defeated by epidemics. The British attack of 1797 ended this phase of Puerto Rican history.

Released from their immediate concerns with defense (and having exhausted what little mineral wealth was exploitable at the time), attention was turned to agriculture and commerce. The lack of interest of the Spanish government in the welfare of its overseas colonies assured that the development of the island would be minimal, as is evident from the fact that only 21 percent of Puerto Rico's arable land was in cultivation by 1898 (Lewis, 1963). The ferment of revolution was everywhere in the Americas by the eighteenth century, and Spain's main concern was the retention of power over its possessions, including Cuba and Puerto Rico.

The nineteenth century brought increased concerns about internal freedom and the attainment of autonomy or independence from Spain. The issue of the island's relationship to Spain dominated the political life of the island. Many history books note the episodes of violence that occurred during this century. Three involved Spanish soldiers—the "Revolt of the Sergeants" in 1835 and 1838 and the "Mutiny of Artillery Men" in 1867. In 1868 the most noted armed revolt by creoles against the Spanish government in the island's history took place in the mountainous, coffee-producing region. A group of approximately 400 men took over the town of Lares and held it for two days. The revolt has come to be known as *El Grita de Lares* (the Cry at Lares). A smaller and even less successful attempt took place in the same region of the island in 1897, this time in the town of Yauco. The emancipation of slaves occurred in 1873 under pressure but without open conflict, although there had been disturbances two years before. In that same year there was a violent confrontation between conservatives and liberals that left three people dead (Bayrón-Toro, 1984). In 1887 the Spanish governor of the island openly persecuted autonomists (those advocating for administrative autonomy *within* the Spanish system), torturing and incarcerating many leaders and followers.

The next episode of military conflict did not involve a Puerto Rican rebellion. In one of the actions of the Hispanic American War, American troops entered the island through the southern town of Guanica on July 25, 1898, and gained control of the whole island in 19 days without much opposition from Puerto Ricans (Ribes Tovar, 1973). The Spanish government officially surrendered three months later on October 18, 1898. Puerto Ricans found themselves freed of 405 years of Spanish domination but still not in control of their government.

Ethnic Identity

The personal version of the culture, and the cultural integrity of the Puerto Rican society, have been the central concerns of Puerto Ricans since inhabitants started to claim for themselves a sense of identity separate from Spain. It is estimated that 30,000 Tainos inhabited the island when the Spaniards arrived (Wagenheim, 1975). The Tainos' initial welcome of the Spaniards turned to resistance once it became clear that the Spaniards would take over the land and force them into labor. Outbreaks of violence against the Spaniards occurred sporadically in the early years of colonization until the Tainos resistance was broken down. In the census of 1530 only 1,148 full-blooded Tainos were counted. The Tainos early demise was brought about as much by hard labor as by diseases for which they had no resistance.

Slaves from West Africa had been brought into the island since 1511, adding the third significant component of the Puerto Rican population. Until 1815 only Spaniards and slaves entered the island, thus forming the bulk of the Puerto Rican population. From 1815, when Spain declared Puerto Rico a haven of refuge, to 1898 the island has received a considerable number of migrants from France, Corsica, Ireland, and Germany. Other immigrants came from American lands fleeing the changes in government or jurisdiction, such as loyalists fleeing the independence struggles in Latin America and French Catholics fleeing the Protestant United States government after the 1803 Louisiana Purchase. The population of the island increased from 155,000 in 1815 to almost 900,000 by 1898, in that process shifting the racial balance from Black to White; by 1830 Whites were a majority.

The mixing of the three groups occurred from the beginning; as early as 1505 warnings against the forced concubinage of Indian women were issued, and in 1539 edicts were sent ordering all Spanish males to formalize their unions with Indian women or loose their claims to the lands granted them (Steiner, 1974). Spaniards intermarried with both Tainos and Africans to such a degree that the distinctiveness of the three ethnic groups was blurred. The result is a multicolored society with no clear boundaries between the ethnoracial groups.

At the time Puerto Rico became a possession of the United States the descendants of the Tainos, Spaniards, West Africans, and the melange of immigrants that arrived in the nineteenth century had given form to the Puerto Rican culture and to an unmistakable Puerto Rican identity. The moment that the inhabitants of Puerto Rico stopped thinking of themselves as Spaniards and identified as Puerto Ricans, the ethnic relations and conflicts in the island were dramatically redefined. Those who had been opponents—natives and foreign-born, masters and slaves—became allies in defining a relationship with Spain.

By the time the U.S. invasion summarily solved the issue of the relationship of the island to Spain, the basic postures about the possible relationship of the island to the metropolis had been defined: autonomy, independence, and integration into the central government. It was only a matter of time before parallel positions were developed in relation to the United States, underpinned by the same kinds of concerns: economic development, cultural integrity, and identity. By the elections in 1900 two parties were established that represented two of the proposed models for relating to the United States: integration into the central government (statehood), and autonomy. Independence supporters did not have a party to represent their interests until 1904.

Each of these positions is still present today. The autonomist posture is supported by *estadolibristas*, those who believe that the present status of the island (*Estada Libre Asociado*, or Commonwealth) is a permanent solution to the island's political status. The integrationist posture is supported by *estadistas*, those who believe that becoming the fifty-first state of the Union is the ultimate outcome for the island. The separatist posture is supported by *independentistas*, those who believe that Puerto Rico should become an independent country. Each of these proposals claims to maintain Puerto Rico's integrity and identity and to promote the island's economic development—a claim challenged by proponents of the other positions.

Open Conflict

From the moment the Spaniards set foot on the island and met the native Tainos the history of Puerto Rico has been characterized by ethnic contact. Since the use of force is essential to the establishment and maintenance of a colony and of slavery, it can be deduced that a state of conflict existed between conquerors and natives, and once Africans were introduced, between slaves and masters. History records instances of open rebellion by slaves and Tainos; Spanish force overcame both (Diaz-Soler, 1953).

The history of open conflict in Puerto Rico is as long as its history of ethnic contact. As the brief historical outline presented above indicates, violent incidents have not been long lasting. During the Spanish regime, apart from the defensive encounters against invading forces from other countries—none of which resulted in significant ethnic contact since the longest occupation was less than six months—there were relatively few instances of open conflict.

What follows is a list of major incidents of open conflict not already mentioned:

- 1935, during a meeting of the Nationalist Party in Rio Piedras there is a confrontation between the police and the nationalists; four nationalists and one policeman die, 40 are injured. Shortly after, two nationalists assassinate the chief of the Puerto Rican police, Colonel Francis Riggs. They in turn are killed a few days later while in the police's custody.

- 1937, the Palm Sunday or Ponce Massacre takes place in which the police fire upon a demonstration by the Nationalist Party, killing 19 and injuring over 100 people.

- 1938, there is an assassination attempt on the American governor of the island; a police colonel is killed.

- 1950, an uprising in various towns in the island by followers of the Nationalist Party, the mountain town of Jayuya is taken for a few hours by the rebels; 25 dead, hundreds injured, more than 1,000 *nacionalistas* (members of the *Partido Nationalista*) jailed.

- 1950, two days after the uprising in Puerto Rico two *nacionalistas* attack Blair House, temporary residence of President Truman, killing one guard and injuring another; one nacionalista is killed, the other injured.

- 1954, four Puerto Rican Nationalists start shooting inside the U.S. Congress, injuring five congressmen.

- 1960s-70s, student protests at the University of Puerto Rico led by the Federation of Pro-Independence University Students (FUPI), where smoke and Molotov bombs are used. Four people are killed in two separate incidents: two policemen, one ROTC cadet, and a female *independentista* bystander. In Vieques and Culebra, islands used as targets by the Navy, continuous protests are led by Puerto Rican Independence party leaders, who are repeatedly jailed.

- 1970s-80s, bomb attacks in both Puerto Rico and the mainland against banks, corporation headquarters, Fraunces Tavern, and other symbols of capitalism. The National Front of Armed Liberation (FALN) and a group called *Los Macheteros* (the Machete Wielders) claim responsibility for these.

- 1978, two independence supporters are killed by the police while intending to blow up an electric tower in what was later acknowledged by the police to be an ambush.

- 1979 and 1985, attacks against personnel of the armed forces stationed in Puerto Rico; three Marines are killed and one Army recruiter injured.

With but one exception, all the instances of open conflict in Puerto Rico since 1898 have revolved around issues of political status and have involved supporters of the independence of the island. (The one exception was the takeover of the island by the U.S. troops during the Hispanic-American War.)

Each of these incidents can be subsumed as accurately under political conflict as under ethnic conflict. They are political because each deals with the political relationship between Puerto Rico and the metropolis—whether it be Puerto Rico and Spain or Puerto Rico and the United States. They are also ethnic conflict because many of the main arguments used to support one political position or the other are based on issues of cultural integrity and ethnic identity. These arguments center on the viability of a Puerto Rican identity under each one of the three statuses, as well as the survival of the cultural characteristics that identify the Puerto Rican society: the Spanish language; the centrality of the family; a sense of *personalismo* (emphasis on the individual rather than systems or institutions), *respeto* (respect), and *dignidad* (dignity) in all interactions; the Catholic flavor if not practice of the culture.

Formalized Political Conflict

Although the history of open conflict in Puerto Rico has been characterized by the limited scope of the incidents and the relatively small number of casualties, the history of formalized conflict through political parties has been a pervasive element of the daily life of all Puerto Ricans. Three political alternatives have been proposed for the destiny of Puerto Rico: autonomy, independence, and statehood. The political parties of Puerto Rico have served not only their traditional functions of obtaining power, they have also given a formal manifestation to these conflicting proposals (Bayrón-Toro, 1984). The position that the party holds regarding the political status of the island is the most fundamental difference among the parties (Ramos de Santiago, 1970). Throughout this century each of these proposals has been the basis for the organization of most political parties in Puerto Rico. In the most recent elections held in November of 1984, four political parties participated: *Partido Popular Democrático*—supporting the current status of Commonwealth; *Partido Independentista Puertorriqueño*—supporting independence; *Partido Nuevo Progresista* and *Partida de Renovación Puertorriqueña*—both supporting statehood.

Internalization of Political Conflict

The internalization of Puerto Rico's overriding concern with political status leads to the third form of conflict present among Puerto Ricans. This conflict is most evident in the prejudices expressed by Puerto Ricans about other ethnic groups. Among Puerto Ricans political status preferences are paramount in affecting the definitions of and attitudes toward outgroups, overriding other factors that have been reported in the social sciences literature, such as cultural similarity, religion, geographical proximity, and race (Bogardus, 1967).

In a 1972 study Ginorio, Luiggi, Olmo, Santos, Navas, and de Jesús administered a scale to 68 college students at the University of Puerto Rico in which 10 countries were used as stimuli and evaluated using paired comparisons. When analyzed according to the political party preference of the respondents, it was found that the countries with the most divergent evaluations were Puerto Rico, the United States, and Cuba. These divergences in evaluation corresponded to the political status preferences of the students; for example independentistas gave positive evaluations to Cuba and negative ones to the United States.

In a 1977 study using a modified version of the Bogardus Social Distance Scale, Jiménez-Santiago found that the greatest social distances reported by a sample of 279 University of Puerto Rico students were toward North Vietnamese, American Jews, Cubans, Russians, and Mohammedans. On the other end of the scale the least social distances were reported toward Puerto Ricans, Catholics, trigueños (literally translated as "the color of wheat," this is a racial category based on a tone of skin intermediate between black and white), Protestants, and Spanish—the first three of these traits describing the typical Puerto Rican. However, when analyses were done according to the political status preferences of the respondents, differences occurred in the rankings that reflected the respondents' beliefs about how those groups fostered or hindered their preferred political status. For example, while statehood supporters ranked U.S. Whites 3rd (right behind Puerto Ricans and Catholics) and Commonwealth supporters ranked them 6th, independentistas ranked the U.S. Whites 45th out of a possible 47. Similarly, Cubans were ranked 24th, 30th, and 47th by these same groups. It should be noted that the closeness to White Americans expressed by estadistas and estadolibristas does not extend to Black Americans (ranked 22nd and 19th, respectively) or American Indians (34th and 23rd rank, respectively). The response of Puerto Ricans to White Americans is dictated primarily by the respondents' political status preference. The response to Black Americans reflects also the prejudice present in the island. However, the social distance of independentistas toward Blacks is less than toward American Blacks, 11th verses 22nd. Corresponding ranks for estadistas and estadolibristas are 19th and 21st, almost identical to Black Americans. It should be noted also that while there is total agreement in placing Puerto Ricans and Catholics first and second across politi-

cal status preferences, trigueño is ranked 3rd, 4th, and 6th by independentistas, estadolibristas, and estadistas, respectively.

Two things are of interest in this study to the present discussion
of internalized conflict: (a) the social distance shifts toward various
ethnic groups according to the political status preferences of the
respondents, in particular Cubans and *americanos;* and (b) the overall as well as subgroup social distance toward the racial categories.
(The common usage in the island is to refer to Anglo-Americans
from the United States as *americanos,* a usage that will be followed
in this chapter. It should be noted, however, that all Latin Americans claim for themselves the title of *americanos*—of the Americas.) The former is of note for all the reasons already discussed;
the latter is of note because race is one of the main bases of ethnic
identity in the United States. The first of these points is essential to
understanding the dynamics of conflict in the island, and the second is essential to understanding the dynamics of conflict to be
found among Puerto Ricans in the mainland.

Attitudes of Puerto Ricans Toward Cubans and Americanos

The attitudes of Puerto Ricans toward both americanos and
Cubans during the last half of the nineteenth century were very
positive. Most Puerto Ricans still know by heart a verse from a
poem by Lola Rodríguez de Tió, a famous Puerto Rican poet:

Cuba y Puerto Rico son	Cuba and Puerto Rico
De un pájara las dos alas	Are two wings of a bird
Reciben flores y balas	Bullets and flowers
En un mismo corazón.	Hit them in the same heart.

The poem reflects a shared feeling that is also demonstrated in the
fact that the Cuban and Puerto Rican flags are identical in design
with the colors red and blue transposed. In 1898 the two islands
had continuous exchanges in commerce and saw themselves pursuing parallel courses toward independence from Spain. Cuba had
been waging a war of independence against Spain while Puerto Rico
was pursuing its goal within the structures of the Spanish government. In both islands independence supporters anticipated that the
United States—considered a promoter of causes of independence—

would grant each island its independence. When the United States did not, Cubans continued their fight until independence was granted in 1902. The less powerful Puerto Rican independence movement continued its pursuit through political negotiations and participation in the electoral processes punctuated by occasional outbursts of violence, as the incidents of open conflict listed above indicate.

As the years went by, attitudes toward the United States differentiated in Puerto Rico according to the political status preference while attitudes toward Cuba remained consistently positive. The 1959 ascent to power by Fidel Castro in Cuba started a chain of events that has affected this positive feeling in complex ways. The communist identification of the Cuban government means that the pro- or anticommunist attitudes of Puerto Ricans will make a distinction between their attitudes toward the government and the people of Cuba (and of the United States or any other country); as the Jimenez-Santiago study (1977) above shows, neither Cubans nor U.S. citizens are perceived as close as their geographical proximity, cultural similarity, and/or former history would warrant.

But an equally important factor affecting Puerto Ricans' attitudes towards Cubans is the increased migration into the island of those fleeing the Castro regime. At a time when many Cubans saw themselves in need of refuge, Puerto Ricans offered them a warm welcome. Between 1959 and 1964, 20,000 Cubans entered the island. As refugees are likely to do, Cubans were eager to work and many entered jobs at the lowest level—accepting at times below standard work conditions or wages; many also went into middle-level positions. In Light's (1981) words, the latter "leap-frogged" the normal chain of succession. The sudden increase in number of job seekers into an already depressed economy (Puerto Rico's acknowledged unemployment rate hovers around 20 percent) and the prompt entry of Cubans into the entrepreneurial ranks in the island created a sense of displacement and unfair competition among Puerto Ricans. Many Puerto Ricans felt like friends who have had their hospitality abused by an unexpectedly pushy guest. In the words of a popular folk saying, *Se la dió de comer del ala y se comieron la pechuga* ("They were offered the chicken wings but they ate the breast").

While Puerto Ricans have become used to U.S. citizens entering the economic structure in Puerto Rico at middle or upper levels, this was seen as part of the disadvantages of the colonial state of the island and one of the prerogatives of controlling capital. Of Cubans, who were their equals, this was not expected. Newspapers carried accounts of resentments and proposed solutions to the situation with the Cubans. At the height of the controversy the list of characteristics attributed to the Cubans included hard-working, show-off, arrogant, uppity, and pushy. Some observers compared this response to that received by other successful newcomers in other settings such as Jews in the United States and Puerto Ricans in the island of St. Croix (U.S. Virgin Islands).

Some would argue that Jiménez-Santiago's report (1977) of a high social distance toward Cubans is not a good measure of Puerto Ricans' attitudes toward Cubans since distinction was not made in the scale between those living in Cuba and those living in Puerto Rico. Seda-Bonilla (1977) notes that the resentment against Cubans was a temporary phenomenon which he attributed to an "Americanized attitude" (p. 108). However, in a 1979 study on social identity, Giles, Lladó, McKirnan, and Taylor asked questions specifically about Cubans living in the island. Among the 10- and 17-year-olds they surveyed, the perceived similarity between themselves and Cubans was consistently smaller than that perceived with "americanos."

In the early 1980s a similar phenomenon occurred with Dominicans who came to the island in search of jobs and other economic benefits. This group swelled the ranks of the 10,000 Dominicans who had come to the island fleeing the 1965 civil war in Santo Domingo. The information available about the most recently arrived group is still at the level of newspaper accounts and word of mouth.

Attitudes of Puerto Ricans Toward Other Puerto Ricans

The internalized conflict of Puerto Ricans is reflected not only in their attitudes toward other ethnic groups but also toward other Puerto Ricans. The social science literature reports that factors such as race, religion, and socioeconomic status are relevant in determining the interethnic social distance in other groups. There are studies that explore how such factors affect the social distance reported by Puerto Ricans toward other Puerto Ricans. In her 1977 study Jiménez-Santiago presents five racial categories that are commonly used in Puerto Rico—Black, Caucasian, *moreno,* mulatto, and trigueño—the last three being gradations of color between black and white. Elicited responses of social distance range from a rank 3 for trigueño, 8 for mullatto, 9 for moreno, 10 for Caucasian, and 14 for Black. Even when broken down by political party preference, as noted above, there is a consistently lower social distance toward trigueño and a higher one for Blacks. Giles et al. (1979), using only two racial categories, "white skin" and "brown skin," reported a slightly closer identification of their respondents with brown- rather than white-skinned people, consistent with Jiménez-Santiago's report.

In terms of religion Jiménez-Santiago (1977) reports overall social distance ranks of 3 for Catholics and 4 for Protestants. In their study Giles et al. (1979) obtained rankings only for Catholics and Protestants. The 10-year-old students reported a closer similarity with Catholics; this disappears among 17-year-olds, who ranked them equally close.

Jiménez-Santiago (1977) does not present socioeconomic status as a stimulus, but the Giles et al. study (1979) contains some statements about similarities between the respondents and designated stimuli of varying social class. The young Puerto Ricans who answered the Giles et al. survey saw themselves as more similar to working-class people than any of the other classes mentioned.

While studies such as those of Ginorio et al. (1972) and Jiménez-Santiago (1977) would seem to indicate that in the popular mind social distance is also affected by a political status preference component, the Giles et al. (1979) study does not evidence this. Students in their sample—10- and 17-year-olds, as opposed to college students for the other two studies—reported a general dislike and distance from anyone for whom political status is a salient identificatory feature. Unfortunately, no other studies appear in the published literature that indicate what would be the social distance felt toward people that support the various political solutions. With the exception of the Giles et al. study, political status preference is used as an independent rather than a dependent variable. Thus Jiménez-Santiago reports that the greatest average social distance scores toward the 47 racial, religious, and nationality groups in her scale are reported by estadolibristas (1.8)—not significantly different from the 1.784 reported by independentistas and 1.547 reported by the estadistas.

A chapter about ethnic conflict in Puerto Rico that ends here would lead the reader to conclude that the main dimension that defines ethnic relations in Puerto Rico is political status preference. The logical extension of this conclusion would be that conflict in Puerto Rico is as much directed toward americanos as toward each other, although open conflict incidents seem to be mainly focused on Americans. The formalized conflict, on the other hand, primarily involves Puerto Ricans.

The Giles et al. (1979) study provides some evidence that other factors enter into social distance judgments of Puerto Ricans toward other Puerto Ricans. These are place of birth and language dominance—both of which are associated with residence outside the island. Although Spanish language dominance was not a significant component of the self-identity of the respondents, it was a significant one when they judged their social environment—with Spanish dominant speakers seen as more similar than either bilingual English speakers, or even Spanish speakers with an American accent. Likewise, New York-born Puerto Ricans—whether still living in the mainland or having returned to Puerto Rico—are perceived as more dissimilar from the self than americanos residing in the island. The Giles et al. (1979) study brings us to a significant group of Puerto Ricans not mentioned before in this chapter: Puerto Ricans in the U.S. mainland (PR-US).

Almost one-third of all Puerto Ricans in the world live in the mainland. Although the discussion that follows is also applicable to persons living in or moving from other countries, the issues are phrased in terms of the United States because of the large numbers of Puerto Ricans living in the mainland: 1,443,862 by the 1980 census (Bureau of the Census, 1983). New York is the second largest Puerto Rican city in the world.

Puerto Ricans in the United States

By placing Puerto Ricans living in the U.S. within the category of Puerto Ricans, I have taken a position within a controversy that has been ongoing both in the island and in the mainland. What defines a Puerto Rican?

Can a person who speaks Spanish with an English accent or who does not speak Spanish at all be a Puerto Rican?

Is a Puerto Rican born person who lives most of her or his life in the
United States Puerto Rican?

Is a person born on the island but raised in the United States a Puerto
Rican?

Is a person of Puerto Rican ancestry who remains in the United States
a Puerto Rican?

In the eyes of many Puerto Ricans a negative answer to any of
these questions may deny the claim to Puertoricaness of PR-US. In
that respect these questions differ from those asked when the issue
is political status preference; what is questioned then is the "kind"
of Puerto Rican that a supporter of the various political formulas is.

In the sections that follow the conflicts experienced by PR-US
will be considered. Open conflict will not be considered since
it has been limited to gang wars, a phenomenon too complex to
include within the context of this chapter. Formalized conflict will
be considered within the sections dealing with PR-US relations
with Blacks and other Latinos.

Internalized Conflict among PR-US

In a partial replication of the Jiménez-Santiago study (1977) done
in New York City, Ginorio (1972) reports that the social distance
scores of Puerto Ricans in New York (PR-NY) are higher than those
of Puerto Ricans, higher even than the average U.S. score of 1.92.
This score becomes more significant when it is considered that the
highest average in Puerto Rico is 1.8. In the small New York City
sample (N = 20), members of a college-level independence organization had higher social distance scores than did nonmembers.
However, when rank-orders are correlated for Puerto Ricans and
PR-NY, it is .64, significant at the .01 level. A similar comparison
of PR-NY with White Americans yielded nonsignificant correla-
tions: −.62 for independence supporters and .29 for nonsupporters.

It should be pointed out that the rank orders of independence
supporters in New York City are more similar to those of independence supporters in the island than to those of nonindependence
supporters in New York. This is surprising in view of the fact that

these respondents were born in New York, feel more at ease speaking English, and some have not even visited the island. Once more this is an instance of political status preferences overriding cultural or geographic proximity factors.

The responses of PR-NY differ from those of Puerto Ricans in that the smallest social distance scores are reserved not for ethnic groups that are culturally similar but for ethnic minorities of color in New York City. In addition to the Ginorio (1972) study in which smaller social distances were reported toward Black Americans than toward White ethnics (Italians, Jews, Irish) or White Americans, there is a later study that provided information about the relations of PR-NY to Black Americans. In a study of 381 high-school students in New York City, 82 percent of the students had non-Puerto Rican friends; among those, Blacks were the most likely choice (82 percent) followed by Dominicans (44 percent)—another population with high interracial mix (Ginorio, 1979). The low social distance toward Blacks may be explained by at least three reasons: (1) the high proportion of Blacks attending the schools sampled, (2) the common experience of being minorities in New York City, and (3) the racial traditions of Puerto Ricans that do not impose large social distance toward Blacks—except perhaps at the level of marriage, if the results of a study done by Díaz-Boulón (1971) in the island were to hold in this population. Similarly, the high social distance that PR-NY expressed toward Irish, Italians, or Jews might indicate the resentment of the PR-NY toward those groups that are directly above them in the social ladder.

Conflicts with Blacks

While their identity as Puerto Ricans may be an important concern for PR-US, a more pressing immediate concern is economic survival. With the lowest median income of any of the Hispanic groups in the mainland, Puerto Ricans compete with Black Americans and other recent immigrants for scarce resources available to the poor (Ford Foundation, 1984). Some Blacks have attributed the Puerto Ricans' insistence on their identity as Puerto Ricans first and Black, trigueño, and so forth second as a denial of their negritude (Rodríguez, 1974). Apart from the benefits that may befall any group in a racist society for distancing themselves from the outgroup, this Puerto Rican response is more properly understood as the outward manifestation of a different, culturally based, system of racial definitions than of discrimination of the U.S. type. Because of the large degree of intermingling that has occurred in Puerto Rico during the last five centuries there are no pure racial types. As a result of the great variety of phenotypes in the population the racial definition system prevalent in the island—as well as the rest of the Caribbean basin—is very fluid (Ginorio, 1979, 1981). This fluidity is evident in at least two ways: the importance of nonracial factors in the definition of racial identity, and the resulting ambiguity of verbal labels when used to name racial types (Harris, 1970; Jiménez-Santiago, 1977; Mörner, 1967; Rogler, 1940). As a result of all the extensive racial mixture and the fluidity of racial definitions, the conception of race in Latin America is one of a continuum with no clear demarcation between categories (Ginorio & Berry, 1972; Hoetink, 1972; Pitt-Rivers, 1967).

In contrast to this racial system, in the U.S. race is seen as a dichotomous variable of white or black (Hoetink, 1967, 1972; Mörner, 1967). Not only does the U.S. racial system differ from the Latin American one in recognizing discrete as opposed to continuous groups, it also limits racial distinctions to a very small number of categories—four, perhaps five, if in addition to white and black, yellow, red and brown are seen as distinct racial categories. The basis for such distinctions in the U.S. is genealogical—if an arbitrarily set amount of Black blood can be determined to exist, the individual is classified as Black. Thus an individual is racially defined at birth and can change that identity only by "passing." In contrast in Latin America the racial identification of an individual depends as much on the physical appearance as on nonracial factors such as the socioeconomic status of the individual being labeled (Hoetink, 1967; Mörner, 1967; Pitt-Rivers, 1967; Rogler, 1948; Wagley, 1965). It can be said then that while in Latin America racial identity can be achieved, in the United States it is ascribed.

When faced with the U.S. racial system, what are the choices for a Puerto Rican living in the United States? Social scientists who have considered this question predict that the phenotypically White will assimilate to the White groups while the phenotypically non-White will assimilate to the Black groups (Gordon, 1964; Herberg, 1960; Seda-Bonilla, 1961). To accept the present racial definitions in the United States would imply not only the division of their community along racial lines but the division of entire extended families. Thus Puerto Ricans insist that they are Puerto Ricans first and a given color second. Were the Latinos to maintain an ethnic or racial identity that encompasses the racial heterogeneity that characterizes Puerto Ricans, Chicanos, Cubans, Dominicans, and many other Latino groups they might add a new dimension to the ethnic history of the United States. While Puerto Ricans and other Latinos may see the continuation of such amalgam as an extension of their own racial system, the North Americans may see the establishment of this brown group as an expansion of their discrete racial system. The labeling of Latinos as brown could formalize a barrier between them and non-Latinos since all of them would be in a class by themselves. La Raza (the Race, name of the Latin American people) may acquire a different meaning in the context of the U.S. system of racial and ethnic relations.

To the degree that American Blacks interpret the system of racial definitions of Puerto Ricans from the dichotomous perspective they will see Puerto Ricans as identifying with Whites. Even if the differences in racial definitions between Puerto Ricans and Blacks were not recognized and surmounted, it would still seem logical to expect common goals given the similarities in socioeconomic status and the proximity of their neighborhoods. The 1980 census data indicate that Puerto Ricans and Blacks are among the poorest citizens. In analyses of residential segregation in the U.S. using 1970 census data, Massey (1981) reported on eight cities with high enough concentrations of Puerto Ricans, Mexicans, and Cubans to allow for significant examination of the data. Massey's analysis indicates that Puerto Ricans are the least segregated of the three groups and that their greatest segregation is from the White groups. The residential proximity of Puerto Ricans to Blacks is particularly noticeable in Boston and New York.

In spite of these similarities, there have been hard-to-bridge differences between these two communities based on access to resources—most notable have been political power and concomitant allocations. Given that Blacks are the closest ethnic group to the Puerto Ricans in socioeconomic status, tensions with the Black community have been most pronounced over a number of issues of access. Organizations such as the Puerto Rican Development Project (for control of antipoverty funds in the 1960s) and Aspira (for educational access) have given form to some of these concerns of the Puerto Rican community in the United States.

In most cities where Puerto Ricans have settled, the Black community is better established in terms of their access to both government and private sectors as well as to the existence of individual
organizations such as the Black churches (Backstrand & Schensul,
1982; Falcón, 1985). To identify totally with the Black community
would subsume Puerto Rican interests to Black interests. According to Padilla (1970), poverty programs of the 1960s brought Puerto
Rican and Black needs closer and into clearer opposition. The
insistence on a Puerto Rican as opposed to a Black identity insured
Puerto Ricans of their share in the "anti-poverty pie," in Padilla's
words.

In issues of education, another major concern of Hispanics,
Black and Puerto Rican interests clash. Blacks emphasize integration as a way of ensuring better facilities for their schools. Since
integration is a fact of life in any Puerto Rican classroom, Puerto
Ricans and other Latinos emphasize bilingual education as their
means of obtaining quality education for their children. Thus some
Puerto Rican leaders opposed decentralization plans for the school
system in New York City in 1969 for fear of Black control at the
local level that would be insensitive to their needs (Fitzpatrick,
1971).

Puerto Ricans and Blacks have worked together, usually in coalitions aimed at specific issues such as an experimental school district in New York (Fitzpatrick, 1971), the 1980 election of Harold
Washington in Chicago, or in order to maintain affordable housing
within the city of Hartford (Backstrand & Schensul, 1982). But the
failure of other coalition attempts, such as the 1984 drive to unseat
Edward Koch as Mayor of New York (Falcón, 1985) or Jesse Jackson's Rainbow Coalition to attract sizable numbers of Hispanics,
gives evidence to the lack of an across-the-board common vision
between Hispanics and Blacks.

Contacts with Other Latinos in the United States

No reliable studies exist about the conflicts, formal or internalized, that may exist between PR-US and Cubans, Chicanos, Dominicans, or other Latinos. Fitzpatrick and Gurak's (1979) study of
Hispanic intermarriage in New York City documents the high incidence of intermarriage of Puerto Ricans, Dominicans, Cubans,
Mexicans, and other Latinos in the city. Second generation Puerto

Ricans, however, are the least exogamous of all the groups studied.

It can be safely assumed that in spite of common cultural roots, whenever the situation between Puerto Ricans and other Latinos places them in some kind of competition for resources conflict will occur. The recent mayoral campaign in Miami brought many of the differences between Cubans and Puerto Ricans to the surface. Furthermore, some of the dynamics operating in the island between Puerto Ricans and Cubans could extend to the mainland.

Chicanos and Puerto Ricans have pursued the same issues in the area of bilingual education. However, a potential for conflict exists over the issue of migration. Puerto Ricans, being American citizens, have had no worries about entry into the United States or return to Puerto Rico while for the Chicano community immigration laws are of paramount importance.

For some political pursuits it has proven expedient to collapse these diverse ethnic identities into a single one of "latinos" or "hispanos"—in a process that Light (1981) calls "ethnic identity expansion and intensification." But there are many more instances of parallel organizations competing for the same funds. One of the examples discussed even in the majority press is that of the differences between the League of United Latin American Cities and Aspira over educational representation in some Eastern cities.

It must not be forgotten either that there is great diversity within each one of these ethnic groups, the most easily observed differences being those based on class and recency of migration. An upper-middle-class Puerto Rican might find more commonalities with a middle-class Mexican than with a poor Puerto Rican. When to class differences that of recency of migration is added—such as the most recent immigration of Cubans, the Marielitos—the situation becomes too complex to even try to speculate about how that relationship will develop.

Those That Return

While many Puerto Ricans come to the United States and stay, there are many who return to Puerto Rico. Among second-generation high school students, 38 percent reported a desire to move to Puerto Rico (Ginorio, 1979). While many PR-US live in the hope of returning to the island, for many that remains a dream. What is a reality is that since some time in the 1960s the migratory flow out of the island has reversed. (Borton places the first instance in 1964, with 8,000 more returnees than migrants, while the Puerto Rican Planning Board places it in 1969 with 7,047 more returned than migrated [Fitzpatrick, 1971].) Hernández-Alvarez (1967) calculates that about 7,500 more Puerto Ricans return to the island yearly than leave it. It is estimated that between 250,000 and 350,000 Puerto Ricans have returned to the island from the mainland.

These Puerto Ricans often return expecting a true homecoming. But to the degree that these returning Puerto Ricans have acquired different expectations and values about things as central as racial definitions, gender roles, or other central cultural concerns, there is bound to be conflict between two groups of Puerto Ricans who claim for themselves that identity but who interpret it differently. Unlike the dictum about poetic forms, "A poem should not mean but be" (MacLeish, 1981), cultural relations demand that an individual not only be but behave in a meaningful manner. Flores, Attinasi, and Pedraza's (1981) vision may be representative of what other PR-US feel:

> Puerto Rican roots lead neither to the folkloric jíbaro, content under the Commonwealth, nor to the glorified pantheon of the national elite. . . . Rather, going back to Puerto Rico evokes the popular culture of an Afro-Caribbean island, the birthplace of musical and poetic forms like la bomba, la plena, la décima, and el seis. It is a culture of the slave and peasant masses, the culture of a colonial people who have known not only misery and submission—and pious "decency"—but also joy, creativity, and struggle. (p. 205)

If so, then there are as many discrepancies between a Puerto Rican's vision and the reality of what *Newyorricans* are as there are between the Newyorrican's vision and what Puerto Rico and Puerto Ricans are all about.

The 10- and 17-year-olds in Giles et al. study (1979) saw PR-US as less similar to them then *americanos* residing in the island. This distancing effect was more pronounced among the 17-year-olds than among the 10-year-olds. The popular press also reports that many Puerto Ricans in Puerto Rico perceive non-Spanish-speaking and/or otherwise acculturated Puerto Ricans as non-Puerto Ricans.

Puerto Ricans who live in the United States, on the other hand, claim for themselves the identity of Puerto Ricans (Laviera, 1979). Exactly what being Puerto Rican means in the United States ranges from a reestablishment of Puerto Rican ways in the metropolis (Fitzpatrick, 1971) to the creation of a New York-based Puerto Rican culture that focuses on "national resistance and the vantage point of the have-nots" (Flores et al., 1981). One of the things it does not necessarily mean is to be born in Puerto Rico or to speak Spanish in a standard manner—or at all.

The Puerto Rican Family Institute, founded in New York City in 1960 to serve the needs of Puerto Rican families, in 1977 established a branch in Puerto Rico to fulfill the needs of returning families and individuals. This agency provides information and help in the areas of housing, employment, health, and education. According to its director, Marcelino Oyola, "the most difficult task is to place the migrant in the context of time and space. To make them understand that present day Puerto Rico is not the same as the Puerto Rico they left behind" (Millán-Pabón, 1985, p. 19). According to their records the most frequently given reasons for returning were that other family members had returned, the climate was too harsh in the states, and they had reached their goals.

The returning Puerto Ricans who felt very Puerto Rican in *el barrio* feel alienated and out of place when back in the island. The locals call them "Neoricans" or "Newyorricans"—whether they have actually returned from New York or not. For these Puerto Ricans the internalized conflict might be one of self-definition, a conflict that if unresolved will add a new layer to those already existing in this society.

Summary

This chapter has presented the kinds of conflict evident among Puerto Ricans both in the island and in the United States. Other chapters in this book that deal with transplanted populations (e.g., Chinese in Malaysia, Tamils in Sri Lanka) argue that the migrants' behavior in the new situation strongly resembles that seen in the country of origin. This chapter provides some information on how the individual traits of Puerto Ricans are manifested in the new context (racial definitions); it also presents information that indicates

TABLE 8.1:   Types of Conflict

	Open	Formalized	Internalized
Puerto Ricans	Indian rebellions Slave rebellions Defensive battles Independence	political parties	prejudices and stereotypes based on political status preference
Puerto Ricans in the United States	Gang wars	ethnic-based organizations	prejudices and stereotypes based on ethnic identity and race

how the content of the conflict is affected by that new situation. Table 8.1 summarizes these findings.

If we had more information on PR-US who had returned to Puerto Rico, a third layer might be added to Table 8.1. There is some evidence of internalized conflict among them about their own identity, and some evidence of antagonism from Puerto Ricans toward them based on perceived differences in language and perhaps behavior. It is a matter of future speculation whether open and formalized forms of conflict will develop between returned Puerto Ricans and Puerto Ricans in Puerto Rico. There is no doubt that internalized conflict already exists.

References

Backstrand, J. R., & Schensul, S. (1982). Co-evolution in an outlying ethnic community: The Puerto Ricans of Hartford, Connecticut. *Urban Anthropology, 11*(1), pp. 9-37.

Bayrón-Toro, F. (1984). *Elecciones y partidos politicos de Puerto Rico* [Elections and political parties of Puerto Rico] (rev. ed.). Mayagüez, PR: Editorial Isla.

Bogardus, E.S. (1967). *A forty year racial distance study.* Los Angeles: University of Southern California.

Bureau of the Census. (1983). *Ancestry of Population by State: 1980,* Supplementary Report, PC80-S1-10.

Díaz-Boulón, F. (1971). *Aceptación ey rechazo de personas de la raza Negra por estudiantes de la universidad* [Acceptance and rejection of persons of the Black race by students of the University]. Unpublished master's thesis, Universidad de Puerto Rico, Río Piedras.

Díaz-Soler, L.M. (1953). *La historia de la esclavitud negra en Puerto Rico, 1493-1890* [The history of black slavery in Puerto Rico, 1493-1890]. Rio Piedras: Universidad de Puerto Rico.

Falcón, A. (1985, June). Puerto Rican and Black electoral politics in NYC in the "Decade of the Hispanic." *Centro de estudios Puertorriqueños at Hunter College Newsletter.* (Available from Centro de Estudios Puertorriqueños, Hunter College, 695 Park Avenue, Box #548, New York, NY 10021)

Fitzpatrick, J.P. (1971). *Puerto Rican Americans: The meaning of migration to the mainland.* Englewood Cliffs, NJ: Prentice-Hall.

Fitzpatrick, J. P., & Gurak, D. T. (1979). Hispanic intermarriage in New York City: 1975. (Hispanic Research Center Monograph No. 2). Bronx, NY: Fordham University, Hispanic Research Center.

Flores, J., Attinasi, J., & Pedraza, P., Jr. (1981). La carreta made a u-turn: Puerto Rican language and culture in the United States. *Daedalus, 110*(2), 193-217.

Ford Foundation. (1984). *Hispanics: Challenges and opportunities* (Working paper No. 436). New York: Ford Foundation.

Giles, H., Lladó, N., McKirnan, D. J., & Taylor, D. M. (1979). Social identity in Puerto Rico. *International Journal of Psychology, 14*, 185-201.

Ginorio, A. B. (1971). *A study of racial perception in Puerto Rico.* Unpublished master's thesis, Universidad de Puerto Rico, Río Piedras.

Ginorio, A. B. (1972). A measure of social distance as a correlate of acculturation. In A. I. Del Campo, F. Estrada, L. Jiménez, M. L. Ramos, & C. N. Velez (Eds.), *Antología de lecturas para psicología general* [Anthology of readings for general psychology] (pp. 189-202). Rio Piedras: Universidad de Puerto Rico.

Ginorio, A.B. (1979). A comparison of Puerto Ricans in New York with native Puerto Ricans and Caucasian and Black Americans on two measures of acculturation: Gender role and racial identification. (Doctoral dissertation, Fordham University, 1979). *Dissertation Abstracts International, 40*, 983B-984B.

Ginorio, A.B. (1981, June). *Race as a factor in acculturation of Puerto Ricans in the United States.* Paper presented at the meeting of the 18th Interamerican Congress of Psychology, Santo Domingo, Dominican Republic.

Ginorio, A.B., & Berry, P.C. (1972). Measuring Puerto Ricans' perceptions of racial characteristics [Summary]. *Proceedings of the 80th Annual Convention of the American Psychological Association, 7*, 287-288.

Ginorio, A. B., Luiggi, N., Olmo, M., Santos, S., Navas, G., & de Jesús, M. (1972). El efecto de la preferencia destatus en Puerto Rico sobre la percepción de otros países. In A. I. Del Campo, F. Estrada, L. Jiménez, M. L. Ramos, & C. N. Vélez (Eds.), *Antología de lecturas para psicología general* [Anthology of readings for general psychology] (pp. 71-90). Río Piedras: Universidad de Puerto Rico.

Gordon, M. M. (1964). *Assimilation in American life: The role of race, religion, and national origin.* New York: Oxford University Press.

Harris, M. (1970). Referential ambiguity in the calculus of Brazilian racial identity. *Southwestern Journal of Anthropology, 26,* 1-14.

Herberg, W. (1960). *Protestant, Catholic, Jew* (rev. ed.). Garden City, NY: Doubleday.

Hernández-Alvarez, J. (1967). *Return migration to Puerto Rico* [Population Monograph Series No. 1]. Berkeley: University of California Press, Institute of International Studies.

Hoetink, H. (1967). *The two variants in Caribbean race relations.* London: Oxford University Press.

Hoetink, H. (1972). National identity, culture, and race in the Caribbean. In E. Qu. Campbell (Ed.), *Racial tensions and national identity* (pp. 17-42). Nashville, TN: Vanderbilt University Press.

Jiménez-Santiago, L. (1977). *Influence of sex and political preference on social distance scores.* Unpublished master's thesis, Universidad de Puerto Rico, Río Piedras.

Laviera, T. (1979). *La carreta made a u-turn.* Gary, IN: Arte Público Press.

Lewis, G. K. (1963). *Puerto Rico: Freedom and power in the Caribbean.* New York: MR Press.

Light, I. (1981). Ethnic succession. In C. F. Keyes (Ed.), *Ethnic change* (pp. 53-86). Seattle: University of Washington Press.

MacLeish, A. (1981). Ars Poetica. In J. F. Nims (Ed.), *The Harper Anthology of Poetry.* New York: Harper & Row.

Massey, D.S. (1981). Hispanic residential segregation: A comparison of Mexicans, Cubans, and Puerto Ricans. *Sociology and Social Research, 65*(3), 311-322.

Millán-Pabón, C. (1985, March 10). Cuando pasa el espejismo [When the mirage is over]. *El Mundo,* p. 19.

Mörner, M. (1967). *Race mixture in the history of Latin America.* Boston: Little, Brown.

Padilla, E. (1970). Race relations: A Puerto Rican view. In L. C. Fitch & A. H. Walsh (Eds.), *Agenda for a city: Issues confronting New York* (pp. 16-20). Newbury Park, CA: Sage.

Pitt-Rivers, J. (1967). Race, color, and class in Central America and the Andes. *Daedalus, 96,* 542-559.

Ramos de Santiago, C. (1970). *El gobierno de Puerto Rico* [The government of Puerto Rico] (2nd. rev. ed.). Río Piedras, PR: Editorial Universitaria.

Ribes Tovar, F. (1973). *Historia cronológica de Puerto Rico* [Chronological history of Puerto Rico]. New York: Plus Ultra Educational Publishers.

Rodriguez, C. (1974). Puerto Ricans: Between black and white. *New York Affairs: New York in the Year 2000, 1,* 92-101.

Rogler, C. C. (1940). *Comerio: A study of a Puerto Rican town.*

Rogler, C. C. (1948). Some situational aspects of race relations in Puerto Rico. *Social Forces, 27,* 72-77.

Seda-Bonilla, E. (1961). Social structure and race relations. *Social Forces, 40,* 141-148.

Seda-Bonilla, E. (1977). Who is a Puerto Rican: Problems of socio cultural identity in Puerto Rico [Review of *Hot land, cold season*]. *Caribbean Review, 17,* 105-121.

Steiner, S. (1974). *The islands: The worlds of the Puerto Ricans.* New York: Harper & Row.

Wagenheim, K. (1975). *Puerto Rico: A profile* (2nd ed.). New York: Praeger.

Wagley, C. (1965). On the concept of social race in the Americas. In D. B. Heath & R. N. Adams (Eds.), *Contemporary cultures and societies of Latin America* (pp. 531-545). New York: Random House.

Chapter Summary

Joseph E. Trimble uses sociopsychological theories of intergroup relations as the basis for a discussion of the experience of American Indians from the time of Columbus to the present. His discussion of stereotyping, for example, centers on the functions of particular images generated by White settlers in order to view the hundreds of distinct tribes as a unified group and justify their treatment of these people.

Trimble reviews various demographic characteristics of the American Indian population and asserts that their birth-death pattern resembles that of a Third World nation with regard to the high percentage of individuals not living beyond early adulthood.

The major portion of this chapter focuses on the key historical events that resulted in conflict between Indian and White groups. This conflict, Trimble suggests, centers primarily on the use and ownership of land. The author examines the "doctrine of discovery" concept of land ownership and the ways in which this view led to efforts to organize White-Indian relations through a series of government regulations. Trimble shows how such government policy, continually masked as protection for Indian groups, was actually a method by which Indians could be controlled and coerced into assimilation.

The author describes how in more recent years the failures of government policy toward Indians has become more obvious (in terms of poor economic, employment, and health conditions), resulting in claims against the Bureau of Indian Affairs, and the government's tendency to decrease aid as evidence of decreased control.

Finally, Trimble looks at the 1960s actions of Indian rights groups and how, in contrast to the goals of other minorities, their emphasis was on tribal rights rather than civil rights. Trimble reflects on the ability of Indians to survive this severe history and examines ethnic identity as a source of survival.

—Susan Goldstein

9

American Indians and Interethnic Conflict

JOSEPH E. TRIMBLE

If you do take it (our land) you must blame yourself as the cause of
trouble between us and the tribes who sold it to you. I want the
present boundary line to continue. Should you cross it, I assure you
it will be productive of bad consequences.

> —*Tecumseh, nineteenth-century
> leader of the Shawnee in response
> to William Henry Harrison, Au-
> gust 21, 1810*

Contact between the natives of the western hemisphere and Europeans began innocently enough. As most every schoolchild knows,
an Italian seafarer flying under a Spanish flag sought to discover
a westward route to India. Upon landing on the islands off of the
southern seaboard of the now United States he made contact with
the then peaceful Arawak people. Columbus and his crew mistak-
enly labeled the natives *los Indios,* or Indians. The name stuck and
is now used as a generic gloss to refer to most natives residing in the
Americas.

Of these people Columbus noted in his journal,

they are so guileless and so generous with all that they possess . . .
they refuse nothing that they possess, if it be asked of them; on the
contrary they invite anyone to share it and display as much love as if

they would give their hearts. They are content with whatever trifle or whatever kind that may be given to them. (Vignaras, 1960, p. 194 ff)

Suffice to say if future colonists and explorers of the Americas had retained the image found by Columbus, the status of the first American might have fared much differently.

The "loving people" image noted by Columbus changed as waves of explorers and colonists made their way to various sections in the Americas. The Spanish, Portuguese and Italians focused their explorations on the southern tier area of the United States including Central and South America. Exploration and settlement of the Mid-Atlantic, northeastern states, and eastern Canada fell to the British, Dutch, and the French. Relationships between the Europeans, the tribes, and the villages were conflict-ridden and strained indeed. The image of the "timid, shy, and sharing" native vanished, to be replaced with a host of stereotypic characterizations that served to justify eventual congressional policies, religious interventions, military massacres, and land settlement policies.

Early explorers and settlers' attitudes and policies toward the first American closely follow social psychological theory concerning intergroup relations and conflict. In many ways early colonial attitudes stemmed from a social Darwinist position: The ethnic traits of the Indian were seen as naturally determined and fixed and because of their alleged lack of progress were deemed inferior. To promote colonization and the interest of European governments and financiers, settlers created an all encompassing collective label—"Indian"—to refer to what amounted to a land of hundreds of different languages and over 2,000 different societies, each with a distinct ethos. According to the historian Robert Berkhofer "the Indian was a White invention and still remains largely a White image, if not stereotype" (1978, p. 3).

Many of the colonial settlers and explorers were outcasts in their country. Several European groups preferred the wilderness of the new frontier to the religious persecution they received in their homelands. Since the Indian was occupying this new frontier it was merely a matter of time before conflict ensued over land proprietorship. Settlement was often justified on the grounds that Indians were deficient—deficient in their knowledge of land use, in adequate living and domestic conditions, in military weapons. Berk-hofer notes that

> the history of White-Indian contact increasingly proved to Whites, particularly in the late eighteenth and nineteenth centuries that civilization and Indianness were inherently incompatible and *verified* the initial conception that gave rise to the imagery (1978, p. 29; italics added)

Thus the view of the Indian as inferior to the Whites led to a stratification process in which (in the Weberian tradition) the Indian was seen as the lowest *class* with little or no *status* and little *power* to ward off colonization and the grim consequences.

The effects and consequences of colonization on the American Indian form the major topic of this chapter. Organized around the major assumptions of intergroup conflict theory, the patterns of influence largely promoted by the United States government are presented to: (1) stimulate discussion about the nature of interethnic group relations; (2) provide evidence for the systematic effects produced by colonialism; and (3) promote the discussion of measures to reduce interethnic group conflict, and to prevent future conflicts, between the indigenous and the immigrant.

Demographic Characteristics

There are various estimates of the number of natives residing in North America at the time of Columbus. Approximate totals range from as few as 800,000 to 9 million. Whatever the number, America's indigenous people were and are extraordinarily diverse socially, culturally, and in physical appearance. In fact, it's relatively safe to conclude that far more diversity existed among the American Indians than among *all* of the populations of Europe, Scandinavia, and countries of the Middle East.

Josephy (1968) points out that Indians were speaking no less than 2,200 different languages and that there were some 200 languages that were mutually unintelligible. In physical appearance there were and are some similarities; hair and eye color, dental patterns, amount of body and facial hair, and skin tone are the most distinguishable. There is evidence though of a subband of the Mandan Hidatsu, among whom blue eyes, blond and brown hair, and light skin tone were prevalent. Today, largely because of intermarriage between Whites and Blacks, the physical characteristics have changed dramatically. And the diversity of languages has decreased largely due to nonuse and diffusion of one dialect over another.

After the arrival of Columbus the native population was reduced considerably. Josephy (1968) remarked, "No one will ever know how many Indians of how many tribes were enslaved, tortured, debauched, and killed" (p. 278). Diseases such as smallpox, measles, diphtheria, and typhoid fever, unknown to most Indians, led to the deaths of thousands. About 1837 the Mandan tribe of the Dakotas were all but exterminated by a smallpox epidemic; no one knows how many other bands from other tribes suffered a similar fate. The devastation and destruction of some 350 years reduced the Indian population to about 250,000 in 1850. People were talking then about the "vanishing American" and the complete submission of the rebellious "savage."

The Indian population increased slowly to about 650,000 in 1960. The growth spurt since then has been quite dramatic, as the 1980 figure increased to slightly over 1.5 million. Figures 9.1, 9.2, and 9.3 depict the current population distribution of Indians by age and sex. Figure 9.1 shows the total distribution of all Indians residing in the United States in 1980. Figure 9.2 shows the distribution of Indians living in urban areas, and Figure 9.3 reflects the pattern for rural and reservation areas. The patterns displayed in the figures closely resemble a pyramid—a pattern typical of populations living in the Third World underdeveloped countries. That being the case, then, the first Americans' birth-death rate represents that of an underdeveloped nation *within* a nation that prides itself in setting the worldwide standard for technological and industrial development.

Slightly more than half of the present-day Indians reside in urban and metropolitan areas. California is the largest Indian-populated state (with 201,000), followed by Oklahoma (170,000), Arizona (153,000), and New Mexico (105,000). Vermont is the state with the least number of Indians (an estimated 984 in 1980). The Navajo, who reside on a New Mexico and Arizona reservation comparable in size to the state of West Virginia, is the largest tribe, with over 110,000 members. There are numerous tribes with as few as 5 members and probably some with only 1 remaining survivor.

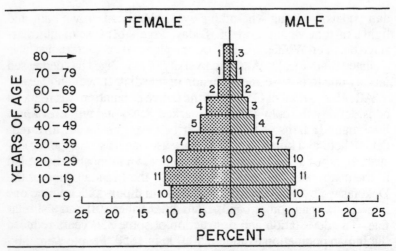

Figure 9.1 Distribution of Total American Indian and Alaska Native Populations, 1980

The American Indian and Alaska Native hold a unique relationship with the federal government of the United States.[1] The nature and development of that relationship will be explored later in the chapter. Because of the relationship though, and owing to the social, cultural, and political diversity of the Indian, the United States Congress was compelled to formulate a legal definition of an Indian. The legal definition enabled government agencies, principally the Bureau of Indian Affairs (BIA), to determine if an individual claiming to be Indian in fact is entitled to government services. Basically the BIA defines an Indian as one who is (1) an enrolled or registered member of a federally recognized Indian tribe; or (2) is at least one-fourth or more in blood quantum and can legally demonstrate that fact to BIA officials.

The legal definition concept was first set forth in the Curtis Act of 1898, when the BIA had to authorize land allotments to members of the Five Civilized Tribes of Oklahoma. Since then the legal definition has undergone few revisions. Nonetheless, many tribes have established their own blood quantum criteria ranging from whatever one could prove (among the Creek of Oklahoma) to more than one-half (among the Utes on the Uintah and Ouray Reservation). Intermarriage has been largely responsible for eroding the question of Indianness. As a consequence it has been estimated that

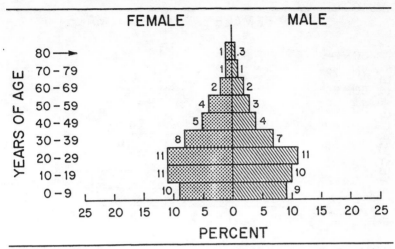

Figure 9.2   Distribution of Urban American Indian and Alaska Native Populations, 1980

between 10 and 20 million people in the United States have some Indian blood (Taylor, 1984).

Svensson (1973) asserts that "Indianness is a state of being, a cast of mind, a relationship to the Universe. It is undefinable" (p. 9). And in a report filed in 1982 to the U.S. Department of Education (DOE) the authors concluded that the "term Indian has no *singular* meaning" (U.S. Department of Education, 1982; italics added). Yet despite the agreement on the elusiveness of the definition, government and the public persist in knowing who is an Indian. The BIA and the tribes have their own definitions, and the U.S. Bureau of Census and DOE have yet another. The Bureau of Census definition is self-enumerative: If one indicates on the census form that he or she is an Indian then the bureau accepts that declaration as sufficient. As a consequence the bureau now recognizes more than 500 tribes and 187 Indian languages—far more than the number recognized by the BIA. DOE has a slightly more rigid definition that parallels closely the one used by the BIA but will accept a person who claims he or she is a descendant of anyone who was at one time a member of a tribe. Population counts generated by each of the definitions produce a rather skewed pattern, so much so that the DOE was compelled to investigate Indian enrollment patterns in many of the nation's schools. As reported in the

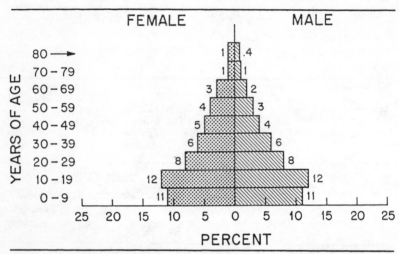

Figure 9.3   Distribution of Rural and Reservation American Indian and Alaska Native
Populations, 1980

DOE document, "the Federal government took a number of steps calculated to heighten or validate racial or ethnic self-awareness and our evidence shows there were substantial shifts in the population toward Indian identification" (U.S. Department of Education, 1982, p. 62).

The American Indian is the *only* ethnic group residing in the United States that has been legally defined. Many Indians and non-Indians, however, simply refuse to accept the criteria. For many non-Indians, an Indian must resemble a historical image, one frozen in the past and in historical archives—the noble, proud warrior dancing about and worshipping nature's mysteries. For still others an Indian is only an Indian if he or she is a full blood. Thus an Indian in the twentieth century is surely distinctive: a victim of colonization, battered about by state and federal government agencies, and subjugated to wardship status by a system that still does not fully understand how the Indian has managed to survive.

Patterns of Conflict

Gunnar Myrdal (1944), the Swedish social scientist responsible for a major study of American Blacks in the early 1940s, suggested then that Whites were basically *ambivalent* toward Blacks. While that point may be disputed, European immigrants historically have *never* been ambivalent toward American Indians. Quoted by Berkhofer (1978) Francis Parkman stated over 100 years ago that "Spanish civilization crushed the Indian; English civilization scorned and neglected him; French civilization embraced and cherished him" (p. 115). Almost at the outset of American colonization the Indian was seen as a hindrance, a nuisance, and the source of conflict. And the history of the Indian is really one of a series of attempts on the part of colonialists and subsequent governments to resolve the conflict over the Indians' presence.

The next section highlights some of the key historical events that served to promote interethnic conflict between Whites and Indians. Woven into the fabric of the information are fundamental social science principles concerning intergroup and interethnic relations. The intent here is to provide familiarity with the substantive historical events and short hypothetical reference points.

Colonial Period Through Removal

Sociologist Lewis Coser (1956) sees conflict as a struggle over values and claims to scarce status, power, and resources, where the aims of the opponents are to neutralize, injure, or eliminate their rivals. Early struggles between the colonialists and Indians were based largely on the premise that one group had what the other wanted; the source of the conflict, in a word, was land. The conflict over land, however, did not begin with the arrival of Columbus. It took almost 200 years for the colonialists to achieve a critical mass that could challenge the Indian.

In 1926, the sociologist Robert Park put forth his linear evolutionary model of race relations. "The race relations cycle takes the form . . . of contact, competition, accommodation and eventual assimilation, [and] is apparently progressive and irreversible" (1950, p. 150). To an extent early Indian-White relations followed Park's evolutionary path. Initially the Indian accommodated the immigrant Whites and in many cases assisted them in surviving the harsh New England winters. But tolerance and accommodation were soon overshadowed by the settlers need for more land, which in turn heightened competition. Oddly enough the need for new land on the part of the colonists led to alliances that would have never occurred in their homelands. Thus the Indian became the natural enemy. To this point Hraba (1979) asserts that "alliances are often created in conflict, and new forms of association emerge out of it. In-group solidarity is strengthened, in-group authority is centralized and consciousness of kind is intensified" (p. 115). Thus competition and ensuing conflict between Whites and Indians was functional. Conflict served to unite factions within both groups that never would have unified without the conflict of group interests.

To obtain the land, colonists, principally the British, resorted to legal theory and the so-called doctrine of discovery, both of which were of course totally foreign to the Indian. The colonialists recognized aboriginal rights but somehow managed to redefine the meaning of these over the course of several hundred years. Moreover, it was generally understood that Indians occupied a land mass far in excess of their needs.

The underlying principle of the "doctrine of discovery" was simple: If no one occupied the land, it was yours for the taking. This led to a number of skirmishes between Indians and Whites, but also led to efforts on behalf of the British government to develop a plan to organize the affairs with the Indians. Out of those efforts came the Royal Proclamation of 1763. The order established that the Indians were entitled to occupy their lands undisturbed, that non-Indian settlers must remove themselves, and that no future land purchases could be consummated without the consent of the British and the Indians (McNickle, 1973). The order also established a containment line in the Appalachian region where no White could settle. Nevertheless, many Whites violated the principle and set up homesteads without much retribution.

The proclamation actually served notice to the Indian that they were no longer in control. Their destiny and that of the colonists was in the hands of the Crown. About 13 years after the proclamation the destiny of the Indian would be transferred to the hands of the first constitutional Congress and the fledgling United States.

One of the first acts of the Continental Congress was to grant itself power to manage the affairs of Indians *not* residing in any of the states and also to turn over Indian jurisdiction to the States. In 1778 Congress negotiated its first treaty with the Delaware, thus establishing a precedent for the recognition of a tribe as "domestic dependent nations" and as a governmental unit. The precedent was to direct monumental treaty agreements in the 1830s that would shape the destiny of Indian law.

The first Congress also set forth a resolution providing that "no land (shall) be sold or ceded by any of the said Indians, either as individuals or as a nation, unless to the United States of America, or by the consent of Congress" (see McNickle, 1973, p. 49). Of the young nation's policy toward the Indian, a United States Civil Rights Commission report quoted George Washington as saying that "there is nothing to be obtained by an Indian war but the soil they live on and this can be had by purchase at less expense, and without that bloodshed" (U.S. Commission on Civil Rights, 1981, p. 18).

As a reflection of Washington's commitment the young Congress proclaimed in 1786 the Ordinance for the Regulation of Indian Affairs. In 1787, providing for the organization of the lands in the Northwest Territory and trying to encourage settlement and self-government, the Congress proclaimed that

> the utmost good faith shall always be observed towards the Indians; their lands and property shall never be taken from them without their consent; and, in their property, rights, and liberty, they shall never be invaded or disturbed. (U.S. Commission on Civil Rights, 1981, p. 18)

The Ordinances of 1786 and 1787, formally ratified by Congress in 1789, essentially maintained that the United States was embarking on a mission to accommodate (and maybe assimilate) the Indian rather than adopting a policy of genocide. Many young bureaucrats, members of the militia, and colonists themselves wanted to exterminate the Indian once and for all. Level heads prevailed, but that did not stop efforts at coercion by force (McNickle, 1973).

Apfelbaum (1979) hypothesizes that power often serves to cement and prolong conflict. A controlling group brings about unequal power relationships and enacts rules and laws that determine how power may be obtained; these laws favor the controlling group and insure that the subordinate will remain so. And so it was with the immigrant and colonist, for they now controlled the direction of Indian-White relations.

The Cherokee and Choctaw tribes of the Southeastern United States were creating more than the usual problems in the 1820s. In 1832 the Supreme Court advised in *Worcester v. Georgia* that the Cherokee tribe was a distinct community and that the state of Georgia could not enact any laws which would encroach upon them (cf. Cohen, 1942). In essence, Georgia law was replaced with Cherokee law (see Svensson, 1973; McNickle, 1973). At that time Andrew Jackson was president. His reaction to the Court's advice was hardly complimentary. A noted Indian fighter himself and an alleged proponent of extermination, and said to have stated in 1817, "I have long viewed treaties with the Indians as an absurdity," (quoted in Svensson, 1973, p. 19), Jackson urged that the Cherokee and other tribes be moved from their ancestral homes to "safe" lands west of the Mississippi River. At about the same time Georgia, Alabama, and Mississippi passed legislation that, in the final analysis, placed Indian jurisdiction under state control. Such actions were viewed by Whites as tantamount to open warfare. More turmoil intensified Indian-White relations. In the end, though, despite protests—many from Northern White *sympaticos*—the Indian lost out. On May 28, 1830, President Jackson signed the Removal Bill giving *him* power to "exchange land west of the Mississippi River for territory still held in the Southeast by the tribes" (Josephy, 1968, p. 323).

With the treaty of Dancing Rabbit Creek the Choctaw tribe was the first to consent to removal. And with the Treaty of New Echota in 1835 the Cherokee tribe ceded all of their lands east of the Mississippi for $5 million and about 7 million acres of land west of the Mississippi (Taylor, 1984). The Creek and Seminole tribes put up a bitter defense and refused to be removed. The Seminoles, led by the young Osceola, put up such a strong resistance that the battle between the American troops and the Seminoles lasted from 1835 to 1842 at a cost of over 2,000 White soldiers and between $40 and $60 million in expenses (Josephy, 1968). Many of the Seminoles escaped to the southern area of Florida where they reside today on three reservations, while many of their kindred were captured and forced to march to new land in "Indian Territory," which is present-day Oklahoma.

The greed for land and the idea that the Indian posed a threat to expansionism led to the Removal Act, an act that in effect meant that the "only good Indian was one you couldn't see." President Jackson's isolationism policy has been described as "one of the blackest chapters in American history" (Josephy, 1968, p. 323) and is referred to as the "Trail of Tears." Josephy comments,

> Tens of thousands of helpless Indians, many of whom had white blood, were wholly or partly civilized . . . suffered incredible hardships. Some of them went reluctantly but without defiance; others went in chains. Most of them streamed westward under the watchful eyes of troops who made sure that they kept moving. (1968, p. 323)

In time some 40 different tribes were relocated to Oklahoma, which in the Choctaw language means "the land of the red people."

The immigrant and colonial Whites simply did not trust the Indian. After all he was *inferior,* a savage either to be annihilated or civilized to live along with all of the other nationalistic and ethnic groups in America. More important, numerous distortions, misperceptions, and misunderstandings occurring between the two groups fanned the flames of mistrust. In addition, many tribes felt that they had been betrayed—and rightfully so, since many agreements forged by Whites were maliciously violated. Worchel (1979) argues that feelings of betrayal and perceptual distortions are potent ingredients for promoting untrustworthiness. Distrust soon leads to the tendency for one group to view the other as a threat and, as such, leads to intergroup conflict. The distrust between Whites and Indians eventually led the federal government to further control the affairs of the Indian in every respect.

Indian removal was a distinct form of ethnic pluralism. As a policy it served to isolate many Indians from encroaching civilization. At the same time it further subordinated the Indian and in so doing prolonged any assimilation whatsoever. Warner and Srole (1945) hypothesize that when combined cultural and biological traits are visibly divergent the subordination of one group by another will be intense, the *subsystem strong,* the period of assimilation long, and the process slow and painful. Somehow the federal government's knowledge anticipated the later work of the sociologist W. Lloyd Warner.

In an effort to consolidate and centralize Indian activities, in 1832 Congress authorized an Office of Indian affairs and appointed a commissioner. The office occupied a convenient place in the War Department. In 1849 the Office was transferred to the Department of Interior, a newly formed organizational entity at that time. The move brought to an end an era of Indian-White relations steeped in turmoil, racism, inequities, brutality, and inconsistencies. Establishment of an Office of Indian Affairs centralized the federal government's commitments to the Indians. It also provided a target for Indians and non-Indian supporters to single out when policies, procedures, and the like were not congruent with expectations. And it also marked a beginning of a new and different approach to dealing with the Indians.

Isolationism and Assimilation Era

From about 1850 to about 1885 Indian-White relations, especially those west of the Mississippi, became severely strained. The discovery of gold in California in 1849, in Colorado in 1852, and in the Black Hills of South Dakota in 1875 generated a mass migration of prospectors, adventurers, and fortune hunters. Railroads closely followed in the dust of the trail wagons. And all of the activity also served to rudely introduce the Plains, Plateau, and West Coast Indian to the United States Army.

The Indian resisted the settlement of the West. The ghastly story of the resistance is found in one form or another in American History textbooks where an Indian victory is usually referred to as a "massacre" and one by the U.S. Calvary as a "battle" (Costo, 1970). To add insult to injury the government pitted tribe against tribe, furthering the fermentation of hatred, distrust, and militancy.

Indian land was a prized commodity and there seemed to be no end to the White man's schemes for taking possession. Treaties were signed with no less than 53 Indian groups between 1853 and 1856; but that did not seem to thwart the taking of Indian lands. McNickle (1973) quotes a Senator as saying of the era,

> When we were weak and the Indians were strong, we were glad to make treaties with them and live up to those treaties. Now we [the Whites] have grown powerful and they [the Indian] have grown weak, and it does not become this nation to turn around and trample on the rights of the weak. (p. 76)

Treaties provided a means for the government to both protect and control the Indian. Beginning with the Removal Act of 1830, tribes were confined to land *reserved* exclusively for them. Taylor (1984) argues that the "establishment of reservations was similar to the concept of removal" (p. 15)—a form of isolationism and a weak example of ethnic pluralism. Herding the tribes on to reservations was intended to give the Indian an opportunity to control and govern. To assure that self-sufficiency would occur, however, the Office of Indian Affairs assigned an agent to each of the reservations. That policy was tantamount to ethnocide, as

> many reservations had come under the authority of what had amounted to stern missionary dictatorships whose fanatic zealousness had crushed Indian culture and institutions, suppressed religions and other liberties, and punished Indians for the least show of independence. (Josephy, 1968, p. 340)

Indeed, many reservations were more like internment or concentration camps rather than havens of peace and prosperity.

In 1871 the federal government issued the Appropriation Act, which in effect meant that tribes were no longer recognized as an independent nation and that treaties would not be negotiated with any tribe on that basis. The act set the stage for opening up Indian lands for yet more settlement and the implementation of a full-scale assimilationist philosophy. Merril Gates, a "friend" of the Indian and quoted in Berkhofer (1978), summed up the policy rather succinctly when he stated,

> We have found it necessary, as one of the first steps in developing a stronger personality in the Indian, *to make him responsible for property*. Even if he learns its value only by losing it, and going without it until he works for more, the educational process has begun. (p. 173)

To promote the assimilationist policy the General Allotment Act was passed under the guidance of Senator Henry L. Dawes in 1887, under which each Indian family received 160 acres and a single person 60 acres. The land title was held in trust by the government for 25 years. In addition "citizenship was conferred upon all allotees and upon other Indians who abandoned their lands and adopted 'the habits of civilized life'" (McNickle, 1973, pp. 82-83).

The net result of the so-called Dawes Act was staggering. At the time of the act about 140 million acres were owned jointly by Indians; but in the span of 45 additional years some 90 million of the 140 million acres would be transferred from Indians to Whites. In effect some 65 percent of Indian land would be wrested away from the original inhabitants, courtesy of the government.

The act also provided "citizenship" to those Indians who opted for assimilation, a policy that was actually initiated as early as 1817. In effect, the policy meant that Indians must abandon their "Indianness" in favor of a more civilized lifestyle. The capstone to this policy occurred in 1924 when the U.S. Congress conferred full citizenship rights to Indians born within the territorial boundaries of the United States (Taylor, 1984). Bestowing citizenship upon a defeated nation of original inhabitants has a rather unsettling quality about it; perhaps this is the ultimate insult to the vanquished.

According to social evolutionists and assimilationists, ethnicity usually disappears as industrialization and the elements of modernity increase in society. In essence, "rationality replaces sentimentality in the modern order" (Hraba, 1979, p. 97). With the passage of the Dawes Act, Indians were introduced rather abruptly to industrialization and mechanized agriculture, not to mention the rapid advances of American society. And while the act was intended to provide a vehicle for Indian assimilation it was merely a form of insidious accommodation.

Newman (1973) reminds us that America was basically a competitive society founded in part on social Darwinian principles. Rather than being assimilated most Indians who opted for citizenship and the government's offer of achieving the "American Dream" were relegated to an oppressed status: They no longer possessed the ability to ward off conflict nor did they possess the skills to compete with the White man on their terms. As long as Indians were identified as such they would be viewed as a separate ethnic identity to be dominated—not only by Whites but by the oppressive nature of the Office of Indian Affairs.

Because of intermarriage many Indians were able to pass for White; for them the opportunity to "assimilate" in a highly competitive society was greater than for their kin on the reservations. The restrictions associated with reservation life, the everpresent paternalistic orientation of the federal government, and the lack of desire to farm and ranch tended to further alienate Indians from the main flow of society, leaving them with nothing more than customs and traditions to sustain life. The federal government with the zealous assistance of Christian missionaries even attempted to govern and regulate the banning of ceremonies such as the Ghost and Sun Dances among the Sioux.

In the very early part of the twentieth century America was pre-occupied with growth through industrialization and the seemingly inexhaustible flow of immigrants, mainly from Europe, Scandinavia, and parts of Asia. With the closing of the nineteenth century the "Indian problem" seemed to be settled and America had to get on to the business of ordering growth. Most people concerned with Indian affairs readily accepted the idea that the first American would all but disappear, vanishing into the mainstream of American life. Whatever problems occurred in Indian country could be handled by the Bureau of Indian Affairs through their "trusted" Indian agents. The ancestors of fur traders, frontiersmen, pioneers, miners, and colonists could breath easily at last.

Reorganization and Revivalism

Around 1913 a land dispute complaint was filed by the Pueblo villages of New Mexico that served to call attention, once again, to the status of the Indian. The Pueblos pointed out that many non-Indians were settling on their lands under the aegis of a homestead policy, or were purchasing Indian land as though it was legal to do so. About 1922 the homesteading and the purchases were judged illegal by the federal government. Congress, in turn, created the All Pueblo Lands Board and developed a procedure whereby the Pueblo groups could determine actual ownership of disputed lands (see McNickle, 1973). In addition, groups sympathetic to the Indian also pointed out that the Indian policies then currently in effect had led to the most tragic of conditions—poverty. Moreover, pan-Indian organizations formed in the early part of this century also began pressuring Congress to investigate reported high incidences of disease, deplorable housing conditions, and low educational status within Indian communities. Something was dreadfully wrong with the government's grand plan for the Indian; forced assimilation was failing.

The Indian Reorganization Act

The impoverished condition of the American Indian in the 1920s caught the attention of several congressional members. Mounting pressure was placed on the Department of the Interior to investigate the claims against the BIA and concerning the current status of Indians. In 1928, Lewis Meriam, together with his research team of the Institute of Government Research (now the Brookings Institute) reported on the "Problem of Indian Administration." The Meriam Report essentially called attention to the fact that the federal government's one-sided policy of assimilation was not working. The institute recommended in its 800-page document that the procedures of the social sciences be implemented to further survey the Indian situation, and that "Indian culture" and all its strengths be given some attention in future planning. Furthermore, the report advocated more appropriate educational programs for Indians, of a type that would produce leaders who could facilitate a tribe's eventual and "inevitable" assimilation into modern society. The sociologist Robert Park would be proud of the Meriam Report findings and recommendations as it, like most other federal policies, predicted assimilation but under the guise of "separate but equal"— the motto of the cultural pluralist.

The findings of the Meriam Report stimulated the guilt of sympathetic members of the U.S. Congress. Under President Roosevelt's administration and as part of his grand New Deal scheme for America, the Indian Reorganization Act (IRA) of 1934 was authorized. The IRA gave recognition to the tribe as a controlling entity where, at minimum, decisions about the tribe's welfare could be made at the local level, pending approval (of course) from the Secretary of Interior. "The tribes," commented the Indian historian D'Arcy McNickle, "that made the most effective use of their political powers [granted by the IRA] became, in effect, operating municipalities" (1973, p. 95). With the passage of the IRA the control of Indian affairs was finally back where it was before White contact, or at least that is what many Indians felt and what many government officials wanted to believe. The control, however, was an illusion.

In the years following the IRA, tribes were busy attempting to manage their affairs. During this time other Indian-related developments were being formulated by the Congress. Under the inspired direction of the conservative Senator Arthur Watkins from Utah, steps were initiated to terminate once and for all the federal government's responsibility for Indian affairs. His efforts led to the passage of House Concurrent Resolution 108 in 1953, which in effect provided for the termination of all federal services and the federal trusteeship and the elimination of the special status of the Indian in the scheme of government and treaty obligation (Berkhofer, 1978).

The results of House Resolution 108 were devastating. At the time of the bill's passage some 10 tribes were believed to be ready for termination and another 20 tribes were thought to be ready within 10 years. The history of 2 tribes, the Klamath of Oregon and Menominee of Wisconsin, epitomize the extent of the hardships generated by 108. Although both tribes protested the termination policy, it went through: Some 12,000 lost their tribal right and their status as Indians. For both tribes unemployment rates soared and the level of confusion, depression, and social disorganization climbed to an alarming height. While both tribes received "fair" market value for their right to "free status" most of the millions of dollars vanished into the hands of the unscrupulous, uneducated, and well-intentioned but poorly informed managers. Word of the travesty and the effect of termination rapidly spread in Indian country, sending the level of distrust for the government to an all-time high.

In yet another insidious attempt to absolve the government's responsibility to treaty obligations and to once again push assimilation, in 1956 the BIA under directives from President Eisenhower developed the Employment Relocation Program (now referred to as the Employment Assistance Program). Reservation Indians, mainly males, were essentially given the promise of jobs in major urban areas. The BIA provided applicants with a "one-way bus ticket," the promise of temporary housing, job orientation training, and a job suited to their skills. During the height of the relocation efforts, while many appeared to take advantage of the program, in fact one in every four families who relocated eventually returned to the reservation. The fact that promised jobs often were slow in coming and the pace and pressure of urban life were two factors contributing to "reverse relocation." Once again the government's attempt to assimilate the Indian failed.

Rebellion and Revitalization

The 1960s in the United States was a time for revolution, rebellion, and protest. And White America symbolically was the target. The patience of Blacks had run out—the promise of civil rights was far too slow in coming. College students attacked the entrenched attitudes of the "establishment" and led the protest against the United States' involvement in a "senseless" war. Hispanics, too, joined the liberation effort and called for their due process in the schools, courts, and the labor force. Blacks, Hispanics, and Asian Americans in a sense wanted a piece of the White man's action. But when the Indian joined the protest force the cry was just the opposite. Indians simply were fed up with continued government attempts at assimilation through isolationism, pluralism, and relocation. In fact, the principal Indian protest groups, the National Indian Youth Council (NIYC) and the American Indian Movement (AIM) attacked the very source of their ills—the BIA offices in Washington, D.C.— and called for an end to government control but *not* an end to the government's treaty agreements.

Ironically, many Indian protestors were not asserting their civil rights as other ethnic minority groups did. They reasoned that tribal rights were far more significant and salient, and to emphasize one right over another might jeopardize them both. In effect, Indian activists wanted equal rights but not the assimilation that went with it; they and their ancestors knew all too well the history of past attempts and their grim consequences.

In the course of Indian-White relations—through the genocide, the religious conversions, the removal, isolationism, and termination—Indians somehow managed to survive. Indians not only physically resisted land settlement and encroachment of the colonists, but also psychologically resisted assimilation. The Indian anthropologist Beatrice Medicine points out that the strength of the American Indian lies in a particular world view that "allow[s] for alternatives for changing adaptations which threaten tribal and individual mazeways" (1981, p. 277). And while many Indians have abandoned tribal custom and religious belief, there are still others who prospered in the tradition and legend of their ancestors. For others, descendants of many who followed the way of the White man, the lure of the sacred ceremonials, belief systems, customs, and generalized ethos is compelling.

At this point in history the federal government is *ambivalent* toward the Indian, a posture Myrdal (1944) maintained that Whites held toward Blacks in the 1940s. The ambivalence stems in part from the failure of past efforts to meet the needs of Indian people; from *inherited guilt* derived from past failures including the illegal land claims, genocide, and the prolonged impoverished state of Indian communities; and from pressure from congressional and industrial types to terminate federal responsibility and abrogate treaty agreements. The Reagan administration of the 1980s desperately wants to terminate federal relations and in an effort to achieve this has cut BIA appropriations from $1.2 billion in past years to $900 million and has accelerated efforts for tribal self-determination. But the administration's policy will fail, in part because of ambivalence. Budgets will be slashed and tribes will continue to receive encouragement to accelerate efforts at self-government.

An examination of the social indicators of America's ethnic minority populations reveals a startling pattern of neglect, discrimination, and repeated violations of civil rights. It also reveals that the four principal groups—Asian Americans, Blacks, Hispanics, and Indians—occupy the low rung of the socioeconomic ladder. That representation is most evident for Indians, whose unemployment rates, median years of education, mortality rates, per capita income, rates of alcoholism and drug abuse, incidence of suicides, and incidence of certain diseases are *worse* than any other ethnic group in North America (Medicine, 1981)—this despite a budget of well over $2 billion budgeted exclusively for Indian affairs (Taylor, 1984). In other words, despite the government's best effort to ameliorate the circumstances inherited through historical fiat, they have failed.

Yet in spite of all the failures the indigenous American perseveres. Perhaps the strength to survive is embedded in an identification with one's ethnicity, as suggested by the psychologist-anthropologist George DeVos (1975). Ethnicity is part of one's definition of self, and through it one's past and present are defined. The federal government has attempted to erode and chip away at the ethnic ethos of tribal life; at the core though was a strong sense of what it meant to be Lakota, Navajo, Iroquois, Seminole, Lummi, Cherokee, Choctaw, Ote, and hundreds of other distinctive sources of strength. Ethnicity most likely then is a source of psychological survival that transcends all other forms of intervention.

But along with ethnic identity there is a need to recognize the integrity of pluralism and the inalienable right to live in freedom. Perhaps this thought was best expressed by Chief Joseph of the Nez Perce in 1877:

I know that my race must change. We cannot hold our own with the white man as we are. We only ask an even chance to live as other men live. We ask to be recognized as men. We ask that the same law shall work alike on all men. . . .

Let me be a free man—free to travel, free to stop, free to work, free to trade where I choose, free to choose my own teachers, free to follow the religion of my fathers, free to think and talk and act for myself. . . .

[And when this comes] the Great Spirit Chief who rules above will smile upon this land and send rain to wash out the bloody spots made by brothers' hands from the face of the earth. For this time the Indian race are waiting and praying. (Council on Interracial Books for Children, 1971, p. 256)

NOTE

1. Hereafter the term "Indian" will be used in lieu of American Indian and Alaska Native. Such practice is customary in historical and social writing about the first American.

References

Apfelbaum, E. (1979). Relations of domination and movements for liberation: An analysis of power between groups (I. Woek, Trans.). In W. G. Austin & S. Worchel (Eds.), *The social psychology of intergroup relations*. Belmont, CA: Brooks/Cole.

Berkhofer, R. F. (1978). *The White man's Indian: Images of the American Indian from Columbus to the present*. New York: Vintage.

Cohen, F. (1942). *Handbook of federal Indian law*. Albuquerque: University of New Mexico Press.

Coser, L. (1956). *The functions of social conflict*. New York: Free Press.

Costo, R. (Ed.). (1970). *Textbooks and the American Indian*. San Francisco: Indian Historian Press.

Council of Interracial Books for Children (Ed.). (1971). *Chronicles of American Indian protest*. Greenwich, CT: Fawcett.

DeVos, G. (1975). Ethnic pluralism: Conflict and accommodation. In G. DeVos & L. Romanucci-Ross (Eds.), *Ethnic identity: Cultural continuities and change* (pp. 5-41). Palo Alto, CA: Mayfield Publishing.

Hraba, J. (1979). *American ethnicity*. Itasca, IL: F.E. Peacock.

Josephy, A. M. (1968). *The Indian heritage of America*. New York: Knopf.

McNickle, D. (1973). *Native American tribalism: Indian survivals and renewals*. New York: Oxford University Press.

Medicine, B. (1981). Native American resistance to integration: Contemporary confrontations and religious revitalization. *Plains Anthropologist, 94*, 227-286.

Myrdal, G. (1944). *An American dilemma: The Negro problem and modern democracy*. New York: Harper & Row.

Newman W. M. (1973). *American pluralism*. New York: Harper & Row.

Park, R. E. (1950). *Race and culture*. New York: Free Press.

Svensson, F. (1973). *The ethnics in American politics: American Indians*. Minneapolis: Burgess Publishing Company.

Taylor, T. W. (1984). *The Bureau of Indian Affairs*. Boulder, CO: Westview.

United States Commission on Civil Rights. (1981). *Indian tribes: A continuing quest for survival*. Washington, DC: Government Printing Office.

United States Department of Education. (1982). *A study of alternative definitions and measures relating to eligibility and service under Part A of the Indian Education Act*. Unpublished report, United States Department of Education, Washington, DC.

Vignaras, L. A. (1960). *The journal of Christopher Columbus* (C. Jane, Trans. rev.). London: Hakluyt Society.

Warner, W.L., & Srole, L. (1945). *The social systems of American ethnic groups*. New Haven, CT: Yale University Press.

Worchel, P. (1979). Trust and distrust. In W.G. Austin & S. Worchel (Eds.), *The social psychology of intergroup relations*. Belmont, CA: Brooks/Cole.

Chapter Summary

Eric S. Casiño deals with interethnic conflicts involving the Moros of the Philippines. Casiño explains that although this conflict has been labeled a Muslim-Christian problem, the issues involved go beyond religion. The author suggests that sociological and anthropological perspectives are necessary in order to consider the nonreligious variables. The main proposition advanced in this chapter is that interethnic conflicts are influenced by classificatory and psychological dynamics as well as political motivations.

The extensive background of the Moros presented here revolves around the fact that the Moros comprise several distinct ethnolinguistic groups. The demographic and ethnographic characteristics of the Moros are presented through an overview of Philippine geography and anthropology. Four Philippine population types based on economic orientation and ecological niche are described.

Casiño discusses the Muslim secession movement of the Southern Philippines and the Moro National Liberation Front (MNLF), which spearheaded the movement, as well as other organizations playing major roles in Philippine interethnic relations. He explains further that although the Tripoli Agreement of 1976 granted autonomy to 13 regions claimed as Moro homelands, a 1977 referendum found that not all of the inhabitants of these provinces were in accord with the proposals of the agreement. Casiño discusses a subsequent rebellion of the MNLF and its support from other Islamic states, including groups in Malaysia and Libya.

Casiño's approach to classificatory ethnicity takes a dialectical view, which considers the larger context of both the minority and the majority together. Ethnic categories are viewed within a chain of classification.

The author analyzes the changing use of the term "Moro" throughout Philippine's history. A distinction is drawn between exonyms, or externally imposed categories such as Moro, and autonyms, or self-designations. Casiño asserts that when the Spaniards introduced the term "Moro," a group identity was given to the various Islamic ethnolinguistic groups. Changes in the application of the term "Filipino" are also discussed. Casiño points out that American political administrators used "Filipino" in reference to those who were Christianized to distinguish them from the "pagans" and Moros. Later, nationalist movements based on the *Liga Filipina* advocated the avoidance of all Spanish exonyms. Casiño draws a relationship between the semantic ambiguity of the term "Filipino" and the political claim that Moros are not Filipinos.

Ingroup-outgroup analysis is recommended, and examples of its application to the Moro situation are provided. Three ingroup-outgroup levels are described: the primary, precolonial ethnolinguistic level; the secondary, colonial-religious level; and the tertiary, postcolonial national-society level.

In the final section Casiño relates the Moro situation to interethnic conflict theory regarding (1) possible responses of the minority to perceived majority oppression; (2) the role of international relations in interethnic conflict; (3) the relevance of ingroup-outgroup analysis; and (4) the formulation of ethnocentrism.

—Susan Goldstein

10

Interethnic Conflict
in the Philippine Archipelago

ERIC S. CASIÑO

The main proposition of this chapter is that interethnic conflict is governed not only by political and economic factors, but also by logical and psychological determinants. Indeed the treatment of group psychology within the classic ingroup-outgroup formulation is the best illustration that interethnic conflict involves not only sentiments but the delineation of boundary markers that follow the laws of *logical typing* (Bateson, 1972). In this chapter I base my argument for this proposition on the historic struggle of the Moros of the Philippines to maintain their Islamic identity and culture against a series of outgroups that includes not only foreign powers such as the Spanish, the Japanese, and the Americans, but also against fellow inhabitants of the Philippines, the so-called Christian Filipinos and the Philippine government. The Moro case is important in terms of its substantive as well as its methodological focus. Substantively, the Moro case highlights a major difference between those types of interethnic struggle in which national territory is involved (e.g., the secessionist struggles of the Moros, or the Quebecois) and those where only ethnic boundries and status positions are at issue (as among the Blacks and Jews in New York). Methodologically, the Moro case, or the approach I use in its analysis, suggests that the concept of levels of logical typing is an unavoidable analytical issue in all cases of interethnic conflict. Such a "classifi-

231

catory" approach might have a useful application in understanding other instances of interethnic conflict worldwide.

The general purpose of this chapter, then, is a reciprocal enrichment of both the specific case and the generic phenomenon of social action and culture change under the impetus of ethnic motivation. To reach this objective I will adopt a number of theoretical insights from three comparative studies. Specifically, these insights are (1) the dialectic relations between systems theory and power-conflict theory from Schermerhorn's book, *Comparative Ethnic Relations* (1978); (2) the role of international relations in the escalation and moderation of interethnic conflict within a pluralistic nation, as suggested by Suhrke and Noble in *Ethnic Conflict in International Relations* (1977); and (3) the psychological dynamics of ingroup-outgroup sentiments and perceptions, as developed by Levine and Campbell in *Ethnocentrism* (1972).

In analyzing the Moros of the Philippines, it will be useful to distinguish three aspects of ethnicity, which I described elsewhere as political, classificatory, and psychological (Casiño, 1985). Briefly defined, *political ethnicity* is that aspect of the phenomenon that pertains to the political action of groups and parties to obtain or defend what they consider to be the benefits due to them as a group. *Classificatory ethnicity* is that aspect of the phenomenon that pertains to the logical imperatives to distinguish the ingroup from the outgroup. *Psychological ethnicity,* finally, is that aspect of the phenomenon that appears as a struggle to redefine status and create pride and dignity for the ingroup. The Moro case can be shown to involve all three aspects insofar as the Moros want to achieve autonomy in a definite territory, to distinguish themselves as a separate "nationality"—a *Bangsa Moro,* and to create pride in the achievement and dignity of their Islamic heritage.

Background

The Moros are those native inhabitants of the Southern Philippines who had been converted to Islam before the rest of the natives of the Philippines were converted to Christianity (Casiño, 1982, pp. 78-85). The Moros do not form a single ethnic group but consist of a series of distinct ethnolinguistic communities, of which 13 have been identified. Altogether they number less than five percent of the total Philippine population of over 50 million people.

The Philippine island world is geographically divided into three segments strung along a north-south axis. These three segments are popularly identified with the principal islands of Luzon, Visayas, and Mindanao. Philippine nationalists have always recognized this threefold arrangement of the Filipino homeland, so much so that the national flag carries three stars to symbolize this threefold division. The Moro secessionist movement questions the integration of parts of this southern third of the Philippine territory with the Philippine state. The Islamization of the Philippines may have started from the thirteenth century as a result of trade contacts with the Indo-Malaysian world. Today, the Filipino Muslims are found in those areas adjacent to Indonesia and Malaysia, namely the islands of Mindanao, Sulu, and Palawan.[1] The Southern Philippines, in its largest extent, comprises the islands of Mindanao, Basilan, Sulu, Tawi-Tawi, and Palawan, with a combined area of 11.5 million hectares or 39 percent of the total area of the Philippines.

Sulu became one historic center of Islamic consciousness in the Southern Philippines. The other historic center was Magindanao, the present area of Cotabato in Western Mindanao. Both served as centers of resistance to all efforts from the North to integrate the Southern Philippines with a Philippine-wide polity under the Spanish, American, and now Filipino sovereignty.

The Southern Philippines' total population according to the 1980 census data is 10.5 million. The provinces where a significant number of Muslims are found are the following: Sulu (94 percent Muslim); Tawi-Tawi (96 percent); Lanao del Sur (92 percent); Basilan (61 percent); Sultan Kudarat (22 percent); Lanao del Norte (23 percent); North Catabato (19 percent). Within the Southern Philippines with its population of 10.5 million, Muslims constitute 22 percent of the total.

In their physical characteristics the Moros are clearly Filipinos, that is, belonging to Philippine ethnosomatic types. They also speak languages that relate more closely to the Philippine family of languages than they do the Malay-related languages of Indonesia and Malaysia.

Classificatory Ethnicity

When the Spaniards came to colonize the Philippines in 1521 under Magellan, they generally referred to all natives with the exonymic term *Indios,* the same term they used to designate the natives of the Americas. When they noted that some of the natives were Muslims, they utilized a second exonymic term, *Moros,* to designate such Islamized natives, the same term they used to refer to their historic enemies the Moors of North Africa and southern Spain. When some of the Indios started to convert to Christianity, to become *Christianos,* the Spaniards had to coin a third exonymic term, *Infieles,* to refer to those natives, particularly the highlanders of Luzon and Mindanao, who remained unconverted to either Islam or Christianity. These three exonyms—Indios, Moros, and Infieles—eventually entered the general discourse on the history of ethnography of the Philippines. When the Americans succeeded the Spaniards as colonizers of the Philippines, they tended to lump together the Moros and Infieles under the category "non-Christians," as exemplified by the title of a colonial administrative unit, the "Bureau of Non-Christian Tribes." Subsequently, under the successor Philippine Republic, this category was relabeled "cultural minorities," with the Moros now called Muslims, and the infieles called *Pagans* or Tribals. The Indios who have become Christians were the corresponding cultural majority.

What is important to note in this brief history is that all three exonyms imposed by the Spaniards are second-level categories or social classifications, in so far as they grouped together first-level ethnic identities with autonomic or self-imposed names (e.g., Tagalog, Bisaya, Tausug). The category Moro encompassed 13 ethnolinguistic groups which regarded each other as distinct peoples. Similarly, the category Indio, when confined to the Christianized natives, numbered 8 distinct ethnolinguistic groups distributed throughout the archipelago. Last, the Infieles or Pagans comprised more than a dozen named tribal groups in Northern Luzon and the highlands of the Visayas and Mindanao. In the colonial period there was not a single state or a single nation that could be named coextensively with the totality of Philippine society. When the category Filipino evolved as a name for all the peoples and groups in the islands, it served in effect as a third-level umbrella name for the triple Spanish exonyms (Indios, Moros, Infieles) and the first-level tribal groups under them (Casiño, 1975b, pp. 18-29).

How the name and category "Filipino" was semantically transformed and transvalued from its original meaning of Philippine-born Spaniard to its current meaning of Philippine national inhabitant and citizen is one of the least-researched mysteries of the turn-of-the-century nationalist transformation of Philippine native society.[2] Yankee intervention in Philippine colonial social history has much to do with the adoption of the name Filipino as the name of the national group. The Americans, however, were not disinterested propagators of the national name, for in common practice they had narrowed the name Filipino to mean the Christianized natives, thereby politically distinguishing them from the Moros and Infieles. Part of their reasoning was linked to an attempt to separate Mindanao and Sulu from the Philippines on the supposition that the Moros were not Filipinos (i.e., Christian Filipinos). In the 69th Congress of the United States, Representative Robert L. Bacon (Republican, New York) introduced a bill (H.R. 12772 of June 11, 1926) separating Mindanao, Sulu, and Palawan from the jurisdiction of of the Philippine Government and establishing for those regions a separate form of government directly under American sovereignty. Among the reasons Bacon mentioned were the following:

> that the Moros are essentially a different race from the Filipinos, that for hundreds of years there has existed bitter racial and religious hatreds between the two and that complete union of the Filipinos under one government is distasteful to the Moros, who would prefer a continuance of the American sovereignty. (Churchill, 1983, pp. 134-135)

American political interference in the Philippines, therefore, resulted in three meanings for the name Filipino:

(F-1) Philippine-born Spaniard. It categorically excluded the Indios and other native social categories such as Moros and Infieles.

(F-2) Native inhabitants of the Philippines, irrespective of language, religion, ethnicity, or regional origin. Such a name when extended to total Philippine society is a national name.

(F-3) Christian lowlanders of the Philippines. F-3 logically excludes the Infieles and Moros. In this sense it is not a name for all the members of the total national society.

What is clear from the history of the nationalist revolution in the Philippines is that the idea of a nation was to be coextensive with total Philippine society. The clearest expression of the idea of a

Philippine national society prescinding now from from its culturally conditioned name, is found in Jose Rizal's *Liga Filipina* (1972), the seed of later Philippine state constitutions.[3] The Liga defined its primary goals in the following terms: (1) to unite the whole archipelago into one compact, vigorous, unified nation; (2) mutual protection in every case of trouble and need; (3) defense against every violence and injustice; (4) development of education, agriculture, and commerce; and (5) study and implementation of reforms.

The archipelago-wide vision of peoplehood, a national society, was shared by other nationalist revolutionaries of this period. General Pio del Pilar's version of the Katipunan flag had the color white to symbolize "brightness and equality of all Filipinos in the three islands—Luzon, Visayas, and Mindanao" (Casiño, 1982, p. 215).

Because the idea of a Philippine-wide nationality emerged from the Christian majority and suffered American colonial interference, the name of the national society, Filipino, is subject to ambiguity. This is manifested in the claim that the Moros are not Filipinos. To transfer that semantic argument into the political arena is not just to challenge the name but the national idea and reality behind the name.

Political Ethnicity

The challenge to the political and classificatory status quo in the Philippines was initiated about 1968 by the Moro National Liberation Front (MNLF), whose avowed goal was secession from and dismemberment of the Philippines. The cost of the resulting conflict was tragic and enormous—60,000 dead; 200,000 refugees in Sabah; and more than a million homeless (McAmis, 1983, pp. 38-39). Founded by a small band of Manila-educated young Muslim intellectuals and student activists (the MNLF Chairman, Nur Misuari, was an instructor at the state-run University of the Philippines), the MNLF had an estimated strength of 15,000 to 30,000 armed fighters in the field at the height of the rebellion.

Politics being about the control of people and territories and about the people's recognition of the authority of those who rule over them and their territories, the MNLF act of rebellion by secession was a supreme political act. To understand the structural implications of this act, we need to briefly trace the political history of the Philippines.

At one time there was no such entity as a single Filipino nation or state, nor a single Bangsa Moro nation or state. The congeries of primary-level tribal groupings were loosely organized into membership in three Philippine states. One was the Manila-based Spanish colonial state; the other two were native states with an Islamic ideology: the sultanate of Sulu and the sultanate of Magindanao. Neither of these three states had a Philippine-wide scope of jurisdiction and political control, although Spanish Manila had the largest span of political sovereignty, embracing Luzon, Visayas, and parts of Mindanao. Over the course of the nineteenth century, the contested areas under Sulu and Magindanao control gradually came under Spanish Manila's hegemony, thanks to the recognition of rival Dutch and British colonial expansionists in Indonesia and Borneo who wanted to stabilize their common borders (Warren, 1981, pp. 123-124). The Moro sultans themselves entered into treaties with Spain, recognizing largely the latter's nominal sovereignty over them, because in their internal affairs their Islamic societies were functioning structures.

When Spanish sovereignty was transferred in 1899 to the United States, it was clearly understood that it included the sovereignty over Mindanao and Sulu Muslim territories. This political understanding was underlined most clearly in the instructions furnished by General Bates, then American Military Governor of the Philippines, to General Otis, who was being sent to assume control over Sulu. Bates wrote,

> The United States has succeeded to all the rights which Spain held in the Archipelago, and its sovereignty over the same is an established fact. But the inquiry arises as to the extent to which that sovereignty can be applied under the agreement of 1878 with the Moros. . . . The Moros acknowledged, through their accepted chiefs, Spanish sovereignty and their subjection thereto, and that nation in turn conferred upon their chiefs powers of supervision over them and their affairs. The kingly prerogatives of Spain, thus abridged by solemn concession, have descended to the United States, and conditions existing at the time of transfer should remain. (Gowing, 1977, p. 31)

The same rights that Spain passed on to the United States the latter in turn passed on to the successor Philippine Republic, which declared independence in 1946. It is this political entity that had power, jurisdiction, and authority over all the territories and all the peoples of the Philippines and against which the MNLF raised the banner of revolt. From the internal perspective of the Philippines the MNLF rebellion is a purely internal affair between the state and a segment of the national community. But from the standpoint of international relations, the Moro case involves a number of international players in both the political and military arena.

The young MNLF leaders gained access to international leverage against the abuses of the Philippine government through the Islamic Conference of Foreign Ministers, which met annually on matters affecting Muslim peoples and states around the world. At the fourth Islamic Conference in Bengazi, Libya, in March 1973, it was decided to form the Quadrapartite Commission composed of Foreign Ministers from Libya, Saudi Arabia, Senegal, and Somalia, which was given the task to visit the Philippines and to discuss with the Philippine government the plight of Filipino Muslims. In the 5th Islamic Conference, held in Kuala Lumpur, Malaysia, in January 1974, the conference passed Resolution 18 which suggested some solutions to the Moro problem. It urged the Philippine government

> to find a political and peaceful solution through negotiation with Muslim leaders, particularly with the representative of the Moro National Liberation Front, in order to arrive at a just solution to the plight of Filipino Muslims within the framework of the National sovereignty and territorial integrity of the Philippines.

At the 6th Islamic Conference, held in Jeddah, Saudi Arabia, in July 1975, the Quadrapartite Commission submitted a plan of action approved by the conference and agreed upon by the MNLF, on the basis of which the Quadrapartite would negotiate with the Philippine government over the Moro problem. The following year, December 21, 1976, the MNLF and the Philippine government finally signed the historic and pivotal Tripoli Agreement, with the participation of the Quadripartite Ministerial Commission members of the Islamic Conference and the Secretary General of the Islamic Conference. The key provisions of the Tripoli Agreement were (1) the establishment of autonomy in the Southern Philippines within the realm of the sovereignty and territorial integrity of the Republic of the Philippines; (2) the specification of 13 geographic areas of autonomy for the Muslims in the Southern Philippines; and (3) the promise that all necessary constitutional processes for the implementation of the entire agreement would be taken by the Philippine government.

In accordance with the Philippine constitution, major changes such as those demanded by the MNLF for the areas of autonomy had to be decided through popular referendum, which was held April 17, 1977. The results showed that not all of the 13 provinces wanted to join the proposed areas of autonomy. The provinces that voted against integration were three—namely, Davao del Sur, South Catabato, and Palawan. The remaining 10 provinces were grouped into two autonomous regions, Region 9 and Region 12, comprising 5 provinces each, as follows:

Region 9
(1) Basilan
(2) Sulu
(3) Tawi-Tawi
(4) Zamboanga del Sur
(5) Zamboanga del Norte

Region 12
(1) Lanao del Norte
(2) Lanao del Sur
(3) North Catabato
(4) Magindanao
(4) Sultan Kudarat

Other issues addressed by the referendum pertained to the role of the MNLF in the areas of autonomy and the MNLF demand for statelike powers and prerequisites for the proposed autonomous regional government. The referendum rejected the proposals (1) that the region of autonomy be called Bangsamoro Islamic Region; (2) that it should have its own flag, official language, and seal separate and distinct from the national government; (3) that it should have its own Court of Appeals and Supreme Court; (4) that it be granted power of general legislation including taxation similar to that of the National Assembly of the national government; (5) that the MNLF be empowered to organize a security force to maintain peace and order separate from and outside the supervision of the armed forces of the Philippines, the Integrated National Police, or any other office of the national government; (6) that the executive council of the region of the autonomy he headed by a Chief Minister and a Deputy Chief Minister; and (7) that the accounts of the region of the autonomy be audited only by a regional commission and not by the National Commission on Audit (Implementation of the Tripoli Agreement, 1984).

On the basis of these referendum results, other national political decisions regarding the Southern Philippines were made. On March 20, 1979, the Philippine *Batasang Pambansa* (National Assembly) passed a legislative act, Batas Pambansa, No. 20, providing for the organization of the *Sangguniang Pampook* (Regional Assembly) and the *Lupong Tagapagpaganap* (Regional Executive Council) for the autonomous Regions 9 and 12. Some members of the Assembly and the Executive Council are former MNLF commanders who have surrendered only their violence but not their determination to improve the quality of life of the Muslims of the Southern Philippines. The Philippines is able to justify such major political and administrative decisions because it has in its constitution two provisions allowing autonomous local or regional government within its sovereignty and territorial integrity.

Within a year of the Tripoli Agreement, the MNLF, which boycotted the referendum, broke the ceasefire accord that was part of that agreement and continued the armed struggle, although with less coordination and intensity. The behavior of the MNLF, in both diplomatic and military arenas, needs to be analyzed not just in relation to the Philippine government's responses and reforms but in terms of the international players who played various parts in the circuits of influence behind the rebellion. In their analysis of the international relations angle of the MNLF rebellion, Suhrke and Noble (1977, pp. 178-212) offer strong evidence that Islamic states both encouraged and moderated the MNLF protagonists. Malaysia, a Muslim country, and its state of Sabah offered training to MNLF commanders and guerrillas in the early phase of the rebellion. Indonesia, although predominantly Muslim, always maintained a pro-Philippine position as it saw a successful secession movement could become a threat to the stability of the Asean region. Libya, however, helped finance the buying of arms and logistic supplies.

The series of Islamic Conferences from the second to the eighth (1972-1977) passed resolutions that were generally fair and balanced in their treatment of the interests of the Moros and of the Philippine state. All the resolutions of the Islamic Conference in effect held back the MNLF from pressing for complete independence and advised it to settle for autonomy within the Philippine state. This diplomatic restraint was also a clear signal to the Philippine government that the conference would not interfere with the internal affairs of another sovereign state. All of the international players who were on either side of the issue followed the etiquette of international relations (i.e., respect for the integrity of fellow states). But Suhrke and Noble concluded their discussion with a sober note:

> Thus the basic causes of Muslim-Christian conflict remain unresolved. The separatists and their overseas sympathizers have succeeded in getting concessions that have benefited Muslims, including many against whom the rebellion was presumably directed; they have not succeeded in getting fundamental change. (Suhrke & Noble, 1977, p. 185)

Notwithstanding Suhrke and Noble's judgment, the international angle to the Moro interethnic conflict has grown more visible and serious through the years. Its success in bringing the Philippine government to the conference table at the 1976 Tripoli negotiations has conferred upon the MNLF an international political and legal status. The Philippines accords the MNLF only the status of insurgency, not that of belligerency, which carries a lot more leverage in international law. In 1980 the Moro case was recognized by the Permanent People's Tribunal (PPT), a favorite forum of those in the anti-imperialist camp who are fighting for self-determination. The earlier option between independence and autonomy is now transcended by the rhetoric of self-determination, which elicits much sympathy among other oppressed groups in the world (Gerlack & Hine, 1970, pp. 183-198). Thus the Moro conflict is no longer the concern only of Asean nor of the Islamic Conference political players, but is now in the agenda of the superpowers. Misuari's MNLF faction, having gotten close to Iran and its fundamentalist brand of Islam, threatens the U.S. interest in the Philippines. Apparently to counter this anti-imperialist threat, the U.S. State Department and the Pentagon have started to open lines of communication to the MNLF Reformist group under Dimas Pundato, who was invited, just this year (1985), to Washington, D.C. The Philippine national security aspect of the MNLF rebellion has forced the Philippines to label the Moro fighters as "Muslim terrorists," a practice shared by some U.S. political observers (Mastura, 1984, pp. 24-28). To the MNLF, however, their soldiers are freedom fighters, the strength of their Bangsa Moro Army (BMA) or Bangsamoro Mujahideen. The Moro conflict indeed has serious world-wide ramifications.

Psychological Ethnicity

The reasons for the MNLF failure to obtain the kind of reforms that it could accept are many. Some of these reasons stem from the resistance of the Philippine government to grant all its demands, or the government's method of appointing Muslim leaders not acceptable to the MNLF leadership. The other reasons derive from psychological sources—the internal conflict within the MNLF leadership mirroring the weakness of the *we-group* notion it used as a basis for the rebellion. To continue our analysis of the psychological dimension of the Moro interethnic conflict, it is useful to quote William Graham Sumner (1906):

> *Sentiments in the in-group and towards the out-group.* The relation of comradeship and peace in the we-group and that of hostility and war towards others-group are correlatives to each other. The exigencies of war with outsiders are what make peace inside, lest internal discord should weaken the we-group for war. These exigencies also make government and law in the in-group, in order to prevent quarrels and enforce discipline. Thus war and peace have reacted on each other and developed each other, one within the group, and the other in the intergroup relation. The closer the neighbors, and the stronger they are, the intenser is the warfare, and then the intenser is the internal organization and discipline of each. Sentiments are produced to correspond. Loyalty to the group, sacrifice for it, hatred and contempt for outsiders, brotherhood within, warlike-ness without—all group together, common products of the same situation (Sumner, 1906, pp. 12-13).

If we apply the concept of the IG-OG (ingroup-outgroup) relations to the Moro case, one is confronted with a problem: Which ingroup and which outgroup? In the preceding section on classificatory ethnicity, it was pointed out that there are at least three levels of logical typing of social categories in the Philippines—the tribel, the colonial, and the national. The MNLF Chairman of the Central Committee, Nur Misuari, who is a Tausug, attempted to transcend the tribel or primary IG-OG level by appealing to the all-Moro sentiments of "Minsupala"—the Muslims of Mindanao, Sulu, and Palawan. In his "Appeal Letter to the Islamic Foreign Ministers Conference" (the fifth) on June 21, 1974, he extols the heroism of the Moro people against the tyranny of the Spanish, the Americans, the Japanese, and the Christian Filipino leaders:

> And yet when it comes to the question of defending their national freedom, their homeland and Islam, our people have already repeatedly withstood the test of time. Nearly four centuries of costly fighting, pitted invariably against the mightiest colonial powers (Spanish, American, and Japanese) is great enough evidence to show their unconquerable spirit and determination to assert their inherent desire to remain free, sovereign, and independent. But by a sudden twist of history and mainly due to the criminal manipulations of the Filipino leaders, our people have fallen under the iron-grip of Christian Filipino rule. (Noble, 1983, p. 42)

It is clear from the rhetorical tone and ideological context of this appeal that Misuari is operating on the colonial or secondary level by opposing the Moro ingroup against a series of outgroups.[4] The classic Sumnerian juxtaposition of boundary markers and sentiments attached to the IG-OG opposition is clearly there. The statement was designed to elicit sympathy for the Moro cause, to lobby support from the rich members of the Islamic conference. Rhetorical exaggeration has its uses and also its cost, however. A political scientist with a strong pro-MNLF leaning concluded that the separatist leadership "exaggerated the solidarity and sympathy likely to be coming from other Islamic States" (Noble, 1983, p. 50).

As we shift our attention from the Muslim-versus-Christian level to the Muslim-versus-Muslim level, we encounter IG-OG sentiments opposing Tausug against Maranao, Maranao against Magindanao, Samal against Tausug, and so forth. The separation of the primary from the secondary IG-OG opposition level is not simply a notional distinction in the minds of observers; the distinction is real and is externalized in the thinking, sentiments, and behavior of the people themselves. The weakening of the MNLF struggle may be ultimately traceable not just to the reforms initiated by the Philippine government but also the centrifugal tendencies of the pre-Islamic sentiments at the primary IG-OG level. Noble, who has monitored the rise and fall of the MNLF organization, concluded that the secessionist leadership "vastly overestimated the sense of nationalism of Philippine Muslims, among whom lines of fissure were profound and obvious" (Noble, 1983, p. 49).

The lines of fissure followed ethnic lines as well as ideological convictions. Two new factions split from the original MNLF nucleus and gravitated around Hashim Salamat, a Magindanao, and Dimas Pundato, a Maranao. If we list the three factions on the rebel side and those Moros who are pro-Philippines by being with the government or the opposition—for example, the Philippine Muslim Solidarity Conference and MNLF Returnees—we obtain four basic positions: (1) the Separatist movement of Misuari aspiring to become a distinct nationality; (2) the Islamic movement of Salamat seeking to provide an alternative authentic identity; (3) the Reformist movement of Dimas pursuing to achieve meaningful autonomy; and (4) those partisans and cause-oriented groups who are for the government or with the political opposition (Mastura, 1984, p. 2).

As early as December 1977, Salamat had voiced his doctrinal difference with Misuari. "The MNLF leadership was being manipulated away from Islamic basis, methodologies, and objectives and fast evolving towards Marxist-Maoist orientation" (Mastura, 1984, p. 115). Both Salamat and Pundato considered Misuari a "roadblock towards a just, honorable, and comprehensive settlement of the Bangsamoro problem by insisting on his intransigent terms which are tantamount to abandoning the letter and spirit of the Tripoli Agreement" (Salamat, 1982, p. 19). Salamat's "takeover" bid in 1977 for the revolution's leadership led to a major split in the original group with his proclamation of a new MNLF leadership. The breakup was sealed by his communication to the secretariat of the Organization of Islamic Conference that his new MNLF central committee would change the title of the front to MILF—Moro Islamic Liberation Front.

The biggest breakaway was led in 1979 by Dimas Pundato, who was to form the MNLF Reformist Movement. It is claimed that the Pundato following, forming about 90 percent of Misuari's armed supporters, hurt the old MNLF leadership the most (Mastura, 1984, p. 19). Some of Pundato's Moranao allies are remnants of BMLO (Bangsa Moro Liberation Organization), founded by the late Rashid Lucman, an older generation Maranao political leader. Pandato's group, like Salamat's, is willing to resume the stalled Tripoli Agreement.

In retaliation against Salamat and Pundato, Misuari did not reconvene the central committee, where the two had seats, and cut them off from financial support and communication. The MNLF Reformist Movement countered by convening in Sabah, Malaysia, the National People's Congress in July 1982 at which a resolution was passed abolishing the central committee.

This was by no means the end of Nur Misuari nor of the original MNLF and its secessionist agenda. In 1980 the 11th Islamic Conference reaffirmed its support for the struggle of the Bangsamoro people "under the leadership of the Moro National Liberation Front with a view to achieving self-determination" (Mastura, 1984, p. 12). The 15th Islamic Conference (1984) confirmed Misuari's original MNLF as the "sole legitimate representative of the Bangsamoro people" (Misuari, 1985, p. 200).

The centrifugal tendencies at the primary IG-OG level manifest themselves also in the regional loyalties. In terms of sentiment, there is not a single Moro homeland; the concept of *dar-ul-Islam* remains a jurisprudential notion that has no relevance to existing fragmented turf loyalties. Many Samals still resent Tausug dominance in Sulu and are glad that Tawi-Tawi was finally constituted a separate province from the old province of Sulu. The establishment of the Western Mindanao University in Zamboanga was largely a result of the fact that Tausug and Samal students did not feel safe and at home in the Maranao-dominated Mindanao State University in Marawi.

There is a third-level IG-OG opposition that we must not forget. This is the postcolonial membership level of a national society organized under a single nation-state. Muslims are as much members of this national ingroup as they are in the primary or precolonial (Maranao-versus-Tausug) level, and the secondary or colonial (Muslim-versus-Christian) level. At this tertiary IG-OG level, the outgroups are the other nation-states that had anything to do with the Moro rebellion in the Southern Philippines.

Analysis and Conclusion

Wirth (1945, pp. 354-363) has proposed a fourfold typology of minority response to majority oppression: assimilationist, pluralist, secessionist, and militant. Assimilation is a policy that seeks to merge minority members in the majority culture by abandoning their values and lifestyles. The pluralist policy demands tolerance from the dominant group to allow minorities to retain much of their cultural distinctiveness. The secessionist strategy by definition aims at radical separation from common membership with the dominant group under a single society. And the militant policy is armed attack on the central government, not in support of secession goals but to capture central government power and restructure political power from the center. The current Moro strategy, for instance, clearly belongs to the third type—secession—but its militant thrust does not fit Wirth's fourth type since the Moros are not interested in taking over the central government apparatus of the Philippines.

Schermerhorn criticized Wirth's typology, and rightly so, for its onesidedness. The typology does not take into account the corresponding policy on the part of the majority and the central government. Even if a minority follows a policy of assimilation, that may not work in a society whose majority believe in an apartheid ideology, as in South Africa, or in a castelike ideology, as in preindependence India. It is therefore absolutely necessary that the policy of both the government and the minority be explicitly articulated. In the case of the Philippines, a series of early government policies encouraged assimilation—a move not exactly opposed by the minority, especially as assimilation was understood to pertain to equal access to educational and civil service opportunities. One evidence of this assimilationist thrust is the establishment of the Commission on National Integration (CNI) in 1957, whose basic policy thrust was integration (i.e., assimilation) and whose mission statement was copied almost verbatim from the objectives of the Bureau of Non-Christian Tribes established in 1916 by the American colonial government. The 1916 statement read as follows:

> to foster, by all adequate means and in a systematic, rapid, and complete manner the moral, material, economic, social, and political development of these regions (inhabited by so-called non-Christian Filipinos), always having in view the aim of rendering permanent the mutual intelligence between the complete fusion of all the Christian and Non-Christian elements populating the provinces of the archipelago. (Casiño, 1975a, p. 189)

The interesting change introduced in the CNI mission statement is shown in the following paraphrase: "to make real, complete and permanent the integration of all the National Cultural Minorities into the body politic." One will notice a subtle but real shift in the two statements. The 1916 statement is symmetrical, taking the Christian and non-Christian as elements to be integrated through mutual intelligence. The 1957 statement is asymmetrical, taking the National Cultural Minorities as *the parties to be brought into the body politic*. The shift may be explained as a reflection of the shift of perspective from a colonial government to that of an indigenous state policy. Nevertheless the point is that both policies were assimilationist.

If there is a change now in the central government vis-à-vis the Moros, it appears to be a change from the assimilationist to the pluralist policy, in Wirth's typology (1945). This is the essence of Gowing's observation that neither the old integration position of the central government nor the secessionist goal of the MNLF are realistic solutions (Gowing, 1977, pp. 199-251).

The establishment of regional autonomy, however, should not be interpreted as an absolutely novel administrative and political mechanism in the Southern Philippines. Before the 1976 Tripoli Agreement, there were a number of administrative units created for the non-Christian Filipinos in Mindanao and Sulu and other regions inhabited by non-Hispanized groups. These administrative agencies were (1) the Moro Province, 1903-1914; (2) Department of Mindanao and Sulu, 1914-1920; (3) Bureau of Non-Christian Tribes, 1916-1938; (4) Commission for Mindanao and Sulu, 1936-1941; and (5) the Commission on National Integration (CNI), 1957-1975.

Thus any pluralist interpretation that social scientists might wish to make about the present Southern Philippine situation might well focus on the psychological dimension of the Moro image and not just on the issue of political administration. From being a derogatory item, the name Moro has now become a badge of honor. This is a Philippine parallel to many ethnic slogans, such as Black is Beautiful, in which a minority boosts its image in the eyes of the larger society. Boasting a renewed self-image, however, is meaningless unless you assume the existence of significant others to whom you can boast and display the new image. Again one is forced to posit a larger societal context. To understand the Moro you need to understand the Filipino, and to understand the Filipino you need to appreciate and accept the Moro. But to understand both, you cannot escape a confrontation with *Philippine* historical and social reality.

Noble and Suhrke have contributed significantly to a comparative understanding of interethnic conflict by highlighting the role of international relations in both the escalation and moderation of such conflicts (Suhrke & Noble, 1977, pp. 178-212). However, while the role of external state actors cannot be denied, the intrastate dynamics should not be underestimated. Some evidence may be cited to show how counterenergies were generated to help resolve the conflict within the resources of both governmental and communal organizations in the Philippines.

First, the Philippine government has made progress in the field of education, law, housing, and industrial development. There are now two state universities in the South, the Mindanao State University in Marawi City, in Lanao del Sur; and the Western Mindanao University based in Zamboanga City. The government has promulgated a Muslim Code of Personal Laws and established the nucleus of an Islamic judicial system administered by Shariah Courts to be coordinated with the Philippine legal system. Industrial and economic development is fostered under the Southern Philippine Development Authority. The government responded to specifically religious needs by creating a Philippine Pilgrimage Authority, approving the opening of Madrasah Schools, and encouraging Koran-reading contests. In financial matters, it has maintained the Amanah Bank that caters to the needs of Muslim businesses and entrepreneurs.

Second, among the various Christian churches and religious organizations there has been a genuine expression of humanitarian concern for the sufferings of innocent victims and displaced families from both Muslim and Christian communities.

As the level of fighting increased in the early 1970s, the National Council of Churches in the Philippines (NCCP) formed a Muslim-Christian Reconciliation Study Committee (MCRSC) to promote understanding and seek a non-violent solution to the problems in the Southern Philippines. This committee was composed of representatives of various Protestant Churches and the Roman Catholic Church of the Philippines. One result of the work of the MCRSC was the promotion of National Muslim-Christian Dialogues. This led to dialogues on the local level where Muslims and Christians could listen and learn from each other. Another result was the beginning of a "Program Aimed at Christian Education about Muslims" (PACEM). This also helped to improve relations between Muslim

Filipinos and Christian Filipinos. There were many other efforts made by Christian churches to promote better relationships. It is impossible to measure the full impact of these efforts on changing negative attitudes and removing centuries old prejudices, but a beginning has been made which can only produce positive results in the future. (McAmis, 1983, pp. 33-34).

The Moro case offers us valuable insights into the limits of Sumner's classical formulation of ethnocentrism. As pointed out by Levine and Campbell (1972, pp. 60-71), the whole reference-group theory investigation has shown that not all outgroups are objects of contempt; outgroups who are also reference groups are significant others, to be emulated in their lifestyle, if not always their values. This is true of the Moro case.

Many of these young rebels had emulated the modern Filipino lifestyle—not because it is Christian, but because it is the existing national norm of a successful life in a modernizing Asian country. It was only the thwarting of that drive for success within the existing political system that drove them to a confrontational course, thus confirming again Simmel's words: "Contradiction and conflict not only precede unity but are operative in it at every moment of its existence" (Simmel, 1955, p. 13).

Postscript

In March 1985 the IVth General Meeting of the MNLF Leadership was held in an undisclosed venue. As Chairman of the Central Committee, Nur Misuari signed the official communique. He called upon the Bangsamoro people to "expose and isolate the hypocrites, colonial spies, agent-provacateurs and all unrepentant stooges so as to stop them from obstructing the revolution" (Misuari, 1985 p. 198). He invited the misguided elements to mend their ways and rejoin the MNLF. In reviewing the last 17 years of the Bangsamoro Revolution, he declared March 18, 1968, as the Bangsmoro Freedom Day and announced 1985 as the start of the Second Phase of the revolution. He also described this vision of the Bangsamoro homeland whose boundaries go far beyond the limits agreed upon in the Tripoli Agreement.

The IVth GM THEREFORE opens the door of the MNLF to all those brothers who are ready to show sincerity to rectify their mistakes and resume their service to God, our people and humanity under the banner of the MNLF and the Bangsamoro Revolution for the complete national liberation and independence of the Bangsamoro homeland of Mindanao, Basilan, Sulu and Palawan, including their internationally recognized continental shelves, territorial waters, air spaces, as well as all the islands and islets and other attributes forming parts of our national patrimony and territory as a distinct and separate nation. Our national territory is bounded from the north by Mindanao Sea; and from the south by Celebes Sea; from the west by South-China Sea; and from the east by the Pacific Ocean. We shall fight to the end of time and to the last man in our effort to regain the sovereignty of the Bangsamoro nation. (Misuari, 1985, pp. 199-200)

We thus end with two nationalist visions, a broad pan-Philippine and a narrow and restricted religiously inspired community. The first is Rizal's and that of the revolutionaries of 1896 who saw a homeland for all the "sons of the people" inhabiting Luzon, Visayas, and Mindanao and forming a single national community. The second is Misuari's and the Moro revolutionaries of the 1970s who see only a restricted homeland that excludes Luzon and the Visayas. Only history will determine whether the Philippines will dissolve like Pakistan or be reunited like Vietnam, or restructure itself in some confederation of ethnolinguistic communities that would embrace the aspirations of the Moro ethnohistorical groups in Mindanao and Sulu. Whatever the scenario, the people in the islands now called the Philippines will live, die, and live again as their heroic ancestors before them, caught in the existential dilemma of their desire for dignity and freedom against the forces of colonialism and neocolonialism that suppress and exploit people. In the face of such formidable uncertainty and utmost gravity, the Muslim can only say, *Insha-Allah,* and the Filipino, *Bahala Na.* Man proposes but his history disposes.

NOTES

1. Palawan is often counted as part of the Southern Philippines. Geographically, however, it lies in the latitude of the Visayas but is not part of the Visayan Islands. Administratively, Palawan is part of Region 4, which covers Manila and Southern Luzon.

2. The important point here is that under the Spanish regime the name "Filipino" was never applied to the natives of the Philippines, whether such

natives were pagans, Christians, or Muslims. The name Filipino was reserved for Philippine-born Spaniards to distinguish them from those born in Spain, called *Peninsulares*. Even as late as the 1880s, educated Philippine natives, such as Jose Rizal, were still called *Indios*, prompting Rizal to express an "Indio is beautiful" sentiment by dubbing the Filipino student club in Europe *Los Indios Bravos*. *Indio* historically is a master social category the European colonizers applied to the new peoples in the new world they discovered in their search for a new passage to India. Like its Anglo-Saxon equivalent, Indian, this name basically means native, a term used to distinguish persons so designated from the Western colonizers.

3. The political organization that attempted to transform the *Liga* ideas into living social reality was the *Katipunan*, a grassroots organization that did not use any of the Spanish-imposed exonyms. The reason for this is partly linguistic. Although Rizal wrote the *Liga* (1972) in Spanish, the grassroots *Katipunan* partisans were predominantly from the Tagalog-speaking region. Being anti-Spanish and masonic-secularists in inspiration, the *Katipunan* organizers made no mention of the name *Filipino, Indio, Cristiano,* or *Infieles.* What they frequently used were the terms *bayan* and *katipunan. Katipunan* (association) is from the root word *tipon* (grouping) and cognate to *lipunan* (society). The full phrase was *Katipunan nang manga anac nang bayan,* that is, sons/daughters of the people/nation.

Bansa is a second key term, in addition to *bayan,* commonly used as a gloss for nation or national. Thus the Philippine national anthem (which incidentally does not contain the word Philippines or Filipino) is called *Pambansang Awit*. It is significant to note that the MNLF also uses a cognate of this Southeast Asian social category in the term *Bangsa Moro*.

4. Misuari's version of the "Moro Wars" is based largely on a religious interpretation by a Muslim political scientist, Cesar A. Majul (1973). Two other interpretations are current in Philippine historiography: (1) the "decay theory" advanced by British colonial apologists who saw Muslim piracy and aggression as symptoms of decaying native maritime kingdoms, no longer able to control their people, which must therefore be destroyed as a menace to European civilizing missions (Reber, 1966); and (2) the "trade and slave-manpower theory" by James A. Warren (1981), which argues that the Sulu maritime state (after 1768) systematically captured slaves all over island Southeast Asia including Spanish-controlled Philippines in order to generate revenue by selling them and to use slave power for production and trading (for example, slave rowers for sea mobility in an era before steam-powered boats). Majul's and thus Misuari's interpretation, being more theological than political or economic, reinforces the Muslim-Christian character of the Moro interethnic conflict.

References

Bateson, G. (1972). *Steps to an ecology of mind.* New York: Ballantine Books.
Casiño, E. S. (1975a). *The history of Philippine anthropology.* Unpublished manuscript, Philippine Social Science Council, Quezon City.

Casiño, E. S. (1975b). Structuralism in Philippine cultural diversities. *Solidarity, 10*(6), 18-29.

Casiño, E. S. (1982) *The Philippines: Lands and peoples. A cultural geography: Vol. 2. The Filipino nation.* New York: Grolier International.

Casiño, E. S. (1985). The parameters of ethnicity research. In F. W. Riggins (Ed.) *Intercocta glossary: Concepts and terms used in ethnicity research* (pp. 1-40). Honolulu: International Social Science Council.

Churchill, B. R. (1983). *The Philippine independence missions to the United States, 1919-1934.* Manila: National Historical Institute.

Gerlack, L. P., & Hine, V. H. (1970). *People, power, change.* New York: Bobbs-Merrill.

Gowing, P. G. (1977). *Mandate in Moroland.* Quezon City: Philippine Center for Advanced Studies.

Implementation of the Tripoli Agreement. (1984). In *Philippines.* Manila: Office of Media Affairs.

Levine, R. A., & Campbell, D. T. (1972). *Ethnocentrism.* New York: John Wiley.

Majul, C. A. (1973). *Muslims in the Philippines.* Quezon City: University of the Philippines Press.

Mastura, M. O. (1984). MNLF's path to parliamentary struggle. In M. O. Mastura (Ed.), *Muslim Filipino experience* (pp. 109-128). Manila: Ministry of Muslim Affairs.

McAmis, R. D. (1983). Muslim Filipinos in the 1980s. *Solidarity, 4,* (1983), 32-40.

Misuari, N. (1985). Communique of the IVth General Meeting of the MNLF Leadership. In *Selected documents for the Conference on the Tripoli Agreement.* Quezon City: International Studies Institute of the Philippines, University of the Philippines.

Noble, L. G. (1983). Roots of the Bangsa Moro revolution. *Solidarity, 4,* 41-50.

Reber, A. L. (1966). *The Sulu world in the eighteenth and early nineteenth centuries: A historiographical problem in British writings on Malay piracy.* Unpublished master's thesis, Cornell University, Ithaca, New York.

Rizal, J. (1972). The Philippines a century hence. In *Political and historical writings.* Manila: National Historical Commission.

Salamat, H. (1982). A position paper of Hashim Salamat. (Presented in Third Session of the Moro Congress, June 1982, in Sabah.) In *Selected documents for the Conference on the Tripoli Agreement.* Quezon City: International Studies Institute of the Philippines, University of the Philippines.

Schermerhorn, R. A. (1978). *Comparative ethnic relations.* Chicago: University of Chicago Press.

Simmel, G. (1955). *Conflict and the web of group-affiliations* (K. H. Wolff & R. Bendix, Trans.). New York: Free Press.

Suhrke, A., & Noble, L. G. (1977). *Ethnic conflict in international relations.* New York: Praeger.

Sumner, W. G. (1906). *Folkways.* New York: Ginn.

Warren, J. F. (1981). *The Sulu zone, 1768-1898.* Singapore: Singapore University Press. '

Wirth, L. (1945). The problem of minority groups. In R. Linton (Ed.), *The science of man in the world crisis* (pp. 354-363). New York: Columbia University Press.

Chapter Summary

M. Joycelyn Armstrong's chapter concentrates on events that have recently focused attention on the Treaty of Waitangi, the original charter for Maori-Pakeha relations.

Armstrong states that New Zealand has had both an international reputation and a national self-image of interethnic harmony, and that the phrase "one people" is often used in oral and written descriptions of New Zealanders. The author indicates that in comparative studies of interethnic conflict, New Zealand is consistently ranked low. Armstrong goes on to explain that the use of the terms "Maori," referring to the indigenous Polynesian people, and "Pakeha," referring to the immigrant Whites, have been said to be illustrative of good interethnic relations since both are Maori language terms.

There is, however, a growing sentiment that the "one people" concept is a myth. Armstrong reviews the race-relations literature on these divergent views and finds that although opinions differ as to the nature and extent of the difficulties in Maori-Pakeha relations, there is general agreement as to their source: the socioeconomic disadvantage of the Maoris and the increased interethnic contact due to large-scale urbanization.

Armstrong explains that with increased interethnic tension there has been a stronger focus on the Treaty of Waitangi and the greater expression of Maori discontent, especially during Waitangi Day—a yearly event when the signing of the treaty is reenacted.

According to the author, the British viewed the 1840 signing of the Treaty of Waitangi as distinguishing New Zealand from other colonies as a case of cooperation with, and protection for, the indigenous people. Armstrong presents an analysis of both the written content and the application of the treaty. She states that the Treaty of Waitangi had three articles: (1) Maoris ceded their sovereignty to Queen Victoria; (2) the Queen guaranteed the Maoris possession of their lands but retained the sole right to purchase these lands; and (3) Maoris were given the rights of British subjects. Various claims against the treaty are detailed, including the existence of differences in the Maori and English versions of the text. Armstrong emphasizes the role of land-related grievances stemming from the treaty in current Maori-Pakeha relations and reviews British acts and ordinances that were used to reinterpret the treaty in this regard. The author discusses four main stages of Maori-Pakeha relations in terms of public policy since the Treaty of Waitangi: amalgamation; assimilation; integration; and biculturalism.

Two Maori views of the treaty are presented. One is that the treaty symbolizes Pakeha oppression and that it should be recognized as a legal document in order to allow for challenging of government acts and ordinances. The other view is that the treaty illustrates New Zealand's commitment to Maori-Pakeha equality. Ratification is opposed as it would detract from its sacredness and subject it to legal manipulation. Armstrong suggests that although these differing views do not cause division in the Maori community, they are associated with differing styles of protest, seen during recent Waitangi Day events.

The author concludes with a discussion of the new urgency in the Treaty of Waitangi debate and asserts that although interethnic relations in New Zealand may have become tense, they have not reached a level of interethnic violence.

—Susan Goldstein

11

Interethnic Conflict
In New Zealand

M. JOCELYN ARMSTRONG

New Zealand has long enjoyed an international reputation for successful management of its ethnic relations. The national self-image has, likewise, long been one of ethnic harmony, both as a fact and as something of value. History has bequeathed the description of New Zealanders as "one people." It has been widely used in both oral and written discourse and it connotes both unity and equality.

In broad-based comparative studies of ethnic situations, New Zealand is typically placed toward the harmony end of any ethnic-tension/ethnic-harmony scale. On a scale designed to measure the presence and significance of ethnic divisions in a worldwide sample of over 100 multiethnic nations, New Zealand scored 1 on a scale of 0 to 8 with 0 signifying a "negligible" amount of tension (Haug, 1967). In a comparative survey of ethnic violence around the world between 1940 and 1975, New Zealand ranked 19th among the 19 societies examined for both the level of violence and for the characteristics of intergroup relations seen to explain the violence (Hewitt, 1977).

The ethnic relations being referred to in the comparisons just cited are the relations between New Zealand's *Maori* minority and its *Pakeha*, or European, majority. Guidelines for harmonious relations between the two groups are available in the Treaty of Waitangi of 1840. According to established contemporary opinion, the treaty decreed that Maori and Pakeha, then relating to each other as native and immigrant colonial, were to live in unity and equality as "one people." In other words, ethnic conflict was to be avoided, or at least controlled, through a blueprint for ethnic harmony.

Colonialism is well known as a major context of interethnic encounters around the world but by no means always with similar outcomes for the peoples involved. The most common relationship established between nineteenth-century colonials and native peoples was a relationship of stratification. Alternatively, a relationship of opposition developed. A relationship of cooperation as equals as envisaged for new Zealand compares in frequency as "rare" (Royce, 1982, pp. 63-71). In short, for its time, the Treaty of Waitangi was a landmark. Over the years it has frequently been looked to as having indeed made a difference, for the better, to the management of ethnic relations in New Zealand. As we seek to understand and deal with ethnic-based conflict as a pervasively serious problem in the world today, influences for tolerance and harmony and attempts to organize "good" relations deserve our attention along with the sources of conflict and efforts at conflict resolution. It is the purpose of this paper to review the status of New Zealand's Treaty of Waitangi as a charter for "good" relations between Maori and Pakeha over the last century and a half, giving particular attention to public debate of the issue by New Zealanders themselves during the 1980s.[1]

The General Environment of Maori-Pakeha Relations

Relations between New Zealand's native Maori and immigrant Pakeha populations were early established as minority-majority relations in demographic terms. In 1840, at the signing of the Treaty of Waitangi, Maoris made up more than 90 percent of a total population of around 120,000, but by 1860 there were already more Pakehas than Maoris and, by 1900, the 1840 proportions had been essentially reversed and would remain so (Baker, 1966). In the 1981 census, New Zealand's population was recorded as 3.1 million. The Pakeha majority accounted for 87 percent of the total. Maoris were the largest of several ethnic minorities, numbering almost 290,000 and representing 9 percent of the total (New Zealand Department of Statistics, 1983).

Significant clues as to the general character of interethnic relations are available in how the people involved talk about those relations. Conventional presentation of relations between New Zealand's indigenous Polynesian minority and its immigrant White majority as between "Maori" and "Pakeha" expresses the model of "good" relations. Pakeha is a Maori-language term. Both terms belong to the postcontact period of New Zealand history and have been in use for about the same length of time, at least a century and a half. The conformity of language and age alone implies an equal footing and social closeness for the people named. Maori translates into English as "normal" or "ordinary" people; Pakeha compares the immigrants as "strangers," but with a significant connotation of "not very different strangers." There are other pairs of terms for expressing more separation. Sometimes, the majority is identified or identifies itself as "European" and as such, for the time being, more socially distant and more politically and economically as well as demographically dominant. The label "European" was in common use during the focal decades of the colonial period (1850-1900) and, with "Native" for the minority, was regularly used in the public documentation of minority-majority relations into the 1940s. But overall, the pairing of Maori with Pakeha prevails. Beyond relative closeness, the terms signify cooperation, mutual respect, a shared valuing of good relations and of New Zealand's one-people image.

Was it easier for native and immigrant to develop good relations in New Zealand than in other comparable places? Were there local circumstances or conditions that made a treaty promising development as equal partners more desirable? Among the more useful comparisons are those with Australia and Canada since in both places native populations also met British colonial immigrants and at about the same time. There are several such comparisons available from historians (Fisher, 1980; Howe, 1977; Sinclair, 1971). They agree in drawing attention to differences in at least three circumstances: geography and demography, the nature of the indigenous cultures, and the attitudes of colonial immigrants.

In all three places the climate was agreeable to Europeans and all became settlement colonies rather than extractive colonies. New Zealand, however, was small in size and its native populations both the largest and most dense. The need for an orderly management of relations was more pressing. This was a very different situation from that of Australia, for example, where the smaller Aborigine population could be pushed aside into the desert expanses of the continent's interior.

As to differences deriving from the indigenous societies and cultures, a marked difference in the precontact period of occupancy may have been important. The Aborigines had been in Australia and the Indians in Canada for at least 30,000 years prior to the coming of the European; Maoris had been in New Zealand perhaps for 3,000 years. Being more "youthful" at the time of contact, Maori society was perhaps more flexible and better equipped for adaptation to the changes introduced with colonization. The first decades of the colonial period saw an enthusiastic adoption of European goods and ways of doing things. Though language differences were everywhere a barrier to communication, Maoris had the advantage of a common native language: In Australia and Canada, the negotiation of relations between native and newcomer had to contend with a multiplicity of native languages. Maori society was at a disadvantage in having been disrupted by serious intertribal warfare in the decades just prior to European colonization. On the other hand, in comparison with Australia's Aborigines and Canada's Indians, New Zealand's Maoris were much better prepared for armed resistance to European encroachment.

In general the early years of native-immigrant interaction in New Zealand were not, in fact, very different from the pattern in Australia and Canada or, for that matter, most other settlement colonies. In New Zealand, as elsewhere, the critical issue was land, and exchanges followed the so-called "settlement cycle" (Forster, 1968, p. 99). After an initial phase of cooperation between newcomer and native, the cycle moves through the following phases: gradual European encroachment on native land resources; increased competition between European and native as the European community grows in size; realization by the natives that their independence and livelihood are at stake and an increasing reluctance to give up their lands; competition for a now scarce resource; more land alienation by the European and an escalation of conflict to the point of open warfare in which the natives are defeated; still greater land acquisition by the Europeans; withdrawal of the defeated native population from further competition and from contact generally, at least for the time being.

In New Zealand, there were outbreaks of war between Maori and European in the 1860s. They were, to say the least, a serious disruption to the Treaty of Waitangi plans for living in harmony as one people; and this was so not only at the time but for the Maoris involved during the aftermath of withdrawal, depression, and population decline that lasted until the 1890s. However, recent reconsiderations by historians of the warring provide several important points of perspective.

Long named the "Maori Wars" and dated 1860-65, the wars have been widely presented as involving all of New Zealand's Maoris and lasting for five years. In fact, the fighting was confined to areas in the country's North Island where conditions of denser Maori populations and less good land combined to make native-settler competition for the land much stronger. As to duration, the fighting was intermittent, not continuous, and it moved from place to place rather than occurring in all of its locations at once. Further, the conflict did not clearly divide Maori and European but involved some Maoris fighting an alliance of Europeans and other Maoris. In the language of the older histories, the wars ended when the "hostile" Maori tribes were defeated by an alliance of British troops and warriors from the "friendly" tribes.

Labeling these the "Maori Wars" has also placed the cause of the conflict too heavily in Maori hands. It is the revised consensus that the Europeans, not the Maoris, were substantially the aggressors. It is now common practice to speak of the "Land Wars" rather than the "Maori Wars" but, in another view (see Ward, 1967), to express the new thinking as to motives—namely, that land was the leading but not the sole motive, so the label "Anglo-Maori Wars" should be promoted. It is a label that better communicates the circumstances of the conflict to non-New Zealand audiences too.

In the long term, the wars compare as considerably less disastrous for Maoris than most other British colonial conquests were for the native peoples involved, and the postwar years saw a number of "reparations" that would advance more equitable Maori participation in the new European-dominated society. Some of the alienated lands were returned, Maori suffrage was introduced, Maori electorates were established, and the Maori school system expanded. Finally, and not incidentally, the wars advanced European respect for Maori military skills and courage. In the words of one British general, the Maoris were "the grandest native enemy" he had ever had to deal with.

Turning to the attitudes of the Europeans generally as an influence on the course of native immigrant relations, the attitudes of the Europeans in New Zealand compare favorably. First, the British among them regarded themselves as a cut above the British in other settlement colonies, and they were especially keen to set themselves apart as voluntary and selected participants in planned colonization from the convicts and their keepers who had been forcibly shipped out to nearby Australia. Second, the New Zealand settlers also brought with them a commitment to egalitarianism; escape from the social class system of Great Britain was one of the leading motivations for emigration. Third, the Maoris were viewed as different from the natives of other colonies. In the ethnic and racial ranking systems of the time, Europeans were invariably at the top, but New Zealand's Maoris were granted a high position among natives. Again, the contrast with Australia was especially striking. In nineteenth-century European eyes, Australia's Aborigines were "horrid blacks" to whom a barely human ranking was ascribed and with whom social closeness was inconceivable. But vis-à-vis the native peoples of British colonies generally New Zealand's Maoris were considered superior: In intelligence, industriousness, and virtue, they came closest to "civilization." They were also physically attractive to the immigrants and cross-ethnic marriages were commonplace from the early days of contact. All in all, European attitudes were more amenable to cooperative native-immigrant relations in New Zealand, and the early attitudes would persist. Toward the end of the nineteenth century, they were sufficiently entrenched to resist the full influence of social Darwinism during the height of its impact (see Sinclair, 1971). Europeans in New Zealand would hold to beliefs in their own race's superiority, but they would not accept the notion of inherent Maori inferiority.

The Idiom and Issues of Maori-Pakeha Conflict

Circumstantial evidence in support of ethnic cooperation and closeness in New Zealand is available in a variety of forms. It includes complete equality under the law; well-established formal as well as informal sanctions against discrimination; English firmly in place as a common language; considerable social mixing in public; a long history of high rates of intermarriage; and over a century of peaceful coexistence. In terms of individual everyday lives, Maori and Pakeha are spouses, neighbors, workmates and playmates, they go to school and church together, they join forces on the football field and the basketball court. The modern-day Maori minority is in many beliefs and behaviors very Pakehafied, but members of the Pakeha majority are also to some extent Maorified. The categorization of individuals is flexible. A person can be Maori in certain sorts of social situations, Pakeha in others. Since contact in the mid-nineteenth century, official policy on Maori-Pakeha relations has changed in name and its specific objectives have been revised, but the policies have always been for ethnic integration as opposed to segregation. The present policy is stated as "biculturalism," which seeks a social equality based on cultural duality.

In keeping with the ideal of good Maori-Pakeha relations bequeathed by the Treaty of Waitangi, when ethnic-based conflict does arise and become the subject of public discourse the language is restrained. The conflict is talked about as "tension," "friction," a "difference of opinion" or a "contention," but not usually as "conflict." Both in the past and recently, there have been occasions of ethnically centered "protests" and "demonstrations" but not "riots" or "violence."

In a related tendency, the problem may be treated as an unfortunate but only temporary departure from the norm or, sometimes, not talked about at all. In reviewing the history of Maori protest behavior in particular, the Maori anthropologist Walker makes the point that because the behavior has been characteristically *ad hoc* and episodic in nature, New Zealanders not involved in the protest could assume that it would go away or die a natural death (Walker, 1984, p. 280). In another recent expression of Maori opinion, the anthropologist Hohepa presents these "typically New Zealand" positions of restraint, disassociation, and disregard on Maori-Pakeha conflict as part of a wider design to maintain "the one-people myth" (Hohepa, 1978).[2]

A review of the literature reveals substantial academic comment on the overrating of Maori-Pakeha accord. Looking back to 1940 and to a symposium in honor of the centennial of Maori-Pakeha interaction as one nation, the Pakeha editor, New Zealand's senior academic psychologist, saw the tradition of interethnic goodwill as sincere and solid but put forth a strong plea for "fuller appreciation of the realities of the present situation" (Sutherland, 1940, pp. 21-22). A review of the research literature on "race relations" in New Zealand through the 1950s by a leading Pakeha sociologist found New Zealand's reputation for ethnic tolerance and harmony to be more "fortuitous" than it was earned or deserved (Thompson, 1963). Research by the American psychologist Ausubel (1977) provided one of the few outside views of modern times. He found "race relations" in New Zealand to be "not bad" and "much better" than in his own United States "or for that matter in most parts of the world" but "not nearly as good as most people think or claim they are." He described the national self-image of one-peoplehood as a "national self-delusion" (Ausubel, 1977, pp. 149-156). For the period under review, the 1950s, Ausubel's judgments seemed to most New Zealanders to be overly harsh, but he was correct in his predictions that a deterioration in Maori-Pakeha relations and an accompanying experience of minor but recurring ethnic-based "explosions" in the 1960s would force New Zealanders "to face up to the problem of growing ethnic tensions." In the opinion of the respected Pakeha anthropologist, Metge, however, at the mid-1970s commitment to ethnic unity and equality as New Zealand's way remained firm. Most New Zealanders still held the one-people model to be the "proper" model of Maori-Pakeha relations. More Pakehas than Maoris, however, accepted it as "an appropriate construction of reality" (Metge, 1976, p. 302).

In 1983, the circumstances of the 1970s were the subject of a research-based review at the annual conference of the New Zealand Sociological Association, and it was generally agreed that the 1970s had brought marked changes in the management of interethnic relations in New Zealand. The language was still of Maori-Pakeha "debates," and outcomes of open conflict that had resulted in connection with two of the debates were referred to as "incidents," but the consensus was, once again, that "race relations would need to be taken more seriously" in the future and that they "would assume a new importance in the 1980s" (Spoonley, Macpherson, Pearson, & Sedgwick, 1984).

The prevailing causes for strain in Maori-Pakeha relations in New Zealand are generally agreed to be the well-known causes of interethnic conflict; that is, they are socioeconomic and demographic in nature. First, an accumulation of socioeconomic divergence has put Maoris at a disadvantage in all major areas—lower levels of education, higher unemployment, lower incomes, more health problems, and shorter life spans. Second, demographic factors are implicated in that large-scale rural-urban migration by Maoris since the 1950s has brought Maori and Pakeha into close proximity in all main cities. This has brought Maori socioeconomic disadvantages into sharper focus on the one hand, while providing the resources and stages for public displays of Maori dissatisfaction and discontent on the other.

To these two internal causes I think we need to add at least two of external origin. During the 1970s New Zealand experienced a marked increase in the in-migration of non-Maori Polynesians and other Pacific Islanders. Sizable populations of Samoans, Tongans, Rartongans, Tokelauans, and Figians, for example, were added to the ethnic scene. Both Maori and Pakeha, long accustomed to behaving as if New Zealand were a biethnic society, now had to face the fact that it was a multiethnic one.[3] For the Pakeha majority, some of its existing attitudes about coexistence with the known Maori minority came under strain. On the Maori side, an initial inclination to cooperate with the newcomers in pursuit of common and overlapping interest soon gave way to demonstrations of Maori independence. Interminority competition for scarce resources was one cause, but much more important was a concern to confirm Maori indigenousness and to protect the rights and privileges that attached to it.

Looking still further afield we should attend to the 1960s and 1970s as decades of marked growth in the "ethnic revival" of modern times (Smith, 1981). Worldwide, the period saw scores of ethnic revitalizations and movements of ethnic nationalism as well as state promotions of ethnic difference and systems of reward for use of one's ethnic identity. The knowledge Maoris had of what other indigenous minorities were doing elsewhere was not only increased but became an important source of support. Since then an information conference of Canadian Indians, American Indians, Hawaiians, and Australian Aborigines has exchanged information and site visits and the network is growing. The status and value of the Treaty of Waitangi has been a topic of discussion on more than one occasion.

The 1980s presents a number of interethnic issues under public debate in New Zealand. The Treaty of Waitangi is one of the more serious but it is not the only one. Others include the following: the future of separate Maori political representation in Parliament; the future of a wide range of Maori-specific social services and of their main administrator, the Department of Maori Affairs; the ethnic composition of national-level executive bodies and of New Zealand's international representatives; the establishment of Maori as one of New Zealand's official languages; and the longstanding, particularly contentious issue of Maori land rights. Each of these by itself could be the subject of lengthy review and comment. Each, however, also falls within the scope of the Treaty of Waitangi debate on two related grounds. The Treaty debate concentrates on the original set of guidelines for managing Maori-Pakeha relations in general, and the debate has been increasingly used as an umbrella for the airing of Maori concerns overall.

The Treaty of Waitangi as a Charter for Ethnic Unity

When Maori and Pakeha signed the Treaty of Waitangi in 1840 the two peoples were, as stated earlier, relating to one another as, respectively, the indigenous population and an immigrant population of (mostly) British colonists. Though circumstances within New Zealand may well have favored the treaty's goal, the push for its negotiation came from outside.

The British government had shown considerable reluctance to annex New Zealand as a colony. When the decision was finally made to do so it was with the firmly stated goal of protecting the natives against the "designs" of the British settlers. The stance put together the experience of colonial activities in Africa, the Americas, Asia, and Australia with the spirit of philanthropy being promoted by the evangelical revival and apparently well represented among the staff of the British Colonial Office.

Accordingly, as the preparations for annexation proceeded, the soon-to-be British governor of New Zealand, William Hobson, was instructed to treat with the Maoris for recognition of British sovereignty. Under specific instructions he was to "deal fairly" with the Maoris; to appoint a protector to guard their welfare once his government was established; to guarantee their rights to New Zealand's lands; and, in order to protect them from the scheming of colonial purchasers, to provide for government supervision of all land transactions. The resulting document was the Treaty of Waitangi, named for the place in the north of New Zealand where it was first presented, discussed, and signed.

The treaty was prepared in both Maori- and English-language versions and contained three concisely stated articles. By the first article, the Maoris ceded their sovereignty to the British Queen Victoria. In return, by the second article the Queen guaranteed the Maoris possession of their lands and other properties, but the Maoris yielded to the Queen the sole right of purchasing their lands. By the third article, the Maoris were given all the rights and privileges of British subjects. As the first complement of Maori leaders signed the Treaty at Waitangi on February 6, 1840, the new governor Hobson is reported to have shaken hands with each of them and said in Maori: *"He iwi tahi tatou"* (We are one people). This was in halting Maori, according to one version (Ross, 1972, p. 154), but so be it: The treaty provided an enduring charter for one-peoplehood.

As presented in the standard history of New Zealand by the Pakeha historian Sinclair,

> The Treaty of Waitangi was intended to lay a basis for a just society in which two races, far apart in civilization, could live in amity. It merited the symbolic significance it came to assume in the minds of both peoples. (1970, p. 73)

At the centennial of the treaty's signing in 1940, the Maori anthropologist Buck spoke for many New Zealanders of both ethnicities regarding the treaty's significance for Maori rights when he wrote,

> The very name Waitangi calls up a picture of tattooed chiefs attaching their symbols to a document as an agreement with the Great White Queen that she and her heirs would give protection and guidance to the Maori people for years to come. (1940, p. 1)

Through the 1950s, what had come to be commonly referred to as "the spirit of the treaty" could still be placed at the base of Maori-

Pakeha relations, as the following statement derived from a thorough review of the relevant literature by Thompson makes clear:

> The belief that Maori and Pakeha were "one people," destined to live together in friendship and equality, goes back to the time of the first European contacts with the Maori, and became symbolized in the Treaty of Waitangi which for one hundred and twenty years has stood as the charter of Maori rights. The spirit of the Treaty has become a very powerful psychological factor in conditioning the relations of the two peoples towards mutual respect and equality and it is constantly reinforced by official statements as well as by private action. (1963, p. 53)

The year 1960 saw official recognition of the Treaty's continuing relevance in Parliament's passage of the Waitangi Day Act. The act provided for February 6 to be officially known as "Waitangi Day" and to be "observed throughout New Zealand as a national day of thanksgiving in commemoration of the signing of the Treaty of Waitangi." In the mid-1970s, public opinion halted a move by Parliament to make the next step naming the day "New Zealand Day" and subsequent legislation dropped the designation "national day of thanksgiving"; but it provided for February 6 to be a public holiday and for annual "celebrations" to be held at Waitangi, the site of the treaty's first signing. Despite 120 years of nationhood, prior to 1960 New Zealand had not observed a national day. In essence, the Waitangi Day legislation made official the treaty's symbolism of nationhood as one-peoplehood.

The Treaty in Application, 1840s to 1970s

It has been said that "the ink on the Treaty of Waitangi was barely dry before it was in trouble" (Clark, 1984-85, p. 9). The treaty provided principles for interaction but said little about how to put them into practice. Its brevity left room for varying interpretations as well as loopholes for sidestepping the principles. Almost immediately Maoris felt cheated when the terms for land sales, as they had understood the treaty to establish them, were not followed and before too long were legally contravened. From the Maori viewpoint, the land-related grievances would accumulate at an alarming rate and persist as burning ones. It is beyond the scope of this chapter to review completely even just the legal contradictions and contraventions of the Treaty of Waitangi between the 1840s and 1970s, but a selection is needed in order to understand the treaty debate of the 1980s.

Of the long sequence of laws seen to violate guarantees given to Maoris under the treaty, most have been directly or indirectly aimed at facilitating Pakeha acquisition of Maori land. Only 20 years after the Treaty's signing, there would be Land Wars.

Little more than a year after the signing of the treaty, under the Land Claims Ordinance of 1841, all "unappropriated" or "waste" land, apart from what was needed for the "rightful and necessary occupation of the aboriginal inhabitants," was deemed to be Crown land. Laws passed in 1844, 1846, 1862, and 1893, respectively, abandoned, restored, then abandoned, then restored again the Crown's right of preemption in land sales, and on each occasion the reasons stated were specific to Pakeha needs and desires. In 1928, the Public Works Act gave the government power to take land for a wide variety of purposes including just "better utilization." In 1953, a comprehensive Maori Affairs Act continued legal violation of the Treaty of Waitangi's provisions regarding land by (among other things) providing for a Maori trustee who, as agent of the Crown, could buy Maori land he considered "uneconomic" without the owner's consent and use it as he saw fit. At the mid-1970s, Maoris retained at most about 15 percent of the lands they originally possessed, and much of it was inferior in quality and difficult to access.

Over the years, the courts have been equally involved in overruling the provisions of the treaty by declaring them to be legally irrelevant. A review prepared by a present member of New Zealand's legal profession (Kelsey, 1984) shows the two reasons used most often and for the longest time to be (1) that the Treaty was merely morally binding on the Crown and hence could be discarded at the discretion of the Crown, (2) that even moral obligations to honor the treaty were offset since Maoris had been granted all the rights and privileges of British subjects so Maori and Pakeha were therefore "alike under the law." It is the conclusion of Kelsey's review of the 130 years from 1840 into the 1970s that, as far as land-related cases are concerned, the courts consistently decided conflicts between Maori and Pakeha in favor of the Pakeha.

Beyond land alienation, abuse of the treaty has been more diffuse; but some of the long-term effects for Maoris and Maori-Pakeha relations have been no less profound. Translation of the treaty's goals into New Zealand's official policies for interethnic relations has produced a sequence of four differently named policies. A first short stage of amalgamation (in the 1840s) was followed by a long period of assimilation (1850s-1960s). However, since it is generally agreed that the two policies were different in name only, the first 120 years of Maori-Pakeha interaction were based on a policy of assimilation. The Treaty of Waitangi's promise of unity was sought through uniformity. Under the facilitating legislation Maoris were to become "absorbed" and "blended" into Pakeha society and culture with "complete loss of Maori culture" (Hunn, 1961, p. 15). They were to become "brown-skinned Pakehas" as it became fashionable to say. By no means all the legislation was as ruthless as most of the land-related laws described above, but neither did it achieve the absorption of most Maori into Pakeha styles of living, much less Pakeha standards of living. Rather, it had led them by the 1940s to marked second-class citizenship in socioeconomic terms, and strong feelings of cultural deprivation as well.

A shift to a policy of integration in the 1960s was supposed to return relations to a more equal footing. According to its official definition, integration would "combine (not fuse) the Maori and Pakeha elements to form one nation wherein Maori culture remains distinct" (Hunn, 1961, p. 15). In the view of many Maoris, integration in practice worked like assimilation. Unity was still to be achieved through uniformity. However, the policy produced considerable legislative support for the revitalization of Maori arts and crafts, the Maori language, and Maori forms of association, leadership, and decision making. It helped prepare New Zealanders for transition to the fourth and current policy of biculturalism during the 1970s.

In an early scholarly presentation by a Pakeha anthropologist, biculturalism was defined as "the conscious confrontation and reconciliation of two conflicting value systems both of which were accepted as valid" (Schwimmer, 1968, p. 13). In New Zealand, commitment to biculturalism at the national level would require a shift from virtually exclusive reference to Pakeha values in the shaping of national institutions to equal reference to both Maori and Pakeha values. In the words of a recent definition by a Maori spokesperson, a bicultural New Zealand will be "one in which taha Maori [the Maori side] receives an equal consideration with, and equally determines the course of this country as taha Pakeha" (Awatere, 1984, p. 10). In the late 1960s, the institutionalization of biculturism was "a Maori aspiration" that Pakehas, for the most part, resisted. During the 1970s, biculturalism became "the Maori agenda"; and, as evidenced in the adjustments in government departments, the legal system, educational institutions, industry, churches, and the mass media, for example, which could not have resulted from Maori effort alone, the Pakeha resistance diminished.

Biculturalism clearly raises new kinds of questions about the status and value of the Treaty of Waitangi's guidelines for present-day Maori-Pakeha relations. At the same time, the equal-footing/ equal-opportunity focus on biculturalism makes public debate of the issue fully proper.

Maori protest over Pakeha interpretations of the Treaty of Waitangi is by no means new, and action today builds on past efforts. But as Walker (1984) has pointed out for the history of Maori protest movements at large, there has been a significant change in leadership. Whereas earlier protest movements were led first by traditional-style leaders—older males of chiefly rank, and then by male charismatic leaders or intellectuals—in more modern (post-World War II) times, the leadership has diversified, with young people and women as notable additions.

Protest in the form of public demonstrations first occurred in the 1970s. A large-scale campaign organized in general protest of continuing nonsettlement of the land issue and two major confrontations about particular cases of land alienation earned the 1970s a description as "the angry decade." In 1971, protesters took up organized disruption of the annual celebration of the Treaty of Waitangi Day. The outspoken style and the urgent tone of the organizers were new to New Zealand's interethnic scene, but the aim of the Waitangi Day protesters was the same aim of previous generations of treaty protesters—to "focus attention on Maori grievances."

A new kind of response from the government, one which was intended to meet the new wave of Maori objections by firmly establishing the importance of the treaty in New Zealand law, was forthcoming in 1975. This was passage of the Treaty of Waitangi Act. The act set up a Waitangi Tribunal to hear and make recommendations on claims relating to the practical application of the principles of the treaty, and to critically preview any proposed legislation that related to the substance of the treaty. In a significant bicultural instruction as to procedure, the tribunal was to consult both the English and Maori texts of the treaty—all previous legislative and judicial bodies had relied only on an English version—and, as necessary, to "decide issues raised by differences between them."

Some observers saw the Waitangi Tribunal as a "reprieve" for the treaty (see Kelsey, 1984). Because it is only a quasijudicial body and can only make recommendations, others called it "toothless." But to a Maori judge on the tribunal, the confinement to recommendations was a strength. The power of final determinations that would affect the rights and duties of individuals would oblige the tribunal to follow formal legal procedures. An informal path aimed at compromise and consensus took Maori forms of dispute settlement into better account. In addition, by the end of the 1970s, I think the charge of toothlessness was looking less serious in the light of close public attention to the tribunal's deliberations and the government's acceptance of certain major recommendations. Because the enacting legislation provided for a mostly Maori membership and for claims by Maoris only, the tribunal had been criticized as "not in the spirit of biculturalism." Since few would dispute that Maoris had by far the greater cause for claims, this criticism may not seem serious; but its phrasing may have represented an important shift in thinking. In one older argument against the large and varied body of legislation that gives special assistance to Maoris, its mere existence was described as "discriminatory." All in all, establishment of the tribunal brought Maori-Pakeha negotiations regarding the Treaty of Waitangi's place in modern New Zealand to a new threshold.

The Treaty of Waitangi in the 1980s

The Treaty of Waitangi debate and its use for the airing of Maori grievances in general expanded during the 1980s, in the number of people involved, in the range of topics discussed, and in overall intensity.

One new, or newly public, topic of debate was the treaty document itself. First, the text was called into question. An English-language text had long stood as the "official" text but other, differing ones were prepared; more than one Maori-language version also existed and they too showed discrepancies. Second, minor parts of the English text were left out of at least some of the Maori versions and there was inadequate translation of abstract but basic concepts like sovereignty. The Maori member of Parliament and author, Apirana Ngata, had explained some of these problems to Maoris as early as the 1920s (Ngata, 1963), and the historian Ross (1972) had informed the academic community, but the problems were now being made known to a much wider audience of Maori and Pakeha through educational institutions and the mass media. Reference to the Maori text at hearings of claims by the Waitangi Tribunal had given the Maori text an "official blessing" and also brought expert Maori comment on it to public notice. The tribunal's chief (Maori) judge presented "a Maori approach to the Treaty" as one that centered still on its spirit since the spirit was "something more than a literal construction of the actual words used can provide" and put "narrow or literal interpretations out of place." In related comments on the broad and general words of the treaty, the tribunal looked to the treaty not as a one-time pact between Maori and Pakeha in 1840 but "as the foundation for a developing social contract." Most significant, it gave articulate voice to a growing sense of the treaty as providing the guidelines for Maori and Pakeha to live as two equal peoples rather than one people, and for development of today's policy of cultural duality or biculturalism. As presented by the tribunal's spokespersons, the treaty went beyond acknowledgment of Maori existence in New Zealand in 1840 to intend that "the Maori presence remain and be respected." It "established the regime not for uni-culturalism but for biculturalism." A related activity of the 1980s involved reeducation of New Zealanders at large as to both the circumstances of the treaty's signing and the historical record of Pakeha disregard of its provisions.

Some of the debators wanted the standard history book descriptions of the treaty, which stressed its uniqueness, humanitarianism, and sincerity as to one-peoplehood (e.g., Sinclair, 1970), dismissed as "romantic nonsense" or "Pakeha mythology." Others were writing new "true" descriptions of the day of signing in 1840 that documented dispute and disorder rather than the pomp and ceremony that the standard histories portrayed (see my earlier quote from Buck, 1940, p. 1) and that modern celebrations of the signing were designed to "reenact." There was a general concern to uncover "what the Maori really did" about signing and "what the Pakeha really said" soon afterward. Some of the more powerful Maori leaders of the day did not sign, for example, while others had second thoughts and subsequently withdrew initial endorsement. One backgrounding of the treaty cited a British signatory's description of it "as a harmless device for pacifying naked savages" and two opinions from colonial officials on the Treaty's recognition of Maori rights to their land as "absurd" and as something to be "relegated to the waste paper basket" (Simpson, 1984). Two booklets of additional backgrounding together with eye-witness accounts from both Maori and Pakeha of protest demonstrations on Waitangi Day were prepared and widely distributed by New Zealand's respected National Council of Churches (1983, 1984). The Anglican Church of New Zealand set up a high-level commission to gather submissions nationwide on understandings of the treaty's principles and their meaning for the planning of future ethnic relations (Treaty of Waitangi Commission, 1984). The increasingly cooperative attitude of the treaty reeducation program was evident in plans to consult with "Maori and non-Maori," the selection of three Maori and three Pakeha members for the six-member commission, and a careful presentation of the body as a "bicultural commission."

The 1980s also brought to frontstage debates about the treaty that were in important ways intra-Maori but, in turn, made debate at the Maori-Pakeha level more complex. There had always been regional and tribal variation in Maori opinion about the treaty and some of it was finding renewed expression. In one nineteenth-century division of opinion, the treaty and its application were seen to be chiefly "Ngapuhi's affair." This implicated the northern Ngapuhi Maoris as having played an important part in the treaty making and as the first Maori signatories at Waitangi in 1840 (Orange, 1980, pp. 67-68). In modern times, Ngapuhi Maoris had been hosts for the official Waitangi Day celebrations held at Waitangi each year, leaving some nonnorthern Maoris feeling "left out" and even "deliberately ignored." Positions of relative passivity with roots in the past also persisted.

An intra-Maori debate about the present-day symbolism of the treaty was more developed and of more consequence. It was initially revived by Maoris and it remained Maori-organized and Maori-centered; but the 1980s saw more active if low-key Pakeha participation and, as with the reeducation program, substantially more organizational input from the Pakeha side. In one body of opinion the treaty was a symbol of Pakeha dominance and disregard for Maori rights and of Maori oppression. Maoris and their supporters must press for recognition of the treaty as a "fraud." At demonstrations on Waitangi Day and on other occasions of protest, "the treaty is a fraud" became familiar as a slogan and catchcry. In a modification of this general view, the need was for recognition that the treaty had been "defrauded"—that is, "by a long succession of acts by many Pakeha governments," as one resource person put it. The main push was for ratification, for recognition and future interpretation of the treaty as a legal document. Meanwhile, the treaty was no cause for celebration. As Turner put it (1982, p. 16), when a nation celebrates its national independence or national day it also "celebrates itself . . . it attempts to manifest in symbolic form what it considers to be its essential life." By the 1980s, demonstrations at Waitangi during the Waitangi Day celebrations had become a well-planned annual event. They had established the day that was supposed to celebrate New Zealand's charter for ethnic unity and equality as its annual "demo day," an annual occasion for interethnic conflict.

To other Maoris, the treaty persisted as a no less potent symbol of New Zealand's commitment to Maori-Pakeha equality. Further, Maoris in particular must value the treaty as the only official document that gave the Maori minority a special place in contemporary New Zealand as the country's indigenous people. To many proponents of this view the treaty had a sacred character; it was signed by their ancestors and should be cherished as were other of the ancestors' bequests. Ratification of the treaty was thereby actively opposed. It would be demeaning to the sacredness of the treaty to subject it to (approved) legal interpretation and manipulation. Instead the call was to "honor" the treaty through amends for past abuses, in present-day action, and in planning for the future. There was some support for a moratorium on the Waitangi Day observances but more for change in the tradition of Pakeha-styled ceremonies.

Maori thinking does not readily link differences of opinion with a division of the community. On the contrary, the Maori way to consensus specifically allows for an airing of differences and, for the most part, this approach prevailed in the 1980s debate of the treaty. The proper setting for intro-Maori consultations is a Maori-style gathering or *hui* on a traditional meeting site, a *marae*. The outstanding example of hui on the Treaty of Waitangi through the mid-1980s was a national meeting held in September 1984.

Talked and written about simply as "the Treaty *hui*," it attracted more than 1,000 participants from all parts of the country for a full weekend of discussions. On the long list of organizations and individuals calling for the hui were representatives of conservative as well as "new wave" Maori opinion; established multipurpose associations as well as younger ones formed for the specific purpose of addressing the treaty issue; representatives from Maori separatist movements and Maori representatives of the Pakeha-dominated government. The message of Maori solidarity was to be made as strong as possible.

The hui passed a series of resolutions and the attending Maori Minister of Maori Affairs was asked to submit them to the government. In evidence of the treaty debate of the 1980s as still very much an umbrella for Maori grievances in general, there were resolutions that addressed the unfavorable status of Maori women and one that called for the Department of Maori Affairs to be made accountable to the people for its actions and especially for its frequent underspending of its budget when "Maori needs are so widespread and critical." Among matters specific to the treaty, it was resolved that a law be enacted to ensure that all legislation was consistent with the principles of the treaty. Another resolution addressed the Waitangi Day celebrations asking that the celebrations in their present form be stopped and, in particular, that "all symbols of Maori oppression, such as the police, army and navy" be withdrawn from their traditional involvement with Waitangi Day. To this recommendation the government made a prompt response in announcements that the official observation of Waitangi Day in 1985 would indeed involve a "significant break from traditions of the past."

One change involved plans for a new official Waitangi Day function in addition to the traditional ceremonies at Waitangi itself. The new function was held 400 miles to the south in the nation's capital, Wellington. It took place in the Parliament Buildings and was hosted by the Pakeha Prime Minister for guests representing Parliament, government departments, the Maori community, New Zealand's other ethnic minorities, and diplomats from other countries. One aim was clearly a reaffirmation of Waitangi Day as New Zealand's national day, and thus of the Treaty of Waitangi as still the foundation of nationhood. The new venue for official observations also heeded the feelings of inequity that the former concentration of activities at Waitangi had given some nonnorthern Maoris. Another effect was to take attention away from Waitangi as a place of protest—about 300 people participated in a "very peaceful" demonstration at The Parliament Buildings as the guests arrived for the Wellington function.

More significant perhaps were changes in the Waitangi Day observations at Waitangi itself on February 6, 1985. The official "celebrations" of past years were replaced with a "commemoration." The commemoration was more restrained in terms of being shorter, and more bicultural in format in that it made more use of Maori forms of ceremony. In addition, there was a separate two-day hui at Waitangi on February 4 and 5. Convened by the Maori members of Parliament and staged in part at government expense, it was opened to 2,000 participants for discussion of the future of the Waitangi Day observances and of the Waitangi Tribunal's role as official protector of the treaty. Protesters staged what were reported as "noisy interruptions" during the February 6 ceremonies; but numbering only 100 the demonstration was much smaller and quieter than in previous years. At the least, the treaty debate had reached another turning point.

Conclusion

At the mid-1980s the intensification of interethnic "debates" such as the Treaty of Waitangi debate and the recurrence of ethnic-related incidents such as the Waitangi Day demonstrations had brought New Zealand's image of good ethnic relations into serious and broad-based question. As one grassroots observation summed up the new state of affairs, whether Maori or Pakeha, it was hard to ignore the fact that "we're not quite the success story we thought we were."

Intense debate about the Treaty of Waitangi itself had brought the original and cherished charter for comparatively good relations between Maori and Pakeha under attack. The debate had also given new voice to the treaty's very checkered career, and to its central theme of one-peoplehood—proposed in good faith but never seriously pursued and, in Maori eyes especially, now obsolete. But the debate had also attested to a continuing shared respect for the treaty—it was worthy of long and deep public debate; and, further, to a shared interest in its preservation. A key had been found in a new sense of the treaty's guidelines as more flexible than past views had allowed and, hence, as open to rethinking to fit the demands of new sets of circumstances. In a finding of particular import for a future of harmonious Maori-Pakeha relations, the treaty was now held to support an official policy of biculturalism and of Maori-Pakeha equality through an integrated duality rather than uniformity. As with the original one-people goal, many of the details for implementing the new one remained to be worked out, but substantial experience in the management of ethnic relations and other new resources were now on hand.

NOTES

1. Discussions draw on a variety of historical materials, a wide range of local newspaper and other journalistic sources among secondary contemporary materials, and field research that I have conducted into Maori ethnicity relations during the last 15 years, most recently in December 1984 to January 1985.

2. Because my chapter reports in some detail on one of New Zealand's interethnic debates, I shall identify most of the New Zealand writers cited by ethnicity as well as discipline or profession. I myself am an anthropologist. I was born a Pakeha New Zealander, began my education in anthropology in New Zealand and completed it in the United States. My firsthand fieldwork in New Zealand has been mainly with Maoris in the South Island.

3. The Pakeha majority and the Maori minority have always made up most of New Zealand's population but smaller minorities have long been present (notably Chinese, Indian, Fijian, other Polynesian). The original biethnic model had remained in place, however.

References

Ausubel, D. P. (1977). *The fern and the tiki. An American view of New Zealand national character, social attitudes, and race relations* (rev. ed.). North Quincy, MA: Christopher Publishing House.

Awatere, D. (1984). *Maori sovereignty.* Auckland, NZ: Boradsheet.

Baker, J.V.T. (1966). Population. In A.H. McLintock (Ed.), *An encyclopedia of New Zealand* (Vol. 2, pp. 821-833). Wellington, NZ: Government Printer.

Buck, P. H. (1940). Foreword. In I.L.G. Sutherland (Ed.), *The Maori people today: A general survey* (pp. 1-17). Christchurch, NZ: Whitcombe and Tombs.

Clark, C. (1984-85). Report on Waitangi hui. *Tu Tangata: Maori News Magazine, 21,* 8-15.

Fisher, R. (1980). The impact of European settlement on the indigenous peoples of Australia, New Zealand, and British Columbia: Some comparative dimensions. *Canadian Ethnic Studies, 12,* 1-14.

Forster, J. (1968). The social position of the Maori. In E. Schwimmer (Ed.), *The Maori people in the nineteen-sixties, a symposium* (pp. 97-117). Auckland, NZ: Blackwood and Janet Paul.

Haug, M. R. (1967). Social and cultural pluralism as a concept in social system analysis. *American Journal of Sociology, 73,* 294-304.

Hewitt, C. (1977). Majorities and minorities: A comparative survey of ethnic violence. *Annals of the American Academy of Political and Social Science, 433,* 150-160.

Hohepa, P. (1978). Maori and Pakeha: The one-people myth. In M. King (Ed.), *Te Maori Ora: Aspects of Maoritanga* (pp. 98-111). Wellington, NZ: Methuen.

Howe, K. R. (1977). *Race relations. Australia and New Zealand: A comparative survey 1770's - 1970's.* Wellington, NZ: Methuen.

Hunn, J. K. (1961). *Report on Department of Maori Affairs with statistical supplement (24 August 1960).* Wellington, NZ: Government Printer.

Kelsey, J. (1984). Legal imperialism and the colonization of Aotearoa. In P. Spoonley, C. Macpherson, D. Pearson, & C. Sedgwick (Eds.), *Tauiwi: Racism and ethnicity in New Zealand.* Palmerston North, NZ: Dunsmore Press.

Metge, J. (1976). *The Maoris of New Zealand, Rautahi* (rev. ed.). London: Routledge & Kegan Paul.

National Council of Churches in New Zealand. (1983). *What happened at Waitangi in 1983? A report to the New Zealand churches concerning the Treaty of Waitangi, its observance and its ceremonial.* Auckland, NZ: Author.

National Council of Churches in New Zealand. (1984). *Waitangi 1984—a turning point? A report to the New Zealand churches concerning the Treaty of Waitangi, and its ceremonial commemoration.* Christchurch, NZ: Author.

New Zealand Department of Statistics. (1983). *New Zealand census of population and dwellings: 1981. Vol. 1. Increase and location of population.* Wellington, NZ: Government Printer.

Ngata, A. (1963). *The Treaty of Waitangi: An explanation.* Wellington, NZ: Maori Purposes Fund Board. (Original work published 1922)

Orange, C. (1980). The covenant of Kohimaramara: A ratification of the Treaty of Waitangi. *New Zealand Journal of History, 14,* 61-82.

Ross, R. M. (1972). The Tiriti of Waitangi: Texts and Translations. *New Zealand Journal of History, 6,* 129-157.

Royce, A. P. (1982). *Ethnic identity: Strategies of diversity.* Bloomington: Indiana University Press.

Schwimmer, E. (1968). The aspirations of the contemporary Maori. In E. Schwimmer (Ed.), *The Maori people in the nineteen sixties: A symposium* (pp. 9-64). Auckland, NZ: Blackwood and Janet Paul.

Simpson, T. (1984). Waitangi: Backgrounding the Treaty. *Tu Tangata: Maori News Magazine, 16,* 26-27.

Sinclair, K. (1970). *A history of New Zealand.* Harmondsworth, Middlesex, England: Penguin.

Sinclair, K. (1971). Why are race relations in New Zealand better than in South Africa, South Australia or South Dakota? *New Zealand Journal of History, 5,* 121-127.

Smith, A. D. (1981). *The ethnic revival in the modern world.* Cambridge: Cambridge University Press.

Spoonley, P., Macpherson, C., Pearson, D., & Sedgwick, C. (Eds.). (1984). *Tauiwi: Racism and ethnicity in New Zealand.* Palmerston North, NZ: Dunsmore Press.

Sutherland, I.L.G. (1940). Introduction. In I.L.G. Sutherland (Ed.), *The Maori people today: A general survey* (pp. 19-48). Christchurch, NZ: Whitcombe and Tombs.

Thompson, R. (1963). *Race relations in New Zealand. A review of the literature.* Christchurch, NZ: National Council of Churches.

Treaty of Waitangi Commission, Anglican Church. (1984). *The Treaty of Waitangi. Discussion Paper.* Rotorua, NZ: Author.

Turner, V. (1982). Introduction. In V. Turner (Ed.), *Celebrations: Studies in festivity and ritual* (pp. 11-30). Washington, DC: Smithsonian Institution Press.

Walker, R. J. (1984). The genesis of Maori activism. *Journal of the Polynesian Society, 93,* 267-281.

Ward, A. D. (1967). The origins of the Anglo-Maori Wars: A reconsideration. *New Zealand Journal of History, 1,* 148-170.

Chapter Summary

Rolf Kuschel focuses on a society with one of the highest known levels of aggression, the people of Bellona in the Solomon Islands. This chapter examines the nature of this aggressive behavior as well as the conditions that produce and maintain such conflict.

According to Kuschel, the history and organization of Bellona had inherent potential for conflict. As recorded in oral tradition, the island began with eight original couples, each of whom formed their own clan. From the start there was a sense of antagonism since seven of these clans had arrived from the Loyalty Islands and had distinguished themselves as a group from the other clan, originating in Wallis Island.

Kuschel lists numerous areas of conflict and discusses aspects of Bellona's social organization contributing to the generation of aggression, including the lack of a formal chief endowed with power to make societywide decisions. The author describes Bellona culture as strongly valuing revenge, especially in response to more serious offenses. He explains that hostile acts are never forgotten and storytelling is used to convey obligations of revenge from one generation to another. Conditions for the development and escalation of conflicts are delineated, the most important of which is that the perpetrator have a large powerful kin group to support him.

Kuschel observes that killings and other aggressive behavior are far more prevalent among men than women. He draws a distinction between public and private aggressive acts. Marital conflict, for example, is viewed as private aggression until a certain degree of violence is reached. The author describes reasons for and consequences of the killings in Bellona. One of the main consequences is that six of the original clans are now extinct.

Aspects of the sociocultural makeup of Bellona that encourage violence include the value placed on killing as an honorable form of problem solving and on retaliation (even above kin-group loyalties) and a patrilineal and patrilocal structure that facilitates the formation of power groups.

Finally, Kuschel stresses the need to solve certain problems in aggression research including the definition of phenomena and the recognition of behavior as multiply determined. Methodological suggestions for future research on aggression are presented.

—Susan Goldstein

12

Twenty-Four Generations of Intergroup Conflicts on Bellona Island (Solomon Islands)

ROLF KUSCHEL

More than 50 years ago, Albert Einstein and Sigmund Freud attempted a dialogue about "the causes and cure of wars." Although Einstein in his letter to Freud explicitly talks of international conflicts, he also makes it clear that he is referring to "civil wars" and "the persecutions of racial minorities." The dialogue almost stopped even before it got started, primarily because the theory of psychoanalysis was unable to give sufficient answers to complex sociological problems. In the psychoanalyst's reply to Einstein, Freud seems very pessimistic and does not foresee any efficient solution to either violence in general or to structural violence. Freud mentions that he has learned that "in some happy corners of the earth, they say, where nature brings forth abundantly whatever man desires, there flourish races whose lives go gently by, unknowing of aggression or constraint. This I can hardly credit; I would like further details about these happy folk" (Nathan & Norden, 1960, p. 199).

Today we know more about aggression. We know that there are certain societies whose members have generally been able to live peacefully with one another without taking to violence (Montagu, 1978; Nance, 1975). But our present knowledge is still fragmented. So far we have no cogent explanation of the nature of aggression and especially no means for its prevention and elimination. There may be several reasons for this state of affairs. I shall only mention a few of them.

Despite the fact that most scientists have realized that human beings are complex entities that interact with their surroundings in multiple ways, the study of aggression and violence still treats the human being as either a biological, psychological, social, or economic animal.

Individual psychologists focus on the intrapsychic processes of the individual, innate dispositions, or personal dispositions, but they ignore the importance of social interaction influences upon the individual. Certain social psychologists emphasize what happens in the first years of the life of a child, but all too often forget that development does not stop at puberty and that the human being is an active individual who at any time can manipulate what has been learned during childhood. On the other hand, sociologists focus on the structure and organization of a society and its importance for furthering—or restraining—aggressive patterns of action. In other fields of science, such as social anthropology, human ethology, and neurophysiology, we find similar restrictions (for references to the different approaches, see Lange & Westin, 1981; Moyer, 1976). Because human beings are simultaneously biological, psychological, and sociological creatures actively interacting with their surroundings, it is unlikely that narrow research on aggression will come to a general conclusion. Aggressive behavior has multiple determinants. There is no single answer. If we really wish to understand the nature of aggression, cooperation between many specialists from the social, behavioral, and natural sciences is necessary.

There are many other problems connected with research on aggression. Definitions are often so vague and broad that phenomena such as atomic bombings, sadistic murders, terrorism, women's defense against rapists, game hunting, and punching a naughty child may be included within the same category. See for example Zillman who defines aggression as "attempts to produce bodily or physical injury to others" (Zillman, 1978). Baron has given a similar vague definition: "Aggression is any form of behavior directed towards the goal of harming or injuring another living being who is motivated to avoid such treatment" (Baron, 1977; for further examples of definitions of aggression, see van der Dennen,

1980, who collected 106 definitions). To further our understanding of aggression, fundamental conceptual analyses are necessary in order to avoid mixing up and comparing phenomena whose functions are widely different (see Goodenough, 1980). What has been said about the difficulties in research on aggression is equally valid for conceptual demarcation and research paradigms in interethnic research (see Lange & Westin, 1981).

Too many theories are nomothetic, formulating general or even universal laws about aggression and violent behavior. They do not take into consideration that human beings live under different ecological conditions and have developed a diversity of social organizations to cope with these differing conditions. We need to look more carefully at cultural variations. We will have to investigate, too, which conditions create relations furthering peacefulness in certain societies. It is only through understanding the contrast of aggression that we can understand what promotes and determines aggression.

Many theories are much too broad in their explanations. It is imperative that research be initiated that attempts, in a more concrete form than previous studies have, to clarify how the individual in communications with the surroundings forms a subjective perception of the social reality. It is only when we understand this complex interaction that we may perhaps hope to teach the future generations to live in greater harmony than many do today.

I shall now turn to social conflicts on the island of Bellona in the Solomon Islands. I shall look at conditions that generate and maintain these conflicts, and I shall present an analysis explaining why it has been virtually impossible to keep conflicts under control in traditional Bellonese society.

In a brief chapter such as this it is impossible to present in a satisfactory way the nuances that appear in the course of social conflicts on Bellona. I shall therefore mainly concentrate on conflicts that have resulted in killings. (For a more detailed exposition, see Kuschel, in press.)

A Brief History of Bellona

Although Bellona is a very small island of only 17 square kilometers whose population has probably never exceeded 500 or 600 individuals at a time,[1] the islanders have lived in a world of strife and social unrest for the past 600 years.

What makes Bellona an interesting site for study is not only its small size and population, but its long isolation, too. Before the introduction of Christianity, contacts with the outside world were scarce, in terms of interaction with other South Pacific islanders as well as with Europeans and Americans. Ships that called on the island only stayed for a few hours or a few days. Their visits did not have any impact on the islanders' traditions and patterns of behavior.

In the early 1930s, missionaries started a campaign to "save" the islanders' souls. They removed young Rennellese and Bellonese boys from the islands, took them to their missionary schools on other islands in the Solomons, and taught them a crude form of Christianity. Finally the missionaries' aggressive and ruthless removal of young people from their traditional culture bore fruit. In October of 1938 Christianity was introduced to Rennell Island; two months later some converted Rennellese went to Bellona, and in one week they managed to convince the Bellonese that the Christian god was stronger than their own. The process was completed without bloodshed. Internal social unrest at the time ensured the speedy acceptance of Christianity. A few years before, men from the eastern part of the island had been killed, a few acts of revenge had ensued, and when the Rennellese arrived everyone was waiting for the decisive battle. Several years in hiding in the forest and fear of the battle ahead made the promise of a peaceful future appear particularly tantalizing. The Seventh-Day Adventists won the first battle. But a few months later representatives of the South Sea Evangelical Mission attempted to win proselytes among the 440 inhabitants then living on Bellona. At first there was little tension between the two missions, but later violent clashes occurred in which the Bible was brought into active service.

The change to the new religion as well as the social changes were gradual at first. The first teacher came into residence on Bellona in 1949. He did little to change the patterns of the settlements. In the late 1960s contacts with ships from the outside world increased, and the changes became more rapid. Young people went to Honiara, the capital in the Solomon Islands, and returned with new ideas, new sets of values, and new patterns of behavior. In the 1970s their culture was changed through the deaths of old men and women who had been bearers of the traditional culture. The mission succeeded and the traditional culture died.

To the Bellonese their recorded past started 24 generations before 1950, when their forefathers left Ubeangango (West Ubea) and Ubeamatangi (East Ubea). (West and East Ubea have been tentatively identified by Elbert & Monberg, 1965, as Uvea of the Loyalty Islands and Uvea of Wallis Island, respectively.) Their forefathers set out on a perilous voyage several thousand kilometers across the open sea and landed on Bellona and Rennell Islands. It is not known how many individuals originally left western Polynesia, but there must have been many more than the eight couples who are said to have arrived at their destination. According to their oral tradition some were killed in battles during the voyage and 100 were drowned in a flood. But according to the oral traditions, only eight couples arrived on the islands of Rennell and Bellona. Upon arrival on Bellona each of the eight men formed his own clan.

Even before the permanent settlement on the two islands, the immigrants had formed specific social groups. Seven forefathers came from the Loyalty Islands and considered themselves one group and took the name the "Seven Original Clans." The eighth ancestor, Kaitu'u, came from Wallis Island and thus did not belong to the Seven Original Clans. Even from the beginning there were feelings of antagonism between the two groups. This was because Kaitu'u was born out of wedlock and thus stigmatized; and when the immigrants decided to select their respective gods, Kaitu'u spoke first and selected two of the most significant and sacred gods as his. Because of this greediness another immigrant, Taupongi, became so outraged that he said to Kaitu'u, "You are showing how to select the best food and have got hermit-crab teeth" (Elbert & Monberg, 1965). Because he originated in a different geographical area from that of the other immigrants, Kaitu'u' is considered an outsider with a different social identity. By being fatherless among men to whom patrilineality is so important he is stigmatized, and "by claiming the more powerful deities of the pantheon as his protectors" (Elbert & Monberg, 1965) he shows an arrogance that does not befit his social status.

Thus the scene is set for the social drama that developed over the next 24 generations, in which bloodshed, revenge, and feuds between the Seven Original Clans and the Kaitu'u Clan set a pattern for their social relations. After the Kaitu'u Clan had severely reduced the Seven Original Clans, some of which were later annihilated, members of the Kaitu'u Clan started fighting and killing among themselves. Intraclan feuds started as a clash between the two subclans within the Kaitu'u Clan, but later on they developed into severe fights even within one of the subclans. Almost two-thirds of all intraclan raids became parts of three feuds, one of which covered a period of approximately 125 years. The reason for these are apparently minor incidents such as the death of a borrowed decoy pigeon. Due to the social organization it is tremendously difficult to control a conflict once it has resulted in a killing. Despite the fact that killings between agnatic kinsmen should be avoided, reality shows another picture. Saint-Exupéry once described this discrepancy between the formal rules and the actual behavior by saying, *"La vie, toujours, fait craquer les formules"* (1942, p. 139). This is especially valid for a society such as Bellona, which stresses individual freedom to act as one pleases and in which there are almost no effective social control devices that can prevent a man from killing, seeking revenge, or counterrevenge.

This brief historical sketch is based upon the oral traditions of the island. The following deductions can be made: (1) Killing was a well-established pattern of action among the immigrants even before their arrival on Bellona; (2) the groups viewed their social identity differently; (3) stigmatization formed a dichotomization among the immigrants. The result of this is the formation of a majority group (the Seven Original Clans) and a minority group (the members of the Kaitu'u Clan).

Social Organization

In the generations to come the immigrants developed a social organization consisting of clans, subclans, and lineages. The nuclear family was the smallest social unit. The social hierarchy consisted of lineage heads, common landowners, and low-status persons. Bellona is patrilineal and has a patrilocal settlement pattern. Formally the firstborn son succeeds in the role as head of the lineage. This person must have certain characteristics: He must be active, industrious, and always helpful to others. Through his own contribution he must add to the prosperity of the entire island as well as provide for himself.

The social organization contains many possibilities for conflicts:

(1) No "chief" is provided with legitimate authority, that is, with the right or power to make decisions on behalf of the society as a whole.

(2) Great value is placed on the individual's freedom to make one's own decisions. This principle does not, however, apply to low-status persons.

(3) The traditional principles of land tenure contain a permanent source of possible conflicts. Even though there are principles stressing the right of a firstborn son to inherit most of the land, a father can at any time ignore this rule according to (2). This often means status rivalry between brothers.

Down through the centuries Bellona has been exposed to controversies and feuds. The areas of conflicts are numerous, including land feuds, disputes over borderlines of a few inches, access to fruit trees and timber for building canoes, theft, deceit, spreading of rumors, insults, taunt songs, jealousy, and marital troubles, just to mention a few causes. Most of these conflicts are often brought to a *temporary* halt. When I speak of a temporary halt the reason is that the Bellonese rarely forget previous events. Items of conflict belong to what Rubin (see From, 1971, p. 44) has termed "easily arising entities." This means that even the smallest occasion can bring these entities into consciousness. Feelings are believed to be seated in the larynx and may spontaneously be activated through any associative connection to the event or by seeing the person who once has been the cause of one's anger. A legend may clarify the origin of conflict.

There is a story about a man by the name of Panio who one day unintentionally pushed another man named Uao. Uao had just received a bowl containing the blood of a killed turtle (a rare and highly valued beverage). When the bowl with the blood fell to the ground he became so furious that he many years later let Panio pay for this with his life. They were both at sea between Rennell and Bellona, when Panio's canoe sank. When Panio swam over to the canoe belonging to Uao and tried to enter it, Uao hit Panio's fingers so hard with a club that Panio in tears had to release the rail and submit to the elements of the sea. This little episode shows how the Bellonese never forget or forgive what has happened to them.

The Bellonese recall humiliations received by their ancestors 24 generations ago. How is it possible for the Bellonese to remember their oral traditions so long back as that, though they do not have a written language? Training in oral presentation takes place informally anywhere and at any time. However, it is most common for the children and young people to congregate around the older people in the evenings and listen to their stories. When the story concerns the humiliating events such as the killing of an ancestor, it is said especially to the boys, "Your grandfather has been killed by so and so, but [the death] has not yet been revenged. You have to revenge it!" In this way the children become prepared for the kind of life they can expect, and the boys are indoctrinated. If too much time elapses before an adult lives up to the expectations, he is exposed to social pressure from other kinsmen who may say, "This old man killed so and so's father, but nobody cares about it, either because it was alright, or because he is afraid!" (Kuschel, forthcoming). This group pressure is constantly at work. A person who does not respond to it is stigmatized as a weakling and risks deprecatory remarks from others. Sometimes, though, it will be more convenient to wait for a retaliation rather than to act immediately. This may be the case when a patrilineal descent group is too small to retaliate with success. In such a case one will wait until the lineage has grown. There is one case in which an attack of retaliation has waited for nine generations, approximately 200 years.

Conflict Development

The development of conflicts is dependent upon various conditions: the reasons for the conflict; the presence of power groups; the personalities of those involved; and admission of guilt and payment of propitiatory sacrifice. In short this means that the more grave the offense the more likely that the conflict will develop into killing, counterkilling, and perhaps into the beginning of a new feud. But one condition for such a development is that the insulted party belong to a large power group and has kin and friends who will support him in the escalation of the conflict. Conditions of personality are also relevant. Some men have a more violent temper than others. Therefore, lesser offenses will cause them to act more violently than more docile individuals. Especially in the beginning, a conflict may be brought to a halt if the offender admits the wrongdoing and sends a gift of atonement consisting of crops, mats, necklaces, clothes, or perhaps even donates some land to the offended.

The general development of a serious social conflict that leads to killings is as follows: (1) verbal accusation, exchanging insults; (2) threatening with or without weapons; (3) wrestling or hairpulling without wounding opponent; (4) wounding each other with fingernails, fists, clubs, or heavy sticks; (5) destruction of valuables such as coconut palms or canoes; (6) planning a raid; (7) killing the enemy; (8) destroying the enemy's settlement; (9) seeking refuge on a hillock; (10) conclusion of peace; and (11) planning revenge.

The structure presented above is theoretical in the sense that development does not have to follow the pattern (1) to (10). Conflicts may start on different levels and can even skip several steps. If phase (7) has been reached, phases (8) to (10) are obligatory, whereafter the conflict can continue over the years and generations to come as well as killings of revenge as counterrevenge takes place.

During each phase of the conflict, enemies will perform "magic" acts, consisting of verbal spells to the gods asking them to bring their enemies' lives into danger and ultimately to death. The intensity of the magic acts reaches its peak just before the launching of an attack. Afterward the attackers continue performing their magic spells against their foes, but with less intensity.

If a man decides to kill his adversary, he assembles a small group of men. (Only men are involved in raiding activities; females are not informed about a planned attack because it is thought they might be tempted to reveal the plans due to a feeling of loyalty to their own relatives.) In the dark they sneak up to the homestead of the enemy. Every man who does not manage to escape the place is killed. Women and children are usually not killed though there are exceptions. Afterward the attackers destroy the victim's settlement.

On their way home they shout short songs, announcing their successful deed. Arriving at their own settlement the fighters celebrate their victory. They dress up as if they were going to a feast, they perform rituals, eat, and dance. There are no specific "war dances," but each man selects one of the traditional songs that alludes to the place or person who has just been killed. After the celebration the attackers retreat to the bush. For several months they live on small hillocks in the bush, as do those out to revenge the raid. Nobody feels secure—the possibility of an ambush is always present. Hiding in the bush is a very strenuous time. Scarcity of food, the long period of inactivity where they cannot garden, go fishing, or have social interaction with their families creates and builds up tension among the men. Sometimes the tension gets so intense that the group of attackers splits up and lives on different hillocks. Meanwhile, males or females, who have relatives among the attackers and the attacked, are sent back and forth between the two antagonistic groups, trying to find out whether they are ready to make peace. If they are, the time for the peace ritual is negotiated. The peace ceremony is a very complicated ritual during which everybody is frightened because this is the first time the enemies will sit face to face with each other. Everybody knows that the peace is only temporary because the society demands that revenge has to take place in the years to come.

The quarrels between women will hardly ever generate into more than verbal accusations, hairpulling, or scratching each other with fingernails. On rare occasions women will beat one another with thick sticks. There is only one recorded example of a woman killing her cowife in jealousy.

Conflicts between men and women who are not their wives may result in exchanges of invectives and threats. Such behavior may infuriate the agnatic or affinal kinsmen of the woman. Even in exchanging invectives one has to be careful because many of these concern tabooed subjects, such as copulation with a consanguineal kinsman or kinswoman.

Marital conflicts are fairly common; the reasons given are laziness, selfishness, neglect of the children, spreading rumors, using bad language, jealousy, adultery, or a woman's refusal to satisfy her husband's sexual desires. In a few cases marital conflicts can lead to homicide, as in the following case: Ta'akihenua had an argument with his wife, Tekata'angaba, because she did not take out the tendons of a coconut crab before serving the food. The tendons stuck in her husband's teeth, whereupon he struck her with a stick. The woman cried and grabbed a beam in the hut. This position revealed love-scratches, made by a lover, in her armpits. Ta'akihenua "pulled out [his] stone adze and smashed its butt end at the neck of Tekata'angaba and [she fell forward and lay there]. When [her husband] lifted [her] up [she] was already dead."

Marital conflicts can develop in different ways depending on whether the means of action under consideration are those of the husband toward his wife or those of the wife toward her husband. The means of action available to the husband are (1) verbal accusations; (2) slap, strike, or knock with fist; (3) kick with foot; (4)

beat with stick; (5) twist hair and beat the body; (6) strike back with club or blunt edge of axe; (7) strike or knock mouth with fist; (8) tear apart earlobe; (9) lacerate forehead; (10) burn body with hot stone or stick; (11) get divorce; and (12) beat to death. Of the behaviors listed, (1) through (6) are regarded as private affairs, while the remaining behaviors are regarded as nonprivate affairs. The means of action available to the wife are: (1) verbal accusations; (2) cursing, as by telling husband to eat undesirable food; (3) ridicule; (4) slap, strike, or knock *own* children with hands; (5) kick or beat own children with foot or stick; (6) flight into exile; and (7) get divorce.

I want to stress the following points concerning the actions available to husbands and wives:

(1) The woman has fewer means of action than has a man.
(2) When the Bellonese say that women beat or kick their own children, it must be understood as an act of humiliation against her husband, especially if the action is to a male child. According to Prætorius (1970, p. 75), more than half of the interviewed women said that they had struck their own children during or after a quarrel with their husbands. When beaten or scolded by grown-ups, older children frequently beat their younger siblings.
(3) There are limits to what a man is allowed to do toward his wife, even in great anger. If he surpasses the patterns of action described as private affairs, it is no longer a private affair but becomes public. The agnatic kinsmen of the woman, commonly her brothers or father, may step in and revenge the woman.

Reasons for Conflict

We may now ask what the reasons are for all these conflicts. Concentrating on conflicts leading to killings, Table 12.1 indicates that approximately half of the killings are caused by revenge or counterrevenge (feuds). This is due to a social demand that any killing shall, if possible, be revenged so that the survivors will not be considered weaklings or indifferent to the fate of their killed kinsmen. This attitude has a spiral effect as it causes perpetual regress. The analysis shows that most of the initiated killings result in feuds of which the longest has lasted about 240 years. Killings of revenge

TABLE 12.1:   Ostensible Reasons for Attacks

General Reasons for Attacks	Samples of Particular Reasons for Attacks	Number of Episodes	Percentage of Episodes
Revenges and counter-revenges		101	53.2
Infringement against or negligent treatment of property	theft	20	
	annexation of land	9	
	destruction of property	7	20.5
	usurpation of title to fruit trees	3	
Violation of social esteem	humiliating behavior and verbal insults	25	
	adultery	6	17.4
	rejected suitor	2	
Individually inherent conditions	enviousness	4	
	jealousy between co-wives	1	4.2
	wanting fame	3	
Unknown		9	4.7
Total		190	100.0

that do not develop into feuds are terminated because of lack of fighters on one side who can continue the killings. The few cases in which killings are unrevenged usually concern the killing of a low-status person, whom no one will bother to revenge in order to avoid being involved in counterrevenge.

There have been numerous consequences of the social unrest that has dominated Bellona during the years. Social interaction between members of the various districts of the island has periodically been very scant. Due to fear of being killed or attacked by enemies or the fear of the uncontrollable behavior of certain gods and supernaturals (see Monberg, 1966), men dared not travel freely on the island. In 1968 I met a man who during the first 40 years of his lifetime had never seen the other end of the island, even though the distance between the two ends is only seven miles. Only when the missionaries came with their message of peace did he dare walk to the other end. Garden areas lying far from one's own settlement are only rarely cultivated during times of social unrest because of fear of enemies waiting their in ambush. What has been even more significant for the society was that six out of the eight clans have become extinct through killings. Today there is only one clan left from the Seven Original Clans. This clan, the Taupongi Clan, and the Kaitu'u Clan have through the years fought each other to such a degree that each of them has twice been close to complete extermination. At one stage only one married couple of the Taupongi Clan was left; they did manage to multiply while hiding in the bush.

The many conflicts between the majority group and the minority caused much irreconcilable hatred. Even intergroup marriages did not reduce these feelings. The hatred leads to many prejudices, as when one side accuses the other side of descending from a fatherless ancestor. Conversely, rumors have it that members of the enemy clan are descended from incestuous relations (it is said that the surviving couple of the Taupongi Clan consisted of such a relationship). Prejudices cause discrimination. There are a number of cases in which a member of one clan tries to prevent his own children from marrying persons of the other clan because all of them are accused of bad behavior, such as being filthy, belonging to a family or lineage in which members eat unclean food, or belonging to a family of thieves. Everything that takes place within the other group is registered. If a person does something degrading, his behavior immediately is generalized to the entire group. If something positive is done, the other group tries to minimize its importance.

Can aggression on Bellona be explained through the influence on the young people by adults—especially parents and grandparents? According to some theories of socialization, it is through the influence in the early years that the young people's picture of the social reality is created. This picture influences their future patterns of actions and evaluations. The theories of socialization are essential for an understanding of why violence plays such an important role in Bellonese solutions of social conflicts. Through their upbringing children learn partly by direct verbal instruction and partly through imitating behavior patterns of adults that violence is not only allowed but even in certain cases an expected action. This is the case when one's own honor and pride or that of one's kinsmen is sullied.

There are, however, certain difficulties in using theories of socialization to explain the behavior of the Bellonese. They cannot tell us why violence has emerged as a form of problem solving, what makes the human being act in this way. The theories of socialization can only explain why certain social patterns of acts and norms of value are maintained and transferred from generation to generation. It is also difficult to explain through the theories of socialization how individual variations emerge. Among a set of siblings some children may sometimes be more violent than the others. Why is that?

A considerable part of the social unrest, especially killings, on Bellona have to do with the culture's social organization and the concept of values:

(1) In the Bellonese society there exists a cultural ethos that (a) considers killings as a historically determined means of solving problems; (b) demands that any kind of wrongdoing is revenged unless the offender somehow admits his offense and pays a propitiatory sacrifice; and (c) requires every group (lineage, subclan, clan, subdistrict, or district) to be very conscious of its social identity. Any attack or threat against its honor and dignity is looked upon as a severe offense.

(2) The society has a patrilineal and patrilocal structure. The latter makes the formation of power groups possible. A power group is "a group which resorts to aggression when the interest of one of its members is threatened" (van Velzen & van Wetering, 1960, p. 179). These power groups are mainly recruited among agnatic kinsmen (mostly brothers) but may also include maternal kin and affines.

These factors make it difficult to limit the extent of conflicts:

(1) One of the fundamental principles of the society is the high value of and respect for individual entrepreneurs.

(2) A superior person, with formal and real authority to interfere with resolutions and acts of other independent landowners, does not exist. Because any independent landowner is basically self-supporting, he is not dependent on others in any respect.

(3) Peace making is looked upon by everybody as something temporary and a kind of armed neutrality. As one informant said, "Peace is but a deception."

Conclusions

It may be said that it is difficult to create a durable peace in a society in which (1) demands for retaliation are strong; (2) the form of organization and settlement facilitates the formation of male power groups; and (3) there is no formal possibility that a third party can actively and forcefully intervene as a peacemaker in a conflict.

Fortunately, there are exceptions. Because humans are freely acting and most commonly also rationally acting, we can influence our own lives. This was the case on Bellona about 50 years ago when two districts, who through generations had fought with one another, decided to put an end to their hostilities. A man said to his son, "Ngango and Matangi [the two districts] have been fighting each other for generations, but we are [because of intermarriage between the two districts] like two eyes. If one eye is hurt, the other one cries, so let's stop the fighting between the two districts."

Despite our rudimentary understanding of what causes and perpetuates aggressive patterns of action and how these can be changed to more positive and peaceful forms of interaction, our knowledge today is fortunately deeper than it was at Freud's time. We need not be as pessimistic as the founder of psychoanalysis. The sociologist, Ilfeld, once said, "Hope is provided by knowing that all peoples are equally violent; violent behaviors which are learned can be unlearned; frustrations can be alleviated; weapons can be limited; and men can find peaceful alternatives for resolving conflicts" (1970, p. 93). The important point in Ilfeld's writing is that he regards violent behavior as something that has been learned and thus can be unlearned too. Since 1938, when the Bellonese increased their interaction with the outside world and when government ships started to visit the island more regularly, killings have almost totally stopped. The Bellonese were told that they would be sent to prison if they continued killing each other, and the missionaries told them in a vivid fashion that those who killed would burn in hell for 1,000 years. Almost from one day to another they desisted from committing homicide. This does not mean that Bellona has turned into a completely peaceful society. They still have a tremendous amount of internal strife and social unrest. This, I believe, can only be changed when some of the main causes for conflicts (e.g., fights about land and borderlines) are settled and when a radical change in their social organization has taken place. What is needed are institutions furnished with legitimate power to control the individuals' acts of hostility.

NOTE

1. The first systematic census is from 1938. At that time 440 people lived on the island.

References

Baron, R. A. (1977). *Human aggression.* New York: Plenum Press.

Christiansen, S. (1975). *Subsistence on Bellona Island (Mungiki).* Copenhagen: C.A. Reitzels Forlag.

Elbert, S., & Monberg, T. (1965). *From the two canoes: Oral traditions of Rennell and Bellona Islands.* Honolulu/Copenhagen: Danish National Museum in cooperation with the University of Hawaii Press.

From, F. (1971). *Perception of other people.* New York: Columbia University Press.

Goodenough, W. H. (1980). *Description and comparison in cultural anthropology.* Cambridge: Cambridge University Press.

Ilfeld, F. W., Jr. (1970). Environmental theories of violence. In D.N. Daniels, M.F. Gilula, & F.M. Ochberg (Eds.), *Violence and the struggle for existence.* Boston: Little, Brown.

Kuschel, R. (in press). *Vengeance is their reply: Bloodshed, vengeance, and feuds on Bellona Island (Mungiki)* (Vols. 1-2).

Lange, A., & Westin, C. (1981). *Etnisk diskriminering och social identitet.* Helsingborg.

Monberg, T. (1966). *The religion of Bellona Island.* Copenhagen: National Museum of Denmark.

Montagu, A. (Ed.). (1978). *Learning non-aggression.* Oxford: Oxford University Press.

Moyer, K. E. (1976). *The psychology of aggression.* New York: Harper & Row.

Nance, J. (1975). *The gentle Tasaday.* New York: Harcourt Brace Jovanovich.

Nathan, O., & Norden, H. (1960). *Einstein on peace.* New York: Avenel Books.

Prætorious, U. (1970). *Aggressionsmønstre og deres socialisation på Bellona - et polynesisk ø-samfund.* Unpublished master's thesis, Copenhagen.

Saint-Exupéry, Antoine de. (1942). *Pilote de guerre.* Gallimard.

van der Dennen, J.M.G. (1980). *Problems in the concepts and definitions of aggression, violence, and some related terms.* Rijsuniversiteit Groningen.

van Velzen, H.E.E.T., & van Wetering, W. (1960). Residence, power groups and intra-societal aggression. *International Archives of Ethnography, 49* (p. 1), 169-200.

Zillman, D. (1978). *Hostility and aggression.* Hillsdale: Lawrence & Erlbaum.

Chapter Summary

Kirkpatrick stresses the complexity of ethnic relations as a key factor contributing to the relative lack of interethnic conflict throughout the history of Hawaii. According to the author, these low levels of interethnic aggression exist despite a history of socioeconomic structures often associated with ethnic divisiveness. Kirkpatrick discusses these structures in terms of three phases of development: (1) the plantation system, (2) the expanded social system of a closed economy, and (3) the postwar development of a service economy dependent on outside capital.

Also limiting the probability of interethnic aggression are problems involved in clearly defining ethnic groups in Hawaii. According to Kirkpatrick these stem from the existence of important subethnic distinctions in terms of tradition or descent, high rates of intermarriage, the use of ethnic terms to describe lifestyle characteristics rather than lineage, the fluidity of ethnic categories, and what is termed a "Local" ethnic identification that consolidates certain ethnic groups. Factors contributing to the emergence of a Local identity are discussed, including the increased use across ethnic groups of a common form of Pidgin English among individuals raised in Hawaii.

Kirkpatrick presents some of the main concerns of specific ethnic groups, concentrating primarily on Filipinos, Hawaiians, and Haoles (Caucasians). Reasons for the absence of high levels of interethnic conflict discussed emphasize the lack of a single dominant group, high rates of intermarriage, a suspicion toward ethnic-based organizations, a tendency to withdraw from potential conflict, and a cultural value of "Aloha" and tolerance.

Kirkpatrick concludes with a discussion of future prospects for the Hawaiian Islands in which he predicts worsening interethnic relations with increased Haole domination.

—Susan Goldstein

13

Ethnic Antagonism and Innovation in Hawaii

JOHN KIRKPATRICK

In 1800, ethnic relations hardly existed in Hawaii. A few sailors were the only foreigners in the islands. By 1900, Hawaiians were no longer the largest population group, and Hawaii had become a territory controlled by Caucasian entrepreneurs and administrators. In 1959, statehood was finally granted. At that time, the concentration of political and economic power in the hands of a resident Caucasian elite was ending. Nowadays, political slates are multiethnic; Americans of Japanese ancestry are more likely than Caucasians or Hawaiians to be accused of taking more than their share of the spoils; the state's economy depends on decision makers on the United States (U.S.) mainland and in Japan.

This chapter surveys the historical context of Hawaii's ethnic relations. Those relations have been extensively studied by others; this account is a summary one. With ethnic conflicts elsewhere in mind, I emphasize (1) that ethnic antagonisms have led to relatively little violence; (2) that such antagonisms in a multiethnic polity may work for stability; and (3) that a quasiethnic Local identity has emerged, reinforcing some ethnic divisions and crosscutting others. Hawaii's people can draw on ethnic traditions to support particular identities and to oppose forms of discrimination, but they

AUTHOR'S NOTE: I thank Steve Boggs, John D'Amato, Cora Jordan, Vivian Murray, and Eugene Ogan for helpful and perceptive comments.

can also transcend the limits of particularistic traditions without renouncing ethnic identities.[1]

To explore the dynamics and meaning of ethnicity in Hawaii, a précis of the islands' social history identifies the changing contexts of ethnic relations. Next, closer attention is given to those relations in recent decades. The account of the Hawaiian situation deals with historical particulars. A thorough restatement of the situation so that it is fully comparable with other cases in this volume would demand another essay, so a partial comparative perspective is developed in conclusion.

Historical Overview

Political Foundations

Rapid social change in Hawaii has been encouraged and eased by political centralization. By 1810, the islands were unified under King Kamehameha I. His successors maintained a unified kingdom while Christianity and new relations between rulers and ruled were introduced. The Hawaiian monarchs dealt as best they could with catastrophic population declines, threats from European powers, the establishment of a cash economy, and the conversion of much of Hawaii's land into plantations owned by Haole (Caucasian) merchants and worked by laborers imported from Asia and Europe.[2] The monarchy had made the growth of the plantations possible, through land laws, immigration laws, and treaties. The Reciprocity Treaty of 1876, for example, assured the importation of Hawaiian sugar into the United States without duty. Yet, the concessions made by the Hawaiian government to the planters did not assure their loyalty: The revolt that led to the Hawaiian Republic (1894-98) was instigated by the Haoles of Honolulu and backed by the U.S. Marines. Annexation by the United States was sought largely to preserve the plantation economy. Annexation occurred during the Spanish-American War, when expansionist enthusiasm swept aside questions of the venal motives behind the revolt, the legality of the republic, or the advisability of gaining a territory with a non-Caucasian population.

As a U.S. territory, Hawaii elected a legislature and a delegate to Congress, but all administrative positions were appointive. Governors did not depend on local party organizations for their position, so their own party affiliation had little effect on their policies and commitments. By and large, they cooperated with the territory's business leaders. Since the Organic Act imposed universal manhood suffrage for citizens of Hawaii, the legislature was at first more Hawaiian than under the republic. The cooperation of elected representatives was gained after 1902 in an alliance of Haole business leaders and Hawaiians, under the aegis of the Republican Party.

During World War II, residents of Japanese ancestry experienced hostility and discrimination, but few were interned. On the other hand, martial law was imposed on the territory for three years, and the liberties of all residents were sharply curtailed.

After the war, successful union organizing, strikes, and a resurgent Democratic Party raised the possibility of a new distribution of power. Statehood was granted in 1959, after many delays. What had been an isolated bastion of conservatism became a state notable for long-range planning: Hawaii is the first state to create a statewide general plan and to use it as a basis for land use regulations. (See Farell, 1982 for a thoughtful account of planning processes and their consequences.) Such planning implies that the political system is so centralized that an attempt to control the destiny of the state remains credible today.

Socioeconomic Structures

The distribution of population in Hawaii and many of the ethnic interactions found in the islands are grounded in structures that have evolved through three distinct phases: the plantation system; the expanded social system of a closed economy; and the postwar development of a service economy dependent on outside capital.

The plantation economy depended on continuous immigration, access to export markets, and enough political power to ensure that these relations continued. The growth of the plantations focused the interests of Hawaii's Haoles so that a cohesive faction emerged, which was not only intolerant of the monarchy and citizenry but largely committed to close ties with the United States.

The plantation system was socially unstable. Chinese, Portuguese, Japanese, Filipino, Korean, and other workers were recruited not only in hopes that they would work hard in the fields, but also to check the possibility that a single group, predominating in the labor force, would pose an economic or political threat. Low wages and harsh conditions made most workers unlikely to remain long on the plantations, so one immigrant group (Chinese, then Japanese, then Filipino) provided the majority of laborers at any one time (Robinson, 1935). When workers' associations emerged in the strikes of 1909 and 1920, they were organized on ethnic lines but sought interethnic cooperation; the need for such cooperation became especially evident as the planters, who acted as one in all labor disputes, tried to set Japanese and Filipino workers against each other (Takaki, 1983).

The plantation economy perpetuated itself by helping to create a larger social system of a different character. In a period of increasing paternalism and less marked ethnic differentiation on the plantations (1920-40), Hawaii gained both a local-born urban and small-farming population and a large number of Haole immigrants, both civilian and military. Many plantation laborers came as single men, and intermarriage with the resident population was high. Moreover, after moving off the plantations the exlaborers did not form tight ethnic enclaves, although some neighborhoods were identified with particular groups. Nowadays, it is the Caucasian population that is most likely to congregate exclusively, in the military areas and the most expensive suburbs (Armstrong, 1983, pp. 115-118).

Given the policy of ethnic separation and competition on the plantations, the ethnocentrism that can be expected among newcomers to a multiethnic setting, the international rivalries of the times, and the difficulties of securing a living on or off the plantations, there are good reasons for Hawaiians, Chinese, Japanese, and Filipinos to have engaged in bitter conflicts in Hawaii during this century. That they largely did not do so is testimony to the positive effects of intermarriage, to traditions of tolerance, and to the everpresent reality of Haole domination. Okamura (1980) points out that immigrant groups had to accommodate to a Haole social system both on the plantations and off; a leveling of cultural differences among them resulted, as well as similar orientations to "American" social patterns and success ideals. These processes will be discussed below, in relation to Local identity.

World War II crystallized existing patterns. Island residents and soldiers gained extensive experience of mainlanders' assumption of superiority. Often, they also learned that Haoles were no more skilled than themselves (Wilson, 1944). People of Japanese ancestry suffered discrimination and triumphed over it. The political outcome, however, was not exclusive organization, but a victory over the elite and the Haole-dominated Republican Party by a coalition, headed by a Haole, John Burns, in which the various ethnic populations were represented.

The poststatehood economy has two bases: defense and tourism. With jet travel, Hawaii became a major tourist destination, and investment in hotels and resorts boomed. By 1982, the number of visitors per year exceeded 4 million, and the average number in the state at any time was over 100,000 (Farrell, 1982; Hawaii, Department of Planning and Economic Development [DPED], 1983). Visitor expenditures rose from $24 million in 1950 to over $4 billion in 1982. Tourism has come to generate nearly 90,000 jobs directly, and 161,000 "direct, indirect and induced" jobs (Hawaii, DPED, 1983). On Oahu, the tourists are concentrated in a few blocks at Waikiki; on other islands the tourist boom has consumed more space, with resorts spreading along beachfronts.

The economic expansion of the postwar years brought a social system no less unstable than the plantation system. Economic gains were registered by many, notably among Hawaii's Chinese and Japanese. The children and grandchildren of laborers now have college degrees. Yet, the service economy tends to create jobs demanding few skills and offering little hope of advancement. Again, the Democratic Party achieved a victory for Locals over Haoles, but the demographic trend is one of immigration from the mainland: At current rates, Haoles could become the majority of the population in decades. Overpopulation and the influx of mainlanders have concerned islanders. In the 1970s, Governor Ariyoshi called for curbs on immigration and residence requirements for state jobs or welfare payments; legislators expressed "a degree of sympathy and understanding, but generally his views were regarded as unrealistic" (Farrell, 1982, p. 117; for further discussion of the positions taken, see Phillips, 1982).

The contemporary economy depends on the attractiveness of the islands to outsiders and outside capital. As a result, elected officials find themselves responding to conditions of scarcity by seeking advantages for outsiders, such as new housing for sailors from a flotilla that might be based in Honolulu, when their constituents need the same scarce resources. By and large, elected officials have supported resort investments as well, and it is hard to see how they could do otherwise while trying to maintain or increase the number of jobs. Consequently, islanders' political power does not counterbalance the economic control exerted by outside investors. Large-scale tourism has made a distinctive local society prosperous, but only on the condition that it serve outside interests and play host to large numbers of visitors.

Ethnic Populations and Groups

Problems of defining ethnic units have not been discussed so far, but they deserve some attention. The tasks of identifying units relevant to interaction and assessing their properties as groups are complex in Hawaii for five reasons.

First, the distinctive populations named above are hardly each the product of shared descent and tradition. For immigrants, divisions within a national population, such as between Ilocanos and Viscayans, loomed large at the time of arrival, and may still be recognized. (Members of Filipino voluntary associations are predominantly immigrants, not Hawaii-born, since members are recruited on the basis of their home areas or particular friendship ties; Okamura, 1982.) Again, successive waves of immigrants may have different experiences and problems. Hawaii's Filipinos include the grandchildren of the first immigrants, along with many more-recent immigrants. The Chinese population largely consists of the descendents of nineteenth-century immigrants, but substantial numbers have arrived since 1970, as the U.S. immigration laws changed. In this respect, Haoles are the most diverse population, including the established elite families, more recent immigrant residents, and most of the military and tourist populations.

Next, with high rates of intermarriage—now over 40 percent of all marriages of Hawaii residents (Hawaii, DPED, 1983)—a person's ethnicity is not easily defined. In the 1980 census, 29.8 percent of the population reported themselves as of more than one national ancestry; using different categories, the Hawaii Health Surveillance Program estimates the "mixed" group at 28.8 percent of the 1982 population (Hawaii, DPED, 1983). For statistical purposes, matters are simplified by viewing part-Hawaiians (18.3 percent of the population in 1982) as members of one group with unmixed Hawaiians (0.9 percent). This reflects social trends, since many people of mixed ancestry view themselves as Hawaiian; but it neither suffices to predict the self-identification of particular persons nor indicates the other ethnic allegiances they may claim.

In a genealogically complex situation, the tendency for ethnic units to have different lifestyles may be transformed, so that ethnicity maps a choice of lifestyle and association with some ascendants rather than others. In Keanae on Maui, known as a Hawaiian village largely because of its taro (now grown for sale, not subsistence), residents "identify themselves as Hawaiian, regardless of their percentage of Hawaiian ancestry" (Linnekin, 1984, p. 32) although only one family is reputedly of "pure" descent; in other contexts, such unanimity is unlikely. Ethnicity can become situational: A person may be Chinese in relation to Chinese (or identifying-as-Chinese) kinsmen, Hawaiian in relation to Hawaiian kinsmen, and Local in many encounters.

Changes in the definition and valuation of ethnic categories may also be under way. Portuguese of Hawaii (descended from immigrants from the Azores and Madeira) have at times been identified as "Cosmopolitan." Some may now insist on being termed Local or Portuguese, to avoid presenting themselves as Caucasian (Correa & Knowlton, 1982; MacDonald, 1983). Since this category has long been a medial one, its status is highly reactive to changes in the valuation of other categories.

Finally, *Local* has emerged as a significant category for interaction and self-identification. The term may be used to separate island-born members of ethnic groups from new immigrants; it also brings together the Hawaii-born in opposition to Haoles. Insofar as the label is associated with shared experiences, a history of struggle, and easy, egalitarian social relations, it tends not to apply to any Haole, whether immigrant or Hawaii-born (S. Boggs, personal communication, March and August, 1984; Okamura, 1980).

With these issues in mind, it should be apparent that counts of ethnic groups in Hawaii are to be taken with a grain of salt. Ethnic populations do not have exclusive memberships, nor do they form solidary collectivities. Tendencies toward exclusiveness are highest among Haoles and Japanese; these have, both in the past and currently, significantly lower rates of outmarriage than other island populations (Lind, 1980). (The rates of outmarriage for persons of Japanese ancestry are increasing; for Caucasians, the rates have decreased from a postwar peak.)

Ethnicity in Hawaii may form a basis for developing interpersonal ties or for associations. Effective groups organizing entire populations, or able to speak for much of a population, are another matter. The issues raised above militate against a stable, loyal, and broad membership in ethnic organizations, while the minority status of all ethnic populations makes ethnic organization a risky basis for political action. Ethnicity may ease the formation of groups to deal with a particular problem or issue, but getting groups representing a single ethnic population to cooperate on more general aims may be laborious. (Haas and Resurrection, 1976, report problems of coordination in the 1970s for Hawaiians and Filipinos alike.)

Before World War II, ethnic politics were overt. The first territorial elections were won by the Home Rule Party, which admonished voters to "look to the skin" and elect fellow Hawaiians. The Haole elite's subsequent political dominance depended on an alliance with Hawaiians. The alliance cost little. Hawaiians filled many lower-level administrative positions and the Hawaiian Homes Commission leased some land to persons of at least 50 percent Hawaiian ancestry. This program was supposed to enable Hawaiians to live on the land, but farming was rarely possible on the plots allotted (Fuchs, 1983).

In the postwar period, bloc voting has been a concern in island politics, but not a predictable factor at the state level. According to a reporter (in 1972), the politicians' rule of thumb is that explicit appeals for bloc voting fail: "If anyone tries to make a big thing of ethnic factors it seems to backfire in Hawaii" (Keir, cited in Haas & Resurrection, 1976, p. 97).

Broadly speaking, ethnicity no longer seems a sufficient factor for the organization of cohesive interest groups in Hawaii. The record, in island politics and newspaper debates, shows ethnic sensitivity rather than successful ethnic competition: Nearly all populations have representatives who argue that they have been victimized by discrimination (Keir, cited in Haas & Resurrection, 1976). In this context, any ethnic or ethnic-based organization may be suspected of acting to renew discrimination against others unless it is restricted to apolitical activities.

Such apolitical activities as the celebration of traditions are not, of course, without political impact (Linnekin, 1983). Both the heirs to ethnic traditions and the public at large have a stake in such celebrations. For example, the centennial of the major phase of Japanese immigration to Hawaii has recently been observed with speeches, books, and exhibits that blend particularistic and broader messages. The immigrants are celebrated as carriers of a distinctive tradition, hardworking, dedicated to making a better life for their children, contributors to the success of today's Americans of Japanese ancestry—but these attributes and actions are also treated as helping to make Hawaii what it is today.

Along with ethnicity in general, Hawaiian culture has come to be celebrated by a larger audience than those of Hawaiian ancestry. With commercial forms of Hawaiian entertainment consumed by tourists, the revival of Hawaiian arts may serve most clearly to express an identity distinct from that of the transients—tourists and the military—on whom the islands' economy depends. Haole immigrants are most obviously in need of a means to indicate their commitment to island social life and the differences between them and transients. They are not alone, however, in finding ethnic identities constraining: Yamamoto (1974) reports that many young persons of Japanese ancestry reject being identified with outside investors and with the islands' Japanese stereotypes.

Local Identity

Localism transcends ethnic particularism in a different way. The notion that ethnicity is a good thing for all is mainly voiced in public discourse; in contrast, Local identity bridges ethnic distinctions on an interpersonal level.

> Locals describe themselves in terms such as easy-going, friendly, open, trusting, non-aggressive, generous, indifferent to achieved status distinctions, and loyal to family and friends. . . . [L]ocal has come to represent the people who are of Hawaii and their appreciation of the inherent values of the land, peoples, and cultures of the islands. For them, Hawaii is a special place to live and to raise their children, not only because of its leisurely pace of life, mild climate, and scenic landscape, but also because the diversity of peoples affords an uncommon opportunity for unique social relationships. (Okamura, 1982)

Many of Hawaii's Haoles appreciate the land and cultures of Hawaii. They are, however, less enmeshed in the "unique social relationships" Okamura (1982) notes. Those relationships took root in earlier decades, as Haoles' intransigence helped to unite non-white populations.

The term "Local" was first used prominently for the five Honolulu youths accused in the Massie Case (1930-1931). Two were of Japanese descent, two Hawaiian, and one Chinese-Hawaiian. A Honolulu jury could not reach a verdict on the questionable evidence presented, but mainland newspapers, at least one Honolulu newspaper, and Navy leaders were ready to convict them. The attitudes expressed at the time made it clear, to a Hawaii public increasingly literate in English, that racism was not just a matter of plantation policy but rather was pervasive among Haoles. At the same time, the mixed composition of the group of accused youths, who were found riding together in a car, testifies to the opportunities for interethnic friendships that Honolulu's poorer districts afforded.

Many island Haoles viewed such friendships with alarm where their own children were concerned. In debates over public schooling, they argued for linguistic segregation: "English Standard" schools were established from 1924 on to provide education uncontaminated by "Pidgin,"—that is, rural or working-class Hawaiian English. The result was a two-track system, with the best facilities provided to those, mainly Haoles, who could prove to selection boards that they were not tainted by fluency in island dialects.

Fuchs (1983) emphasizes the influence of Haole teachers in the non-Standard schools, who infused their students with ideals of individual achievement. (So, however, did those students' parents.) A greater impact of the two-track system may lie in the ways that it formulated goals for educational achievement and lumped together the various island populations as speakers of Pidgin. The vast majority of the islands' people were treated as sharing a common tongue, not several languages and a range of dialects along a continuum (Carr, 1972); and as distinct from both the Haole elite and newcomers. The notion that Hawaii's people speak a distinctive idiom has been a sign of continuity and solidarity across generational and ethnic differences. By now, Hawaiian English varies little from mainland dialects, but Pidgin is still viewed as a shared island dialect and may still be seen by islanders as "broken English" (i.e., dysfluency).

Educational attainments have been a source of pride for many descendants of immigrants to Hawaii. Yet standard English, the vehicle for such accomplishments, has been contested; since it has been used to separate Haoles from nonwhites, it can be taken as a sign that someone is "Haolefied" and looks down on others. This means that considerable opposition exists in interpersonal networks to linguistic practices that would ease occupational mobility in Haole-controlled enterprises. (For years, of course, Haole attitudes made such mobility impossible.)

More than linguistic details are at issue here. Hawaii's people have striven hard to become "Americanized"; but this trend has been accompanied by a recognition of Haole separation, and in response, strong pressures to remain distinct from Haoles. Pidgin has provided a medium for equating the close interpersonal bonds of peer networks with a broader non-Haole solidarity.

As Okamura (1980) notes, Local identity has been linked with efforts to control social and economic change in Hawaii. Those efforts have been successful largely in mobilizing opposition to specific projects, not in charting an alternative, autonomous future for Hawaii. Even attempts to mobilize Local sentiments against newcomers meet the objection that Hawaii is a state of immigrants: Anti-immigration measures would replicate the disadvantages against which earlier generations struggled. (Another factor at issue here is that Local culture is strongly egalitarian, and hence a poor basis for recruiting followers to any leader's program.) A Local populism may reemerge as a significant political force. To achieve organization and continuing purpose, however, it will be challenged to formulate a vision that is widely accepted as coherent, realistic, and valuable.

Concerns and Conflicts

A focus on economic change and economic aspirations may mislead: Ethnic populations are not only stereotyped in class terms (with partial accuracy) but may express distinct attitudes toward economic competition. In any event, ethnic populations' concerns involve distinctive historical views, ranging from some Haoles' sense that they have no part in Hawaii's history of ethnic stratification, to visions of generational progress, to a view of the last two centuries as a series of crimes against the Hawaiian people and land. Again, while any population can suspect that it is a victim of derogatory treatment—and harsh ethnic stereotypes give some substance to suspicions—the concerns at issue vary. Some of these concerns can be listed, with the proviso that they are held by some, not all, members of each population.

For persons of Filipino ancestry, awareness of their relatively low economic position, the large numbers of recent immigrants in unskilled jobs, and others' derogatory views make appealing the hope that they are the next in Hawaii "to make it" (Okamura, 1982). Whether economic mobility on a large scale is still possible is, however, not clear.

The concerns of many Hawaiians have to do with more than income levels and stereotypes. On the one hand, land issues are important. Development often involves the dispossession of rural communities with a substantial proportion of Hawaiians. Access to the land as a resource for identity has also been important—in the Moloka'i marches for beach access (across land that was being converted from ranching to a resort), the occupation of Sand Island, in Honolulu, and in the movement to end the military's use of Kaho'olawe as an artillery target. Most generally, Hawaiians can claim to be dispossessed as original inhabitants, whose islands were taken by merchants, planters, and the U.S. government. A related idea has emerged, that Hawaiians are characterized by *aloha 'aina* (love of the land): They are its stewards, in opposition to those who use it for profit.

Haoles, immigrant or island-born, express concern with others' attitudes. These are focused on such institutions as the public schools, where parents fear that teachers may discriminate against Haole children, as other students certainly do. Haole newcomers often find the local ethnic situation confusing, the prevalence of ethnic stereotypes appalling, and the Haole stereotype—as materialistic, self-serving, cold or uncommitted to interpersonal relations, pushy, and arrogant—a source of anger or soul-searching (Maretzki & McDermott, 1980; Rapson, 1980; Whittaker, 1973). A common pattern is for recent immigrants to become enamored of Hawaii's life and fiercely protective of the environment, only to find themselves eventually rebuffed as "pushy Haoles" by island-born associates in community action groups. Withdrawal from such interethnic encounters and negative views of other ethnicities are then likely (S. Boggs, personal communication, March and August, 1984; Yamamoto, 1974). While a pattern of Haole dominance is assumed by many to exist, some Haoles feel they are victimized by the stereotype and by islanders' discrimination against them (Samuels, 1970).

This discussion may suffice to show that ethnicity does much to formulate the concerns of Hawaii's residents. They do not point to violent encounters, however. Instead, they help to identify why large-scale ethnic conflict has been absent.

First, no single group has in recent years combined economic dominance and a commitment to control over the local social system. (While mainland corporations dominate the economy, they have no reason to invest in Haole dominance. The tourist industry depends on social peace, not ties to any one group.) The transition from the period in which those factors were combined, in Haole elite control, to the present was eased by an expanding economy that allowed success for many at little risk to those more advantaged.

Next, the extent of interethnic marriage works against systematic discrimination. The populations that still tend to marry exclusively—Haoles and Americans of Japanese ancestry—are, however, also those who may arouse others' ire as wealthy, residentially more exclusive, and the cause of displacement of lower-income groups. Unless practices of cross-ethnic contact and economic mobility continue, a risk that Hawaii's people will form a new two-class system, with ethnic and even racial bases, is evident.

Next, concerns over possible victimization motivate suspicion of others' ethnic organizations and may impede such forms of collective action as bloc voting. Defensive political action (e.g., to augment tenants' rights against eviction) may gain widespread support, but this hardly amounts to a program of Local rights or of Local control over the economy.

Withdrawal is a common response to perceived threats. For example, private school attendance is exceptionally high in Hawaii: Those who can afford to avoid the violence and anti-intellectual youth culture of the public schools do so. This tactic avoids conflict, but perpetuates fear: "Kill a Haole Day" (or "Zap a Jap Day") is believed to be a common occurrence in the public high schools.[3]

Finally, a cultural emphasis on tolerance and acceptance is no less evident than are ethnic antagonisms. To an extent, these are complementary. The harsher the ethnic stereotypes, the more the creation of personal ties is a momentous accomplishment, a demonstration of valued *aloha*.

I have delayed consideration of aloha and the value of tolerance in order to suggest that these are neither unchanged survivals from the Hawaiian past nor free-floating, inexplicable attitudes. "Aloha spirit" is so often mentioned in Hawaii's public rhetoric that it may seem a sham. Yet the values associated with Local identity foreground a commitment to personal ties (Okamura, 1980; Yamamoto, 1974). Rural traditions of hospitality and exchange have been amplified by urban experiences—of intermarriage, schooling, limited employment and similar economic mobility, discrimination, and the exchange of others' foods, festivals, and customs. Moreover, the "no make waves" response to authority, the response of a powerless working class, carries over to a degree to an economic setting in which island institutions are relatively impotent. Locals are far more ready to assert their rights than in 1940, but are not blind to the limits imposed by their dependence on sources of capital that make Hawaii both prosperous and endangered.

Concluding Remarks

The Present Situation

Hawaii's people have ample reason to fear and suspect ethnic antagonism, and they express ethnic tensions in many ways. Clearcut ethnic conflict has erupted only rarely, mainly in the form of attacks and discrimination by Haoles (during the strikes, in the Massie Case, and during the World War II occupation of the islands; Lind, 1947). In response to Haole domination, a quasiethnic Local identity, substantial solidarity among islanders, and an ethic of tolerance that can even encompass Haoles in limited encounters have arisen. Acts of anti-Haole discrimination and crimes directed at tourists (above all, crimes against property) indicate that past intolerance may now be reciprocated. But the scope of ethnic conflict remains small. I have argued that this derives from structural factors.

The outlook for the future suggested here is, however, far from optimistic. Without continuing economic expansion, the aspirations of many islanders must be frustrated; the cost of such expansion may be the degradation of the islands' environment. Intolerance toward Haole newcomers may well increase. The phrasing of current and future antagonisms in ethnic or quasiethnic terms, however, limits the possibility of conflict. Several island populations can view their own positions as threatened by gains for those now at the bottom of economic and social rankings. Also, the available symbols for coordinating a broad community—Local identity, aloha, support for Hawaiian culture and the land—have provided only weak bases for organization against other groups. (Organization to oppose specific projects is another matter.) The cultural assumption that islanders and Haoles are profoundly dissimilar, most notable in the persistence of Pidgin, may however make such symbols unnecessary in opposing Haole newcomers.

Dominance by a Haole minority has produced more ethnic antagonism than conflict. If the Haole population swells and others' economic mobility stagnates, as seems likely, the possibility that ethnic and class divisions could lead to extensive conflict must be seriously considered. In the past, however, those who have suffered the worst effects of Haole domination have considered reemigration, to the mainland or to their homeland (Wright, 1983). As Hawaii becomes less distinctive and more limited in its opportunity structure, such movements may again do much to defuse tensions.

Toward Comparative Understandings

As Cohen (1981) remarks, "There is ethnicity and ethnicity": Identifiable ethnic groups and relations vary in definition, in organization, in the extent to which they channel social functions and cultural ideas, and the extent to which they are central to social conflict. Some attempt must be made to place definitions, functions, and processes of ethnic relations in a broader framework, despite the difficulties of creating a rigorous language and theory for comparison. The special position of Hawaii as a part of American society separated by geography and history from the continent allows some rather crude comparisons to convey detailed analytic points.

When contrasted with other states, Hawaii stands out because of its ethnic composition, its rate of intermarriage, and attitudes toward ethnicity. Compared to accounts of ethnic relations elsewhere, Hawaii is obviously marked by American themes. The population is largely descended from immigrants. Ethnic traditions are hence relatively simplified, and can be easily transformed into spectacles for an interethnic audience. Despite the diversity of ethnic origins, one language is widely shared, and both local and national values are widespread. Ethnic competition has largely been channeled into attempts to advance economic and social status. When, as on the plantations, attempts to gain greater resources may

benefit the majority at the expense of only a few, interethnic solidarity may result from labor struggles. Again, when an expanding
economy makes individuals' economic advance easier, personal
and group ambitions may be realized without great competition
among groups for scarce resources.

Elsewhere in the United States, Americanism and assimilation to a majority population could be equated during much of this
century. No such majority existed in Hawaii. Hawaiians have been
generally receptive to newcomers, with the consequences that
genetically pure Hawaiians are few and predominantly Hawaiian communities generally exist only on sites with legislatively
imposed residence requirements. Hawaiians hardly embody a reference group for successful assimilation to American ideals. On
the mainland, people who were "100 percent American" or "just
American" could be contrasted with "ethnics" descended from
more recent immigrants. In Hawaii, Haoles have formed a distinctive minority, not an assimilationist ideal. The tension between
"Americanization" and becoming Haolefied thus remains, even
when contradictions between ethnic traditions or values and American goals are muted as those traditions are dropped and as ethnic
consciousness becomes widely acceptable.

Furthermore, for most of Hawaii's people, Hawaii's "unique
social relationships" are evidently preferable to alternatives elsewhere. The island-born largely lack the linguistic and cultural skills
necessary to live outside the United States; on the mainland they
are likely to be viewed as members of low-status racial minorities.
(Hawaiian informants tell of being categorized as Mexicans or simply "dark" on the mainland, while Asian Americans express a
sense of distance from both mainland-born and foreign groups of
ancestry similar to theirs.) Hence circular migration, from Hawaii
to the mainland and back, is usually experienced as a success, not
as a failure: Hawaii, for all its faults, is home (Wright, 1983). The
situation resembles that described by Bond (this volume) for Hong
Kong, inasmuch as people are aware that no satisfactory alternative
to Hawaii can be found or created.

The emergence of Local identity and the limited extent of ethnic
conflict can be explained in part as reflexes of Hawaii's marginal
position in a larger socioeconomic system. Except for Haoles and
recent immigrants, Hawaii's people share experiences and similar
limitations on their options. They may differ in their aims: Those

Hawaiians who seek land or reparations for land taken by the government have goals distinct from, and possibly in conflict with, others' striving for economic success and security. Yet their attachment to Hawaii as a place to live, work, and maintain family ties outweighs many differences.

One reason why ethnic conflict is likely to be muted in Hawaii is, then, that it amounts to fouling the nest. Another is that defensive ethnic orientations, derived from the immigrant and plantation experiences, induce an extreme sensitivity to such conflict. Moreover, the presence of new immigrants, whose behavior may embarrass or anger the island-born, can reinforce ethnic stereotypes and the fear of victimization. Okamura (1983) argues that when island-born Filipinos see Filipinos as a group as embroiled in fights, they refer to them as immigrants. Many may wish to dissociate themselves, as Locals, from blame for violence. But ethnic identities are not easily lost. Continuing immigration poses a problem for several groups, who may be identified with the misdeeds and social position of newcomers. Certainly, continuing immigration makes any population's sense of social and economic security highly vulnerable.

One expression of contentment with the islands, "Lucky you live Hawaii," suggests that the blessings of life in Hawaii rest as much on chance as they do on human choice and stable social structures. That idea may have little empirical basis; the defensiveness it expresses, and the search for consensus and controls on conflict that have resulted, are, however, important in understanding the structure of a multiethnic polity that has managed to limit ethnic conflict.

NOTES

1. Some anachronisms are inevitable in this chapter. "Hawaii's people" and "Hawaiians" are not the same, for present purposes. The term "Hawaiian" is reserved for persons descended from the Polynesian people of the islands, a population that now contains few genetically "pure" Hawaiians. I use the word Local to describe a population that did not have a distinctive political voice before statehood, and may have had little sense of cultural sharing before that time.

Some ethnic groups go unmentioned here, notably Southeast Asians, Samoans, and Tongans. On the broad historical issues sketched here, Daws (1968), Fuchs (1983), and Kent (1983) are critical readings.

2. The term "Haole" is far more often used in Hawaii than "Caucasian." It usually does not cover Portuguese and people of Hispanic origin. Hence it is not fully equivalent to the racial category, Caucasian, while it may reflect the racial views of many Caucasians.

3. It is difficult to specify the level of violence in the schools and the extent to which it is aimed at upper-income groups. Some Haoles have experienced beatings at school; others clearly limit their movements to avoid threatening situations. Yet, the major episodes of school violence have involved others: Two Filipinos were killed in the early 1970s. In one case, tension between island-born and immigrant Filipinos was the context in which the death occurred. The newspaper stories reprinted by Haas and Resurrection (1976) attest to violence and to residents' readiness to understand it in ethnic terms. Yet some perspective may be called for. A man in his twenties noted that the youth of his generation were not organized for confrontations, while nowadays "they're even forming gangs, like the mainland, . . . wow, big time now." Again, hostility against outsiders is far more often expressed in thefts from rental cars than in muggings or rapes. Victims may see these crimes as proof that "many young Hawaiians are anti-American"—a view that ignores both local ethnic categories and citizenship—while island officials suspect that tourists are victimized in part because they are unlikely to prosecute (Haas and Resurrection, 1976; Farrell, 1982).

References

Armstrong, R. W. (Ed.). (1983). *Atlas of Hawaii* (2nd ed.). Honolulu: University of Hawaii Press.
Carr, E. B. (1972). *Da kine talk.* Honolulu: University Press of Hawaii.
Cohen, A. (1981). Variables in ethnicity. In C. F. Keyes (Ed.), *Ethnic change* (pp. 306-332). Seattle: University of Washington Press.
Correa, G. B., & Knowlton, E. W., Jr. (1982). The Portuguese in Hawai'i. *Social Process in Hawaii, 29,* 70-77.
Daws, G. (1968). *Shoal of time.* Honolulu: University of Hawaii Press.
Farrell, B. H. (1982). *Hawaii: The legend that sells.* Honolulu: University Press of Hawaii.
Fuchs, L. H. (1983). *Hawaii pono* (2nd ed.). New York: Harcourt Brace Jovanovich.
Haas, M., & Resurrection, P. P. (1976). *Politics and prejudice in contemporary Hawaii.* Honolulu: Coventry Press.
Hawaii, Department of Planning and Economic Development (DPED). (1983). *The state of Hawaii data book: 1983.* Honolulu: Author.
Kent, N. J. (1983). *Hawaii: Islands under the influence.* New York: Monthly Review Press.
Lind, A. W. (1947). Service-civilian tensions in Honolulu. *Social Process in Hawaii, 11,* 93-99.
Lind, A. W. (1980). *Hawaii's people* (4th ed.). Honolulu: University Press of Hawaii.
Linnekin, J. (1983). Defining tradition: Variations on the Hawaiian identity. *American Ethnologist, 10,* 241-252.

Linnekin, J. (1984). *Children of the land.* New Brunswick, NJ: Rutgers University Press.

MacDonald, J. J. (1983). Cognitive aggregate and social group: The ethnic Portuguese of Honolulu (Ph.D. dissertation, University of Hawaii). *Dissertation Abstracts International, 44,* 527A. (University Microfilms No. 83-13,522)

Maretzki, T. W., & McDermott, J. F., Jr. (1980). The Caucasians. In J. F. McDermott, Jr., W.-S. Tseng, & T. W. Maretzki (Eds.), *Peoples and cultures of Hawaii* (pp. 25-52). Honolulu: University Press of Hawaii.

Okamura, J. Y. (1980). Aloha kanaka me ke aloha 'aina: Local culture and society in Hawaii. *Amerasia, 7,* 119-137.

Okamura, J. Y. (1982). Ethnicity and ethnic relations in Hawaii. In D. Wu (Ed.), *Ethnicity and interpersonal interaction* (pp. 213-236). Singapore: Maruzen.

Okamura, J. Y. (1983). Immigrant and local Filipino perceptions of ethnic conflict. In W. C. McCready (Ed.), *Culture, ethnicity, and identity* (pp. 241-263). New York: Academic.

Phillips, P. C. (1982). *Hawaii's Democrats: Chasing the American dream.* Washington, DC: University Press of America.

Rapson, R. L. (1980). *Fairly lucky you live Hawaii!* Washington, DC: University Press of America.

Robinson, C. R. (1935). Occupational succession on the plantation. *Social Process in Hawaii, 1,* 21-25.

Samuels, F. (1970). *The Japanese and the Haoles of Honolulu.* New Haven, CT: College and University Press.

Takaki, R. (1983). *Pau hana: Plantation life and labor in Hawaii.* Honolulu: University of Hawaii Press.

Whittaker, E. W. (1973). *The Malihini: The ideological and experiential world of the mainland expatriate in Hawaii.* Unpublished doctoral dissertation, University of California, Berkeley.

Wilson, C. (1944). Some social aspects of mainland defense workers in Honolulu. *Social Process in Hawaii, 8,* 60-65.

Wright, P. (1983). Ethnic differences in the outmigration of local-born residents from Hawaii. *Social Process in Hawaii, 30,* 7-31.

Yamamoto, E. (1974). *From "Japanee" to Local: Community change and the redefinition of Sansei identity in Hawaii.* Unpublished senior thesis, University of Hawaii.

14

Some Thoughts on Ethnic Conflict

WINTHROP D. JORDAN

Any attempt to offer an overview of the chapters in this volume runs into immediate difficulty. Not all chapters deal with interethnic conflict. Some are concerned primarily with human aggression, as in Bellona; others with societies such as Hong Kong that are not fundamentally multi- or even biethnic and where harmony is much more notable than conflict. Some chapters aim to be primarily theoretical; others, as with Sri Lanka, are primarily descriptive. Accordingly, this overview will be highly selective and idiosyncratic in its approach.

Conflict often involves physical violence, but not necessarily and always. Such a statement may be almost a truism, though sometimes truisms are overlooked because they are so obvious. Many scholarly papers—and many social scientists generally—seem to regard conflict as normally involving physical violence, or at least that conflict always has the potential for escalating to the level of physical injury and death. That group conflict has this tendency is undeniable. In our world of atomic weapons, our attention quite naturally focuses on the possibility and even probability of such a progression. What is striking about this assumption is that it is just that, an assumption rather than a demonstrable (let alone demonstrated) fact. The obverse of this assumption is our tendency to assume—even though we know better—that absence of violence means absence of conflict. Many readers will object that social scientists are not sufficiently naive to make such assumptions. To such objection I can only reply that, at least as I read many papers and hear other discussions of group conflict, this assumption is not consciously and intentionally "made" but does in fact exist.

The complex nature of the relationship between conflict and violence is not a trivial matter, and I wish present-day research met it more squarely. Not only can conflict exist without violence; but nonviolence can be and has been very consciously adopted as a weapon in major conflicts. With Gandhi and Martin Luther King, nonviolence has been shaped into a formal ideology. Indeed in their hands nonviolence came to include an enormous range of functions, all the way from a tactical and strategic weapon to a fundamental religious principle that was considered pertinent to all realms of human behavior.

A similar ethic has had an influence in several of the societies discussed in this chapter. While Gandhi and King wrote formal defenses and elaborations of the principle of nonviolence, in other societies such as China, Hong Kong, New Zealand, and Hawaii, a generally agreed-upon ethic on the matter has proved to be a strong community norm. In these cases we are not dealing with a formal ideology but with prevailing values that reprobate violence as a means of conflict resolution. The *reasons* for the prevalence of such values vary greatly from one society to another, depending especially upon past and present demographic and socioeconomic circumstances and the historic cultures of the participants. In contrast, the negative valuation of violence seems to be much less prevalent in other societies, such as Sri Lanka, Malaysia, the Basque country, and the Philippines; and in the striking instance of Bellona the ethic is marked by its nonexistence.

Indeed in many cases it is clear that a small minority of an ethnic group can reject a prevailing ethic and bring about violence that the majority's values repudiate. The Puerto Rican situation shows this possibility most clearly, though the evidence in these chapters seems to suggest that relatively small minorities can very readily escalate the level of interethnic violence, especially when their thinking takes place in a self-perceived context of national liberation—in short, when ethnicity becomes linked with questions of nationality, as it most patently has for the Basques and Moros but not for residents of Hawaii. This is to say that many social scientists tend to define a framework of conflict that is often more consistent with their own categories and expectations than with the actualities of the various situations they study.

This point raises a problem that seems to permeate the study of interethnic conflict. The problem is generic to the field of inquiry as it is usually defined. By definition, such inquiries segment societies along ethnic lines and ask how these various sentiments are getting along with one another. There are—as we know perfectly well but tend to forget when asking about ethnicity—other ways of analyzing societies, other lines along which societies may be segmented, such as gender, age, and economic status. By framing our questions in terms of ethnic groups alone, we beg a central question concerning exactly who is engaging actively in conflict. What about conflicts between men and women, young and old, rich and poor?

Of course social scientists do not agree among themselves about the proper social categories for studying intergroup conflict. Very commonly they treat intergroup conflict as a rather different phenomenon from intragroup (or interpersonal) conflict. Indeed these two categories present sufficiently different kinds of problems that they tend to attract two rather different kinds of social scientists. While we are dealing here with an objectively real distinction between in- and outgroup conflicts, we need to bear in mind that the two phenomena are not so clear-cut as they are sometimes treated. Quarrels within a family, for instance, are clearly intragroup interactions, but they may involve the intrusion of values and assumptions that derive from larger age or gender groupings and, of course in some cases, from religious or ethnic differences. The sort of overlapping involved between the two kinds of conflict could easily be diagrammed, but as an historian I am radically disinclined to do so.

What is striking about these chapters in particular is that they have, collectively, a certain difficulty with the problem of intergroup conflict because it is defined at the outset as "interethnic." This latter term is not defined. And is anyone really certain what an "ethnic" group actually is? Presumably such a group involves a collective sense of being a people, and derives its cohesion primarily from self-conscious identification with the group by its constituent members. But such a definition rather nicely suits a "group" of almost any kind, including clans, classes, lineages, and the U.S. Marine Corps. What, then, is ethnicity? There seems to be general agreement that the term carries different connotations than "racial." "Ethnicity" may be associated with, but is not normally tightly interlocked with, physiognomic characteristics. It suggests the inheritance of qualities that are cultural rather than physical.

Very often, ethnic groups are set apart by linguistic difference. More precisely, they are distinguished by distinct linguistic histories that differ from that of the majority or dominant group. The many groups living in the Hawaiian islands originally spoke different languages, though English is now the primary language of most Hawaiians and is of course a powerful unifying force. Originally, American Indians and American Blacks spoke hundreds of different languages, and the fact that English is now the predominant tongue of these peoples does not prevent their being regarded as distinct ethnic groups. So much depends on the social context, both past and present, as these chapters collectively make clear. Sometimes language appears to lie at the core of ethnicity, as in China, where some "minorities" are distinguished not only by distinct language but the absence of a written version. It is well to bear in mind, though, that pronounced linguistic differences exist even among the majority Han Chinese. On the opposite side of the globe, social circumstances make for a very different situation. On the island of Puerto Rico there has been so much racial intermixture and such long predominance of the Spanish language that Puerto Ricans regard themselves as one people, even while recognizing differences in shades of complexion and hence distinctions in racial ancestry. On their home island, Puerto Ricans are not an ethnic group, yet when they move to New York City they become one. Finally, one might point to the Basques, some of whom can speak an ancient language that is radically different from both French and Spanish while others cannot. Thus the case of the Basques suggests that the *degree* of linguistic difference is not the determining factor in making language the key to an ethnic group's identity.

A sense of a shared, common history seems fully as important as language for the formation of ethnic identity. Most of the chapters in this book have not been formulated by professional historians, yet almost all the authors have felt it necessary to discuss the past of the ethnic groups in question. They have handled history in two ways, sometimes almost simultaneously. On the one hand they have reviewed the objective historic past of the group's formation and conflicts with others. Second, many of the chapters discuss the ethnic group's own consciousness of its past development and its past relations with other (usually dominant) groups. It seems to me that such consciousness is crucial to the formation of ethnic groups as such. In some cultures this sense of separateness may be diffuse and poorly articulated, but nonetheless very real. In Bellona, by way of contrast, a highly articulated past that appears to be heavily mythological apparently forms the sole basis for group indentification and conflict—a situation that may lead many readers to question whether the conflicts on that little island may properly be termed ethnic in the first place. A different and very instructive use of the past shows up in New Zealand, where both Maori and British settlers place formal and even ritualized reliance on an old written document, the Treaty of Waitangi, which is taken by both parties to be a kind of prescriptive constitution for proper relations between the two groups. Obviously literate cultures are the only ones that can fall back on such charters, though few if any place such importance on a single treaty that defines (ostensibly for all time) proper ethnic relations.

This reliance on historic written documents has perhaps been strongest in areas touched by English overseas expansion, which has usually carried with it a long history of documenting limitations on arbitrary government and by implication the proper relationships among the constituent groups of society. The conflict between Sinhalese and Tamils in Sri Lanka has been affected by values and assumptions that derive from the parliamentary tradition of the old British Raj. In the United States the Constitution has had enormous impact on interethnic relations. So has the Declaration of Independence, as powerfully and explicitly suggested in Frederick Douglass's famous speech, "What the Fourth of July Means to Me."

The importance of historical experience is underlined by the fact that there are no instant ethnic groups except those created by migration, as is so clearly the case in Hawaii. Ethnic identity may be latent in the sense that Samoans are not an ethnic group in Samoa but are in the Hawaiian islands. But the sense of being a people is the result of accretive, cumulative processes. We need to bear in mind this obvious fact because some varieties of intergroup conflict may not have a long history of group self-consciousness, such as the conflicts between Protestants and Catholics during the Reformation. Of course over the years such religious conflicts can take on historical dimensions and perhaps even come to resemble interethnic struggles, as the situation of the Moros in the Philippines makes clear.

Looked at historically, it is also clear that ethnic groups can disappear, but over relatively long periods of time—most certainly not overnight. Their disappearance most usually comes about through intermarriage and other forms of genetic intermixture. Such a process is taking place before our eyes in Hawaii. There are of course other possibilities, such as cultural absorption—a complicated process often marked by conscious resistance—which may be taking place today with Native Americans. Such absorption seems most likely to occur when an ethnic group is numerically small in relation to the dominant majority. In this connection it is hard to see how the "minority" groups in China, no matter how geographically isolated, can maintain their distinctiveness through many more generations, given the homogenizing pressures generated by modern technology, political ideology, and nationalism.

These homogenizing pressures are worth our attention because in the long run they have done a great deal to create the very concept of ethnicity. All the societies discussed in this volume have been affected by the overseas expansion of the people who lived in the western, Atlantic parts of the European continent. The people in that geographical region have had a profound impact, and in turn have been affected by that thrust overseas.

The overseas expansion and imperialism of the nations of Western Europe have done a great deal to shape the way we think about ethnicity and ethnic conflicts. It is important that we bear in mind that the overseas thrust of the Atlantic nations of Western Europe was fueled in large part by a burgeoning sense of nationalism and national rivalry, which in turn was complicated and exacerbated in certain instances by a feeling of righteous struggle between Roman Catholics and Protestants. We do not tend to think of these well-known rivalries and conflicts as being ethnic in nature. Ordinarily we call them international conflicts, just as we use that term to describe the relationship between the Chinese and Japanese during the 1930s and 1940s. Yet if we look more objectively at the Atlantic nations of Western Europe during their age of expansion overseas, it is hard to distinguish their conflicts from ethnic ones. Differences in language were very clearly important. So was a sense of peoplehood, though this sense was then a rather recent one. One might argue that conflicts among the five Atlantic nations were distinguished by pronounced territoriality, by the fact that these five groups occupied distinct and mutually exclusive territories; yet such an argument comes close to saying that *ethnic* conflict can take place only among neighbors. While there may be some validity to this latter proposition, it comes dangerously close to the truism that conflict cannot occur without contact. Such a proposition also runs into the historical fact that territorial claims in Western Europe had overlapped for centuries before and even during the thrust overseas: The English and French had finally finished a period of conflict long enough to be called the Hundred Years War in which there was a great deal of contact between two peoples on what is now regarded as French soil, and the provinces of the Netherlands were owned and governed by the King of Spain and occupied by his soldiery and political commissars.

What is most important about this historical "background," which after all covers only about 500 years, is that these Atlantic nations were quite new and modern political entities. They were themselves composed of what would today be called a variety of ethnic groups. None of these newfangled modern monarchies were linguistically homogenous. Entirely apart from class and educational differences within these five nations, all of them had distinct and in some cases profound regional differences in languages. In Spain, the Catalan language of northern Aragon was so different from Castillian Spanish that it constituted much more than a separate dialect. Parisian French did not dominate the new nation of France; the Langue d'Oc of the south was then one of several strong competitors. Many residents of the peninsula of Brittany, which was part of the French nation, did not speak French at all, but rather Breton, a language closely related to the now extinct Celtic language then spoken in Cornwall at England's southwest tip. Many of the Welsh people, who became permanent subjects of the English monarch only seven years before Columbus's first voyage, spoke a Celtic rather than a Germanic language. The separate kingdom of Scotland, which occupied the northern half of that island, was itself split into two radically different linguistic parts. Even in the most homogeneous of the colonizing Atlantic nations, the northern Netherlands and Portugal, there were pronounced dialectical differences in different regions.

These linguistic differences were accompanied by other reasons that made certain human groups identify themselves as "a people" separate from other peoples. Sometimes, as with the Basques and in the region now called Belgium, the boundaries of the new nations divided rather than united previously existing groups of people. But as the new monarchies developed some 500 years ago, a sense of national loyalty grew among the peoples within their boundaries. In many cases that new sense of nationalism has pronounced religious overtones, most conspicuously in Spain, the Netherlands, and even in England.

As those new nations settled and grabbed territories overseas, the colonizers' sense of nationalism strengthened. As they encountered groups of newly "discovered" people around the world, they saw and felt cultural (and physical) differences that seemed radical and compelling, so much so that they tended to mute previously important perceived differences in their original homelands. A different aspect of this same process was fully as important: Europeans tended to homogenize overseas peoples, or at least to lump them into the more manageable categories of race. Thus hundreds of distinct West African and Native American peoples were tossed into only two groupings (universally named but variously spelled and pronounced by the colonizers) as Negroes and Indians. Then, later on as things got really sticky when so many islands turned up in the Pacific Ocean, the colonizers opted for more scientific sounding terms such as Polynesian and Melanesian.

If such a brisk review can have any implication at all, it would seem to be that the very concept of ethnicity is itself an artifact of our own culture. To suggest this is most emphatically *not* to suggest that interethnic conflict is a mirage. On the contrary it is real, dangerous, and damaging, as these chapters make clear. I retain, however, the conviction that it is always important to ask how one is framing one's terms of inquiry. Indeed it might be well to look back to the origin of the critical word *ethnos*. It has been passed down to us, over a period of several thousand years, from some intellectuals living on a peninsula whose populace had had considerable experience of conflict with other "peoples."

About the Contributors

Sinnappah Arasaratnam, a native of Ceylon (Sri Lanka), was educated at the University of Ceylon and University of London. He has held academic positions at the University of Ceylon (1956-61), University of Malaya (1961-72), and University of New England (from 1973), as well as visiting academic positions at the University of London, University of Texas at Austin, University of Hawaii, University of Cambridge, and University of Madras. He has been awarded the following fellowships: Carnegie Traveling Fellow in the United States; Rockefeller Research Fellow, London; Smuts Fellow in Commonwealth Studies, Cambridge; Visiting Fellow, Calcutta. He has held the following editorships: *Ceylon Journal of Historical and Social Studies* (1958-62), *Journal of Malaysian Branch Royal Asiatic Society* (1968-72) and *South Asia—Journal of South Asian Studies* (from 1984). He serves as President of the South Asian Studies Association (Australia). His publications include books, chapters, articles, and published lectures on South and Southeast Asian History.

M. Jocelyn Armstrong, a cultural anthropologist, completed her undergraduate education at the University of Auckland and Victoria University of Wellington in New Zealand, and her graduate degrees at the University of Illinois at Urbana-Champaign (Ph.D., 1971). Between 1974 and 1985, she taught anthropology at the University of Hawaii at Manoa and, from 1983 to 1985, organized seminars on ethnicity for the university's interdisciplinary Honors Program. She is currently a research anthropologist at the Institute for Child Behavior and Development, College for Applied Life Studies, University of Illinois at Urbana-Champaign. Her research interests combine ethnicity and interethnic relations with urban ways of life, women's lives, and the social contexts of health and disease in the Polynesian Pacific, Southeast Asia, and the United States. She has published on ethnic topics in *Social Science in Medicine, Ecology of Disease, Sex Roles,* and other journals, and in symposia on ethnicity.

Ronald Bailey is Associate Professor of History and Director of Afro-American Studies at the University of Mississippi. He holds a B.A. from Michigan State, an M.A. in political science, and a Ph.D. in Black studies from Stanford, and has taught at Fisk University, Cornell, University of California at Santa Barbara, and Northwestern University. His publications include *Black Business Enterprise* (1971), *Introduction to Afro-American Studies* (1976), and *Black People and the 1980 Census: Proceedings from a Conference on the Population Undercount* (1980), and his articles have appeared in *The Black Scholar, The Review of Black Political Economy,* and the *Journal of Social Issues.* His recent articles focus on Black Studies curricula and Harold Washington's election as mayor of Chicago, and he is currently working on a book on the history of the slave trade and its role in the development of industrial capitalism.

Michael Harris Bond was born in Canada of Anglo-Saxon stock, journeyed to America for graduate study in social psychology, and landed unprepared in Japan shortly thereafter. He did research and struggled with Oriental culture shock for three years at Kwansei Gakuin University before assuming duties at the Chinese University of Hong Kong. Over the last 12 years he has been fascinated by the intergroup situation in Hong Kong, exploring its outcroppings in such areas as bilingualism, stereotypes, and conflict management. He has brazenly edited a book titled *The Psychology of the Chinese People,* but hopes to remain in Hong Kong long enough to put some of that book's speculations on more solid empirical footing.

Jerry Boucher is a Research Associate on the Staff of the East-West Center in Honolulu, Hawaii. After receiving his Ph.D. in psychology in 1971 from the University of California, San Francisco Medical Center, he was appointed as a Research Psychologist on the staff of the UCSF Department of International Health on a two-year assignment to the Institute for Medical Research in Kuala Lumpur, Malaysia. He is on the editorial boards of the *Journal of*

Cross-Culture Psychology and the *International Journal of Intercultural Relations.* His research interests include aggression and interethnic conflict, and he has performed studies of emotions and emotional behavior in 10 cultures.

Eric S. Casiño, a social anthropologist, is a specialist on the Muslim cultures of the Southern Philippines and related Islamic traditions in Southeast Asia. He was chief anthropologist of the National Museum of the Philippines before he joined the East-West Center as a senior research associate for four years, 1977-81. He graduated with a Ph.D. from Sydney University in 1973, where he served as a teaching fellow for two years. He has taught in several universities in the Philippines, Australia, and the United States. He has recently served as an educational specialist with the Hawaii State Department of Education, where he directed a federal project in bilingual education for Samoan and Filipino immigrant students. Currently he is a Visiting Research Associate at the Academy of Asean Law and Jurisprudence, University of the Philippines.

Karen Arnold Clark is a doctoral student in clinical psychology at the University of Mississippi. She received her B.S. degree from the University of Alabama in psychology. She currently serves as Managing Editor of the *International Journal of Intercultural Relations* and as a member of the research team for the Center for Applied Research and Evaluation (University of Mississippi). Her research interests are in the areas of mental health program evaluation and relationship issues in chronic psychiatric populations.

Angela B. Ginorio received her undergraduate education at the University of Puerto Rico and received her Ph.D. in social psychology from Fordham University in 1979. Currently she is Director of the Women's Information Center at the University of Washington. Her research interests are gender roles and racial identity in the context of acculturation, particularly in Puerto Ricans.

Winthrop D. Jordan is Professor of History and Afro-American Studies at the University of Mississippi. From 1963 until 1982 he taught at the University of California, Berkeley, where he was Associate Dean of Minority Affairs, Graduate Division, for two years. He has written about race relations in articles, reviews, and in his prize-winning book, *White Over Black: American Attitudes Toward the Negro, 1550-1812* (1968).

John Kirkpatrick is an anthropologist (Ph.D., University of Chicago) with field experience in both Micronesia and Polynesia. His first book, *The Marquesan Notion of the Person*, shows how Marquesans' conceptions fit together to form an ideological system. He has organized a collaborative investigation of cultural understandings of psychology in Pacific societies; some of the resulting analyses are in *Person, Self, and Experience: Exploring Pacific Ethnopsychologies*, edited by Geoffrey M. White and John Kirkpatrick. He has taught at Brown University and Wesleyan University. He is now conducting research on ethnic labeling and the presentation of self in interethnic encounters.

Rolf Kuschel received a master's degree (1969) in social psychology from the Psychological Laboratory, University of Copenhagen, Denmark, where he received the Gold Medal from the University of Copenhagen, Denmark, where he received the Gold Medal from the University of Copenhagen for a thesis titled "A Critical Evaluation of the Term 'Taboo' and Its Application in Psychology." He has served as Assistant (1969-73) and Associate Professor (1973-present) at the University of Copenhagen. He has conducted field research in 1968, 1971, 1972, 1977, and 1983 on Bellona and Rennell Islands, Solomon Islands, and in 1971 on Nggatokae, Solomon Islands. The field researchers were sponsored by the Danish National Council of the Humanities, Copenhagen, Denmark.

Dan Landis is Professor of Psychology and Director, Center for Applied Research and Evaluation, University of Mississippi. He is the coeditor of the three-volume *Handbook of Interethnic Training*, as well as the editor and founder of the *International Journal of Intercultural Relations*, and serves on the editorial boards of several other journals. His published papers cover a wide variety of topics, including cross-cultural investigations, race-relations training in a number of settings, methodological and statistical approaches to individual differences, and studies of perception, human sexuality, and decision making. He received his Ph.D. in general-theoretical psychology from Wayne State University in 1963, and has held research positions at the Franklin Institute Research Laboratories, Educational Testing Service, Riverside Research Institute, and the University City Science Center. His prior academic appointments include the Chairship of Psychology at Indiana

University—Purdue University in Indianapolis, and the Deanship of the College of Liberal Arts at the University of Mississippi. He was a Fellow at the East-West Center in Honolulu during 1983.

Ronald Provencher (Ph.D., University of California, Berkeley) is Professor of Anthropology and Director of the Center for Southeast Asian Studies at Northern Illinois University. He has taught at Rice University, San Diego State University, Universiti Kebangsaan Malaysia (the National University of Malaysia), and Chiang Mai University (in Thailand). Among his publications are *Two Malay Worlds: Interaction in Urban and Rural Settings* (Research Monograph 4, Center for South and Southeast Asian Studies, University of California, Berkeley, 1971); *Mainland Southeast Asia: An Anthropological Perspective* (Goodyear, 1975); "Orality as a Pattern of Symbolism in Malay Psychiatry" (in A. L. Becker & A. A. Yengoyan, Eds., *The Imagination of Reality: Essays in Southeast Asian Coherence Systems,* Ablex, 1979); "Islam in Malaysia and Thailand" (in R. Israeli, Ed., *The Crescent in the East: Islam in Asia Major,* Curzon, 1982); and "'Mother Needles': Lessons on Inter-Ethnic Psychiatry in Malaysian Society" (*Social Science and Medicine,* Vol. 18).

J. Martín Ramirez graduated in medicine and philosophy, and received a Ph.D. in neuroscience and a Ph.D. in education. He was trained in psychobiology at Frie Universitat Berlin, Ruhr Universitat, and Stanford University. Previously, he was on the Faculty of the Psychology Department and Director of the Gabinete de Estudios of the Universidad Autonoma de Madrid, and was Research Fellow at the Centro Ramon y Cajal in Madrid. Currently, he is Head of the Department of Psychobiology at the University of Seville and is a member of the adjunct Faculty of Troy State University. His research interests include the biological basis of behavior and aggression in humans and animals, and he is presently heading a research project engaged in the cross-cultural study of social interactions from a bioethological perspective. He is the author of eight books and more than 170 articles in seven languages.

Ross Stagner is Professor Emeritus of Psychology at Wayne State University and Visiting Professor of Organizational Psychology at Texas A&M University. He is the author of a dozen books, including major works on psychology of personality (1937, 1948, 1961, and 1974), social psychology (1952), and industrial and international conflict (1956, 1960, 1967). He is also the author of over 100 papers and chapters in books. He has been President of Divisions 8 and 14 of APA, President of the Midwestern Psychological Association, and served on the National Research Council from 1964 to 67. He served as Chair of the Psychology Department at Wayne State University from 1957 to 1972.

Bobbie Sullivan is a doctoral candidate in psychology at the University of Hawaii and a doctoral participant at the East-West Center. She has worked extensively in France, Greece, and most of the countries in the Middle East. She received the B.A. from the University of Maryland and the M.A. from the University of Hawaii, both in psychology.

Joseph E. Trimble (Ph.D., University of Oklahoma) is a Professor of Psychology at Western Washington University in Bellingham, Washington. His principal research efforts are concentrated in the mental health and substance abuse problems of native populations, particularly American Indian and Alaska Native groups. He also has written extensively in the field of cross-cultural counseling and delivering mental health services to American Indian communities. In addition, he has conducted research on the effects of life-threatening events on ethnic-minority elderly populations, and self-image and value orientations of American Indian youth. He is currently developing a cognitive-behavioral model for use in preventing drug abuse among American Indian youth.

David Y. H. Wu has been a Research Associate at the East-West Center since 1974. He is currently also an affiliate Professor of Anthropology and Associate Clinical Professor of Psychiatry at the University of Hawaii. He is a native of Taiwan (now a naturalized American citizen). He received a B.A. degree in archaeology and anthropology from the National Taiwan University, his master's degree (and a Ph.D. candidacy) from the University of Hawaii, and his doctorate in anthropology from the Australian National University. He has conducted field research in Hawaii, Papua New Guinea, Singapore, and other Southeast Asian countries, most recently in China. His contribution on the subjects of overseas Chinese, ethnic minorities, child socialization, and mental health have appeared in books and journals published in Australia, Singapore, Taiwan, and the United States. He has also authored two books on the subject of interethnic relations and coedited a third. In the past few years he has been in charge of research projects on ethnicity and ethnic relations in Asian and Pacific countries, and has coordinated research and international conferences on culture and mental health.

Zhang Shifu Associate Professor and Chairperson of the Department of Psychology at the Kunming Normal College, Kunming, Yunnan Province, People's Republic of China (PRC). He also serves as Chair of the Board of Directors of both the Psychological Association and the Association of Social Psychology, PRC, and as Director of the Executive Committee for the Association of Ethnic Psychology, PRC. He received a bachelor's degree in psychology from the South-West Associated University (1944) and a master's in psychology from Ching-Hua University (1946).

NOTES

NOTES

NOTES